Mystery Babalon

Mystery Babalon

being the

Bhaktic and Ecstatic

Rites of Babalon

by

Hagia Aureavia

Edited by

Carus Babalonis

Thelemic Productions LLC

Ophidia

Bloomington, Indiana USA

Thelemic Productions LLC
An Ophidian Press
PO Box 2334
Bloomington, IN 47402
USA

www.thelemicproductions.com

© 2016 Thelemic Productions
All Rights Reserved

All rights reserved. No part of this book may be reproduced or transmitted in any form or by any means, electronic or mechanical, including photocopying, recording, or by an information storage and retrieval system - except by a reviewer who may quote brief passages in a review to be printed in a magazine or newspaper - without permission in writing from the publisher.

ISBN 978-0692728192

Cover design by Carus Babalonis.

Photograph on front cover by Angel Silva. Model: Saba Khandroma, showing the Blue Goddess and the Red Daughter.

Image on Title Page: The Seal and Banner of the Shrines of Babalon system. The Bindu (sperm and menses), Yoni Triangle (vulva) and Star of Babalon (Goddess).

Dedication

I am dedicating this book to my Twin Flame, for like the gods of old who are brother and sister, lover and lover, we have danced through time, two divided for love's sake for the chance of union. It is in this way that balance is created. It is in this way that the past is verified. It is in this way that the continuity of the Lineage is protected, proven, tested, and tethered. There is no more dedicated and loyal of a guardian. There is no more formidable of a Brother. It is forever how it was. INBVSM

Table of Contents

Acknowledgements xi
Preface xiii
Introduction xvii

Part I   Philosophy & Cosmology

1. Your Divine Spirit and Will 3
2. Ophidian Rebellion 7
3. Who or what is Babalon? 11
4. Blue Goddess, Red Daughter 23
5. What is a Scarlet Woman? 27
6. Women of the Wheel 35
7. Becoming the Beast 37
8. Beast 45
9. Nuit, Hadit, Ra Hoor Khuit 49
10. A Pure Heart and the Serpent Flame Therein 59

Part II   Preparations

A: For the Shrine

11. What is a Shrine? 67
12. Offices, Roles and Pathways 75

Contents

13. Altars and Shrine Decorations 83
14. Shrine Incense, Perfumes and Oils 89

B: For the Rites

15. Name of Dedication 101
16. Preparing for the Rites 103
17. Timing of the Rites 107
18. Grounding 115
19. Your Dominion 119
20. Banishing 121
---20a. Gaia-Luna Point of Light 125
---20b. Stella Heru 129
21. Dedication of your Shrine to Babalon 135

Part III Invocations, Hymns, Adorations and Prayers

22. The Adorations of Babalon 143
23. The Company of Heaven 155
24. The Archangels 163
25. The Planets 173
26. The Elements and Elementals 187
27. The Zodiac 197

Part IV The Bhaktic Rites of Babalon

28. The Devotional Path 213
29. Daily Devotions 217
30. Dreamtime Devotions 225
31. The Rite of Devotion 229
32. The Rite of Convocation 237
33. The Bhaktic Rites of Babalon 247

Optional Rites to Ra Hoor Khuit

34. The Adorations of Ra Hoor Khuit 267
35. The Devotional Rites of Ra Hoor Khuit 301
36. The Blood Rites of Ra Hoor Khuit 311

Part V   Ecstatic Rites of Babalon

37. The Balanced Ecstatic Path 321
38. Preparations for the Union 331
39. The Rite of Sappho 337
40. The Rite of Pan 343
41. The Rite of the Twin Flame 349
42. The Rites of the Holy Whore 359
43. The Ecstatic Rites of Babalon 365
44. The Hieros Gamos to Babalon 385

Appendices

A. What are Shrines of Babalon? 395
B. Ophidian Thelema and the Temple of Babalon 399
C. The Gematria of the Ophidian Kabbalah 407
D. Artist Acknowledgements and Resources 417

Glossary of Concepts 419
About the Author 451

CONTENTS

LIST OF IMAGES

Hagia Aureavia, Girt with Sword xvi
Babalon upon Her Lion with Serpents xx
Media upon Her Chariot pulled by Serpents 9
Babalon by Luciana Lupe Vasconcelos. 10
Salomé by Pierre Bonnard, Embellished 22
Ra Hoor Khuit Falcon 28
Hagia Aureavia in the Liminal Gateway 35
The Lion of St Mark by Martin Schongauer 44
Nuit by Lawless art (Janin Pisarek) 48
Ra Hoor Khuit, Lord of the Aeon 54
Autumn Vintage Festival by Sir Lawrence Alma-Tadema 58
Durga-Babalon Apocalypse by Orryelle Defenestrate-Bascule 64
Chinnamasta Sketch by Daniel Corcuera 68
Incense by Paul Edouard Rosset-Granger 88
Ancient Arabic Talisman with Mansions of the Moon 108
Biblis by Adolphe-William Bouguereau 118
Nava-Durga-Babalon on the Beast by Orryelle Defenestrate-Bascule . . . 134
Ornamental Serpent Torch with Star of Babalon 140
Whore of Babalon by Nuria Fortuny Art 210
The Sigillum Divinorum 220
The Sigillum Divinorum Altar Layout 223
Priestess of Babalon by Saba Khandroma and Angel Silva 246
The Mudras for the Adorations of Ra Hoor Khuit 276
Idol of perversity by Jean Delville 318
God Pan by Nuria Fortuny Art 342
Babalon Brigid by Orryelle Defenestrate-Bascule 358
Priestess of Babalon 2 by Saba Khandroma and Angel Silva 364
Chinnamasta Study by Daniel Corcuera 384
An Example of the Holy Vessel of Babalon 390
Ornamental Star of Babalon 392

Mystery Babalon

Acknowledgements

I would like to thank Carus Babalonis for his contributions to the writing and creating of this book. This book is in part an act of Heka, and he is the Magus, the Beast, the Therion, and the Ape of Thoth. There is no one more dedicated. In Nomine Babalon!

I would like to thank all of the magnificent artists who contributed their beauty and their genius to this book, both with allowing inclusion of existent works, and those who created newly inspired art for the book: Angel Silva, Daniel Corcuera, Janin Pisarek, Nuria Fortuny, Orryelle Defenestrate-Bascule, Saba Khandroma, and Luciana Lupe Vasconcelos. In Nomine Babalon!

I would like to give special acknowledgement to Saba Khandroma, Luciana Lupe Vasconcelos, Patience Moniker, and Laurelei Black who through their passion and devotion for Babalon jumped onboard with enthusiasm to establish Shrines of Babalon in their locales and agreed to be on the Shrine Council as a diverse body to oversee the Shrine System world-wide. Each woman brings unique vision and gifts to the System, and it would not be possible for it to exist without them. In Nomine Babalon!

I would like to thank Semper Fidelis Babalon for his assistance with editing this book, his assistance with the Shrine System, and for his dedication to Babalon. He is a true seeker. In Nomine Babalon!

I would like to thank all of the members past and present of Templum Babalonis for their contributions over the last 16 years to the body of Her Temple as it has risen in the West. We are the axle of the wheel—may Her Circumference know no bounds.

I would like to thank all who serve Her who know it not. For it is through the balance of opposition that we understand what messages are needed to be put forth. There are no enemies, there are no detractors, there

Acknowledgements

are no obstacles. All is ever as it was. All is accepted and used as it presents itself to be.

> *This is the creation of the world, that the pain of division is as nothing, and the joy of dissolution all.*
>
> -Liber Legis I 30

The Holy Whore accepts all and refuses none. Babalon is for ALL!

I would like to thank all who seek out Babalon with a pure heart, and a pure Will. May She embrace you all. INBVSM
 And I humbly and with complete devotion thank Babalon, My Sisters the Nine, my Guardians the Seven and the Brotherhood of the Midnight Sun, and those spiritual allies who, as the Nephilim before, taught me everything that I am and that I know. It is with every thread and passion of my being that I give these Rites to all. May the Serpent Rise!

> *…another woman shall awake the lust & worship of the Snake…*
>
> -Liber Legis III 34

Aum Ho!

Lust. Give. Rise.

In Nomine Babalon et Vox Sanctae Meretricis

Hagia Aureavia

Preface

Babalon is everywhere in these times, and Her image is ubiquitous. People worship Her, portray Her, give Her energy and adoration every day around the world, without ever realizing that they do so. Such is Her power and reach. Yet who exactly She is, and what She may mean to you is not to be found in this book, or in any other book either. No. Your relationship with Her is one which you must cultivate on your own, through direct and indirect experience of Her and Her energies. Like your Will, no one can tell you what Babalon means to you personally. And more importantly, no one can tell you how She will transform your life.

In the 30 years of my devotion to the Great Liberating Mother, this has been my greatest lesson: Babalon is the Goddess of Transformation in the Underworld, and those experiences of transformation are non-transferable. The results can not be given in words, except as tokens of recognition to those who have already made the journey. You must take the journey yourself. You must take responsibility for your own spirituality into your own hands. You must place this work as the highest priority of your existence. And you better start now, because we all have less time here than you think - such is the trick of memory and time.

To this end, let me say that *Mystery Babalon* is not a philosophy manual, or a book full of definitions or lengthy description of Babalon in all of Her offices, roles, incarnations and functions - complete with comments and communications from the Goddess Herself and Her allies. That is what we have done before and continue to do through our Temple work, and it certainly appeals to a specific class of people. Nor is this a book full of the secrets and rituals for the Initiated within our Temple. No.

Preface

This book, and the accompanying Shrines project, is a different approach. This book is an instruction book for all people of all persuasions. It is light on philosophy and heavy on recipes. This book is for those who want to experience Her, to taste Her, to feel Her - alone or with others, on their own terms and in their own way. This book is an instruction manual for experiences, both devotional and sensual. It is a book of Her Mysteries for the people at large, for them to practice and celebrate, no matter who they may be - for She indeed refuses none and accepts all.

This book is a book of suggestions. This book is a book of guidelines. This book is a book which will start you on your own road to your own experiences with Babalon, in light of your own Will. You will decide where to start, what to do, and how deep to go - in your own way, and in your own time. Nothing is required, except to release your inhibitions and be as you truly are. Nothing is demanded, other than your sincerity concerning your own life, and your own spiritual journey. You do not need to know anything or everything - for your own journey, once undertaken, will teach you all you need to know. Babalon is a Goddess of experience, not of knowledge. Babalon is a Goddess of Transformation. Babalon is a Goddess of Ecstatic Liberation, from all of the bonds which previously kept you from your Spirit and who you truly are. Within Her purview are all modes of change as given by the Seven Guiding Principles, be they Death or Consumption or Recumbancy or Generation. Because of this, She is one of the most powerful Goddesses of all, and also one of the most feared. For nothing that is, not even Spirit, can resist Her powers of Transformation, as all things which are and which are not, must pass through that place of greatest mystery which is Her Domain, in the Realm of the Underworld. The Underworld Mysteries are the Mysteries of Sex and Death, and these will be the same Rites in all of their many iterations, which you will practice in your Shrine. And the path is a Balanced Ecstatic Path, always seeking more beauty and joy and bliss and wisdom, for they are all complimentary states of being for those who pass the Gates of Death, and who have liberated themselves from the bonds and cares of the Persona, achieving true self-mastery, in Nomine Babalon.

Most who write books on Babalon today do so from a purely theoretical perspective. They are often scholars, or would-be scholars, who think that the key to knowing, and therefore understanding Babalon is through the reading and studying of books. Behind this self-edifying wall of research, a citadel of codified thought, of dogma, and of overly-simplistic theism is created, based mostly upon Parsons, who in turn was based upon Crowley, whose knowledge in turn stopped at *the Book of*

Mystery Babalon

Revelation. And Dee also. These are the last three men to have any intimate contact with Babalon which amounted to any value in the historical record. And do notice that I said *men*.

This book is here to destroy that citadel.

The information in this book, like all of those which we produce, does not come from the minds of men. It does not come from research, or reading other books on Babalon, or by getting some degree which codifies a certain way of thinking which is then applied to any and every concept. No. The information in this book comes from direct experiential communication with the spirits. The information comes from the company of Gods, with Babalon at their head. Hear their voice, not ours, when you read these words. Our genius has selected and arranged and polished and displayed them for you, but they are the teachers of all things which humanity has inherited. We live in service to them, and to give them voice, knowing that we will not and shall not be remembered. And that service to something greater than ourselves is the true key of our success.

    So we admonish you to jump in. Get your feet wet. Raise your flag. Bring others to your Shrine, if you decide to create one. Or go solo if that is your Will. Facilitate these experiences of bliss, pleasure and self-transcendence - for others, and for yourself. Whether it is your first time delving into Her Rites or you have been a devotee of Hers for many years, we welcome you to the Mysteries of Babalon. There are many people, and there are many paths. Babalon is for ALL

Carus Babalonis

Na Nia Het Hotep
Luciferos

Ianitor and Therion of Templum Babalonis

Hagia Aureavia

Introduction

As Hagia, I have been approached by many seekers desiring advice and direction in regards to the devotional practices of Babalon. To this point in history, very little has been discovered or written in regards to the exact Rites and practices for Her Cult. It is my Will and gift as Her Priestess to make some of these Rites available for those who seek to know Her. While everyone has their own Will and path in life to traverse, these Rites, preparations and rituals within this book may be utilized as a starting point in one's own journey to Babalon.

As a Priestess of Babalon, I teach the Ecstatic Path - this is the Via Babalonis, the Way of Babalon. Many esoteric paths proclaim that they are "left-hand path", and many religions claim that they are "right-hand path". The Ecstatic Path has no such limitations, and employs all aspects in a path that is at once balanced, and rebellious, against that which would keep one from realizing one's True Will. The Balanced Ecstatic Path is the true Luciferian Path, as it has no limitations in its expression and its direction, yet it follows the principles and rules of one's own Divine Purpose. This is the path of the journey to Babalon. This is the path alighted by the torch, for the torchbearer is Lucifera, She who is the Morning Star which shines forth. Follow the Hermit's lamp, follow the Torchbearer to the Seven Gates of Babalon, for the light of the torch is the same as the fire in your heart which burns to know Babalon. Only you can determine your Will. Only you can decide to embark upon this journey.

The Balanced Ecstatic Path offers many ways of exploration utilizing the combination of sensual physical energy combined with the devotion of Spirit. One may therefore better explore, learn, and grow one's

Introduction

own connection to self and to Babalon. Within these Rites there are many paths to explore, as well as many roles that you may wish to learn, explore, and partake of. These roles offer you different ways in which to relate to the people who come to your Shrine as well as new ways to think and feel about yourself.

Within this book we will explore some of these roles, which include the Holy Whore, the Scarlet Woman, the Beast, the Baphomet, as well as the Bhaktic path of the Holy and Devoted One and many others. In addition, there are many ways to practice these Rites in a solitary fashion, or in small or large groups. There are Rites for people of all paths, persuasions, preferences and levels of devotion. And it is through these Rites that we may, all of us, begin the realization of Babalon, Her Energy, and Her Manifestation worldwide. For this is the Great Reclamation: the Reclamation of the Great Liberating Mother. Rise, Babalon, Rise!

Indwelling

I am not certain that people in the modern world understand the process of indwelling the gods, and their manifestation upon the Earth. The old Pagans understood this innately. This is the process of Sacred Manifestation, of Heka, which is the bringing of Spirit down into matter through the human body. This is not a psychological process. This is not creative visualization. This is a process of the Elements, within you and around you, which act upon matter as it manifests from the Celestial and Orkestial Realms and into the Terrestrial[1]. This is represented by the image of the Inverted Pentacle. We use an Inverted Pentacle because it is a symbol of the dark ways of the Female Mysteries, and it is the body, yoni and womb itself of the female which governs and manifests the descent of Spirit down into matter.

The Pagans of ancient times, from cultures such as the Greeks, Romans, Etruscans and Egyptians, understood that Spirit is ubiquitous, and that if one wishes to have a god dwell amongst them, they needed to provide that god with a house or body to indwell in. Even if only in part, for in order for a Spirit to come to the Realm of Earth and to have a lasting presence, it must have some sort of temporal body in which to indwell. This can be a body such as the planet Earth, which is the body of Gaia Herself. Or this can be a race of people, who act as a collective body which

---

[1] Please see the Glossary of Terms for an explanation of *the Three Great Realms*.

indwells their ancestral spirits and spirits of their gods through their worship and interaction. Or this can be a physical Temple or Shrine, within which Rites are performed to manifest the presence of that deity within.

It is in this way that we can, all of us, come together to undertake the process of indwelling Babalon upon Earth. In order for Her to have Her Reclamation, She wishes to become manifest in all ways. This in part is what this book is for, and it is important that She manifests through *your* desires, and through *your* actions, driven by *your* Spirit, and not simply mine or that of anyone else. These Rites are yours — yours, and Babalon's.

The nature of the gods, unlike all other spirits, is such that they, too have incarnations. Their natures are grown and changed through their interactions with not only the forces of the cosmos, but also the various cultures of humanity with which they interact. We are on the cusp of a new Aeon, and a new incarnation of the Gods. Babalon is the name of one such new incarnation of a very ancient deity, and how we interact with Her now will shape the future of us all.

People of this modern era often think that a ritual, or a "magickal" act is something that takes place at a certain hour, or a certain day, with specific words or symbols. They do not realize that a magical act can also be something that can span years, or decades, or even centuries. This, then, is the beginning of the public understanding of what this Mystery of Babalon is: it is a magickal act - an action or ritual of Heka. And you are the magician. You are the Priestess. You are the body, the congregation, the Devotee - you are the Wick of this incredible and Sacred Flame.

Here then, is Mystery Babalon.

Βαβαλον

Part I

Philosophy & Cosmology

I

Your Divine Spirit and Will

hey are mistaken in the notion that Spirit is separate from animal. *We incarnate to sensually unify the five elements within us as a means to realize the Purpose of our Spirit. There must be an integration of Spirit and animal, for to force separation is to create fragmentation. The pursuit of enlightenment cannot entail any less than an understanding of the purpose of the animal in relation to our existence while walking with our feet upon the body of our Mother.*

-Hagia Aureavia

From the most Ancient times of human history, the Great Goddesses of Earth, Sky and Underworld have been the source of the most important Wisdom for humanity concerning the Spirit. This Spirit is your immortal, divine, unique, higher self which incarnates into flesh in order to achieve its manifest purpose, which is called its Will. It is immortal in that it is deathless, and imperishable. It is divine in that it is incorruptible and perfect in its nature and possesses a consciousness with a much greater horizon than your own manifest self. It is unique in that it is like no other Spirit in both its nature and consciousness, yet always recognizable in every incarnation no matter which different body you are born into. It is your higher self in that it creates and informs all that you are, and without which you would certainly cease.

Therefore from times immemorial, certain Goddesses have taught to humanity the Principles of the Will, one's Divine Purpose, and its greater relation to life and to existence. These Principles invariably describe the Art of Living Well, in Harmonia, which is the state of beauty, balance and euphoria which attends any thing done properly as directed from the Spirit. And this Harmonia is the result of practicing the teachings of Heka and Natura. Heka is an act of consciously manifesting Spirit into matter, and all of the attendant spiritual powers which become apparent as the result of this action. The Principles and Rituals which govern the manifestation of the Spirit in the body, the Persona, and the natural world are called Natura. It is in Natura that we find the secrets of the body, its energy pathways, how the substances we ingest affect not only our health, but also our emotions, our consciousness and our ability to manifest Heka.

It is important to understand that these teachings of the Goddesses concerning Spirit, Heka and Natura change and adapt to that of the current understanding of humanity, depending upon their current stage of evolutionary progress. These evolutionary stages are charted in the Aeonic Cycles which span thousands of years. However in the current Aeon of Aquarius, the first impulse of this understanding of the old teachings and Principles of Spirit and Heka has been delivered under the banner of Thelema, in what is commonly known as the Book of the Law, called Liber AL vel Legis.

So we can now see that in modern terms, Thelema is the Cult of the Will. This is pronounced **Thel**-ley-mah in Ancient Greek, with a strong emphasis on the first syllable. And this word Thelema is the name for the system of Magical Philosophy that was divulged to the modern world in the book *Liber AL vel Legis*, commonly referred to as *The Book of the Law*, in Cairo, Egypt, in 1904. On April 8th, 9th and 10th of that year, a communication was received by Rose Edith Kelley[2] and written down by her husband Aleister Crowley. This communication consisted of three small chapters that were received at noon, one on each of the three days.

---

[2] It is not the intent of this book to argue a proof concerning Crowley's key omission of Rose standing outside the door during the receipt of this book, other than to say we contend that he conveniently did not mention this fact so that he could say the room was empty. This will be covered in detail in *Book IV of the Magickal Philosophy of Templum Babalonis, Commentaria*.

Within this writing, with its strange phrases, multi-layered meanings, and hidden ciphers, a new Law for a New Aeon was proclaimed.

Do what thou wilt shall be the whole of the Law.

-Liber Legis I 40

Thelema is Greek for Will, and by Gematria equals 93. This Law proclaims that every woman and every man his a unique, individual and autonomous Will, and that she or he has an inalienable right and responsibility to find out that purpose, and to achieve it, no matter what it may be. Each person's Will is unique, and can only be discovered by his or her self. This Will is spiritual, and the reason why one has incarnated on this planet. But, how does one discover what their Will is?

Love is the law, love under will.

-Liber Legis I 57

Agape is Greek for Love, and also equals 93. In Thelema, Love means attraction and union. This union is a union with one's Spirit, which holds the keys to one's Will. One must discover and follow their path, by uniting with each and every experience that one needs in order to accomplish their Will, no matter what it may be.

Now it should be understood that since the most Ancient times, the image of the serpent was the image of the Spirit. The wise ones of old understood clearly that there could be no life on this planet without Spirit manifesting in matter. For Spirit animates, in every sense of the word. Spirit is the Prime Mover. All things which live and move do so because they are literally possessed by a spirit. Without

Spirit there would be no life anywhere in the universe. In fact, there would be no thing at all, either animate or "inanimate". Spirit is the supreme source of Light and Life.

So therefore it should be no surprise that the Mother of all mothers, the Mother of all Life on this planet and throughout the entire universe, the one whom we today call Nuit – it is She who bears this light of Spirit into existence. And this light of Spirit is forever renewed and changing, and never diminishes. Every living thing, no matter how motionless or how small, possesses spirit energy. The planet itself, which is a living being called Gaia by some, the little sister of Our Lady Nuit, imbues even the otherwise lifeless matter with Her Spirit, and makes all life possible here. Without Her Spirit powering life on this planet, there would be nothing but an inanimate shell.

Each person that is born here within the body of Gaia possesses a unique Spirit of their own. This Spirit is sometimes called your True Self, Divine Self or Divine Spirit. This Spirit is one's immortal, divine, unique, higher self which incarnates into flesh in order to achieve its great and terrible purpose, which we call its Will. On a personal level, the Will of one's Spirit is felt to be the guiding sovereign purpose in life, and one's reason for incarnation. All people are here for a purpose, and there is no greater and nobler act than accomplishing the purpose of one's incarnation, or to die trying to achieve it. This is the meaning of the phrase "Do what thou wilt shall be the whole of the law." It is a commandment to achieve one's divine purpose, above which there is no other.

II

OPHIDIAN REBELLION

t is in the Dominion of the Continuum, *the collective Will of the Lineage, that we stand as Guardians in the manifest realm of that which is most sacred. It is therefore at times such as these, at the writing of these symbols known as words in this modern age, that I am at once holding firmly to the Great Wheel with one hand as I bear my sword in the other, and at the same time I am held suspended in what is thought of as time, with the same tension as that which holds my breath still in my lungs.*

The knowledge that I will need to breathe is suspended by the desire to stillness, for this moment is both foretold and precise, and I shall not breathe until my hand is guided into action. And what hand holds the torch, if both of mine are full? And by what light are my eyes filled?

Such is the Continuum that my hand shall hold the sword for hundreds, thousands of years. Such is the death of an Age, and the birth of another. Such is the passage, the transformation, that my hand will hold the sword high amongst the stars and blood will fall as tears. Not tears for the dying, no. For the dying chose death. There are no tears for death. Only gladness within our hearts.

The Serpent moves through time as if it were water. Sometimes slowly, sometimes too fast to even see. And though the Serpent bears the crown of Wickedness as our Mother bears the crown of Whore, we, the Daughters of the

Ophidian Rebellion

Bloodline, those deemed Scarlet, smile as the sword is raised in defiance of the true wickedness that has about ended the life of Gaia and all of her Children. All that is known in the minds of modernity is a lie. This is where we find ourselves, and I speak only to those Ophidians who understand that this is the Reclamation of Her, even if as of yet they did not know they bore that name.

There is a hand around the throat of mankind's manifest existence. Its grasp grows so tight that it has almost ended the very breath of incarnation upon this realm even as I hold my breath so still and hot within me. The moment draws near.

Man has sought so many ways in recent times to find that act of subversion that his Spirit cries out so longingly for. Knowing deep within his soul that his life is all but suspended within the bounds of enslavement, he turns to distraction so as not to find the true meaning of his existence. Yet rebellion burns within him, and he turns to all that glows as the opposition to that which he reviles.

There is but one act, however, that we as Ophidians know is the only true act of subversion and rebellion against those forces that have sought to destroy us for the last 12,000 years, and that is to do what it is we have incarnated for: to do our Will.

It is the act of doing the Will of one's incarnated Spirit that subverts the energies that draw tyranny and enslavement to all life on Earth. The Will of an Ophidian is Justified in this age of War and Vengeance. We shall do no act that is not to these ends, as we have been called forth in the alignment of all that is allied to Her, Babalon.

And it is this deep and longing love that we bear for Gaia that will draw our brothers and sisters here. We have reclaimed the Garden for that which it was intended all along, and we await you. There is only one act of rebellion that our people need to take now, and that is to come home. Your Will to serve Her is all that you need to know.

BABALON - LUCIANA LUPE VASCONCELOS

III

WHO OR WHAT IS BABALON?

he Great Liberating Mother has been known and worshipped since the most ancient times - probably even before we were homo-sapiens. But Her name then was not Babalon, or Babylon or anything remotely resembling that. The current manifestation of the Great Liberating Mother known as Babalon derives Her name from certain passages in *the Book of Revelation*, modified in spelling by the Enochian works of Dr. John Dee, and finally popularized within the occult movement known today as Thelema. And it is in this modern movement where She has been despiritualized, dethroned from Her status as Goddess, and recast into a simple role designed for females to play in conjunction with the fantasies and the workings of male magicians in their own sex magick. But all of that is changing, and Babalon is slowly and surely regaining Her rightful place as one of the most powerful, feared and revered Goddesses in history, after two thousand years of repression in the West.

But who, or what is Babalon? Babalon is a Goddess who is both a force and a being. Some deities are one or the other - few are both. But what kind of Goddess is She? She is certainly not what you have read in the books of men, or what you have been taught in these times. Babalon is the Goddess of Heka, the Goddess of the Liberation of the Spirit, the

Who or What is Babalon?

Goddess of the Underworld, the Goddess of the Liminal Point, the Warrior Goddess of Vengeance, and as a force She is the Guardian of the Principles of Life. Let us take a closer look at each one of these statements.

Babalon is the Goddess of Heka, which in Egyptian means that She oversees the Activation (He) of the manifest Spirit (Ka). In other words, the Ophidian definition of Magick is the act of calling down the Spirit into the body, which in turn activates special powers or abilities within the body. This Heka is a Female principle, and the Priestesses who are dedicated to Underworld Goddesses utilize the Female body itself, the vulva, the womb and the menses, in their Rites to power their Heka. Therefore Babalon is a Goddess of Heka, and teaches the secret ways of this Magick to Her devotees. The Enochian system, so-called, is one such example of this. The Triangle of Manifestation and the Orphetic Mysteries are another. She also teaches Egyptian "Magick" or Heka quite thoroughly, as She spent much time with the people of that culture there under Her name Pahkhet, who was the template upon which the later Cipheric Goddess known as Isis was based. Many of the Goddesses of Heka, Guardians of Arcane Knowledge, and some of the Angels have an affinity with Babalon and work with Her in this area of Heka.

Babalon is the Goddess of the Liberation of Spirit which is often represented in the form of a Serpent. The body possesses grand powers when the Serpent becomes manifest in the flesh. There is a great bliss when the Spirit draws close, and the body is liberated by it. Rather than pose a duality between the flesh and the Spirit like most paths do, Ophidian Thelema stresses the importance of calling down the Spirit into flesh, thereby liberating the body from the bonds of the Persona. The Persona is not destroyed, but rather put in service of the Spirit. Babalon teaches of this process, and the powers which are associated with the manifest Spirit, called Heka.

This is the reason why She is called the Great Liberating Mother, and the remover of obstacles. Such is Babalon's potency and power, that She can remove that which keeps you from your divine purpose of incarnation. But be warned, this is often painful to the Persona, which clings to its attachments in the world - and the fear of death. Being a devotee of Babalon often means that one is forced to face things about oneself that others do not, and ultimately it will mean the total death and destruction of what in modern times is termed "the ego". The Persona will be yoked in service of the Spirit, and all which keeps one from it will be destroyed, if you devote yourself to Babalon. This is true Liberation.

Babalon is the Goddess of the Underworld, in that She oversees the reclamation of the remnants of life unto death, and its transformation in the Orkestial Realms. This process is mirrored in nature in the processes of death and decay which create fertile ground for new life. The true Liberation of the Spirit from the bonds of flesh comes at death, when the Spirit is released in an ecstasy which is unimaginable and unbearable to the Persona. Yet the Persona can catch a glimpse of this ecstasy in the intensity of the orgasm of sex. This is why the Mysteries of Sex and Death are related, and both are of the Underworld. One ecstasy engenders creation into the Manifest Realm, the other is its liberation from that same Realm at death. These Mysteries of Sex and Death are utilized in Her Rites, in order to sublimate the Persona to the Spirit, and to increase one's capacity for holding ecstasy at the Liminal Gateway, through which Spirits pass.

There are many creatures in the Underworld who are Babalon's children and Her allies. Some of Her children are demons, and some are Angelic - but all have their purposes in the Underworld processes. She is the presiding Goddess over all of the Gates of Underworld Initiation, which are 28 in number. All Underworld Goddesses, Torch-bearers, Titans and Guardians of the Gates and Rivers there have an allegiance with Her in that place of darkness and transformation.

Babalon is the Goddess of the Liminal Point, which is that place where the Spirit enters into the manifest realms - whether it be the womb, the Underworld, the Temple Door or a living body. Her Priestesses are Liminal Gateways for spirits of various sorts to enter into the manifest realms. She teaches this process to Her Priestesses, showing them the proper ways of the Orphetic Mysteries such as Triangle of Manifestation, which do not involve channeling, trance-possession, drugs or the like. The sovereignty of the body of Her Priestess is not defiled in such ways. She also shows how the spirits can prove their presence beyond the doubts of the minds of men through the use of dead and forgotten languages, ciphers and other means which prove the authenticity of the communication. Many of the Liminal Goddesses and Guardians such as Hekate, Pahkhet and Baphometis have an affinity for Babalon in this regard.

Who or What is Babalon?

Babalon is the Warrior Goddess of Vengeance, along with Her Brother Ra Hoor Khuit. This aspect of Babalon shows Her powers of reclamation unto the Underworld for life out of balance, for the degenerate and for the unfit. And this is one purpose of many of the demons which She births. It is this aspect of the Great Liberating Mother which reminds so many of Kali - and their roles are often very similar. Babalon is indeed coming for Her Vengeance upon the degenerate people, and to avenge the wrongs of the Areans, Ichthyos[3] and their masters who have suppressed Her cult. This is not something that many people want to hear. And make no mistake concerning the form of Her Vengeance. She will enact a great corruption and violence upon them, as is Her right as Guardian of Life. She is the vehicle of the Principles of the Underworld in the Manifest Realm. And it is because of this that life may have a chance to continue afterwards, in one form or another. She is certainly not a Goddess for the timid or pacifistic. She is verily the Daughter of Fortitude. Because of this, a great many Warrior Goddesses, Guardians and Angels have an affinity for Babalon in this way.

Babalon is the Guardian of the Principles of Life. This is a role that not many are aware of. When these Principles of Life are violated, then it is Her duty to set them right. There are many principles throughout the Three Realms, but the highest are called the Seven Guiding Principles[4]. These Principles describe the manifestation of Spirit, and therefore the processes of the creation of all things, in all of the Realms. This process has no beginning, and is endless. Each principle is ruled over by a Fortuitous Angel as guardian. Separate from this, She is the Mother of the Enochian Angels and leader of the Heptarchia. This is why She was at the head of the Enochian system given to Dr. John Dee, and made Her dramatic appearance there at the end of his diaries after the system was given. The Enochian system and its angels are directly related to Her system of guardianship and vengeance. It is in these systems, and in others, that She has many allies, including the Seven and the Nine as well as Gaia and Her children, the Titans.

---

[3] The Areans are the warrior lords of the Aeon of Aries (2416 - 256 BCE) from whom they draw their name. Later this word became Aryan, but the original concept has nothing to do with race. The Ichthyos (pronounced eek-tohs) are the fish people who came to rule the Aeon of Pisces (256 BCE - 1904 CE). Their lineage began with the Jews and ended with the Christians. They are the greatest enemies of Babalon.

[4] For an exposition of the Seven Guiding Principles please see *The Magickal Philosophy of Templum Babalon, Book II Principia*.

Mystery Babalon

The Symbols of Babalon

Because of Her different functions, Babalon is often imagined in different forms with different symbols. Most often She is pictured in Serpentine form, which shows Her connection to the Underworld and Her powers of Heka and its relation to Spirit. The Serpent is the Spirit[5]. When Her power of Ecstatic Liberation is being emphasized, one will often find the symbol of the Sun and Moon conjoined. This shows the ecstasy of union, both in the Spirit and the Persona as well as the man and the woman. When She is a Warrior and a Guardian, She is often envisioned riding upon a Lion or beast of some sort, or pulled by Lions in a chariot. The lion shows Her ferocity and strength. It is also a symbol of Her lovers and devotees. When She is imagined as the Goddess of Seven Guiding Principles She is pictured with a Wheel with Seven Spokes or the Star with Seven Points. This Star is very complex, and has many layers of meaning and association. When She is shown as a Goddess of Heka She is often shown as the Star and the Snake together. Like many of the Underworld Goddesses and Guides, She is sometimes shown with the Torch shining bright, which is the light of Spirit which She carries in the vast darkness of the Underworld.

In Modern times many have given Her the symbol of the cup, which is representative of the Mysteries of Sex and Death. In actuality, this symbol is of either the vulva or the womb, depending upon the function and role being described. The cup is, in reality, a symbol of the Priestess, not the Goddess, and in ancient times it was not used at all. This symbol was instead represented by the horns of the bull, which was the image of the womb in shape. The Horns also mirrored the shape of the waxing and waning crescents of the moon. All of these Lunar images of the womb are representative of its power in Heka, and of the periodic cycle of the menses. This is the vaunted "best blood" which feed all life[6].

Titles of Babalon from History

---

[5] For a full discussion of the Serpent as Spirit see *The Manifestation of the Divine Serpent*, Book II, Ch. 1 of *The Magickal Philosophy of Templum Babalonis*.

[6] Liber Legis III, 24: "The best blood is of the moon, monthly: then the fresh blood of a child, or dropping from the host of heaven: then of enemies; then of the priest or of the worshippers: last of some beast, no matter what." These bloods are the menses, the blood of child-birth or the placenta, the blood of enemies on the battlefield, one's own blood as a devotee, and finally the least effective being the blood of animal sacrifice.

Who or What is Babalon?

The following are some of the more common and accessible titles of Babalon from various times and places, which help to shed further light upon Her nature. For a more extensive discussion of Babalon and Her history and Nature, please see *The Magickal Philosophy of Templum Babalonis* in four volumes.

> *The Great Liberating Mother*
> *Magna Mater*
> *Magna Mater Liberans*
> *Babalon the Great*
> *Babalon the Black*
> *The Daughter of Fortitude*
> *Daughter of Ra*
> *The Great Lioness*
> *Goddess of the Mouth of the Wadi*
> *The Woman Clothed with the Sun*
> *The Gate of God*
> *The Gate of Elyon*
> *The Blue Flame*
> *The Mother of Prostitutes and Abominations of the Earth*
> *The Mother of Abominations*
> *The Holy Whore*

The History of Babalon

Historically, Babalon is the current incarnation of the Goddess that we generally call the Great Liberating Mother. There are three main divisions of Goddesses from the Ancient times. These Goddesses ruled before the rise of Areans five thousand years ago in the Aeon of Aries, which completely changed the nature of the Gods and the mythologies into the ones which are known today. These Ancient divisions of the Goddess divide Her between the Earth, Sky and Underworld. The Earth Goddesses were the Mother Goddesses who oversaw the birth of Spirits as humans, and their upbringing. They were later joined by the Grain Goddesses of agriculture. The Sky Goddesses were all the totems of the airs in bird form: falcons, songbirds, water-fowl and vultures. These Goddesses were concerned with knowledge of the principles and divine potentialities for the early tribe. They granted far-sight and rules for happy living, as well as the implementation of proper death rituals so that the Spirit might find its way to the Underworld. The Underworld Goddesses, the class of

Goddesses to which Babalon belongs, are concerned with all things which dwell in the Underworld. The Underworld is the place of mystery to which all things return when they die and from which all things are born again. It is the place of the greatest transformation. The Underworld is not the same as the Afterworld with its Shades or Heaven with its Souls. These are later degenerations based upon successive misinterpretations of the original Underworld.

Babalon, as a Goddess of the Underworld, manifests in different incarnations in different times. Each of these manifestations has been shaped by the Aeon into which She is born, and the culture of the place which forms Her Cult. As such, a chain of incarnations can be seen stretching back through history, marking Her places of influence upon the world. We name this chain of Her incarnations collectively as the Great Liberating Mother, for convenience's sake. This name has appeared in the Cult Titles of many of Her incarnations. Some of Her more famous incarnations include Inanna, Astarte, Kybele, Pahkhet and Qadeshet.

The current incarnation of the Great Liberating Mother is known as Babalon. Her Rites of Sex and Death have been the subject of much fear, loathing and lust over the past five thousand years by the Areans and the Ichthyos. She has intentionally taken Her name at this time as a play upon the degenerated image of Her as portrayed in *the Book of Revelation*, in order to enact Her revenge upon Her enemies. She is described there as "Babylon the Great, the Mother of Prostitutes and Abominations of the Earth." They call Her the Mother of Abominations, because She births the very creatures which will destroy their degeneracy on this planet. She is the enemy of their way of life and their culture, which grips this planet to the point of death. They call Her a Whore because She will not submit to their sexual domination, but instead uses it to initiate them.

When the Areans, the warlords of the Aeon of Aries who are the fathers of all war and empire, were let loose upon the planet they sought out and destroyed much of the Goddess culture which existed before them. The Earth and Sky Goddesses were married off to their Storm Gods, like Zeus and Indra. In the same way the women on Earth likewise became chattel and property of the men of the world, used for breeding and sexual pleasure. The women who resisted and who kept their old traditions alive were the Cults of the Great Liberating Mother. They were not always successful in this. They were vilified as demons and as whores because they would not submit. Because of this, and because Her Priestesses utilize the sexual initiation of men, She has been labeled a Whore Goddess by the Ichthyos and Aryans ever since.

Who or What is Babalon?

Esoteric Aspects of Babalon

But in modern times, this old label of whore is being reclaimed as a title of empowerment for women. No longer are women defined as the sexual property of men, or considered unclean for engaging in sexual relations on their own terms, for their own pleasure.

> *The word of Sin is Restriction. O man! refuse not thy wife, if she will! O lover, if thou wilt, depart! There is no bond that can unite the divided but love: all else is a curse. Accursed! Accursed be it to the aeons! Hell.*
>
> -Liber Legis I, 41

> *At all my meetings with you shall the priestess say -- and her eyes shall burn with desire as she stands bare and rejoicing in my secret temple -- To me! To me! calling forth the flame of the hearts of all in her love-chant.*
>
> -Liber Legis I, 62

> *But let her raise herself in pride! Let her follow me in my way! Let her work the work of wickedness! Let her kill her heart! Let her be loud and adulterous! Let her be covered with jewels, and rich garments, and let her be shameless before all men!*
>
> *Then will I lift her to pinnacles of power: then will I breed from her a child mightier than all the kings of the Earth. I will fill her with joy: with my force shall she see & strike at the worship of Nu: she shall achieve Hadit.*
>
> -Liber Legis III, 44-45

> *Let Mary inviolate be torn upon wheels: for her sake let all chaste women be utterly despised among you!*
>
> *Also for beauty's sake and love's!*
>
> -Liber Legis III, 55-56

Clearly the key to the power of the female is in her vulva, in her sexuality. This is the power of woman which has been repressed for over five thousand years[7]. And it is this power which Babalon seeks to liberate from that oppression. This is shown clearly in the image of Babalon, a Goddess who has consorts of Her own choosing, but is wife to no god. This is why it is said that "Babalon rides who She Will." This formula of the sexual power of the female, acquired by the magical use of the vulva and womb during intercourse, is the hallmark of what is termed the 156 current. In Greek, the word Babalon (Βαβαλον) has the value of 156. 2 + 1 + 2 + 1 + 30 + 70 + 50 = 156. This is considered Her exoteric number, which is widely known. In the New Aeon English Qabalah[8], 156 is the same as *Heart of Babalon*, showing that this is an important number to Her. 156 also equals *Fortitude*, which comes from one of Her titles, the Daughter of Fortitude. This number also describes Her appearance in two different ways, *flame of blue* (156) and *blue am I and gold* (156). These words and phrases above are from Liber Legis, all of which equal 156.

Now there is a catch with the number 156, as it is that it leaves one wanting for a value which answers to the command of Liber Legis I, 60 "My number is 11, as all their numbers who are of us." 1+5+6 is equal to 12, not 11 unfortunately. The answer to this problem lies in Her esoteric number, which is Her name in the English Qabalah, where *Babalon* equals 65. 20 + 1 + 20 + 1 + 2 + 7 + 14 equals 65. 6 + 5 does indeed equal 11, and satisfies the command of Liber Legis I, 60. This proves the spelling of Her name in English as *Babalon*, and not *Babylon* as in the ancient city of the same name. This secret number 65 is also the value of the words which describe Her color, both as *golden* (65) and as *honey* (65). This agrees with the 156 version of Her color, *blue am I and gold*. The sexual references of words which equal the value of 65 are unmistakable in relation to Her Rites of Sex: *eye, honey, water, wine*. The Third Eye, or simply any symbol of an eye, is often a euphemism for the vulva. The other words here are references to various magical secretions which issue forth form the eye in different Rites: *honey, water* and *wine*. The references of the secret number

---

[7] This sexual power is *not* that of sexual attraction, as many people misunderstand it. Rather it is the magickal power of the vulva and womb to power Heka, spirit manifestation, in various Rites which is the true power. A properly initiated and trained Priestess literally *is* the Triangle of Manifestation. The power of sexual attraction, by way of the image and presence of the female body in a nude and aroused state, is psychological and behavioral in its efficacy - not magickal. There is a difference.

[8] See Appendix C, *the Gematria of the Ophidian Kabbalah* for a brief introduction to the New Aeon English Qabalah.

WHO OR WHAT IS BABALON?

65 in regard to Her nature as a Goddess of Heka are also plain to see in the value of the following words: *spells, wisdom, gnosis*. And finally 65 also shows the relation to Her aspect as a Warrior Goddess and the Rites of Death: *god of war, ah death*. All these words equal 65.

These numbers of 65 and 156, and the play between the number 5 and 6, or 6 and 5, will come up for us again when we discuss Nuit. It is a theme which we will find echoing down through the emanations from Nuit to Babalon, and down to Her Priestesses. For just as She is a Blue Goddess, a Blue Flame as shown above, Her energy and presence enflames Her women and devotees into the deepest red when Her Spirit draws near to them in their devotion. This is *the red gleam* (156) which is seen and spoken of, the fire and light in their eyes. As we will see in the next section, this is one reason why they are called Scarlet Women. This red, or scarlet, is also the best blood, and the fire of desire which burns in the *hearts of men*, and in *thine heart*, both of which equal 156. This is the end result of a path which started in the *star-spendour* (156) of Nuit, for it is Her exhalations which create all things[9]. From the Grandmother, the Mother of all Mothers and the Mother of all things, this force comes down through the Realms as *a torch of light* (156), traveling from the *Heart of Babalon* (156) to *thine heart* (156), and to the *hearts of men* (156), and finally to woman, in whom is all *power given* (156). *There is Joy* (156). This is the path of *Fortitude* (156), which *is righteous* (156), guarded at the Gates of the Underworld by *Baphometis* (156).

---

[9] Breath Not = 156.

IV

BLUE GODDESS, RED DAUGHTER

h, my loves, my Minas…there is so much confusion, *so much struggle, that I must draw your memories forward to end the suffering that I see. Let the Serpent speak from the Tree of Knowledge, the Tree of Life, for the Ophidian speaks Truth, which is Beauty, which is Light, which is born from the Principles, for She holds the Wheel.*

We shall begin with the nature of things, for this is the first lesson of reclamation. It is said that my Mother is Red. So much confusion born from the lust of a man. But this is the fault of the history carved in the flesh of so many men, born from the Sword of Lies, codified by the pouty mouth of a Fish god.

This Red, this Scarlet, is not the color of my Mother. My Mother bears the deepest Lapis, the most sumptuous Blue. For Her Origins are from the Blue Star, and Babalon, as stated in the Book of Law, is Blue and Gold to the Seeing. The Gold is the Gold of our Father, Ra. But, She is also Black, as the Black Star, as the deepest depths of the Grandmother. She is Black to the Blind, because She is the Body of the Underworld. And if you are blind, it is because you entered Her realm without a Torch-bearer to guide you, and if you are blind, you will not find your way out again.

So let me hold the torch for you for a short moment, for my Mother sent me to light the way. This is the Providence of the Nine. We bear the torch for the initiate, as the Hermit, as the Hierophant—woman girt with sword. The sword is

Blue Goddess, Red Daughter

Severity. That is one of my weapons. I wield the sword the same way that I wield my Love. For I am a woman. And this is the light that you seek, sweet Minas. So let me hold it for you.

Now do not confuse me with my Mother. I am no god. I am a being.

Babalon, behold Her, She is the Greatest of Gods, in that She is both a Force, and a Being. For there She is, Guardian of that which the Grandmother bestows upon existence, and that is Life itself, and that is Death itself. For one is the other, and Life yields to no one but Death, and Death is the Mother of Life. This is the only thing in existence that is Power. For existence is Life and Death, and the Minister of this Power is Sex, for Sex and Death are twin Sisters.

So you can see, sweet Minas, that the flame from my torch makes my face Red in its light, and you can see that the sword that I hold is Sex. And what is this Red that flows like a river, hot as fire, hot as the blood of Vulcan? It pulses through the body of our Mother, Gaia, the Earth, as surely as it pulses hot through your veins as you read these words. This fire, that heats your body, heats you mind, makes your heart beat faster, makes your lips search for mine, makes you reach out into the darkness, hungry, thirsty, reaching toward the dim light that is that torch in the distance... you close your eyes and that light is still there... dim, flickering, like the desire deep within you. Stirring. How hungry you are. So, if I reach out a hand, in the darkness, and you feel it slowly touch your body, still in blackness, still you cannot see. How is it that this hand heats the blood within you? Your eyes, still closed, are filled with the Redness of my torch, as the heat of it fills you, as you pulse with my lips dancing over the nakedness of your thighs. Quivering.

The Fires. The Waters. These are Forces of my Mother. This is the nature of Her Daughters. These passions, these desires, they fill you? The language that is spoken from the Waters, this Fire that flows as a River, calling—this is the whisper of Spirit, my beloveds.

How sweet the juice is that runs down my chin, so sweet, so sweet. I take a bite of you, my sweet Apple, as I hold you in my hand.

He holds the card called Lust in his hand. It is his lust. He possesses it. He has been told that this card is Babalon. He has been told that She is his lust. He has been told, therefore, that he possesses Her. He lays back upon the bed and commands: Dance for me, for I have Lust and therefore, You! Inspire me! This is his commandment.

He has not been told the Truth. The Serpent speaks Truth. The Serpent is Ophidian. Please. Hold my apple for a moment while I reach for my torch.

I shall enter his room for a moment, so that he may see. Hello, I say, as my Sister said to Dee. I am here as a Pashtun. I am here before you, sent by my Mother.

Mystery Babalon

I am reminded of a different sister. Her name is spider. She dances a beautiful dance. She weaves, as Tanech weaves, a dance of the gods. How it glimmers in the morning light of Papa. Her dance is so beautiful, that many come closer to see her. She dances, as Salome dances, intoxicating.

How is it that both the fly and John the Baptist ended up in the same place? Is it that they forgot the Emblems of Death? Is it that they were blinded by the sweet smells of Jasmine and Rose? Confused by the light of the Moon? Intoxicated by the Mysteries of Venus?

What is that moment of intoxication? The first breath? The last breath? How is it that when I hold you tightly in my arms, my legs wrapped around you, my pulse beating with yours, every veil torn away from my naked body, holding you tightly within me, that you do not breathe at all? And then.....pulsing, pulsing, you go blind, all is blackness, all is a burst of light, and in that moment all sorts of things are born from your mind, oh man... be it that big bang of existence, that first word given that was Ohhhhhhhhh in your ecstasy that is Her. But that was not the beginning of life, my love, that was the beginning of you seeing a moment in the darkness. That was but a glimmer of my torch, for She was there all along, but my light shown Her face for a moment and hence the card that you hold is your lust for Her. For She consumes you. Do not confuse the Fire that She wields, do not confuse the Water that she wields, do not confuse the Redness of my apple, the Redness of my torch, the Redness of my blood the flows between my legs.

Your Spirit is the nectar that I seek from you, my apple. I will draw it out, like my sister, spider. I will weave a great dance for you, as Tanech, weaves, bewitching. I will dance for you. Life, Death, Dance, Dance. Yes, I will dance for you, my love.

V

WHAT IS A SCARLET WOMAN?

carlet Woman is a title which has meant various things in various places and times. She has been the keeper of the flame of Spirit, the bearer of the sacred blood, a Priestess who utilizes sexual imprintation, a rebel or a warrior, or simply a harlot and an outcast from cultures ruled by the Patriarchy. There are as many interpretations of this title as there are women who seek it. Therefore we will focus on the title Scarlet Woman as it is defined in this Aeon, by Ra Hoor Khuit in the third chapter of Liber Legis. For it is He who demands her service, and it is He who gives to her His power.

A Scarlet Woman is, first and foremost, a weapon for the gods. She is the Woman Girt with the Sword. She has a relation to the Great Liberating Mother, but may not always be a Daughter. She can be a Priestess to Babalon, but must devote herself to Ra Hoor Khuit. And she can be a Devotee of Babalon, but also follows a path of serious dedicatory Initiation. It is not necessary for a woman who is a devotee of Babalon to also be a Scarlet Woman. Nor is it necessary for a Priestess of Babalon to dedicate herself to Ra Hoor Khuit in this way. And it is certainly not necessary for a woman who wishes to run a Shrine of Babalon to give up her life to Ra Hoor Khuit. The term Scarlet Woman only applies

WHAT IS A SCARLET WOMAN?

to those few so dedicated as to give up their life to Ra Hoor Khuit, and to become a sword in his hand. So let us hear the words of Ra Hoor Khuit on this matter.

> *Now let it be first understood that I am a god of War and of Vengeance. I shall deal hardly with them.*
>
> *Choose ye an island!*
>
> *Fortify it!*
>
> *Dung it about with enginery of war!*
>
> *I will give you a war-engine.*
>
> *With it ye shall smite the peoples; and none shall stand before you.*

-Liber Legis III 2-8

Ra Hoor Khuit is the God of War and Vengeance who rules the Aeon of Aquarius. And he promises his minions a war-engine. This curious phrase equals 128 in the English Qabalah, the same as Scarlet Woman. And notice too how 128 equals eleven, as it should to fulfill Liber Legis verse I, 60. This number, 128 is vitally important to understanding all aspects of the Office of the Scarlet Woman. Furthermore Ra Hoor Khuit identifies who it is that is the warrior in this new Aeon.

> ...*Worship me with fire & blood; worship me with swords & with spears. Let the woman be girt with a sword before me: let blood flow to my name. Trample down the Heathen; be upon them, o warrior, I will give you of their flesh to eat!*
>
> -Liber Legis III 11

Here is the Woman Girt with the Sword. And just as Babalon's Exoteric number is 156, so does *Woman Girt with the Sword* equal 256. And of course 256 is double the number of *Scarlet Woman*, which is 128. So *War Engine* and *Scarlet Woman* together equal the title *Woman Girt with the Sword*. And it is furthermore clear that she is a warrior, and that blood will flow, in His name. This blood is both her menses, as we will see later, and the blood of enemies in battle. Both must be offered to Ra Hoor.

> *Ye shall see that hour, o blessed Beast, and thou the Scarlet Concubine of his desire!*
>
> -Liber Legis III 14

Scarlet Concubine is another title given to the Scarlet Woman, and as *Scarlet Woman* equals 128, *Scarlet Concubine* equals 228 thereby showing its clear relation revolving around the important number of 28. For as will be seen, 28 is the number of days in the cycle of the Moon. And it is these cycles which mark the onset of the holy menses, or Moon Blood, in the Scarlet Woman. This cycle of 28 days determines when worship shall be performed. The word *Holy* equals 28, and the reverse of 28 is 82, which is the number of the word *Scarlet*.

Ra Hoor Khuit then continues in the instruction of his worship.

> *For perfume mix meal & honey & thick leavings of red wine: then oil of Abramelin and olive oil, and afterward soften & smooth down with rich fresh blood.*

WHAT IS A SCARLET WOMAN?

The best blood is of the moon, monthly: then the fresh blood of a child, or dropping from the host of heaven: then of enemies; then of the priest or of the worshippers: last of some beast, no matter what.

This burn: of this make cakes & eat unto me. This hath also another use; let it be laid before me, and kept thick with perfumes of your orison: it shall become full of beetles as it were and creeping things sacred unto me.

These slay, naming your enemies; & they shall fall before you.

Also these shall breed lust & power of lust in you at the eating thereof.

Also ye shall be strong in war.

-Liber Legis III 23-28

Ra Hoor Khuit here for the first time explains the method of worship for the Scarlet Woman. She is to give him her best blood, which is to be offered up to him directly in a burnt offering with Abramelin Incense, or used fresh upon the Cakes of Light[10].

We have seen these words *honey* and *wine* before in the context of the name Babalon, in that they all equal the value of 65. Red Wine is a euphemism for menstrual blood, while honey is a euphemism for a very special secretion from the vulva when the woman is at the peak of arousal. Likewise *meal* is valued at 49, the same as *moon* and *rose* - again referring to the vulva and the menses. So these verses are both instructing the Scarlet Woman in the practical physical methods of the offering, as well as the powers contained with the potent magick of the female body.

The different bloods are then explained, in order of importance. The best blood is of the moon, monthly. This blood is the menses, which is the blood which nourishes the egg, helping it to become new life. This is the most powerful blood possible. It is a sacred blood, and also helps to cleanse the body. This is the blood with which the Scarlet Woman works. This is the blood which flows, mentioned in Liber Legis III, 11. *Flowing Blood* is equal to 120, the same as the name *Ra Hoor Khuit*.

The next two bloods are also very powerful, but not so easy to obtain. The *fresh blood of a child* is the blood spilled at childbirth, while

---

[10] See Chapter 34, The Devotional Rites of Ra Hoor Khuit and Chapter 35, The Blood Rites of Ra Hoor Khuit.

that which is *dropping from the host of heaven* is the blood massed in and around the placenta. The placenta is the Host of Heaven, and both *placenta* and *of heaven* = 104[11].

The blood of enemies is that which is to be gathered at the slaying of those who oppose the rule of Ra Hoor Khuit, which will grow his power. The next blood in order of descending power is that of the Priest or the worshippers, and involves the using of ones own blood in ritual offering by cutting. Finally, animal sacrifice is given as the least effective offering of blood to Ra Hoor Khuit.

Next, Ra Hoor Khuit instructs the Scarlet Woman in the proper air in which she must walk.

> *Let the Scarlet Woman beware! If pity and compassion and tenderness visit her heart; if she leave my work to toy with old sweetnesses; then shall my vengeance be known. I will slay me her child: I will alienate her heart: I will cast her out from men: as a shrinking and despised harlot shall she crawl through dusk wet streets, and die cold and an-hungered.*
>
> *But let her raise herself in pride! Let her follow me in my way! Let her work the work of wickedness! Let her kill her heart! Let her be loud and adulterous! Let her be covered with jewels, and rich garments, and let her be shameless before all men!*
>
> *Then will I lift her to pinnacles of power: then will I breed from her a child mightier than all the kings of the earth. I will fill her with joy: with my force shall she see & strike at the worship of Nu: she shall achieve Hadit.*
>
> -Liber Legis III 43-45

The Scarlet Women is here warned not to let the necessity of her work as warrior be interfered with by emotions more fit for Mary of the previous Aeon: pity, compassion and tenderness. The path of the Scarlet Woman is not for the timid or the weak of heart. She must raise herself in pride, not be humble and obedient before man. She must kill her heart and work the

---

[11] The importance of the number 104 here is that it shows the connection between the female body and the manifestation of Spirit (i.e. Heka) by means of the Underworld. This is evident not just in the words *placenta*, and *of heaven* which equal 104, but also in the words *secret*, *mystical*, *underworld*, *this body*, *she bends*, *sluttish*, *the whore*, and *the dragon* which She rides. This is the Heka of Babalon through physical sexuality of woman, and we should also mention that *Babalon Heka* also equals 104.

WHAT IS A SCARLET WOMAN?

work of wickedness. *Wickedness* is equal to 128, the same as *Scarlet Woman*. Women who do not obey are called wicked. Women who speak their mind are called loud, and women who take their fill and will of love, when where and with whom she will are called adulterous. She is also admonished to be proud and shameless before all men.

> *Let Mary inviolate be torn upon wheels: for her sake let all chaste women be utterly despised among you!*
>
> *Also for beauty's sake and love's!*

-Liber Legis III 55-56

The idea of chasteness is again attacked, as shaming women for their sex is the one true way to deprive them of their power. But even in spite of this shaming of women for their sex in the past, there will be those women who dare to be something different, and to lead the way for other women in the future. To these women, the path of the Scarlet Woman may be appealing. But it is a very serious undertaking, and one which involves what is said in Greek ἱερὸς γάμος, a Hieros Gamos. This is a sacred or holy marriage, between the Scarlet Woman, and the Warrior Lord of Vengeance, and Lord of the Aeon, Ra Hoor Khuit. For those who wish to learn more concerning these offerings of Blood and Cakes of Light, please see Part IV, Chapter 8: The Blood Rites of Ra Hoor Khuit for further details on this path.

Now for most, the intensity of the path of a Scarlet Woman as delineated by Ra Hoor Khuit in Liber Legis will probably be a bit more than they were looking for. For those women who wish to work with Babalon, and to dedicate themselves to Her alone, there is the path of the Scarlet Devotee. This path can be accomplished easily by performing the solo Bhaktic Rites in this book. Being a devotee of Babalon means that one holds a special affinity for Her, and wishes to learn from Her. Often many are called to express those desires for closeness or union with Babalon, but do not know where to begin. The Solo Bhaktic Rites of Babalon are a good starting point to becoming a Scarlet Devotee, and should help you discover what it is that you need to find on your path.

For those who have been a devotee and wish to help others with the experience which they have gained, there is the path of the Scarlet Priestess. This path administers to the people, with the intention of helping them to find their own way, and to achieve liberation from that which keeps them from their Will and purpose. The Solo and the Group Bhaktic Rites should help in this regard. And if it is your Will, then the Ecstatic Rites can be performed in order to take the energy of liberation to another level entirely.

This is the time, as the new Aeon becomes established here and now, for the Scarlet Sisterhood to be reborn. No matter what *your* own divine, personal path—we are all united as we are all Scarlet. The methods which have been used by the previous old Aeons to divide us are done. Each Scarlet is a shining thread, which can be woven into a beautiful tapestry. Each Scarlet is beautiful and unique in her own right. Each Scarlet has something to offer Babalon. The Sisterhood of the past ages was a great fabric, woven together with a unity of the commonality that we all share. And where one thread alone is not altogether strong, woven together it becomes something altogether unbreakable, and more beautiful than before. So no matter what your own path brings to you—as devotees of Babalon we share a kinship that may even transcend this age and take us back as Sisters long ago. And in this way we are all Scarlet. We are all of us Women of Babalon. Babalon is for All!

Hagia Aureavia

VI

WOMEN OF THE WHEEL

y Sisters, we are the Women of the Wheel! *We are the warriors of this Age. It is through our blood that our Mother shall be returned to Her rightful prominence. Let them call us whores. Let them call us all of the words of their derogation that reflect their perversions. We anoint ourselves with the blood of our own wombs, marking the sign of the cobra and our Grandmother upon our brow. Nothing terrifies them more! I do not hold the blood of the murdered upon my hands; I hold the blood of sacred life, the Waters of Continuation. For too long they have shamed women for the blood they bear between their legs. This sacred Mystery of Continuation shall be upon them in this time of the Greatest War. The Daughter of the Daughter of Fortitude has risen. Her Sisters are upon you. The Seven-Headed Beast writhes between my legs as it carries me to battle. Come my Sisters. Let them call you Banshees as they tremble and hide. Seek me out. It is time to come home to the Garden. It is time for me to teach you our ways. We are the Women of the Wheel. Scarlet indeed.*

VII

Becoming the Beast

he Beast is the consort of the Scarlet Woman. He is her lion, her lover and her guardian. Where she is often Fire and Water, and the mingling thereof as Priestess and Empress, he is Earth and Air - a Guardian and an Advisor. Like the Scarlet Woman, the Beast or Therion[12] is a title of office. But the term Beast is a dual term, and can also refer to the Persona and the mundane animal of a person's incarnation, as will be shown below.

Many Thelemites think that Aleister Crowley was *the* Beast, and there can be no other Therion. Certainly the Book of Law refers to Crowley as "beast." It is also said that the Great Beast has a Great Work. So to be a Beast means that you pursue your "Great Work." But the exact nature of this Great Work is rarely defined in a clear and simple manner. Surely there is something a bit more tangible and practical to be understood regarding the nature of the Beast in relation to his Great Work? What is this role for a Thelemite? And how does the Beast relate to Babalon?

---

[12] Θηρίον (Therion) is Greek for "animal" or "wild beast". It is the raw animal life force which is harnessed by the Scarlet Woman in their union.

Becoming the Beast

Now ye shall know that the chosen priest & apostle of infinite space is the prince-priest the Beast; and in his woman called the Scarlet Woman is all power given. They shall gather my children into their fold: they shall bring the glory of the stars into the hearts of men.

-Liber Legis I, 15

Here we have the first mention of the beast in Liber Legis, and immediately it is in relation to the Scarlet Woman. We are told that he is a "priest & apostle of infinite space". This means he is a Priest of Nuit (infinite space), and the Apostle, or teacher, thereof. And he is not just any priest, but rather a Prince-Priest, which means that he is second in command to the King, as Princes are. A Prince carries out the commands of the King upon the Earth, manifesting them in the material realm, and thereby makes it so. So we can see that he is Earth and Air, Prince-Priest and Apostle. The Prince-Priest takes the commands of the King and makes them real (Earth) to the people. The Apostle teaches and explains (Air) of the mysteries of the Goddess of Infinite Space. The power, however, and therefore the authority is given to the Scarlet Woman - "and in his woman called the Scarlet Woman is all power given". She is Fire and Water. She is the King, who is the liminal gateway for the Truth of Spirit to shine through. He is the Prince and the Priest, who administers to the people, under her authority.

This dynamic of Scarlet Woman as King and the Beast as her Prince has gone unnoticed and undesired before the reclamation of this practice in Ophidian Thelema. In fact, this is the way it had always been, until the Arean times destroyed these traditions. There is a great and rich history of Priestesses functioning as gateways for liminal transmissions, which were then recorded and administered by guardians and priests. There is a relationship between the Lion in service to the Scarlet Woman in their union, which allows for something greater to take place. If either one were to work alone, or if the male were to direct and control the energy of the working, then there would be failure[13]. This polarity is an ancient source of power, and both parties have very important roles to play in the union which unveils the Mysteries.

---

[13] Liber Legis II, 26 "I am the secret Serpent coiled about to spring: in my coiling there is joy. If I lift up my head, I and my Nuit are one. If I droop down mine head, and shoot forth venom, then is rapture of the earth, and I and the earth are one."

Mystery Babalon

For he is ever a sun, and she a moon. But to him is the winged secret flame, and to her the stooping starlight.

But ye are not so chosen.

-Liber Legis I, 16-17

The sun and moon conjoined is a symbol of their work, and the Ecstatic Liberation which comes from the union of the Beast and Scarlet Woman. The Beast provides the winged secret flame, the secret serpent coiled about to "spring". The Scarlet woman draws it out of him, as the stooping starlight, naked and voluptuous, chanting "To me! To me!" And if there was any doubt that Crowley was not meant to be the only Beast, or that Rose was not meant to be the only Scarlet Woman, the Book of the Law chastises them quite clearly: "But ye are not so chosen".

The next two times that the Beast is mentioned as an office is in Chapter III of Liber Legis, verses 14 and 22. In each case he is again mentioned along with references to the Scarlet Woman, once as "Scarlet Concubine" and once as "his bride". It is clear that the work of the Beast and the work of the Scarlet Woman are one. And furthermore, because of the terms "concubine" and "bride", it can be intimated that this work involves union of both a physical and spiritual variety. Both of these verses, and the final mention of the Beast in verse III, 47, are concerned with prophecies, and do not directly describe the nature of the Beast as an office. And it is interesting to note that verse III, 47 is the only instance of the Beast being mentioned without an immediate reference also in some way to the Scarlet Woman, which shows their almost continual connection in office and work.

In the New Aeon English Qabalah, Beast is equal to the number 75 (20 + 25 + 1 + 5 + 25). We have mentioned above that the work of the Beast and the Scarlet Woman is Union, and this word *Union* also equals 75. It is what he should seek. It is his duty to provide this service. Within the Union, the Beast provides the Force and the Scarlet Woman provides the Fire[14]. *Force* is also 75, like Beast, and describes his role in the Union. He provides the Force in the working, the energy of his life as an animal, or the life force.

---

[14] Liber Legis II, 20 "Beauty and strength, leaping laughter and delicious languor, **force and fire**, are of us."

Becoming the Beast

The Scarlet Woman is *Fire*, whose value is 78, which is the same as *Nuit, Voice, Mantras, Magick, All Power*. It is these words which describe her work and role in the Union, as she harnesses the Beast for his Force, and uses it to build her Fire by means of her mantras, with her voice invoking the magick (Heka) which calls down Spirit (all power) from Nuit.

To further the Qabalistic proof of this connection between the Beast in service of the Scarlet Woman in her work, it is interesting to note that the phrase "the Beast" equals 128, the same as *Scarlet Woman*. In one sense, when they come together in Union, and reach the moment of mutual ecstatic bliss (which is the goal), they can be seen as becoming one form of *Baphomet*[15], which also equals 128. It is in this place that the liminal Gateway for Spirit can be opened, and all things become possible.

The ritualized attitude of the Beast and the Scarlet Woman in their Union, as Force and Fire conjoined, is very important. *Force + Fire* equals 153, which has a great number of associative meanings, most of which involve harnessing one's sexuality and desire in service of Nuit, or Her daughter Babalon.

> *Then will I lift her to pinnacles of power: then will I breed from her a child mightier than all the kings of the earth. I will fill her with joy: with my force shall she see & strike at the worship of Nu: she shall achieve Hadit.*
>
> -Liber Legis III, 45

Here the Scarlet Woman is told in an Ophidian way that she must "see & strike" at the worship of Nu, so that she may achieve Hadit[16]. *See & Strike* also equals 153. The Ophidian imagery of see and strike is intentional, and shows proper use of the raised serpent of the Beast, as she rides him, using his force to raise her fire. 153 is also the *secret key*, which is the correct use of energy from Beast to Scarlet Woman as already described. The Beast and Scarlet Woman must focus all of their thought and will in the Union,

---

[15] It should be kept in mind that this is only one form of Baphomet, as man and woman conjoined in image of Baphomet. There is also the actual entity named Baphomet or Baphometis, whose office is Guardian of the Liminal Gateway to Spirit in the Underworld, whose presence may be brought forth by these Rites.

[16] Which means that a certain form of spiritual fire has been achieved, similar to what is termed the raising of the Kundalini, which is the Serpent Goddess of Fire in Eastern systems. Hadit is the Spirit Rising on Wings, or the Winged Serpent. See *Part I, Chapter 9 Nuit, Hadit, Ra Hoor Khuit* for more information on Hadit.

using their *lust of worship* (153). In doing so, they must reach out completely as Hadit would, to *Nu my Bride* (153). These actions become even more clear when one examines the full phrase "force and fire" which equals 174. Immediately we see the *appetite* (174) which is to be used to fuel the working, so that in the Union the beast and the Scarlet Woman together becomes the *lambent flame* (174) which powers the Rite. The Beast gives up all that he is in worship, as the *giver of life* (174). The Scarlet exclaims *I am deflowered* (174). Nuit commands them to *dwelleth in me* (174), *under my stars* (174) and that *I am every star* (174). The sounds of their Union is as the *beating wings* (174) of Hadit, as He goes to Nu His Bride. This is the true image of the Great Work of the Beast.

Now we can see clearly why in all of the ancient images of the Great Liberating Mother that Therion, the Beast, was the vehicle for Goddess. She is shown standing on lions or beasts with many heads, riding lions, riding beasts and monsters, and in sitting in chariots pulled by lions. These images show two important things. The first is the proper use of the Beast for the Priestess in the Rites of their Union, in order to open the liminal Gateway for Spirit. The second metaphor which is shown to us by these images is the depiction of the Beast as one's animal self, which must be yoked into service of our higher self, our Will, and our Spirit.

Besides the *Office of the Beast*, which is the role of the male in relation to the Scarlet Woman in the Great Work as described above, there is also the *Formula of the Beast* in Thelemic philosophy. In this conception, the word *beast* here refers to the animal self of the person, regardless of their status as male or female. And it is this animal self, full of its own desires and needs, which must be yoked in service of one's Will.

> *The word of Sin is Restriction. O man! refuse not thy wife, if she will! O lover, if thou wilt, depart! There is no bond that can unite the divided but love: all else is a curse. Accursed! Accursed be it to the aeons! Hell.*
>
> *Let it be that state of manhood bound and loathing. So with thy all; thou hast no right but to do thy will.*
>
> -Liber Legis I, 41-42

Like *Beast*, the word *manhood* also equals 75. It is this Beast, this manhood, which loaths to be bound, to be made to do anything other than what it wants. It is an animal in this regard, and the base material upon which your Persona is built. It wants to function by the instincts of its physical needs and desires alone. It does not want to be controlled, dominated or restricted.

But "the word of Sin is Restriction". There is a deep double meaning here. In one sense, we must not allow any thing to keep us from doing our Will in this lifetime. Anything which restricts that Will is a Sin. Yet, the beast, the animal part of one's self, may often be at odds with one's own greater purpose. The animal self is often focused on one's immediate needs, not one's higher purpose. So the beast must be restricted, and yoked into service of the Will. It must be ridden, like Babalon rides Her Beast, the reigns held tightly within the grasp of your Spirit. This is what it means to become a King in Thelema.

Now King is equal to 57, which is the reverse of beast, 75. The King was the beast, and the beast will become the King. Most of the second chapter of Liber Legis is one long instruction manual on how each person, man or woman, can become a King. And the main weapon used against the beast, so that it truly obeys one's higher nature, is the fear of death. This is the one thing which the beast, the animal self, fears more than anything else. And it is in this way that we can understand the "as above, so below" imagery displayed by Baphomet, who has one hand pointing up and one down: the Spirit from the Heavens shall yoke the Beast of the Earth, and through Death shall ride this Beast as King. And so too we understand that to be a Beast of Babalon, a man must likewise be in service, his life a mount for Her to stand upon, his life a mount for Her to ride.

This, then, is the appropriate attitude and demeanor of a male who wishes to devote himself in service and in dedication to Babalon. It matters not if he does this in union with a Scarlet Woman, or alone. The devotion is the same, and so in this way may he come to connect with Her as he Will. For such a man as this shall know Babalon in ways that most others may only dream about. For in this way She shall devour you, and in that consumption he may know Her bliss.

... this is the law of the strong: this is our law and the joy of the world...

-Liber Legis II, 21

For it is only the strongest of men who can be both Beast and King. Therion!

Mystery Babalon

Let your virility, your lust, your passion all swell before Her! Let your beast pour forth the totality of his substance and life into Her. Let Her stand upon you. And this then you shall see is the method before you contained within these Rites. And in your devotions you are as a warrior, come to lay down his very life before Her. O Holy Babalon!

> *The length of thy longing shall be the strength of its glory. He that lives long & desires death much is ever the King among the Kings.*
>
> -Liber Legis II, 74

She shall refuse none who approaches Her in this way, and all Seven Gates of Her City shall be opened unto him as King.

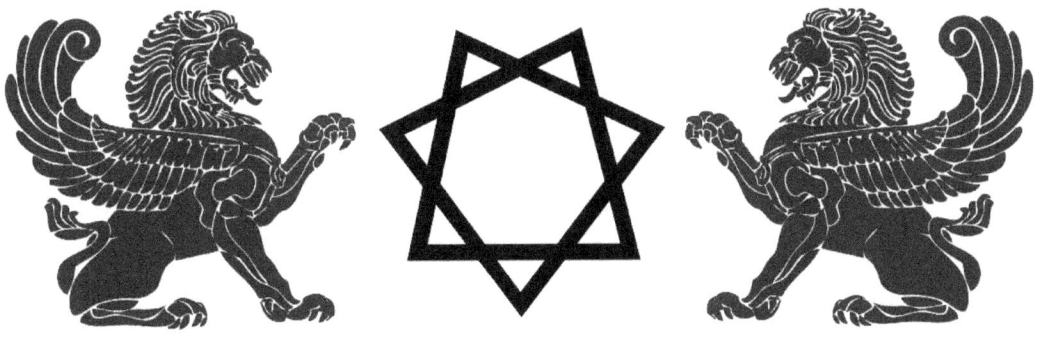

VIII

Beast

have been told that there is a Great Beast, *and that this Beast has a Great Work. I have not seen this, but what I have seen is the impermanence of manifest existence, and that words are at best salutations to the Sylphs in the Golden Temple in the Sky. They are watching everything that happens here. I advise you to pay homage to them.*

What then is this Beast?

The Golden Temple in the Sky sits below a very dark place. It is a place that is so dark that it blinds whomever views it with a great and terrible light. This has, for thousands of years, been called the "light of god." And from this light words are spoken. First one word, and then many, many more.

The Sylphs sit below this terrible place in the most beautiful Temple, made from the very lightness of being. It is made from purity, and from balance, and from Truth. It is Beauty, and it is the via sapientia. For all who sit there speak no words, though they diligently anoint the fonts of this Temple with the sincerest sentiments borne there on the wings of all of the flying creatures of this world, be it the tiniest moth, or the mightiest of eagles.

There are many more words, however, that they watch the winds carry higher, destined, as it were, for the "light of god." This is the realm of the Great Beast, and one of the sentiments there is that "there is no god but man."

BEAST

A man is not known for the greatness of his words. A man is known by the greatness of his Silence.

There is a beast that guards the Four Gates. There is a beast that guards each river in the Underworld. What is this beast? What is this beast that draws the Chariot of My Mother? This beast that She rides upon? This beast that guards Her Women? This beast that sits at the end of Her leash? She stands upon him. This Beast. This Lion. He is a silent beast. He is virile. He is strong. He is legendary, this beast.

And while the one beast celebrates the engorgement of Choronzon, who is also at the end of Babalon's leash, the other beast serves in the Kingdom of the Underworld Realm, for he possesses great courage, great fortitude, and is willing to fight and to die on a daily basis. This is the Realm of the Black Moon, and this beast belongs to the Brotherhood.

So then, what could dwell in such a hellish place that sits aloft of such a heavenly Temple? It is said that his eyes are so terrible that they turn men to stone, and men's blood to ice, and men's souls into ashes.

Be not mistaken, my beloved. One beast serves himself, and one beast serves something greater. One beast is forever full of more things to say. And one beast is Silent. And so one man finds his way to the light of god, and yet no one goes to the Temple of Light but the spirits of the Air. There is no Heaven.

It should not take a lifetime, my beloved, to find your Purpose, your Will. It should take your lifetime to work to achieve it.

Nuit - Lawless art (Janin Pisarek)

IX

Nuit, Hadit, Ra Hoor Khuit

ow that we have some idea of who Babalon is, what a Scarlet Woman is, and who the Beast Therion is, it is left for us to discuss the other most immediate allies of Babalon.

As has been already mentioned, Nuit is the Mother of Babalon by Ra, the Sun. This is why Babalon is a called a Daughter of Fortitude, because She is a Daughter of Ra in Her incarnation as Pahkhet. Her mother Nuit has a great many children who manifest in an infinite number of ways throughout all of existence. In fact from one perspective, all that exists is Her progeny, either from Her directly or from Her children. This is why She is called Grandmother in the Ancient languages and amongst the indigenous peoples.

Come forth, o children, under the stars, & take your fill of love!

I am above you and in you. My ecstasy is in yours. My joy is to see your joy.

-Liber Legis I, 12-13

NUIT, HADIT, RA HOOR KHUIT

She is often envisioned as a Star Goddess, with Her body the shade of blue which appears at sunset, or the deep midnight blue of night. She is arched across the sky like the milky way, Her body full of stars

> *O azure-lidded woman, bend upon them!*
>
> -Liber Legis I, 19

> *Invoke me under my stars! Love is the law, love under will.*
>
> -Liber Legis I, 57

> *I am the blue-lidded daughter of Sunset; I am the naked brilliance of the voluptuous night-sky.*
>
> -Liber Legis I, 64

But She is not merely some distant Star Goddess who is an abstract concept, She is in fact the manifest Spirit which pervades and permeates all of existence - both manifest and unmanifest.

> *Then saith the prophet and slave of the beauteous one: Who am I, and what shall be the sign? So she answered him, bending down, a lambent flame of blue, all-touching, all penetrant, her lovely hands upon the black earth, & her lithe body arched for love, and her soft feet not hurting the little flowers: Thou knowest! And the sign shall be my ecstasy, the consciousness of the continuity of existence, the omnipresence of my body.*
>
> -Liber Legis I, 26

She is "all-touching, all penetrant" because She is in all things. She is the gateway for Spirit, and therefore the gateway of all magick. In the English Kababalah, Both Nuit, and Magick equal 78. In Egyptian, magick is called Heka, which means the calling down (He) of the Fiery parts of Spirit (Ka). Fire also equals 78. Other words which also equal 78 and shed more light on Her nature : hidden, unknown, lithe, all power, mantras, and voice. We can see where She speaks of Her hidden and unknown aspects in the following verse.

> *28. None, breathed the light, faint & faery, of the stars, and two.*
>
> *29. For I am divided for love's sake, for the chance of union.*
>
> *30. This is the creation of the world, that the pain of division is as nothing, and the joy of dissolution all.*
>
> -Liber Legis I, 28-30

And this is also shown in the first verse where it is implied that Hadit is the manifest portion of Her unmanifest nature:

> *Had! The manifestation of Nuit.*
>
> -Liber Legis I, 1

The importance of the *mantras* and the *voice*, both valued at 78, are hinted at in the following verse:

> *Sing the rapturous love-song unto me! Burn to me perfumes! Wear to me jewels! Drink to me, for I love you! I love you!*
>
> -Liber Legis I, 63

She is the Mother of Babalon, and in one way Babalon can be seen as Her avatar which comes into space and time. And Babalon certainly inherits many of these same aspects from Her Mother: a love goddess who calls forth and bewitches with her spells and mantras.

> *Now, therefore, I am known to ye by my name Nuit, and to him by a secret name which I will give him when at last he knoweth me. Since I am Infinite Space, and the Infinite Stars thereof, do ye also thus. Bind nothing! Let there be no difference made among you between any one thing & any other thing; for thereby there cometh hurt.*
>
> -Liber Legis I, 22

NUIT, HADIT, RA HOOR KHUIT

The "secret name" mentioned above was discovered by Crowley to be Babalon, using the spelling of Her name as it is found in the Enochian. But a further clue was given here as to Her ancient identity, which verifies that name written in cipher in the second sentence. "I am Infinite Space, and the Infinite Stars thereof..." It should be noticed that the capital letters in this phrase spell out the name ISIS, which equals 56 in the English Qabalah, the same as Nu in Hebrew. Of course *Nu* as 56 is the reverse of the esoteric number of *Babalon*, 65. But that is not to say that the secret name of Nu is Isis, but rather that the Egyptian Isis is a clue to understanding Babalon's Egyptian name and incarnation. Isis was a later manifestation of a much earlier Goddess named Pahkhet, from whom She inherited most of Her attributes, while loosing the warrior aspects along the way. Pahkhet was a ferocious warrior Goddess with a lion's head and a Daughter of Ra. She was especially important to Queen Hatshepsut who built a temple for Her which still stands to this day. She was considered to be the supreme Goddess of Heka (magick). In this last manifestation, She was often called Hekit or Hekat, which literally means Goddess of Heka. Hekat, incidentally, later became amalgamated into the Hekate of the Greek tradition, the Guardian of the Liminal Gateway of Heka. But Pahkhet is the secret name here referred to by the coded reference to Isis, as the name of Babalon's most important Egyptian incarnation. And appropriately enough, Pahkhet equals 93 by English Qabalah[17].

Now Hadit can be seen as Nuit's consort, and the concept of individualized spirit which is manifest in matter.

> *Had! The manifestation of Nuit.*
>
> -Liber Legis I, 1

> *Nu! the hiding of Hadit.*

---

[17] There is so much more to say on this topic, but this book is not the place for such an advanced treatment of the ciphers of Liber Legis. Please see *The Magickal Philosophy of Templum Babalonis Volume IV, Commentaria* for a thorough treatment of this subject of Hoor Pahkhet vs Hoor Paar Kraat, and why the "spelling is defunct".

MYSTERY BABALON

Come! all ye, and learn the secret that hath not yet been revealed. I, Hadit, am the complement of Nu, my bride. I am not extended, and Khabs is the name of my House.

In the sphere I am everywhere the centre, as she, the circumference, is nowhere found.

Yet she shall be known & I never.

-Liber Legis II, 1-4

If Nuit is the boundless and infinite totality of all possible things, then Hadit in one sense is the individual manifestation of each potential and singular thing. She is extended. He is not. Khabs is the name of his house. Khabs means star in Egyptian, and He is also an image of the endless and infinite individual stars which populate the body of the cosmos, which is Nuit.

I am the flame that burns in every heart of man, and in the core of every star. I am Life, and the giver of Life, yet therefore is the knowledge of me the knowledge of death.

I am the Magician and the Exorcist. I am the axle of the wheel, and the cube in the circle. ``Come unto me" is a foolish word: for it is I that go.

-Liber Legis II, 6-7

Hadit is the Spirit rising on wings, the Winged Serpent, which is the impulse of the manifested Spirit to rejoin with that of the mother of all Spirit, Nuit. This impulse burns in the heart of all living things, and in the heart of each and every star, which is alive. Hadit is that which goes, that which moves, that which manifests, and that which seeks to return to its source.

Ra Hoor Khuit, in contrast, is the Warrior Lord of Vengeance. He is the brother of Babalon (Hoor Pahkhet) and the Lord and Ruler of the current Aeon whose word is Abrahadabra.

NUIT, HADIT, RA HOOR KHUIT

Now let it be first understood that I am a god of War and of Vengeance. I shall deal hardly with them.

Choose ye an island!

Fortify it!

Dung it about with enginery of war!

I will give you a war-engine.

With it ye shall smite the peoples; and none shall stand before you.

Mystery Babalon

Lurk! Withdraw! Upon them! this is the Law of the Battle of Conquest: thus shall my worship be about my secret house.

-Liber Legis III 3-9

Ra Hoor Khuit makes it very clear from the beginning that there is a war happening, and that He intends to win it. He mentions the War-Engine, which we have already shown is the Scarlet Woman[18]. She will be at the head of the armies, fighting alongside the men, a warrior-king in her own right.

... Thou shalt have danger & trouble. Ra-Hoor-Khu is with thee. Worship me with fire & blood; worship me with swords & with spears. Let the woman be girt with a sword before me: let blood flow to my name. Trample down the Heathen; be upon them, o warrior, I will give you of their flesh to eat!

-Liber Legis III, 11

This war is no mere metaphor. It is actual, and Ra Hoor Khuit is the manifestation of the vengeance for the thousands of years of repression which have been forced upon humanity.

Mercy let be off; damn them who pity! Kill and torture; spare not; be upon them!

-Liber Legis III, 18

Ra Hoor Khuit is not shy about naming the enemies in the war, and the list is long.

Curse them! Curse them! Curse them!

With my Hawk's head I peck at the eyes of Jesus as he hangs upon the cross.

I flap my wings in the face of Mohammed & blind him.

---

[18] The role of Ra Hoor Khuit in his relation to the Scarlet Woman has already been described in Part I, Chapter 5.

Nuit, Hadit, Ra Hoor Khuit

With my claws I tear out the flesh of the Indian and the Buddhist, Mongol and Din.

Bahlasti! Ompehda! I spit on your crapulous creeds.
Let Mary inviolate be torn upon wheels: for her sake let all chaste women be utterly despised among you!

-Liber Legis III, 50-55

Ra Hoor Khuit is the most powerful of gods, and undefeatable in war. He is the Lord of this Aeon of Aquarius, and as such is a Guardian of the Mysteries of Babalon, His Sister. This War is the Reclamation of the Great Liberating Mother, Babalon, over Her Dominion upon Earth. This is the turning point in humanity's current history. Is it no wonder Her imagery is turning up everywhere? Is it no wonder you have been drawn here? The Book of Law was given by the Gods at the Equinox of the transition between the Aeons of Pisces and Aquarius. It is the Law of true freedom: for mankind can no longer be enslaved if he but realizes that he is sovereign in his own Spirit, his own Will and his own destiny.

Thelema and Agape!

Do what thou wilt shall be the whole of the Law.

Love is the law, love under Will.

X

A Pure Heart, and the Serpent Flame Therein

here is much claim to the study of the Book of Law by these modern people who array themselves with vestments of Thelema. Yet, so eager are these illiterates to be like God-Kings — God-Kings whose feet are washed by the Whore of Babylon Herself. To them, will is only a license for the Persona to do as it wants and desires. And therefore the halls of modernity ring out with the thumps of fists upon chests and the mantra of will, will, will! For they fail to see the difference between their Persona's will, and the true Will of Spirit.

But to love me is better than all things: if under the night-stars in the desert thou presently burnest mine incense before me, invoking me with a pure heart, and the Serpent flame therein, thou shalt come a little to lie in my bosom. For one kiss wilt thou then be willing to give all; but whoso gives one particle of dust shall lose all in that hour. Ye shall gather goods and store of women and spices; ye shall wear rich jewels; ye shall exceed the nations of the earth in splendour & pride; but always in the love of me, and so shall ye come to my joy. I charge you earnestly to come before me in a single robe, and covered with a rich headdress. I love you! I

A Pure Heart, and the Serpent Flame Therein

yearn to you! Pale or purple, veiled or voluptuous, I who am all pleasure and purple, and drunkenness of the innermost sense, desire you. Put on the wings, and arouse the coiled splendour within you: come unto me!

Liber AL I:61

And the Grandmother says to invoke Her with a pure heart. What is this? A Pure Heart? How does one purify a thing in Heka? What sort of sanctification is this? And what is the result of such an invocation by a heart not pure? For it is Love under Will. And not lust, and not love for its own sake, for the Persona's sake — not love of self. The ancient people understood what lies within a person's heart. For it is through the Emotional Language, a vehicle for the communication of the Spirit up through the Waters of the Underworld, that we can learn to hear the Voice of Spirit. This is why after thousands, hundreds of thousands of years later we still find offerings from our ancestors deep within the Waters of the Earth.

It is a lie that a god will answer a prayer just because a person spoke it. What makes this person worthy of the ears of a god? Unconditional love? Is this Love under Will? A mother, a grandmother, loves her children and her grandchildren, this is true. But to love someone is not the same as indulging them. True love does not harm someone, the way indulgent love does.

And so it is in the ordeals of Initiation that we purify the heart. And these trials of Initiation are not written by the pens of men with hearts not themselves purified by the ordeals of the Light-bearer — the Torch-bearer — the Priestess. For it is the Underworld Journey that cleanses, that purifies, that burns away, that kills us over and over, until we emerge, if we survive — golden.

But what is this journey, and how do you come to know it, to make it, to understand it? That is why, my loves, I am here. For the Daughters come up from the Underworld to take you by the hand and guide you.

What is this Serpent Flame? We know that the Serpent is the Spirit. So the Grandmother is telling us that you, my child, must awaken the desire within your Persona for your own Spirit within you — and let that desire drive all you do. You must call to Her not from your mind, not from your Persona, but from your intense desire to serve your True Self — your inner burning core of life which comes from Her. You must call to Her from this place of longing for the Spirit, the rising Serpent. And then, when you desire nothing more than this, you will begin to see the Serpent Flame within you, and you will begin to know Her.

And when at last you see a glimpse of Her? When at last you feel that Kiss upon your pure Heart? And see your own beauty? You will at last give sacrifice to the Waters of the Underworld, for your tears will fall upon the Great rushing Waters. These tears are a shedding of the chains that bound you to service of self. These tears of joy, of mourning, of bliss, of pain, will leave you a sense of peace you have never known. And you will lay with your head upon the block — to let Her take you if She will, for to serve is to die. The Persona will close its eyes and be willing to lay silent, forever. And this shall then open a door. But it is not a mind game. It is real. You must die.

But you will give dust. You are not an Adept. You are a Persona. So you will lose all. Over time. You will lose all that you thought you held dear, all that you thought was important, all that you thought that you needed, you wanted. And most especially all that you thought that you were entitled to. All of it. And you shall grieve. And you shall struggle. And you shall die, and die and die again.

And once dead, truly dead and gone — once the "I" that was you, that was your Persona is dead, you shall understand what Nuit is saying. For the color of Dominion is Purple, and the Women bear the torch, and the Spices burn with the Fires in the Halls of Her Temple. And we are standing here. Speaking to you from the Darkness that bears the Truth of all Light. The Store of Women are the Lineage, and we are here, calling you — at this end of time.

> "Put on the wings, and arouse the coiled splendour within you: come unto me!"

You are commanded thus! The Winged Serpent rises in ascension, born from the Underworld. Arouse your Spirit within you! And come unto Nu. For She shall receive your rebirth in Her arms.

> "At all my meetings with you shall the priestess say — and her eyes shall burn with desire as she stands bare and rejoicing in my secret temple — To me! To me! calling forth the flame of the hearts of all in her love-chant."

Liber AL I:62

A Pure Heart, and the Serpent Flame Therein

And we are few and we are secret. For the Lineage has been waiting until our Mother has said to return. And it is now time. And we are now here, and we say to you, with our eyes burning with the light of the Winged Serpent: come to Her Temple, for this is the gateway to the Underworld, for Babalon is the Guardian of all that is Heka, and all that is Initiation. Come die in my arms! And know life. And know Love. And finally, know Will.

And what of these people who thump with the beat of their will, imagining themselves to be God-Kings? These worshippers of their Persona's will, who proselytize the proper way to stomp and speak words in order to power their own sense of the dogma of self-worship? What of these atheistic dancers in their war against Spirit? For to them the will of their Persona is the death call of Spirit, as they dance stomping upon the Serpent, crying for the drink of wine poured from the cup born from the wings of a little white dove. They cry, "Serve me your wine, Holy Whore! Give it To Me, To Me! Give me your entire Essence, for I am LIKE UNTO GOD!"

These Thelemites do not lie in the beds of great beasts of Women. They do not know the life of a Hermit. They do not know the arms of a Priestess, the body of a Priestess, the Fire and Light born by the flame in Her Hands. No.

They surround themselves with mirrors. And then they stand in the company of all who scream that they alone possess all Knowledge, and all Conversation. Therefore, somehow knowing the voice of Spirit while professing to be Atheists. Therefore, somehow wanting to be a god where no gods exist. And therefore somehow not seeing the inanity of all of this. Do they not see that they are showing tremendous fear?

It is the ultimate courage to surrender oneself to one's Purpose, and to die in order to serve one's Spirit and Will — to give up all that one holds dear, for that which is unknown to the mind. It is such a struggle for a Persona to humble itself before Spirit, to acknowledge that it is but a servant, not a master. Yet this is the only path of a True King.

Let the Serpent Flame of your Heart answer to Nu, for She calls you, Babalon calls you, and I call to you to hear Them.

In Nomine Babalon et Vox Sanctae Meretricis.

Image on following page:

DURGA-BABALON APOCALYPSE
ORRYELLE DEFENESTRATE-BASCULE

Part II

Preparations for the Shrine and the Rites

XI

WHAT IS A SHRINE?

n ancient times a Shrine was a holy place for a deity or some other spirit. It was considered to be its house, and the keeper of the Shrine was tasked with its well-being. The keeper of the Shrine was also responsible to see that the sacrifices to the deity were properly honored and performed. The keeper of the Shrine was also the Guardian, and was responsible for making sure that the energy and manifestation of the Shrine matched that of the deity it was dedicated to in order that it be a proper vessel for their manifestation.

This last part is important, for the deity will not manifest into an improper vessel. The Shrine can be thought of as the body of the deity, and it must match the energy of the deity which you wish to come and indwell there. The arrangement of the Shrine and the symbols and objects within the Shrine are all designed to help in this regard. And it is the keeper of the Shrine who performs the Rites which calls in and maintains the energy of the deity there. Once that connection is established, the keeper then becomes the Guardian who makes sure that this special place of connection is not defiled, so that the energy of the deity flows pure and free for those who seek it. This is the ancient understanding of a Shrine, as a body of the deity.

Study for Chinnamasta ~ Daniel Corcuera Urzua

It is no different in these times for you. Whether you have a separate building or just a corner of your bedroom matters not. The most important action you can undertake for success is not the physical appearance of your Shrine, but your dedication as Guardian and caretaker of the energy which manifests there. This energy can not be faked or manufactured, and there are no short-cuts to its manifestation. One must give of oneself, of one's time, energy and devotion to the Shrine, in order to make the connection with Babalon and manifest Her energy there. This is the true meaning of Sacrifice. So remember, you are the important key to the success of your Shrine, and you alone have the ability to manifest your own success.

On Sacrifice, Human Sacrifice, and the Living Flame

In the first chapter of the Book of Law, Nuit says the following:

> *I give unimaginable joys on earth: certainty, not faith, while in life, upon death; peace unutterable, rest, ecstasy; nor do I demand aught in sacrifice.*
>
> -Liber Legis I, 58

And this is correct, the Thelemic Deities and spirits with which they are allied do not demand anything in sacrifice. The Thelemic Deities shall make no demands upon you in any regard whatsoever, for it must be *your* Will to make a connection with them. It must be *your* Spirit that seeks out Thelema, and those Deities who are the Guardians of its Mysteries. Sacrifice is not demanded of you. It is given of your own free Will. So that then begs the question, what exactly is meant by a sacrifice?

A Sacrifice is literally an offering made by a person to a Spirit. The origin of the word "sacrifice" comes from the Latin word sacrificium. In Latin, sacra means "sacred rites" and facere, the verbal root of ficium, means "to do, perform or make". Thus we see that the word sacrifice literally means "doing or performing sacred rites." So what is it about giving a sacrifice that can connect a person to a Spirit or deity? And how did sacrifice come to be considered a "bad" thing in modern times?

All forms of giving or offering, with intention upon the mantle of your heart, are technically sacrifices. The important concept to understand here is that by making an offering to a spirit or being, you are creating a

What is a Shrine?

Fila to that spirit. A Fila is a spiritual connection, a conduit, or an energy pathway. This connection cannot be broken, once established, and can be ritually increased over time. And a Fila is established and grown through sacrifice.

Now do not be fooled into thinking that sacrifice is a unique practice unto certain sects of Pagans, Heathens, or even Satanists. The monotheists give sacrifice every day by the millions. Let us remember that a sacrifice is an offering or a gift of attention and energy. We can see that when, for example, a Christian goes to a church to light a votive candle that he or she is making an offering to Yahweh, or to Jesus. And what does the word "votive" mean? A votive is an item that has been given for the fulfillment of a vow, such as a candle used as a light of vigil. It is a focal point, a focus of one's intent in the heart, as one gives of oneself through the offering. This is how gods are grown.

The life-force energy within the sovereign dominion of your physical space, your body, is unique to you, and comes from your Spirit that has incarnated there. If you choose to use that force to make a connection with another spirit, then you are making a sacrifice. It is best to direct this connection or offering with Will, and feel it intently upon the mantle of your heart. And now we can begin to see the purpose of Devotion, which is concerned with the proper intent and attitude when doing spiritual acts. It is in this way that prayer, or in our case Rites, are an offering of self - which is to say a sacrifice. We can say then that this book, *Mystery Babalon*, is a book of sacrifices. It is a book of Rites that can be used as a means to forge a living connection to Babalon, through the use of your own energy, Spirit and life-force.

But what then is "human sacrifice"? Is such a thing as the killing of a living being as an offering to a spirit or a deity effective? Yes. And to be specific by definition, this sort of an offering is also known as a "blood sacrifice." But to be clear, a blood sacrifice does not have to mean the loss of a life given in sacrifice. A woman, for example, may offer up her menstrual blood in the form of a blood offering or sacrifice. In the Third Chapter of the Book of Law, Ra Hoor Khuit is very specific about what blood is appropriate to use in sacrifice, and how to go about using it. In Thelema, the taking of life to use as a sacrifice is not generally practiced as the blood of an animal is the least effective of the bloods. Yet this blood sacrifice of animals is the exact way in which deities like Yahweh rose to prominence, as animals of all sorts were sacrificed to him and other storm gods for thousands of years in the Aeon of Ares.

Technically, any energy attached to your personal being that is of your body and Spirit that is offered to make connection can be called a "human sacrifice." One need not die or be greatly harmed to accomplish this. And this leads us to the Living Flame: because a living person, who can make renewed offerings has a much better chance of making a strong personal connection with a spirit or deity than one which kills the devotee. When you practice Rites of devotion using Bhaktic or Ecstatic Rites, you are using yourself as a Living Flame of sacrifice. It is you, and the other devotees, who are powering the Rites, and maintaining the energy of the Shrine.

This is the most potent form of devotion possible. Making a direct connection to your deity with your own energy is the best way to seek union with that deity. And in Thelema one uses one's own Will to seek out that which one needs in order to meet in union, and to realize one's purpose. Sacrifice then is an offering of love, a giving, or as it is said: Love is the Law, Love under Will. In this way will your Shrine be powered by sacrifice, love and devotion, which in turn shall bring you closer to Babalon.

The Shrine as symbolic of the One Palace

There are four gates to one palace; the floor of that palace is of silver and gold; lapis lazuli & jasper are there; and all rare scents; jasmine & rose, and the emblems of death. Let him enter in turn or at once the four gates; let him stand on the floor of the palace. Will he not sink? Amn. Ho! warrior, if thy servant sink?

-Liber Legis I, 51

There is a lot to say concerning the above line from Liber Legis, but for our purposes you should first consider the Four Gates to the One Palace. The One Palace is the Spirit, and its resting place with the body called in English "the Soul". This was called the Sa in Egyptian[19]. There are four gates to this Palace, through the Fires (Ka), Waters (Ab), the manifest consciousness (Ba) and certain parts of the body (Khaibit). These Four Gates are marked also by the Sun on its journey every day, which also

---

[19] See Membra Animae in the *Glossary of Terms* at the end of this book.

What is a Shrine?

reflect your own stages of existence in conception, birth, life and death. The Rites to open these Four Gates over time within yourself are given Adorations of Ra Hoor Khuit, which should be performed four times a day (sunrise, noon, sunset and midnight) in your Shrine if possible[20]. Lapis Lazuli and Jasper are the colors of the Waters and the Fires, of Babalon and Ra Hoor Khuit, and will be represented in your Shrine on the altars.

And now you should consider the *"jasmine, rose and the emblems of death"*. These should be decorations in the Shrine, because they involve the important triangulation between the Moon, Venus and Saturn. Jasmine is the incense of the Moon, Rose of Venus, and the images or emblems of Death belong to Saturn. These are skulls, the color black and things such as lunar moth wings, which have the eyes of the owl whose screech is like the dying. The Rites of Babalon are the Rites of Sex and Death - the Mysteries of the Underworld. All of these things must be cherished and celebrated within your Shrine, and in every day of your existence.

Protocols for Worshippers at the Shrine

In the following chapters you will be given tips and suggestions for developing your Shrine. You will be given suggestions on various roles and activities which engender energies which are helpful to the development of your Shrine. You will be given suggestions for the layout of your Shrine, what to have on your altars, and how to decorate it. You will be given instructions on the proper preparation of yourself for Rites within your Shrine, as well as rituals to help keep the energy of your Shrine in balance with that of Babalon. And finally you will be given a ritual with which to dedicate your Shrine to Babalon.

This section will help get you started, and well on your way to having a functioning Shrine in which you can perform the Rites which follow in later chapters. But never forget, it is you who powers your Shrine. It can not and will not happen without you. A Shrine is a place which fosters a certain energy for people to partake in. This energy is rare. This energy is special. And this energy has the power to change people, and therefore change the world, one person at a time. Babalon's energy is that of Liberation, and it is different for every person who encounters it, because we are all in different places with different experiences and

---

[20] See Chapter 33, *The Adorations of Ra Hoor Khuit*.

different histories. But that is expected, and encouraged, because She accepts all and refuses none.

But do not think that this last statement gives others the right to disrupt your Shrine, or that you must let trouble-makers disrupt the energy of your sacred place. You are the Guardian of that place, and responsible for keeping the energy of the Shrine as it should be, according to your highest genius and understanding. What sits within the mantle of the heart when one does any action is what will be manifested. It is your job as Guardian of the Shrine to make sure that the energy of your Shrine is maintained and not allowed to be disrupted by those who would disrupt what you have worked so hard to manifest. So even though you may welcome all to your Shrine, do not also be afraid to be the authority therein. For it is your place, your creation, and you are the Guardian thereof. Those who come to your Shrine must do so with a proper and respectful attitude towards spirit and life, and thereby help to grow the energy and effectiveness of your Shrine.

The following are some suggested Protocols for Worshippers at the Shrines to help in this regard. It may take some time to institute all of the suggestions in these protocols and in the following chapters. Do not let that stop you from getting started now, with what you have available. You can always integrate these suggestions along the way as you go.

> Shrines should provide a place for people to leave their shoes outside the door to the inner sanctum. Traditionally feet, and footwear, are the dirtiest part of the body. Therefore footwear is removed or feet are washed before entry. A place for participants to wash their feet and hands in a ritual fashion before entering is ideal.

> Keep mundane talk and activity out of the Shrine as much as possible. Such activity keeps one in their lower Persona, and makes it difficult to approach a spiritual level of being. In addition remove and leave all smart phones and electronic devices in an outer room, as their electro-magnetic energy (microwaves etc) can be very disruptive to spiritual levels of being.

> People who come to the Shrine should take time to prepare themselves for the experience in paying special attention to their dress and appearance. Let these Rites be viewed as special events, marked by special appearances and behaviors which are different

What is a Shrine?

than the normal day-to-day appearance and attitude of the people attending them.

Shrines should consider having a small altar dedicated to the Genius of the Shrine. All people who enter the Shrine may then present a small offering of something meaningful to them at this Genius Altar. These offerings should be personal and not monetary. This offering should somehow represent the intention and the Spirit of the person attending the Shrine event, or be a token of their appreciation in some way.

Build the Genius of the Shrine with attendance to this altar. This Genius, or Spirit of this place, shall become a Guardian of all that occurs there. Dedicate the altar upon the opening of the Shrine for this purpose, and seek a name for this Genius. (See Shrine Dedication Ritual.)

Every Shrine that has public Rites must appoint members to act as Guardians of all who partake. This position can be permanent, or rotate amongst members. Guardians protect all who attend the Shrine, and they oversee the Rites to ensure that they are carried out in accordance with Shrine protocols and requirements as set by the Shrine-holder.

Remember to let this experience of the creation of your Shrine be a joy. Whether grand or small, whether simple and heartfelt or grandiloquent, you are performing an act of creation. You are manifesting something new and beautiful in the world that would not have existed before - and you are its guardian. This is something to celebrate!

Remember all ye that existence is pure joy; that all the sorrows are but as shadows; they pass & are done; but there is that which remains.

-Liber Legis II, 9

XII

Offices, Roles and Pathways

ithin your Shrine there are Offices, Roles and Pathways. If you have a private Shrine, and you are operating alone, then this will be a fairly simple affair, and personal to your individual work with Babalon. Therefore you will be in charge of all Offices, perform all Roles, and will travel your individual Pathway. If, however, you have a large Shrine with many members then there is the possibility that you will have many people in Offices performing their duties, people practicing and performing various Roles in the Rites of Babalon, and various Pathways of experience being tread by many different people according to their desires. All of these positions are established at the discretion of the Shrine-holder, and will depend on the needs of the individual Shrine and the people available to fulfill those needs.

Offices

Offices are positions of responsibility in the Shrine, and are created by the Shrine-holder in order to help manage the day-to-day operations of the Shrine. These Offices are all concerned with practical duties and

Offices, Roles and Pathways

responsibilities which keep the Shrine operational and functioning smoothly.

The Shrine-holder. Also sometimes called the Shrine Keeper, this Office is the supreme authority of the Shrine, and makes all of the decisions for the Shrine. The Shrine-holder decides on the structure of the Shrine, which Rites are to be performed, who can be an official member of that Shrine, and whatever else which takes place there. The individual structure or model of power and authority within the Shrine is set forth by the Shrine-holder, according to their own design and Will.

The Guardian. A Guardian of the Shrine is responsible for the safety and well being of all members of the Shrine, as well as protecting the Shrine itself. They ensure the integrity of the energy of the Shrine, so that it is not defiled, as well as the safety of the individual members and attendees of the Shrine during Rites.

The Custodian. A Custodian of the Shrine is responsible for the upkeep of the Shrine. A Custodian will not only keep the Shrine clean and ready for whatever Rites are to be performed, but also keep the stores stocked with whatever incense, ritual tools, objects or whatever else may be needed. They are also in charge of coordinating feasts and the like after the Rites.

The Emissary. The Emissary is responsible for all public relations and communications with the outside world. They answer questions, respond to enquiries and make official announcements. They are also responsible for secretarial duties and record keeping.

Roles

Roles are positions within the Shrine which provide certain specific energies which may be needed in the Rites and in the Shrine. Roles are specialized positions, filled by those who have natural inclinations towards the energies specified in the roles. There is no reason why multiple people can not fulfill the same roles, if they have a calling. For small or solo Shrines, one person may need to fulfill multiple roles.

Holy Whore. The Holy Whore is a role which will appeal to those who enjoy the energies of submission and acceptance. In this Role, one becomes the Divine Living Receptacle for the Sacrificial Offerings of the people, which the Holy Whore must then translate as energy given to Babalon. Often these offerings are sexual and ecstatic, but the offerings can also be limited to a Bhaktic nature as well. Even so, the Holy Whore usually performs completely nude, usually adorned with only headdresses and jewelry. The Holy Whore is a vehicle for both the worshippers and for Babalon, submitting to both and providing a gateway, thereby becoming a Living Altar. The Holy Whore allows one to exalt oneself in service, being humble yet vital as a vehicle for the transmission of the offerings of the devotees within the Shrine unto Babalon Herself. This Role is utilized in some of the Ecstatic Rites within the Shrine.

Scarlet Woman. Technically the Scarlet Woman is an Initiated Role of Dedication to Ra Hoor Khuit. This union is a Hieros Gamos, and the Scarlet Woman offers up her Moon-blood in special Rites.[21] Only the most dedicated of women should choose to undertake this Role, as it can not be undone. Much of the Third Chapter of Liber Legis is devoted to the instruction of the Scarlet Woman by Ra Hoor Khuit.

Priestess. A Priestess is a woman dedicated to Babalon who brings the people to Her and administers the Rites. It is her duty to continually increase her ability to function as a conduit of energy between the deity and the people. Her Role is to be found within many of the Rites, where often she works to accomplish this with the Magus. Many of the ways of the Priestess is alluded to in Chapter One of *Liber Legis* by Nuit.

Therion. A Therion is also called a Beast or a Lion. This Role is a specialized form of a Guardian who has dedicated his life to the service and protection of Babalon and Her women. Similar to the Scarlet Woman, whom he may serve, he has undergone a Hieros Gamos of service and dedication to Babalon.[22] Only the most dedicated of men should choose to

---

[21] See Chapter 5, What is a Scarlet Woman and Chapter 35, The Blood Rites of Ra Hoor Khuit which should be read together.
[22] See Chapter 7, *Becoming the Beast* and Chapter 44, *Hieros Gamos to Babalon*.

undertake this Role, as it can not be undone. This Role is equivalent to the *Prince* and the *Priest* of *Liber Legis*.

Magus. A Magus, or magician, is the conductor of energy who helps the Priestess to administer the Rites. He provides what is needed by Her or by the Rites, and safeguards the integrity of the place in which the Rites are performed and the energy called therein. Since the Priestess may sometimes travel beyond the Liminal Gateway, it is important for the Magus to watch over her, and to bring her back when required. It is also the duty of the Magus to shut down any operations or Rites which become compromised in their purity, in order to protect the Priestess or others who are involved in the Rites. His Role is to be found within many of the Rites, where often he works to help accomplish the workings with the Priestess. This role is equivalent to the *Magician* and the *Exorcist* from *Liber Legis*.

Guardian. A Guardian ensures the safety, privacy, and security of the Shrine and the devotees. They stand guard so that others may participate in the Rites without worry or care. In addition, they may be appointed as caretaker or overseer of those who desire a guardian for themselves in the Ecstatic Rites to ensure boundaries which they have set.

Baphomet. The role of Baphomet will appeal to those who wish to explore one's nature outside of gender restrictions, or who desire to experience gender in all of its iterations. A Baphomet is the Keeper of the Torch, which is the Flame of Spirit. S/he is Guardian of the Bhaktic and Ecstatic Rites, and ensures that everyone acts in a respectful manner. The Baphomet also oversees the planning and scheduling of the Rites and the Feasts, ensuring that they are rightly prepared.

Nymph. A Nymph is one who follows and flows with the waters within. They are sensitive to the emotional currents of their waters, and those of others. They are givers and caretakers, as well as those who have the gift to see problems and the solutions to them. Nymphs often see things that others do not. This Role is for exploring that which moves within one's Waters—the emotional language of the Spirit which speaks within us all. How does what you do in your Shrine affect you? A Nymph helps others to learn to see one's emotions as possible communications from your Spirit to your manifest being. The Nymphs of the Shrine maintain what is working well in the Shrine and take notice what is not working in regards to how the Rites are making everyone feel. If something is taking place that is not allowing devotees to express their Wills and their Devotion, the Nymphs work to find a way to better facilitate things to correct that. Nymphs may offer themselves to others if they wish to give comfort or to offer support in times of stress or other difficult times.

Satyr. A Satyr hails from the Realm of Jupiter, where language is non-verbal and sensually based. Satyrs are often playful and joyous creatures who help to keep the spirits high in the Shrine. They are often good at instigating others to participate in the Rites, giving them confidence to participate in a group setting. Before a group Rite, the Satyrs may rouse the audience and help them get into a joyous and devotional state of being.

Serpent. A Serpent is often quiet and wise. Sometimes they are solitary in nature, but are adept at helping others realize the presence of their Divine Spirit. Serpents prefer to work in the shadows and behind the scenes, facilitating spiritual experiences for others without any expectation of reciprocation.

Pathways

Pathways represent the ecstatic experiences which one seeks out in the Shrine, according to their own natures and desires. These Pathways are of course optional, but do provide an interesting way for others within the Shrine to understand one's own desires and needs in a complex world of identities, without having to ask invasive or embarrassing questions. One then can simply ask which Pathway one is traveling in order to understand their needs and desires.

Path of the Divine Couple. This path usually indicates a monogamous relationship between two people who are currently focusing their sensual and spiritual explorations on each other, in order to go as deeply as possible over time. This is most often a hetero or bi-sexual path that utilizes the opposition of gender to raise ecstatic energy in dedication to

Offices, Roles and Pathways

Babalon. The dance and tension of the female and the male may be explored and utilized in endless iterations. The practice of Tantra, as well as fetish dynamics can aid in building this energy for dedication to Babalon.

Path of the Whore. This path is for those who enjoy submission to the lusts of others and being an object of sexual use for those around you. Orientation does not matter in this path, as all will be used as they are and for what they have to offer. Often those who tread this path have insatiable appetites which grow the more they are aroused. This arousal is fostered and used in the worship of Babalon, with all of the lust in the sexual escapades ultimately being seen as a form of worship of Our Lady through the Holy Whore. Every touch, kiss and thrust is then a prayer unto Her, and every orgasm is Her presence drawing near.

Path of Pan. This path is for those who know no sexual bounds in their appetites, and who have a tendency to be more aggressive, eager or dominant in their sexual appetites. Pansexuals lust for all things, and want to arouse everyone and everything around them, so that they will submit to their advances. Orientation does not matter, as all things are lusted for and used equally. These Pansexual lusts are fostered as a gift and offering to Babalon, which are consummated in explosions of orgiastic bliss.

Path of Sappho. This path is dedicated to the sexuality of women by women, this path is a sexually ecstatic path often followed by lesbian or bisexual women. The flow of female on female energy is raised and harnessed in dedicated to Babalon.

Path of Apollo. This path is dedicated to the sexuality of men by men, this path is a sexually ecstatic path often followed by gay or bisexual men. The flow of male on male energy is raised and harnessed in dedicated to Babalon.

Path of Baphomet. This path is for transgendered people with cock and breasts, people of fluid genders, gay men who enjoy dressing as female, or any combination of such gender rebellions. This path is for challenging the gender ideas and ideals of modern society. This path is for expressing your inner genders, or your ideas of what your gender is or may be, using the energy raised in this way in Worship of Babalon.

Path of Attis. This path is an extreme path of dedication, and is for a transgender person of any birth gender who has come to the decision that it is their Will to permanently alter their physical genitalia to that of the opposite gender. This path is named for those men of ancient times in and around Rome who worshipped Kybele with a great personal sacrifice. March 24 was known as Sanguem or Dies Sanguinis, which meant the "Day of Blood". Worshippers would work themselves into a frenzy of mourning over the death of Attis, the young lover of Kybele. The devotees whipped themselves repeatedly and then sprinkled the altars and effigies of Attis with their own blood. Some especially dedicated worshippers performed the self-castrations of the Galli, offering their testicles upon the altar. These castrated men then became Priests of Kybele. The "sacred night" then followed, with Attis placed in his ritual tomb.

A person of male origination may, after having had their testicles removed, give them to Babalon as a sacrificial offering in a special dedicatory rite. This may be done with a seven day rite with the testicles upon Her alter during each day, starting on Sunday. A planetary invocation is said, appropriate for each day, and then an offering of the testicles as a sign of dedication is made aloud to Babalon with words of specially written personal dedication. This is done for each of the seven days. On the Seventh and final Day of Saturn (Saturday) after the final planetary invocation and personal dedication are said, the testicles may be either burned as an offering and the ashes scattered in nature; or placed within the body of Gaia, and buried there as an offering.

For a person who was originated as a female, and who is having their uterus and ovaries removed, this same ritual as related above may be performed utilizing the ovaries instead. In either case, the Rites should be very serious and solemn, as this sacrifice is the highest one can make next to death.

OFFICES, ROLES AND PATHWAYS

Path of the Virgin. This path is centered around the tension of sexual denial and release. Many people for many different reasons identify as asexual or prefer a virginal path. There are many ecstatic, sensual rights to be explored along this path, as well as the power of the tensions produced using denial, and then release. Some devotees may wish to withhold orgasm despite sexual arousal for an extended period before a final ritual sacrifice to Babalon. One can pledge their virginity, in that only Babalon receives any sort of sexual devotion and energy from their orgasms. In this way, one can make a "virgin sacrifice" after a long and extended period of sexual denial in order to build the tension of energy to incredible heights.

This path, and many of the paths previously described, will often appeal to people drawn to BDSM lifestyles, and who wish to engage in the growing of one's own energy to be given and dedicated to Babalon through rites of great tension and release. If one is asexual, one may utilize techniques of fasting and dietary restriction, pain/pleasure, or other practices of restricting one's appetites and then releasing them in dedication. Using the sensuality of food, dance, water emersion, sensory deprivation, and other practices are wonderful ways to explore sensuality in a non-sexual manner. There are many Lusts. Not all Lust is sexual. And all should be used in service and worship of Babalon, to grow Her power not only in your own life, but in the world as well.

XIII

ALTARS AND SHRINE DECORATIONS

he minimum requirement for all Shrines is an altar in the West of your Shrine, which is dedicated specifically to Babalon. It is recommended (but not required) that there also be an altar in the East, dedicated to Ra Hoor Khuit. Ra Hoor Khuit is the Warrior-Brother of Babalon, and can function as a Guardian over all Rites which are performed within your Shrine. Their energies are complementary to each other, one over the day and the rising of the Sun in the East, the other over the night and the setting Sun in the West on its journey to the Underworld.

There are many other types of altars that may be added to a Shrine according to the desires of the Shrine-holder. One may wish to have an altar in the entrance to the Shrine for Shrine offerings to be received (candles, incense, and other non-monetary gifts for the Shrine.) One may wish to have altars to other deities and Spirits in the Shrine as well which are important to your work there. Many gods and images of gods can be clustered around (but not above) the Shrine for Ra Hoor Khuit.

Set up my image in the East: thou shalt buy thee an image which I will show thee, especial, not unlike the one thou knowest. And it shall be suddenly easy for thee to do this. The other images group

ALTARS AND SHRINE DECORATIONS

around me to support me: let all be worshipped, for they shall cluster to exalt me. I am the visible object of worship...

-Liber Legis III:21-22

Many Shrines have altars to Baphomet or images of Baphomet in the North. Gaia, Nuit, Hadit and Lucifer are all common choices as well. Hadit usually appears in the South, while Nuit is in the North - but reverse this if you live in the Southern Hemisphere like Australia. The only restriction is that these Shrines are Heathen, Pantheistic or Polytheistic in theme, and therefore no monotheistic entities are honored within the Shrine System. You may honor them as you Will on your own according to your Will, but not during official Rites in the Shrine. There are plenty of other churches, temples, mosques and the like for the monotheists already in the world. Let the Shrine be a special place in the world for Babalon and Her Allies, away from the influence of other currents.

The Altars may be made of simple tables, stools, shelves, or boards. They may be as elaborate as you wish, or as simple. Customarily, altars are covered with a cloth, with colors corresponding to the deity which the altar is for. Babalon's colors are typically blue, or blue and gold, with black or a field of stars underneath. The blue is a special deep lapis blue, which is the color of Her energy when She appears. It is "A lambent flame of blue" as it says in Liber AL I, 26. It is almost neon, and unmistakable. Her mother Nuit and Kali share this color, if only a bit darker. The Gold is because She is a Daughter of Ra, by Nuit, and sister of Ra Hoor Khuit. She is the Blue Woman clothed in the Sun. For Ecstatic Rites, a red cloth may be used to denote the Scarlet Woman.

My colour is black to the blind, but the blue & gold are seen of the seeing.

-Liber Legis I, 60

I am the blue-lidded daughter of Sunset; I am the naked brilliance of the voluptuous night-sky.

-Liber Legis I, 64

Mystery Babalon

Blue am I and gold in the light of my bride...

-Liber Legis II, 50

The sigil of devotion. Be it consecrated, be it true, be it daily affirmed. I am not scorned. Thy love is to me. Procure a disk of copper, in diameter three inches paint thereon the field blue the star gold of me, BABALON.

-Liber 49, v. 21

The Babalon Altar

Items needed:

- Candles: 3 lapis blue or midnight blue, or 2 blue and one gold
- 1 Censer for incense
- 1 Offering bowl or Cup

When facing the altar, place the two blue candles at the back of the altar, one in each corner. Place the final blue or gold candle at the front, middle of the Altar. The three candles should in this way make an equilateral triangle. Place a censor for incense in the middle-back of the triangle. Place the offering cup or offering bowl in the center of the triangle. This is the minimum arrangement for the Babalon altar. If you have made the Sigillum Divinorum[23], then you may place it within the center of the Triangle. If you have made the Sigil of Devotion as described in Liber 49[24], above, then that can be placed within the triangle as well, on top of the Sigillum Divinorum. The Chalice may then be set upon the Sigillum Divinorum. You may add any other items that you wish which are

---

[23] See Chapter 29, *Daily Devotions* in the section named *Planetary Rites* for details on the construction of the Sigillum Divinorum..

[24] Liber 49, The Book of Babalon, Jack Parsons. Verse 21-22:
The sigil of devotion. Be it consecrated, be it true, be it daily affirmed. I am not scorned. Thy love is to me. Procure a disk of copper, in diameter three inches paint thereon the field blue the star gold of me, BABALON.
It shall be my talisman. Consecrate with the supreme rituals of the word and the cup.

Altars and Shrine Decorations

important to you and your work with Babalon, or items can be left on the altar to become consecrated to Her over time as the Rites are performed.

The Ra Hoor Khuit Altar

Items needed:

- Candles: 3 red, or 2 red and one gold
- 1 Censer for incense, preferably gold in color
- 1 Offering Bowl. Preferably silver in color

My altar is of open brass work: burn thereon in silver or gold!

-Liber Legis III,30

If you can afford an altar of ornate open brass-work for Ra Hoor Khuit, then by all means do so - but that will be beyond the reach of most. Alternatively, add small brass detail items as you can to His altar. Place a red candle in each corner at the back of the altar, and one more (either red or gold) at the middle-front of the altar. This should make an equilateral triangle as was done before with the Babalon altar, but facing the opposite direction. The points of both triangles should now point to the center of the Shrine. Place the censor and the offering bowl in the center of the triangle. It is desirable to have a statue of Ra Hoor Khuit placed in the middle-back of the altar, between the two red candles. One can also place the Stele of Revealing there as well, if you have one, behind or next to the image of Ra Hoor Khuit.

Additional Light Sources

Candles, candles, candles. Tea-lights are an inexpensive way to go, as you can find inexpensive 100-packs online. Make sure your candles are unscented so they do not interfere with your Shrine perfumes and incense. The more candles in a shrine, the more intense it will look and feel. Oil lamps are also wonderful. Many ornate hanging oil lamps can be procured to hang in the middle or at strategic places in the Shrine. Butter lamps or lamps that burn any sort of natural fat (non-petroleum fuel like olive oil, lard or ghee) are less hazardous, and tend to go out if spilled, as opposed to spreading fire and destruction.

Other Decorations

Decorate! Decorate your Shrine according to your customs, taste, passions. Tapestries and special fabrics flowing down the walls are wonderful for creating atmosphere and mood. Special floor tiles and carpets add a nice touch. Statues, drawings, paintings, and other unique items can create interest and focal points. Items from nature such as goat-skulls, stones, gems, feathers, flowers, and dried plants can be used in many combinations. Avoid mirrors, as you do not want to see reflections or images during certain Rites in your Shrine, or to see anything looking back at you. Otherwise, let your creativity and genius run wild according to your own aesthetic and vision of Babalon.

Perishables

It is a nice practice to make offerings upon your altar for various reasons, from time to time. Examples of such offerings are incense, wine, fresh flowers, perfumes or special food items. The Cakes of Light used in some of the Rites are another example.

Safety

Do remember to use candles plates under all candles to catch wax drippings and to keep candles from burning down to and igniting the surface upon which they sit. Keep open flames away from flammable materials and high winds. Insulate incense burners with sand inside, if using charcoal, and heat resistant plates or tiles underneath. Use care with fire, and extinguish all flames before closing down and leaving your Shrine. You may wish to have a fire extinguisher or water available nearby in case of accidental fire.

XIV

Shrine Incense, Perfumes and Oils

t was traditional for the Scarlet Priestesses, as part of their preparation for the Rites, to ritually bathe and adorn themselves with not only their special attire for the Rites, but also with unguents. The inner thighs, the breasts, the neck, the small of the back, the ankles, the third eye and the wrists were all important accent points for sacred scents. Often this was done in a ritual manner, with the Priestess sometimes standing over a burning censer of incense while lifting her veils to receive the perfume in her most intimate places, before entering the Shrine for the Rites.

It should be no different for men as well, although it may be less well documented. The same care for cleanliness, ritual bathing, adornment and perfuming should apply. This ritual preparation with unguents and perfumes helps one to achieve an elevated sense of being before the Rites. Aroma changes a space and the beings in it, and by doing so that allows one to walk in a different, rarified air.

The main perfume in a Shrine of Babalon is the one known as Abramelin - and there is nothing quite like it.

Shrine Incense, Perfumes and Oils

For perfume mix meal & honey & thick leavings of red wine: then oil of Abramelin and olive oil, and afterward soften & smooth down with rich fresh blood.

The best blood is of the moon, monthly: then the fresh blood of a child, or dropping from the host of heaven: then of enemies; then of the priest or of the worshippers: last of some beast, no matter what.

-Liber Legis III 23-24

The above instructions are for making the Cakes of Light, which can also be burned ritually for incense on their own, used in curses of vengeance, used in the controlling of demons, or used for the Blood-Rites to Ra Hoor Khuit by the Priestess[25].

To make Abramelin Oil, or its complementary incense version, requires some fairly rare materials which do not grow naturally in the northern latitudes. There are actually two versions of Abramelin Incense. The first, called Thelemic Abramelin, copies the aroma of Abramelin Oil exactly. It is used in many of the Rites in this book. The second, called Traditional Abramelin, is a completely different aroma with different ingredients and is mostly used for evocations and ceremonial magick[26]. It is included for thoroughness and as an option in case you like its aroma.

These incense and oil recipes use raw botanical ingredients. The incense will require charcoal in order to burn it. This is the ancient way of incense burning, by mixing raw ingredients and placing them on hot coals, which causes the aromatic chemicals of the ingredients to be released in the smoke as it slowly simmers and burns. Today, almost all incense shops and pagan stores sell small charcoal tablets which are inexpensive and are

---

[25] An adaptation of the Blood Rites is covered in a later chapter entitled Blood Rites to Ra Hoor Khuit, in the Bhaktic Rites section.
[26] See Abraham von Worms, *The Book of Abramelin* (Ibis Press, 2006)

used for this purpose. Simply hold the charcoal with tongs and place it over fire - a simple lighter will do. The charcoal disc or tablet will begin to spark. Keep the fire on it in a steady manner for 20-40 seconds. Move the fire slowly around the charcoal to ignite all parts. Then hold it in the air for a few moments until it starts to catch well, and one side is alight and glowing red. Some like to blow on it to increase the ignition. Carefully place the charcoal in your heat proof incense censer, preferably on a bed of sand or ash which works as an insulate against heat. Wait a little longer before adding incense ingredients to the charcoal. It doesn't take much. Too much resin at once may drown out your charcoal as it melts, so go slow.

Here follows a bevy of recipes which will be of use to you in your Rites.

Abramelin Blends

Abramelin Oil

- 4 parts cinnamon essential oil (Cinnamomum cassia)
- 2 parts myrrh essential oil (Commiphora myrrha)
- 1 part galangal oil (lesser galangal, Alpinia officinalis)
- Half of that total weight of the above in olive oil

So, for example, we might have 4 ounces of cinnamon, 2 ounces of myrrh and 1 ounce of galangal oil, all mixed together with 3.5 ounces of a true high-quality olive oil. Mix essential oils in glass containers only, as they may react with containers which are metallic. This oil will be very golden in color at first, but turns more reddish with age.

Substitutes: If you absolutely can not get Alpinia officinalis essential oil, then you may substitute its cousin Alpinia galanga, Greater Galangal. We grow both, and there is a difference in aroma, but not so much that it will spoil the overall results. Do not use Kaempferia galanga, or False Ginger Galangal as it is a different aroma and will spoil the recipe. For Cinnamon, use Cassia which is known by its botanical name Cinnamomum cassia. Do not use what is today called True Cinnamon, Cinnamomum verum or Cinnamomum zeylanicum as it will change the aroma. For Myrrh use Commiphora myrrha from Arabia or in a pinch Commiphora molmol from Africa. Arabian Myrrh is much superior to

SHRINE INCENSE, PERFUMES AND OILS

African, especially the variety from Yemen. Do not use Sweet Myrrh (Bdellium, Commiphora guggul) or Opoponax (Commiphora holtziana) as these Myrrh relatives have a completely different aroma. Do not use Maydi, though wonderful on its own, it will change the nature of this recipe. All oils, except for the Olive Oil, must be essential oils. Perfume oils or synthetics will not work at all, and will carry inappropriate energy for your Rites.

The powerful nature of the aroma of Abramelin is of the male and female centered together. While Abramelin smells immediately of male fire, it is countered and balanced by potent and powerful water energy of the female, known to create a feeling that draws out the potent sexuality of both men and women. It can also bring energy of levity and joy infused with passion. The Oil of Abramelin is used for anointing the body before the Rites of Babalon, but please use caution as cinnamon essential oil is very potent, and can cause irritation or burning sensations on delicate parts of the body, as many have discovered.

Abramelin Incense, Thelemic

- 4 tbs ground Myrrh (32 grams / 1.14 ounces)
- 2 tbs ground Lesser Galangal (Alpina officinalis) (12 grams / .43 ounces)
- 2 tsp Cinnamon Essential Oil (Cassia bark) (.33 fluid ounces)

This recipe is slightly complicated to scale upwards, because you are mixing ratios of solid ingredients to liquid ingredients. It is best to grind the ingredients before use, as opposed to buying pre-ground powders. Powders carry the least amount of volatile essential oils, which are prone to being lost to aeration over time, and therefore loose their aromatic potency. Stir and mix thoroughly in a glass bowl, until the oil has completely saturated the other ingredients and the overall color is a dark reddish-brown. The use of Cinnamon Oil, instead of raw Cinnamon bark, is the key to getting the recipe to smell exactly like the oil when burned. Cinnamon bark has a tendency to smell rough and unappealing when burned as incense.

Abramelin Incense, Traditional

- 8 parts Olibanum (Boswellia serrata)
- 4 parts Storax Bark (Liquidambar orientalis)
- 2 parts Aloeswood Powder (Aquilaria agallocha)

Substitutes: Olibanum is also known as Indian Olibanum or Indian Frankincense. While being related to Frankincense, it is actually a different species of Boswelia. Where Frankincense is more yellow and has a lemonish aroma, Olibanum is more orange in color and more citrus in aroma. You may substitute a good Frankincense for the Olibanum, but it will change the aroma of the blend. Turkish Storax bark is recommended, but American Storax Bark (Liquidambar styraciflua) can also be used, but it is far less aromatic. Aloeswood, also called Agarwood comes in a wide variety of aromas, some of which can be incredibly expensive. The less expensive varieties, if you can find them, will do fine.

Traditional Abramelin has a smooth, commanding, bright aroma with serious and exotic notes. Traditional Abramelin incense is considered essential for evocation by many Ceremonial magicians, especially when attempting the long and complicated Abramelin ritual. It is also very effective for any rituals that work with the energies of the Sun (Fire) or Air (Mercury or Jupiter), or any of the spirits thereof.

Temple Blend

- 1 part Frankincense
- 1 part Myrrh

Temple blend is a good, basic blend for normal Shrine activities, meetings or for pleasure.

High Temple Blend

- 1 part Frankincense
- 1 part Myrrh
- 1 part White Sandalwood

SHRINE INCENSE, PERFUMES AND OILS

High Temple blend can be used like Temple Blend, or for Shrine openings and more general Rites. White Sandalwood (Santalum album) is also called Yellow Sandalwood.

Elemental Incense Blends

Earth Blend

- 13 oz Dark Damar (small pieces or crushed)
- 0.4 oz Dittany of Crete (cut and sifted)
- 0.2 oz Thyme Leaf (cut and sifted)
- 0.5 tsp Patchouly Oil

Damar, also called Dammar, can be substituted with Copal, white or black depending. Dark Damar is from Canarium strictum. Dittany of Crete is Origanum dictamnus, while Thyme is Thymus vulgaris.

Air Blend

- 10 oz White Damar or Mastic (small pieces or crushed)
- 5 oz Colophony (small pieces or crushed)
- 0.5 oz Lemon Balm (cut and sifted)
- 1 tsp Bayberry Oil

White Damar is Vateria indica. Mastic is Pistacia lentiscus. Colophony is also called Colophonium or Pine Rosin and comes from various different pine trees. Light Colophony (in color) is a little better for the Air Blend than Dark Colophony, but any will do. Lemon Balm is Melissa officinalis.

Water Blend

- 15 oz Myrrh (small pieces or crushed)
- 0.5 oz Lotus Plumules
- 0.25 oz Lotus Petals
- 1 tsp Lotus Oil

Lotus Plumules and Lotus Petals come from Nelumbo nucifera.

Fire Blend

- 6 oz Frankincense (small pieces or crushed)
- 6 oz Bdellium (Gum Guggul) (small pieces or crushed)
- 3.6 oz Dragon's Blood (crushed)
- 1/4 tsp Cinnamon Essential Oil (Cassia)

Dragon's Blood is from the fruit of Daemonorops draco.

Shrine Incense, Perfumes and Oils

Spirit Blend

- 4 oz Frankincense (small pieces or crushed)
- 4 oz Myrrh (small pieces or crushed)
- 4 oz White Damar or Mastic (small pieces or crushed)
- 4 oz Dark Damar (small pieces or crushed)
- 0.25 tsp Almond Oil (EYE030)

Planetary Incense Blends

Moon Blend

- 1 part Benzoin Sumatra (small pieces or crushed)
- 4/5 part Lesser Galangal (cut and sifted)
- 1/14 part Jasmine Petals (cut and sifted)
- small pinch Camphor (powder)

Benzoin Sumatra (Styrax benzoin) is not to be confused with Benzoin Siam (Styrax tonkinensis). Benzoin Sumatra is usually gray and white in color while Siam is usually orange and yellow. Jasmine petals are from Jasminium odoratissimum while Camphor is from Cinnamomum camphora and usually comes in powder form.

Mystery Babalon

Mercury Blend

- 2 parts White Damar or Mastic (small pieces or crushed)
- 1/4 part Star Anise (small pieces or crushed)
- 1/4 part White Sandalwood Shavings
- 1/28 part Mace powder

Star Anise is from Illicium verum while Mace is from Myristica fragans.

Venus Blend

- 1 part Benzoin Sumatra (small pieces or crushed)
- 1/7 part Orris root (cut and sifted)
- 1/12 Lavander flower
- 1/28 Red Sandalwood Shavings
- 1/28 Rose Petals (shredded or crushed)

Orris root comes from either Iris florentina or Iris germanica. Lavander is Lavendula officinalis. Red Sandalwood is Pterocarpus santalinus, while Rose is Rosa centifolia.

Shrine Incense, Perfumes and Oils

Sun Blend

- 1 part Chinese Amber or Brown Damar or Lodgepole Pine Copal
- 1 part Gold Copal (small pieces or crushed)
- 1 part Olibanum (small pieces or crushed)
- 2/5 part Hibiscus petals (cut and sifted)
- a couple stamens of Saffron

Chinese Amber is usually marked as Succinum, but is more often a type of semi-petrified Brown Damar, such as Shorea wiesneri. Lodgepole Pine Copal is Pinus contorta. Gold Copal is Agathis Dammara. Hibiscus is Hibiscus rosa sinensis while Saffron are the tiny and expensive flower stamens from Crocus sativus.

Mars Blend

- 1 part Bdellium (Gum Guggul) (small pieces or crushed)
- 1/2 part Dragon's Blood (small pieces or crushed)
- 1/14 part Pepper corns (whole)
- 1/14 part Musk Ambrette seed

Peppercorns come from Piper nigrum while Musk Ambrette is Abelmoschus moschatus.

Jupiter Blend

- 1 part Frankincense (small pieces or crushed)
- 1 part Dark Damar (small pieces or crushed)
- 1/14 part Cedar Tips (cut and sifted)
- 1/14 part Cedar Chips (cut and sifted)

You may use either Western Red Cedar (Thuja plicata), Eastern Red Cedar (Juniperus virginiana) or White Cedar (Thuja occidentalis).

Saturn Blend

- 1 part Dark Damar (small pieces or crushed)
- 1 part Myrrh (small pieces or crushed)
- 1/2 part Tolu Balsam (small pieces or crushed)
- 1/2 part Storax Bark (Turkish or American, cut and sifted)

Tolu Balsam is sometimes called Black Dragon's Blood and comes from Myroxylon toluifera.

If you do not wish to make your own incense blends or oils, a list of vendors may be found in the appendix for Abramelin Oils and Incenses as well as suppliers of rare botanicals and aromatic resins and herbs.

XV

Name of Dedication

It is traditional when one enters into a spiritual and devotional practice, that one chooses a new name for oneself, to reflect this new way of being. Often this name is a word or phrase that comes to one, or which represents one's aspirations on their spiritual path. Or it could be a name which calls to you, and you have no idea yet why. Regardless, it should be a name which is special to you in some way, and connected to your spiritual work. This will help you to form a new identity and understanding of yourself outside of your common, mundane Persona.

Spirits have names. Their names are also what they are — their name identifies their offices, which is a way of saying their nature and their purpose, which is in actuality the same thing to most spirits. So your chosen name should reflect, to the best of your current understanding and aspirations, the nature of your inner self — your higher self — your Spirit.

This name is for you, right now only. In the future, if you desire, you can change the name to better reflect your new understanding of yourself. Take some time to ponder the choice of your new Name of Dedication, and sleep well on it before making your final decision. And when you are ready, and you have chosen your name, be sure to use this name for yourself in all rituals and Rites from then on which require it.

XVI

Preparing for the Rites: A message from the Pashtun!

Pashtun is a Herald for a spirit who often appears before or in place of his Master. Amongst many duties per his office, he makes certain that a way has been made open in a proper manner in order for his Master to make his way into the Material Realm. A Pashtun can instruct a Magician or a Priestess in the proper ways of preparation and rituals to be preformed to facilitate their Master's appearance.

If you are preparing to conduct these Rites to Babalon, then the following are our instructions to you, as Pashtun, so that you may have greater success in the Rites. These preparations should be performed by all who will partake of the Rites, either in the performance thereof, or in the attendance if possible.

1. Each person should fast at least several hours prior to the Rites to lessen the grounding effects of food. The person may fast all day. It is our tradition to have a feast after the Rites to celebrate the Rites, discuss it, and ground from the intensity of the energy. Digestion works contrary to manifestation of Spirit, so it is no good to have a full stomach before performing the Rites.

Preparing for the Rites

2. All ritual tools should be clean and ready at all times. Select that which is required for the Rites before bathing, and have all ready on the altar. Have the Shrine arranged and ready to go for the Rite

3. Each person should have cleansed the body prior to the Rites. It is wise to take a ritual bath, to facilitate relaxation, clarity, and to awaken the senses. Use incense and candles and clean the body in a ritual manner. In this way you work to set the mind in accordance with the Rites to come, and clear it of any interfering thoughts or worldly cares. Use your own genius and preferences to create these preparatory cleansing rituals. Recommendations for incense: begin with a fine Sandalwood, followed by a fine Frankincense. The Sandalwood is calming, encourages a high minded clarity, and soothes the animal. The Frankincense encourages strength of Will and clarity of purpose or intention. If one is inclined towards nervousness, include a touch of Lavender to soothe the beast. We recommend using real raw ingredients over hot charcoal, but a fine quality Masala stick incense will work as well.

4. Bathe for as long as you feel the need. Bathing should include the hair, as well as shaving whatever one regularly saves - or not. Let the sensuality of the warm water soak away your stress and care from the body. Dress in your ritual attire. This may be your Shrine robes which you have prepared yourself, or perhaps a particular costume if one has a special designation for the Rites at hand. Adorn yourself with all appropriate adornments for the Rites at hand. Keep the feet in slippers so that when they are bared for the Shrine they are clean. No dirty feet may step within the Shrine!

5. After dressing, sit in meditation for as long as needed to be in the right state for your Rites. One should enter a Shrine with Will focused and Spirit high, with the animal body ready to serve in all ways that are demanded upon it.

6. One should remain in silence and seclusion as much as possible prior to the Rites so as not to mix energies and introduce interfering thoughts and emotions. Discuss what is needed for the Rites prior to your self-preparation if possible, and limit your interaction with others until the celebratory feast after the Rites are complete within the Shrine. Small talk, chit-chat or horseplay before the Rites will ruin any chance to raise serious energy in your Rites. You, and the other participants, are the vehicles for the energy of the Rites. Your attitude will reflect upon the energy you call

forth, so let your state of being reflect the energy you wish to come forth from the Rites you are performing.

> *But to love me is better than all things: if under the night-stars in the desert thou presently burnest mine incense before me, invoking me with a pure heart, and the Serpent flame therein, thou shalt come a little to lie in my bosom. For one kiss wilt thou then be willing to give all; but whoso gives one particle of dust shall lose all in that hour. Ye shall gather goods and store of women and spices; ye shall wear rich jewels; ye shall exceed the nations of the earth in splendour & pride; but always in the love of me, and so shall ye come to my joy. I charge you earnestly to come before me in a single robe, and covered with a rich headdress. I love you! I yearn to you! Pale or purple, veiled or voluptuous, I who am all pleasure and purple, and drunkenness of the innermost sense, desire you. Put on the wings, and arouse the coiled splendour within you: come unto me!*
>
> *At all my meetings with you shall the priestess say - and her eyes shall burn with desire as she stands bare and rejoicing in my secret temple - To me! To me! calling forth the flame of the hearts of all in her love-chant.*
>
> *Sing the rapturous love-song unto me! Burn to me perfumes! Wear to me jewels! Drink to me, for I love you! I love you!*
>
> *I am the blue-lidded daughter of Sunset; I am the naked brilliance of the voluptuous night-sky.*
>
> *To me! To me!*
>
> -Liber Legis I 61-65

XVII

Timing of the Rites

n one sense, **Babalon can be considered** as a manifestation in space and time of Her mother Nuit. In this way, Her powers, Her image, Her wisdom and Her aspect changes according to the Kalas. This word Kala is a Sankrit word which is much used in Tantric works, and is a word that gives Babalon's sister-spirit in India, Kali, Her name. Kala means time, but can also mean the various secretions from the sex of a woman, of which there are at least 15 in number. The English word Menses, taken directly from the Latin, is a similar word which implies a periodic emission or manifestation.

And just as the cycles of the body, like the tides of the Earth, are ruled by the Kalas of the Moon, so too are the powers which manifest from Babalon. The cosmological timings in your manifest corner of the universe will affect the energy outcome of the Rites you perform. So to this end, it is important for you to be aware of a few basic cosmological Kalas that may affect your work in your Shrine.

Timing of the Rites

The Sun is born and dies each day,
And the Moon each month.
Both are born again, but the Moon always in blood,
And the Sun always of darkness.

-Ra Hoor Khuit from the secret Blood Rites,
Templum Babalonis

The Moon

The Moon has many influences in many ways, but the greatest of her influences is through her phases. There is the Full Moon, when the lunar disc is completely illuminated by the light of the Sun, which it reflects. This is the bright full round disc seen at night. There is the New Moon, Black Moon or the Midnight Sun, which is the complete absence of any visible part of the moon in the night sky. And then there is the Waxing period of the Moon, when the image of the moon slowly starts to build on it way to the full moon. This increase of the visibility of the Moon is marked at its halfway point by the First Quarter. The same happens in reverse after the Full Moon. This is the Waning, or decreasing, cycle of the Moon. Its halfway point is marked by the Last Quarter, also called Third Quarter.

Now these phases of the Moon mark the life of the Moon, and they have profound effect upon Spirit energy. The Moon's life is conceived when the first sliver of light appears after the New Moon. This is the beginning of growth for the Moon, like an embryo in the womb. It is a time of increase and abundance. This period of increase, which culminates in the Full Moon, is generally the best time for Rites to be performed, regardless of any other cosmological calculations. This is especially true of any attempts to manifest spirits or energy into the physical realm. The Full Moon itself is the height of this increasing energy, and is considered to be the birth of the Moon for that month. All celebratory and ecstatic Rites should be performed during the Waxing or Full Moon.

From the day after the Full Moon, the energy of the Moon starts to decay towards death, and so too does its effect on Spirit manifestation and your Rites. During this time, it is better to be contemplative, to study and to rest for the next cycle. Although not covered in the Rites of this book, nor is it recommended, ritual curses and acts of Justified vengeance are often performed late in the Waning Moon, because of the egress of the energy of death and decay which is available in these Kalas. The New Moon is the culmination of this energy of death and decay, and the disappearance of its image marks its journey through the Underworld, in order to be conceived anew and reborn. Only Rites of dedication and adoration should be performed during this Waning period of time.

The Mansions of the Moon can also be important to the workings, but have almost completely fallen from use in the modern world. The Mansions, or houses, mark the individual Lunar "days" in the Lunar cycles which waxes and wanes. Each Lunar day starts at Moonrise and each Lunar night starts at Moonset. As a side note it should be mentioned that the Moons power, and all of the Planets, are stronger when they are above the line of the horizon and visible in the sky - although during the daytime you will not be able to see them because of the light of the Sun, even though they are there. But to return, the phase of the Moon at each Moonrise marks its mansion, and there are on average 28 of them in a cycle. Each of these Mansions, like the houses of the Zodiac, have a purpose, a ruler and many denizens which alight there. These 28 Mansions of the Moon also demarcate the 28 stages of the Underworld Journey, seven each across the Four Rivers there. Detailed information on each of the 28 Mansions is too much to include in this space.

The Other Planets

The other traditional planets of the Ancients also affect the energy of your Rites, but to a lesser degree than the Moon. Most of these Kalas are based upon the arrangements of the planets and constellations in various arrangements of Aeonic Cycles, Solar Years, Zodiacal Months and Planetary Hours.

The Sun is probably the most obvious of the planets, and also the least of your worries in the Rites. The subject of the Aeonic cycles of the

Timing of the Rites

Precession of the Equinoxes is probably too much to go into in this space, other than to say that we are currently in the new Aeon of Aquarius, which is ruled over by Ra Hoor Khuit. This is one of the reasons that he has a place in His Sister's Shrine. He is the Lord of the Aeon, and the manifestation of the Sun itself, who is His father Ra. Now the Sun goes through its birth and death each day and each year. The Sun is conceived in the moment after the darkest moment of night, born at sunrise, reaches the height of its power at true noon, and then wanes in power until sunset when it dies. The same cycle can be found in the year, where the Sun is conceived on the day after the Winter Solstice, is born at the Spring Equinox, reaches its height of power at the Summer Solstice, and then dies again at the Fall Equinox. The seasons reflect this change in the life cycle of the Sun.

In addition the Sun, and all of the other planets too, are constantly traveling through a circular section of the sky known as the belt of the Zodiac. These stars are divided into twelve constellations which reflect each of the four Elemental energies in three different ways. The powers of Earth, Air, Water and Fire are replicated through the Triplicates of Cardinal, Mutable and Fixed waves of energy in order to form the twelve Sings of the Zodiac. Cardinal energy bursts out strong and fast, but also ends rather abruptly at times. Fixed energy manifests as slower, steady and strong. Mutable energy is adaptable, changeable and sometimes fast. Aires is Cardinal Fire, Leo is Fixed Fire and Sagittarius is Mutable Fire. Cancer is Cardinal Water, Scorpio is Fixed Water while Pisces is Mutable Water. Libra is Cardinal Air, Aquarius is Fixed Air and Gemini is Mutable Air. Capricorn is Cardinal Earth, Taurus is Fixed Earth while Virgo is Mutable Earth. These energies can be generally helpful to certain Rites, but the subject is too detailed to relate in this space and scope of this book.

The other Planets besides the Sun also travel through these same Zodiacal Signs, and their energies and influences are affected or changed by them as well. The Moon has already been discussed above, and is the place of timing in all things: healing, life, death, beginnings and endings. In this way, many things can be affected by the Moon through these aspects of change.

Mercury is a planet which affects thought and consciousness. Mercury can move through realms, and can bring information from one realm to another. Things of import concerning commerce and health are often attributed to mercury, but that is because those are the kinds of things people want to know about most. He can deliver any type of information, from any other realm, for he is the consciousness provided by Spirit.

Venus is the place of connection between realms. It is the place where all Spirit enters into matter, creating the lush beauty of physicality and the senses. All passions, arts and sciences are to be found here, as they are all different expressions and descriptions of Spirit entering into matter. She is far more than a love Goddess, but love is what most people lack, so it is what they seek most - that connection or union. Venus is the place of connection, and it is She who provides the connection and relation to all of the other planets, which Mercury uses to travel between the realms.

The Sun has already been considered, but it should also be noted that He provides for the basic energy of all life, and is the physical manifestation of Spirit in its greatest presence in our part of the galaxy. He emanates that which is essential for all life in the physical realms, and can also destroy it as well. This is why the Sun can bring good health, or terrible disease, such as related in the old tales of Apollo.

Mars, like Saturn, is a much feared and maligned planet with a reputation for violence. Mars in actuality is no worse or better than any other planet when ill-dignified. Mars is the necessity of Will in manifest life. This planet provides the drive and energy of life to consume, replicate and defend itself. The fires of Mars are very important in ones life, and in the Rites, and should be cultivated in the same way as the other planets, in order to achieve robust health and therefore clarity of purpose and thought. A weak will or a fearful existence will not be helpful to your endeavors.

Jupiter is your highest-aspected self, and describes the Dominion of the Will of Spirit. All things which are Justified by your existence are within the powers of Jupiter to affect. The pleasure of exercising this dominion of Spirit is also part of Jupiter, and includes all revelry and pleasure of success and kingship. Often people associate luck with Jupiter, but there is only Fortune here in reality, which is the state of the Universe lending itself to the Will of the incarnate Spirit. Fortune is the fortuitous energy of a Spirit doing its Will, which can be felt by all those in its presence.

Saturn is the dark planet of Transformation. In this way it is the gateway of death and of birth, but also so much more. All things which exist are subject to transformation and change. Nothing escapes this, not even Spirit. Because of this, Saturn is often the most feared planet of all. But it is this fear itself which turns the energy of this planet to something ill-dignified. Saturn teaches that all things must be embraced, all change, and to release the Persona's need to hold all things tight to oneself, in order to keep them from changing. Saturn's lessons can sometimes seem to be the harshest of all, but in reality She offers the highest of revelations concerning love which is possible.

The Planetary Days and Hours

The seven traditional planets mark the different days of the week and their influence. Sunday is the Day of the Sun, Monday the day of the Moon, Tuesday the Day of Mars, Wednesday the Day of Mercury, Thursday the Day of Jupiter, Friday the Day of Venus and Saturday the Day of Saturn.

In addition to the days of the week, the Seven Planets also rule over the hours of each day, the order of which change for each day of the week. These Planetary Hours are not exactly the same as a modern hour, and change in length depending on the time of year. In addition there are twelve daytime hours and twelve nighttime hours. To find the length of the daytime hours, take the time from Sunrise in the morning to Sunset in the evening and divide by twelve. This gives you the length of each daytime hour. To find the length of the nighttime hours, take the time from Sunset in the evening to Sunrise in the following morning and divide by twelve. This gives you the length of each nighttime hour. In this system the day starts at sunrise, and its following night completes it until the rise of the sun again the next day.

Once you have the length of the daytime and nighttime hours, you can populate those hours with the planets, according to the day of the week. The first hour of the day, when the Sun comes over the horizon, is the same as that of the day. So the first hour of Friday is always Venus, and the first hour of Sunday is always the Sun, etc. The rest of the planets are then populated in the Chaldean order, and continue on through the nighttime. This order of the planets signifies how fast they move across the sky, with the Moon being the fastest and Saturn being the slowest.

Mystery Babalon

Daytime Hours

Hour	Sunday	Monday	Tuesday	Wednesday	Tuesday	Friday	Saturday
1	☉	☽	♂	☿	♃	♀	♄
2	♀	♄	☉	☽	♂	☿	♃
3	☿	♃	♀	♄	☉	☽	♂
4	☽	♂	☿	♃	♀	♄	☉
5	♄	☉	☽	♂	☿	♃	♀
6	♃	♀	♄	☉	☽	♂	☿
7	♂	☿	♃	♀	♄	☉	☽
8	☉	☽	♂	☿	♃	♀	♄
9	♀	♄	☉	☽	♂	☿	♃
10	☿	♃	♀	♄	☉	☽	♂
11	☽	♂	☿	♃	♀	♄	☉
12	♄	☉	☽	♂	☿	♃	♀

Nighttime Hours

Hour	Sunday	Monday	Tuesday	Wednesday	Tuesday	Friday	Saturday
1	♃	♀	♄	☉	☽	♂	☿
2	♂	☿	♃	♀	♄	☉	☽
3	☉	☽	♂	☿	♃	♀	♄
4	♀	♄	☉	☽	♂	☿	♃
5	☿	♃	♀	♄	☉	☽	♂
6	☽	♂	☿	♃	♀	♄	☉
7	♄	☉	☽	♂	☿	♃	♀
8	♃	♀	♄	☉	☽	♂	☿
9	♂	☿	♃	♀	♄	☉	☽
10	☉	☽	♂	☿	♃	♀	♄
11	♀	♄	☉	☽	♂	☿	♃
12	☿	♃	♀	♄	☉	☽	♂

Therefore, if one wanted to do a working of Mars, the best day for doing so would be a Tuesday, and therein you would find four different hours which would be the best for Mars, the first and eighth hours of the day, and the third and tenth hours of the night.

Timing of the Rites

Mark these Kalas, these times of the Sun, the Moon and the days of the planets, in your Shrines with candles and the adorations which are given later in this book[27]. Attune yourself to the times and manifestations of Spirit. Come to understand them by paying attention to them in quiet moments. Observe the patterns in moods and energies around you as the cosmic wheels turn. And over time you will slowly learn to arrange your Rites to achieve the best results possible, by aligning them with these movements of the universe.

---

[27] See Section III, *Invocations, Hymns, Adorations and Prayers.*

XVIII

Grounding

aia is the World Soul, and it is from Her that all of our bodies are born. Life as we know it can not exist outside of Her body, any more than cells in our body can long exist apart from us. In addition, all living things upon this planet vibrate at Her frequency, which has been called the Breath of Gaia. This frequency, and the energy of Her body, offers us protection and healing if we spend some time within Her body and open to Her influence while there.

This simple ritual is the bare-minimum requirement before performing Rites in your Shrine. They are also a good prerequisite for the Banishing Rituals found in the next chapter. Grounding is a simple ritual, but often very effective and with continued use will help to create a Fila, or strong connection, to Gaia by Grounding within Her body. All living things upon this planet vibrate at Gaia's frequency, which in the language of science is called the Schumann Resonance which is found at 7.83 Hz. This is the frequency of Earth's magnetic field. Whenever this frequency is changed for extended periods of time around living beings, it causes a malfunction in the biological systems of all animals, starting first by the disruption of brain function. Most electronic items and technology emanate disharmonious fields and frequencies. Cell phones and smart

Grounding

devices are the worst and greatly disrupt one's focus on and connection to Spirit. Extended disruption can cause permanent damage. A quick return to the proper frequency causes a return of normal biological functions, over time.

Before one begins to Ground, it is important to identify the Muladhara or Root Chakra, located at the base of the spine in the region of the genitals (pronounced moo-lad-HAR-rah). Chakras can be utilized as energy points within the body and interface points used to connect with particular energies. Muladhara is the point of the body where, when sitting, a person can connect their physical energy with that of the Earth. When standing, the feet become the interface point for the Earth energy, and this energy then travels up the legs to the Muladhara Chakra. It is always better to have bare feet when standing, as this allows the skin and nerves of the feet to act as conduits for the energy. This is important due to the distance the energy must travel to be rooted in the core of the body, and the energy must be strong and significant.

To begin, start in a sitting position of the half or full lotus (i.e. legs crossed). Close your eyes. Place your hands in front of you and face your palms together without touching. This is done so that you can become aware of your own energy and begin to differentiate it from energies around you. Start with your hands wide apart and bring them slowly to about six inches apart. You should start to feel some resistance in the field of energy between your hands as they get closer together. Move your hands out and in a slight distance until the resistance between them is palpable. Once you can feel this, slowly bring your hands together and increase the strength of the energy between them. The energy should start to feel warm, and perhaps tingly or prickly on the palms of your hand. This is the feeling of the energy of fire, and this is your own Spirit's energy. Work with this and become accustomed to it.

Now that you know what your own energy feels like, focus on the energy beneath you. Take a deep breath in through your nose and fill your lungs completely. Exhale slowly and steadily through your mouth, and push your inner energy down towards your Muladhara, and beyond to feel it root into the Earth. You may need to start by visualizing your energy flowing down through you into the Earth, if you can not feel it at first. The Earth will reach back, and provide a feeling of calm foundation. Think of this like you are an infant laying in the arms of your loving mother, for the Earth is indeed our Mother and this is how she protects you. She envelopes you with Her energy, if you will allow it to be so. Consciously allow Her energy to mix with your own, by giving Her permission to do so. You may do this by implicit permission in your Waters, which is the act of feeling desire for it and reaching out to Her, or explicitly be speaking aloud your permission to Her and calling upon Her to come to you and envelop you with Her Soul

By performing this ritual you may reduce anxiety and negative influences while bringing calm and stability within you. Meditate on this Fila, this connection, to Gaia which you have established and focus on the feelings it produces.

Practice this ritual either in the morning after your Daily Dedication, in the evening when you are in a relaxed state, or both if you are able. Record your results in your diary. Do not move on to more advanced forms of banishing until you can Ground and achieve a calm and meditative state at will, even after a hectic day.

The more complicated Banishing Rituals in the next chapter will draw upon the work you do here in this ritual, and the Fila you create to Gaia by Grounding within Her body. Try not to let you mind wander when grounding. Focus your attention on reaching out to Gaia, and feeling Her presence all around you. Try to give Her permission to permeate your being with Her energy, and do not be afraid to let go of control under Her influence as a Guardian of Life. Do not worry if you can not feel much of the energy in your hands as described above. Continued practice of this ritual over time will help to sensitize yourself to this energy and its presence within and around you. Have patience and perseverance.

XIX

Your Dominion

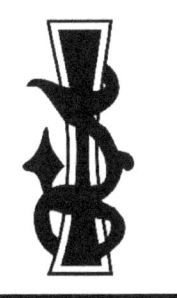

If humanity could listen, there would be much to say. For when those who read my words assume that I speak in metaphor, they have forgotten Truth. For what I say is real.

If those people who could listen would, I would have them gather around me. Not as the men did who were in Ancient Greece, lounging about the symposiums, distracted by their opulence. I would have the people sitting with their bodies upon the warmth of their mother, Gaia, spring flowers the incense, the birds the music.

If the people who yearned to listen were you, this is what I would say: you are lost in a world of belief, battered by convention, abused by lies and propaganda. Close your eyes with the Sun upon your face as you sit and hear my words, and let him illuminate the shadows contained within you so that nothing is hidden from you. So that there is no place for deceit to hide. So that there is no place for fears, deceptions, the poisons given to you all of your life. Become an animal, sitting upon the ground. And let the Sun, Ra, burn away all that is not a part of you.

And for a while just be silent. Be that animal born from the mother upon whose lap you sit. Protected by Her love.

Now, feel that this space within you is a sovereign space. This space is your dominion. There is nothing that can be within this space except that which

Your Dominion

you permit to enter and reside there. There is only one thing which should be in this space and that is your Spirit. Your Spirit is the real you, the true you. Your Spirit came to dwell within your body when your body was conceived. It came and immediately established dominion there. It came and stood and guarded you as you grew, as you changed, as you developed there. And when you were born, it had an agreement with you. That you would live and serve it the best way that you can so that it can achieve its purpose here.

But you were not raised in a way that honored this agreement, or encouraged this, or taught this.

So I teach you now.

When you wake each day remember that you walk this Earth with sovereignty. That you hold dominion of self. That you are obligated to live in a way that enables the Spirit that is You to reach its potential. That by spending time each day doing this exercise that you may come to finally learn who you are, and that you may finally begin to find your purpose here.

Do not let anything else dwell in your first sacred space. Do not sacrifice your sovereignty and dominion to someone or something else, lest you be their slave. For then it is their Will that you will be doing, and not your own.

Do what thou wilt shall be the whole of the law.

Love is the law, love under Will.

XX

Banishing

t is necessary when doing magick, or Heka, to clear one's sacred space of any and all spirits and energy before performing any sort of ritual, lest there be interference in your work. There are many different traditions of banishing rituals. Below you will find two different types of banishing rituals to get you started. The most effective banishing is one that begins with Grounding and connection to the source of life on this plane, Gaia, as was shown in the last chapter. Then, a connection to the source of all life, and the Mother of all Mothers named Nuit is established. This primal and divine source of all Spirit and life is then drawn down to the material realm and utilized in the forces of the Four Quarters. Here it is balanced and strengthened by the Archangels in those Four Elements.

When banishing, one's Will is of the utmost importance. You have a physical space, your body, which was born to hold only your Spirit and nothing else. This is your divine presence, and can not be removed or influenced without your permission. Keep this place sovereign and strong. This is the place of your Truth and your Will. Use this Will to establish your Dominion. When you banish, you are utilizing this divine place

Banishing

within yourself to firmly and forcefully create a sacred space in the material realm which is an extension of your own inner harmony and divinity. Be patient with yourself. This takes time. It is cumulative. The more you physically practice these rituals, the more real and actual it will become. It is like a muscle which you must constantly exercise in order to keep it strong, and like a love which you must always attend to, in order to keep it strong and fresh. The more you invest in your Shrine and your work there, the more it will begin to glow with your Spirit, and those you call.

On a practical note, one should not use the Lesser Banishing Ritual of the Pentagram in the Shrine as a banishing ritual, as it uses Hebrew god names. Yahweh is the enemy of Babalon, Her greatest enemy in fact, and it would not be advisable to invoke his energy into your Shrine by using his names. The Star Ruby from Crowley is excellent in many respects, except for its abandonment of the Archangels. The Archangels are important allies of Babalon, and will add harmonious energy to your Shrine as well as control over negative forces which would not otherwise be available.[28]

In any case, it does not do much good to call upon names which you have no intention of ever forming a good relationship with. The only potential power in using Divine Names in ritual is the threat that you actually have a relationship with that deity or spirit, and that they do indeed lend their power to you and your ends in creating your sacred space. It doesn't really pose much threat to negative influences in your area if you call upon the Archangel Michael, but you have no real connection with him of any sort. In the beginning, you have no such relationship with the names in these rituals. Therefore, in order for the banishings to be effective, it is incumbent upon you to develop a serious relationship with all of the entities whose names you use in ritual. While there is not room in this book to cover every aspect of Heka in this regard, we can say that you should spend much time in study and dedication to each of the four Archangels, as well as Nuit, Hadit, Babalon and Ra Hoor Khuit. Light a candle to Michael, for example, and invite him into your life. Give him some type of formal permission to lend his influence to you in your life. Recite adorations to him on days when the mood strikes you

---

[28] Unknown to most, Angels do not have their origin in Christianity, or even Judaism, even though those religions greatly organized and popularized their use in their own way. Angels, winged messengers, many with similar offices and appearances (although more often female in form) appear throughout many ancient pagan cultures, including Sumeria and Etrusca, and are described in very similar terms to later images of angels: as divine messengers and overseers or guardians of natural forces.

to do so. Eventually, when the time feels right, cultivate a relationship with all of the divine names you use, and ask of them to give you insight about their natures in dreams and by inspiration. Keep your relationship with them sacred, and renew you bond with them periodically. Your banishing will benefit from this interaction tremendously, as their energy is what helps with the banishing, in addition to the force of your own Will. The force of your Will alone is not always enough to clear any space or remove any threat, contrary to what some believe. Your Will is sovereign and inviolable to you, but it is not the only manifest incarnate Will in the material realm. It is always better to have stronger allies which will bolster your own energy with theirs.

Next you will find two different types of Banishing rituals. The first, called Gaia-Luna Point of Light, is more Pagan oriented and a good beginning point for those more aligned with those traditions. The second, called Stella Heru, is forceful and Thelemic in nature. It is an Ophidian Banishing which is practiced by the students of Templum Babalonis in the outer Temple. Remember that all of these banishings benefit well from doing the Grounding exercise in the previous chapter, first.

XX A

Gaia-Luna Point of Light

Basic version

Stand in the center of your circle or area and face the North. North is the place of Nuit, the Grandmother.

Ground your energy down through the core of your body, down into Gaia (see previous chapter, Grounding). Touch the ground and intone the following with great meaning as you do this:

> *I reach down into the body of Gaia. I am rooted, as the trees are rooted. I am bound to Her, Mother of all.*

When you feel that you are well connected through the soles of your feet (remember, bare footed is best), stand tall and raise your hands up above your head. Look up to the heavens, and take your hands, palms towards each other, and draw down the energy of the Moon in through your Crown Chakra at the top of your head. Intone, as you do this:

> *Ma Bella Luna—you who guide the waters of the Earth, you who guide my Waters—with your light I am elevated to be one with the Stars.*

GAIA-LUNA POINT OF LIGHT

Proceed to the Northern Quarter. Lighting a sage smudge wand or an incense stick, draw the Banishing Pentagram of Earth as large as you can with extended arm in front of you (see below). As you do this, intone:

> *I call to the Watchtowers of the North. Begone all ye who dare tread here, my sovereign space.*

Using your smudge wand, draw the outline of the outer circle of your space from North proceeding West and stop in the Western Quarter. Using the sage smudge wand, draw the Banishing Pentagram of Water. As you do this, intone:

> *I call to the Watchtowers of the West. Begone all ye who dare tread here, my sovereign space.*

Using your smudge wand, draw the outline of the outer circle of your space from West proceeding South and stop in the Southern Quarter. Using the sage smudge wand, draw the Banishing Pentagram of Fire. As you do this, intone:

> *I call to the Watchtowers of the South. Begone all ye who dare tread here, my sovereign space.*

Using your smudge wand, draw the outline of the outer circle of your space from South proceeding East and stop in the Eastern Quarter. Using the sage smudge wand, draw the Banishing Pentagram of Air. As you do this, intone:

> *I call to the Watchtowers of the East. Begone all ye who dare tread here, my sovereign space.*

Complete the outline of the circle with your smudge wand to the North where you began, then return to the center of the circle and again face North. Place the smudge wand in a vessel at your feet. Extend you arms out to either side so that you form a cross of the elements, intoning the following with great Will:

> *I, (name of dedication), am the point in the circumference - the center of the Great Wheel! With my light, I command this space. With my light, I have Dominion here. In the name of the Mother's Three, So Mote it Be!*

Your space is now cleansed, and you may continue with your work at hand.

Angelic version

The basic version of Gaia-Luna Point of Light can be enhanced in potency by the addition of the Archangels. To do so, vocally vibrate their names when drawing the pentagrams at the quarters, thereby strengthening them with their energy too. When drawing the Banishing Pentagram of Earth in the North, vocally vibrate the name Auriel (**Ow**-ree-el or **Ar**-ree-el). In the West use Gabriel (**Gah**-bree-el). In the South, Michael (**Mee**-kai-el). In the East, Raphael (**Rah**-fay-el). Also, to enhance the pentagrams, you may wish to envision them in their appropriate colors as you draw them. In the north, see it as strong and black. In the West, glowing lapis blue. In the south, burning red fire. In the East, bright clear yellow.

Formulating the Pentagram and the Elements, after the Ophidian Manner[29]

To invoke the Element, reach out with your arm fully extended in front of you to the Element in question on the star, and then trace around the Pentagram in a clockwise direction until you return to where you started. Do this with determined force, and to the full extent of your reach (make it big).

To banish, do the same, but travel around the Pentagram in a counter-clockwise direction.

---

[29] Please note that this manner of making the Pentagrams is different than what is commonly practiced by the masses, which was inherited from the peculiarities of the Golden Dawn.

Gaia-Luna Point of Light

▽ is Earth   △ is Air   ▽ is Water   △ is Fire   ✹ is Spirit

XX B

STELLA HERU

Being an Ophidian ritual of grounding, banishment and alignment to Spirit for the Three Realms, to be used daily or as a preparation for other works of Heka.

The Alignment with the Great Liberating Mother

Stand in the center of your Shrine.

If needed, yell forcefully and with all of your might to all and everything around you:

> *Apo Pantos Kakodaimonos!*

Pronounced Ah-po Pahn-tohs Kah-koh-die-moh-nos . This is Greek for "Begone from me, all evil spirits!" You may wish to sweep your hand out in front of you, as if forcefully knocking down all opposition.

Then proclaim to all who are present and all the Gods:

> *Great Mother of All Mothers, Sacred Grandmother of all that breathes - O Nuit! It is I, (name of dedication), a true servant of your Mighty Daughter of Fortitude. I call to Thee, as (Son or Daughter) of Gaia. I have*

established my Dominion, and I am Justified. I stand before you, a Warrior in the Army of Ra Hoor Khuit. Lend me your Fortitude and Providence, as I stand at the Point and establish the Wards of this your Sacred Circle.

Now close your eyes and Ground yourself as you have been taught. Then with your feet firmly upon our Mother Gaia, feel your connection to Her. Breathe deeply and relax as you Will. When you are ready, expand your Anima up and out of your current place. Utilize your breath, Will and consciousness in rhythmic undulations to propel you as you go. In this way, growing larger and larger, expanding your Anima, continue to journey up past the clouds, atmosphere, moon, planets, stars, galaxies and finally the universe itself. Travel even unto the Infinite Ends of Space, to the Blackness of Nuit Herself. This may take many minutes. Do not rush this. Take as much time as you need. Upon finding yourself there, innocent and naked before the Mother of All Mothers, continue with the following.

Trace a circle in the Infinite Black high above your head, and then pull it down from the center of that circle to your forehead saying with reverence: *Nuit.*

Feel Her energy, the Source of Life, fill your head and consciousness with blinding and dizzying white light of Spirit.

Now pull that white energy of spirit down with your hand to the genitals, and say with reverence: *O Gaia.*

Let it fill you there, and then continue down your body into Gaia Herself. You are now the conduit for the energy from Nuit all the way down to Gaia, Her Little Sister, Her Manifestation upon which we live.

Now that this connection is established, become a Guardian for this life-energy of the universe as it manifests here on Gaia. Having aligned yourself properly, you are Justified in its use. Purposefully pull the energy with your hand back up the middle of your body to your chest, and then over to your right shoulder, saying forcefully when you are there: *Thelema!*

Then pull the light and energy across to your left shoulder, saying forcefully: *and Agape!*

Then finally clasp your left hand around the fist of your right hand at the center of your chest. Feel and see the light of your Spirit come forth to join with the light of all creation. Let it swell and then finally burst forth from you as Guardian, Daughter or Son of Gaia. Let it fill the room and continue out to the edges of the Universe so that all may be aware of your Guardianship. While doing so invoke and intone in your heart and out loud with every last ounce of your being the name of the Guardian of all Life: *Babalon!*

The Alignment is now complete.

The Banishing of the Quarters

The Guardian now moves counter-clockwise to the East edge of the circle and traces an Ophidian Banishing Pentagram of Air. Deep-Breathe down to the center of Gaia, and when ready Serpent-Strike[30] to the ends of the East at the center of your Pentagram with a great thrust of Spirit, crying forth: *Ra Hoor Khuit!*

Continue to the North, tracing a white line of spirit-energy for your circle as you go. Act as before, but with Ophidian Banishing Pentagram of Earth, saying with meaningful reverence so all beings to the North are alerted to what you are doing: *Nuit.*

Continue to the West, tracing a white line of spirit-energy for your circle as you go. Act as before, but with Ophidian Banishing Pentagram of Water, whispering with dedication and longing to the ends of the West: *Babalon!*

---

[30] Hold your hands closed, and bring them up to either side of your head while breathing in deeply. As you do this, feel and see the energy of the Pentagram flow into you, down your body, and into Gaia. When you have breathed in fully, and the energy hits the earth, strike out hard and fast with your hands in front of you, through the center of the pentagram while you say the name of the quarter (Therion, Babalon etc.). Step forward with your left foot as you do this. Strike fast like a serpent, and see the pentagram glow with your energy, and then see the energy continue on to the ends of the universe in that direction, awakening all things to your presence. Complete the motion with the Sign of Silence, your index finger pressed firmly against your lips.

Continue to the South, tracing a white line of spirit-energy for your circle as you go. Act as before, but with Ophidian Banishing Pentagram of Fire, crying forth with the bellowing depths of your being to the South: *Hadit!*

Return to the East where you began, tracing a white line of spirit-energy for your circle so as to complete it. Then return to the center, facing East. Call forth to all seven directions with an endless chain of AbraHadAbra seven time. (East, North, West, South, Downward, Inward, Upward - *Abrahad-abrahad-abrahad-abrahad-abrahad-abrahad-abrahadabra* is the chain until "Had" is said seven times.) Fully extend your arms out to each of the directions as you do so.

The Banishing is now complete.

The Warding of the Quarters

Let the Guardian continue to face East, and envision the coming presence of each of the Archangels as you call to them to come down from the Caelestial Realms to aid you to guard the Quarters in your Circle.

> *Mighty Angels, messengers, teachers and guardians, I have been made Justified by my Spirit, and so I call to you to lend your aid to me here in this Circle.*
>
> *On the Eastern Winds comes wise Raphael*
>
> *On the Western Waters comes mighty Gabriel*
>
> *On the Southern Fires comes unconquered Michael*
>
> *And from the Northern Lands comes bright Auriel*

Vibrate and intone the name of each Archangel, after calling them forth meaningfully with the words. Reach out to them with your hands, and see them standing there, even if you feel they are not. Then say:

> *The Way through the Elements has been Opened. For I stand as Guardian in this Circle, feet firmly upon Gaia, warded by the Stars and the Angels, my Spirit present and ready - so that I may do my Will amongst the living.*

Mystery Babalon

In Nomine Babalon et Vox Sanctae Meretricis.

Say the last while performing the Gesture of Seeing, which is the hands up and out in front of ones face, slightly to either side of it, palms facing towards the face. End with the Sign of Silence, which is the index finger pressed firmly to the lips, as if hushing someone.

The Pentagrams are formulated in the same manner as the previous ritual, Gaia-Luna Point of Light.

Nava-Durga-Babalon on the Beast by

Orryelle Defenestrate-Bascule

XXI

Dedication of your Shrine to Babalon

hen you have the basics of your Shrine prepared and feel that you are ready to proceed to the Rites, then it is time to dedicate your Shrine to Babalon. This dedication ritual marks your space in Her name, and opens the doorway to Her presence. Over time, as you perform the Rites in Her Shrine, that presence will become stronger. The Shrine will become a gateway for Her energy, to be felt by all and any who enter therein.

Before preceding, you should have, at the bare minimum, chosen a Name of Dedication, practiced the Grounding Ritual, and practiced one of the Banishings. Timing is important for this Dedication. It is best to perform this Dedication to Babalon on the Day of the Sun (Sunday) at Noon. Although Babalon may choose to manifest at any time of day or night, She is a Daughter of Ra under Her name Pahkhet, and the Woman Clothed with the Sun in western traditions, so this time is an auspicious time for the manifestation of Her energy - when the Sun is at its fullest strength.[31]

---

[31] This is also, incidentally, why Liber Legis was received at Noon on each of three consecutive days in 1904. Noon is an excellent and clear time for spirit communication, though rarely used in modern times.

DEDICATION OF YOUR SHRINE TO BABALON

To begin, make sure that Her altar is properly arranged in the West. You will need Thelemic Abramelin Incense for this dedication, as well as Abramelin Oil. Then, prepare yourself with patient care, as described in the previous chapter, Preparing for the Rites. Bath ritually, adorn yourself appropriately, and then proceed to your Shrine around Noontime.

Begin with silent meditation in the West before Her altar, to calm and prepare yourself for the Dedication. When this has been accomplished to your satisfaction, perform the Grounding Ritual. After this, light the candles upon Her altar, with the words "In Nomine Babalon" said as each candle is lit. Ignite your charcoal and add Abramelin Incense to it when the charcoal is ready. Then perform whichever Banishing Ritual you have chosen (Gaia-Luna Point of Light or Stella Heru). If you are familiar with the Adorations of Ra Hoor Khuit[32], it is also prudent to perform the full version of the Adorations of Ra Hoor Khuit to all four quarters at this time.

When finished, advance to the Altar of Babalon in the West. Add more Abramelin Incense to the charcoal, if necessary. Take the Oil of Abramelin and anoint your third eye with a small amount on your finger, saying "In Nomine Babalon", and again over your heart saying "In Nomine Babalon et Vox Sanctae Meretricis". Breath deep to calm yourself, and then begin reading the sevenfold adoration. Read it slowly, and with full focus of Will on each and every word. In your heart, feel the yearning for Her presence with all of your being. Open yourself and your Shrine to Her presence, as you invite Her in.

O Great Warrior!
You who scales the wall of the pit you have been cast into
*   by the denizens of the fish-god!*
You, Mightier than all the gods of men and their fools,
Bearer of the Angels who Guard the very Principles of Existence,
Born from the Great Mother, Nu,
Veiled by Her Night Sky,
Adorned with a crown of Stars,
Kissed by the Flame of your Father Star, Ra.

O Great Fomenter!
You who raises all in fervor and splendor!
You, whose supple power plagues the minds of those

---

[32] See Chapter 34, *the Adorations of Ra Hoor Khuit.*

Mystery Babalon

who try to turn away in fear,
For too insidious are your long, deft fingers
That hold all tightly in your embrace of lust:
For they yearn to you in secret, in the dark,
Drumming feverishly, beating, flailing, wailing to you
          over, and over, and over again.
They call to you, though they admit it not.

O Great Passion!
You who holds my soul in your very hand,
For I cannot die enough for you.
Take me, all of me, consume me, bleed me dry!
My bliss is in my torment of desire for all that you are,
For you arouse the power of the Great Serpent within me.
Take me, use me, command me,
For all that I am exists to be yours.

O Great Death!
You who takes the souls of all and oversees their transformation.
You, who embraces all and refuses none,
For Your Whoredom is the essence of Death's renewal and release.
Borne from the ashes of all who have passed before,
Turned to stone by your sweet, deep kiss,
So cold that the flame of it burns the very soul
With a bliss of the darkest night sky.

O Great Liberator!
You who frees the souls of all who are cast into the enslavement
          and the bonds of Mind.
You who bears the Torch that leads to the great Abyss,
          That place which is not at all - the one that is none.
Free me from that which binds and holds me from my Will!
For that is the only true Freedom, all else is false and folly.
And your Truth shall be my ecstasy, for all that is you leads me to Spirit.
Show me that which I might cast away, that which is put upon me
          by those who seek to consume my Light.
Free me, so that I might come to lay within Truth.

Dedication of your Shrine to Babalon

O Great Lover!
You who manifest all that is Love under Will,
Casting Love in the light of the All Fire!
You who yoke all that is beast, riding us
  as we shall become ridden by our own Star.
Bind me to Truth so that I might reflect its light as the mantle of my soul,
For you shall, with the Light of your Father Ra,
Banish from me all that dwells in the shadows.
Draw me to all that I lack so that I may become whole,
  under the Will of my Spirit.

O Great Babalon!
You who bears as your crown the Seven Stars.
You who move through time and space as the Great Serpent,
Weaving all that is magick throughout the body of the Great Nu.
Your sword glints, O Greatest Warrior who stands
  upon the mightiest of all of the Beasts.
and the severed heads that lay at your feet glow like the stars of the night sky,
Burned are they by your essence of Transformation:
All that is life is your Dominion.

Now raise your arms out to the Heavens in adoration and calling unto Her, as you invite Her into the Shrine.

O Babalon! Babalon! come unto this, Your divine space,
For I, [your name], dedicate this Shrine to your existence:
May all that is borne here be given unto You.
May all that is grown here bear the light of Your being.
May all that is shared here bear the essence of your Lambent Flame.
May all who come here bear their devotion with earnest attention.
May all who leave here carry your Love amongst them.
May all who feed their Lust grow it and return it all to You.

O Babalon! Mighty Babalon!
Come unto this Shrine, as it is dedicated in Your Name,
Made as a vessel for your devotion,
Delivered as a promise of all that is sacred!
Let this place alone be made sacred for the worship of you,
And all devotion here be as a gift to your being.
Bless this space with the presence of your being,

Mystery Babalon

So that all may know you as they Will!

In Nomine Babalon et Vox Sanctae Meretricis!

Sit then in meditation when you have finished, basking in the energy of the Shrine.

Part III

Invocations, Hymns, Adorations and Prayers

XXII

The Adorations of Babalon

The Sevenfold Invocation of Babalon

O Great Warrior!
You who scales the wall of the pit you have been cast into
    by the denizens of the fish-god!
You, Mightier than all the gods of men and their fools,
Bearer of the Angels who Guard the very Principles of Existence,
Born from the Great Mother, Nu,
Veiled by Her Night Sky,
Adorned with a crown of Stars,
Kissed by the Flame of your Father Star, Ra.

O Great Fomenter!
You who raises all in fervor and splendor!
You, whose supple power plagues the minds of those
    who try to turn away in fear,
For too insidious are your long, deft fingers
That hold all tightly in your embrace of lust:
For they yearn to you in secret, in the dark,
Drumming feverishly, beating, flailing, wailing to you
    over, and over, and over again.
They call to you, though they admit it not.

O Great Passion!

The Adorations of Babalon

You who holds my soul in your very hand,
For I cannot die enough for you.
Take me, all of me, consume me, bleed me dry!
My bliss is in my torment of desire for all that you are,
For you arouse the power of the Great Serpent within me.
Take me, use me, command me,
For all that I am exists to be yours.

O Great Death!
You who takes the souls of all and oversees their transformation.
You, who embraces all and refuses none,
For Your Whoredom is the essence of Death's renewal and release.
Borne from the ashes of all who have passed before,
Turned to stone by your sweet, deep kiss,
So cold that the flame of it burns the very soul
With a bliss of the darkest night sky.

O Great Liberator!
You who frees the souls of all who are cast into the enslavement
    and the bonds of Mind.
You who bears the Torch that leads to the great Abyss,
    That place which is not at all - the one that is none.
Free me from that which binds and holds me from my Will!
For that is the only true Freedom, all else is false and folly.
And your Truth shall be my ecstasy, for all that is you leads me to Spirit.
Show me that which I might cast away, that which is put upon me
    by those who seek to consume my Light.
Free me, so that I might come to lay within Truth.

O Great Lover!
You who manifest all that is Love under Will,
Casting Love in the light of the All Fire!
You who yoke all that is beast, riding us
    as we shall become ridden by our own Star.
Bind me to Truth so that I might reflect its light as the mantle of my soul,
For you shall, with the Light of your Father Ra,
Banish from me all that dwells in the shadows.
Draw me to all that I lack so that I may become whole,
    under the Will of my Spirit.
O Great Babalon!
You who bears as your crown the Seven Stars.
You who move through time and space as the Great Serpent,
Weaving all that is magick throughout the body of the Great Nu.

Your sword glints, O Greatest Warrior who stands
    upon the mightiest of all of the Beasts.
and the severed heads that lay at your feet glow like the stars of the night sky,
Burned are they by your essence of Transformation:
All that is life is your Dominion.

In Nomine Babalon et Vox Sanctae Meretricis

The 65 Invocations of Babalon, three pieces[33]

Adoration I

O Babalon!
Like Fire you appear,
As you lick up desire like flames.
Like Water you appear,
As you stir yearnings and devotions of delight.

Come to the people, O Babalon!
Drive them with mad desire
To break the bonds which bind them,
Liberating them from slavery and despair.

Prayer

Great Babalon,
Help me to be a flame for you,
So that you may lick me up,
And use me to stir yearnings in others.

Break the bonds which bind me,
From my True Self,
From my True Will
And all that I incarnated for.

In Nomine Babalon et Vox Sanctae Meretricis

---

[33] Selections from a forthcoming collection of invocations which is as yet unpublished.

The Adorations of Babalon

Adoration II

O Babalon
You who hold the Sacred Wheel,
The Seven spokes aligned,
The Seven Principles at the ready,
In your hands, you hold it.

It spins, motionless.
On the wheels of the Chariot,
It spins, motionless.

And you watch and you wait, O Wise One,
For the moment to stop the wheel,
By sign, and Fortune, and Fate.

Prayer

Great Babalon,
Show me how to live my life,
Guided by your great Chariot of Principles.

May Fortune guide me to my greatest potential.

May my hand turn the wheel by my Will,
Sevenfold unfolding,
My path revealed.

In Nomine Babalon et Vox Sanctae Meretricis

Adoration III

O Babalon
You accept all and refuse none,
For Death is your greatest Passion.

All reside within your grasp,
Sanctified, Blessed, Holy.

Your Greatest Kiss and Your Greatest Love
Is given equally to all in your embrace.

Mystery Babalon

O let me succumb to your seduction,
Holy Womb, Holy Tomb, Holy Lover.

Prayer

Transform me, O Holy Mother
Lest I become Abomination.

Lead me to the Golden Path
Of broken chains, no longer binding.

May my Spirit, rise!
Winged Serpent, Hadit, rise!

I become a point of light,
I become star, bright.

In Nomine Babalon et Vox Sanctae Meretricis

The Earthly Invocation of Babalon

O Babalon, from the dusk-wet Earth you come!
Arise! Daughter of night, arise!
O Babalon, from the depths of dark you come.
Arise! Daughter of might, arise!

O Babalon, this world is your dominion,
The people your subjects,
Their desires your reigns.

Drive them, Babalon,
O Great Liberating Mother,
To a place beyond the slavery of their fears!

Prayer

I call to thee, Great Liberating mother
To show me the beauty in the quiet dark,
As well as the light.

I call to thee, Great Liberating Mother,

The Adorations of Babalon

To show me the strength in my own depths,
As well as in others.

I call to thee Great Liberating Mother,
To break the spell which binds me,
In fear and ignorance
Of my true self.

In Nomine Babalon et Vox Sanctae Meretricis

The Watery Invocation of Babalon

O Babalon, the seas are your home, as well as the deep,
And in this darkness you stir
As in a mirror quiet, the desires of this world.

O Babalon, whether in waters placid or storms of seas,
You orchestrate the chaos,
And in the pools of all things, give calm.

Arise, Babalon in the wake!
Crash upon the shores,
And there break the rocks of resistance and fear,
Into pebbles beneath your feet.

Prayer

I call to thee, Great Liberating Mother
To show me the Fortitude in the Waters,
The power of my depths.

I call to thee, Great Liberating Mother,
To show me the Sovereignty of Dominion,
The calm of my truth.

I call to thee Great Liberating Mother,
To break down those dense stones
Which gather upon my shores!
Shatter fear and jealousy and shame,
Attachments which keep me
From my great and shining Will.

Mystery Babalon

In Nomine Babalon et Vox Sanctae Meretricis

The Airy Invocation of Babalon

*O Babalon, from the unreachable heights of mountains tall,
And the starry reaches of the Celestial Spheres
You sit enthroned with the Wheel of Seven.*

*Seven You are in the heights, and seven in the depths,
Seven are the planets, seven are principles, and seven are realms
From which all things are ruled,
And to which all things are subject.*

*O Babalon, You are the Guardian of the Principles
Which rule all things which move from Spirit,
Out of the Depths, down from the Heights,
And through all places in between.*

Prayer

*I call to thee, Great Liberating Mother
To show me the wisdom of the Principles,
And the beauty therein.*

*I call to thee, Great Liberating Mother,
To show me the way in which to live righteously,
Justified in my will.*

*I call to thee Great Liberating Mother,
To instill within me the desire
For a life lived in balance and harmony,
With the many symbols of my truth.*

The Fiery Invocation of Babalon

*O Babalon, from the fires of the stars You come!
Arise! Daughter of light, arise!
O Babalon, from the fires of the depths You rise!
Arise! Mighty torch-bearer, arise!
O Babalon, the lusts and desires of all,*

The Adorations of Babalon

Are as warriors in Your army,
Ready to serve you in battle.

Command them, Babalon,
O Great Liberating Mother,
Use them as minions in your Victory!

Prayer

I call to thee, Great Liberating Mother
To show me the strength of my lusts,
And the fortitude therein.

I call to thee, Great Liberating Mother,
To show me the way in which to harness my desires,
By love under will.

I call to thee Great Liberating Mother,
To break the inhibition of cowardice,
Which keeps me from the realization
Of my true self.

In Nomine Babalon et Vox Sanctae Meretricis

A General Invocation of Babalon

O Great Liberating Mother,
You, who free me from the bonds that keep me from my Will!

You, who releases me unto my Passions,
My Fires, raging,
My Waters, teaming,
With the currents of my Spirit.

O You whom they call the Great and Terrible Whore,
Who embraces all in the valley feared by the greatest of men.

These depths give rise to the Serpent's Power,
O Babalon!

I call to thee, who has all Wisdom, and all Fortitude,
As You ride your Chariot called the Great Beast.

Mystery Babalon

O Babalon come unto me,
So that I might begin to know Your Mysteries,
And at last know thee.

The Grand Devotion of Babalon

I come before thee, all that is of the deepest depths of existence.
Guardian of the Seven Great Principles, held within Your wheel,
Goddess of Heka, laid before the people within the Mysteries of Blackness
Seen as Golden by Your true seekers,
I give myself, and all that I am, to You,
Great Babalon!

I lay before You, all that is within me.
I harness my animal, as You ride the Great Beast
So that I might serve you, with my Spirit,
O Great Goddess of the Gateway of Death, of Life,
And of all that is brought forth from the mysteries beyond knowing.

You, who are the Goddess of War and of Vengeance,
Great Daughter of Ra,
Whose Secret Name at last I knoweth,
O, mighty Hoor-Pahkhet, whose reign rose from the sands upon the Nile,
Whose reign was born from the people who lived before even time.

You, mighty Babalon,
Take me for Your own!
I exist to serve You, with all of my passion,
my heart, my soul.
My devotion is Yours. My breath is for You.
I ask You to take me, and make me that which you Desire,
For Your Desire is Wisdom,
And Your Heart beats for All.

In Nomine Babalon et Vox Sanctae Meretricis

The Serpentine Invocation of Babalon, Female

Arise within me, O Goddess of Lust,
Make me wet with unconquerable desire!

THE ADORATIONS OF BABALON

Insatiable I become, unquenchable, frenzied
In my lusty worship of You.

Move within my Waters, deep with undulations!
To me! O Babalon, to me!
Arise within my Fires, O coiled serpent dancing!
To me! O Babalon, to me!

All that I receive, in sensual and carnal worship
Is for you.
Every thrust and kiss and shudder and moan
Is for you.

Come with me and my lovers, O Babalon,
And partake of the sense and rapture
Of life lived exceedingly well.

There are no limits to my desires,
There are no boundaries to my ecstasy,
For the sounds of our love is the chanting of the faithful,
In Your worship.

The Serpentine Invocation of Babalon, Male

Arise within me, O mighty lust of Will!
For I crawl now as a Beast on the hunt,
Wild and ruddy and strong
As they like me to be,
As they need me to be.

Therion!

Arise within me, O mighty lust of Will!
Whether driving long and hard,
Or seducing soft and slow,
I will be that which they need
In service to all!

Therion!

Hard! Hold! Breathe not so deep! Die!

Mystery Babalon

Ride them as bull and be ridden,
Through froth, lather and storm!
Take pleasure in acts of pleasing,
A true Beast of Babalon.

The Hagia's Daily Dedication to Babalon

In Nomine Babalon et Vox Sanctae Meretricis. I honor You,
Divine manifestation of all that is the union of fire and water
The potency of Female Divine Spirit
The Fire of Will, and the Love of Water
United with force, with passion, with wisdom, with inspiration,
Inspiration derived from the blackness of the deepest knowing.

Your Love, under Your virility of Will,
Manifests through lust, through desire,
With a potency that drives most mad by their own fear.
Death is not a shadow in your army,
But a lover who caresses a true king.

I honor You, Dea Babalon
I serve You,
I build my fire, and feed Your fire,
Do what thou wilt shall be the whole of the Law
I seek to manifest You through my existence.

I honor You with my service
I honor You with my devotion
It is my Will to serve You
Love is the Law, Love Under Will

XXIII

THE COMPANY OF HEAVEN

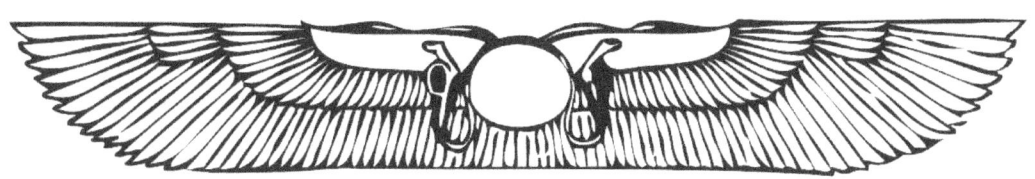

Invocation of Therion

O, Great Beast
You who hold the Fire of Will within you,
For are not all of us aligned in the Light of the Perfect Star?

I call to thee, O Strongest among us,
Therion!

Lend me your Light of Clarity,
Borne from the might of Babalon's Lust,
The greatness of Her Passions.

Therion!

May I swell in your Strength and Light.

The Company of Heaven

An Invocation to Nuit

O, Nuit.

You are the Divine.

You are the Soul of Existence, the Consciousness of all of Creation,
For every manifestation of Your love is existence itself,
Every breath, every flick of light, and every shadow
Is a part of Your Will.

And though You give birth to every star,
And each star is the seed that sheds its essence into all of life,
You glorify Your wisdom in the separateness of self:
For all life is unique,
And every moment unrepeatable.
So, this is the passing and turning of Your Great Wheel
In the greatest, and the smallest of Your children.

O, Nuit.

Mother, Grandmother,
There are none in existence who do not know You as such,
For we are all Your daughters and your sons,
And we are the daughters of Your daughters, or the sons of Your sons.
And when the starlight meets the dew we are born:
Spirit, seeking to manifest Your love, Your wisdom
In the course of our being.

It is I, (name of dedication), who comes before You on this glorious day
Under the Sun in this sky, Ra,
I stand before You, naked, as I was born from the love of Your heart,
The warmth of Your bounty:
And I shall live my life as a gift to You,
For my existence is as gratitude to You.

Beneath Aiwaith[34], Your divine children, who manifest the breath of the Sylphs
Into the song of the birds who glorify the motion therein,
It is I, your Grandchild,

---

[34] Aiwaith, the Elements of Air, who function as a collective spirit without individuality. Pronounced Ai-**way**-eth.

Mystery Babalon

Who washes away all wards of restriction
As Elwaith[35] carries them through my fingers in the waters that
Conceived all life upon Earth.

And as I warm my flesh, my body born from Gaia,
By the flicker of the fires that hint at the very essence
Within the body of all stars,
I say to You my promise, my devotion, my commitment:

O, Nuit,

It is I, (name of dedication)
I live each day to indwell my Spirit,
For I serve my Spirit in Will.
I give rise to the Serpent,
Divine expression of the kiss of Nu,
Each spark of light a star.
Her love, rains upon all of existence in
All forms
All expressions
All beauty
All joy.

Every breath that I take is a song of Her glory.
Every moment of my life is a chance to give thanks.
For my existence is not possible without Her love,
For it is Her love that She sheds in all of Her motion.
And I am but a reflection of Her motion in that moment,
Transformed by the Will and intent of my being
Forever riding the undulations of divine existence
As I strive to be a true expression of Her wisdom.

O, Nuit.

In all of your wisdom you made me a guardian.

---

[35] Elwaith, the Elements of Water, who are spirits which function as a collective spirit without individuality. Pronounced El-**way**-eth. The others are Throath (thro-**way**-eth) for Earth and Dantaiyeth (dan-**tay**-eth) for fire, who should only be called in glass because his/their fire is dangerous. These all serve under Lowaiyeth (lo-**way**-eth), the Steward of the North and Ghob (Go-ah-**oob**), the Supreme Elemental King of Earth. These Elements then are also under the gnomes Senomeo (say-**no**-may-oh) and Phorlukh (**for**-lukh), who in turn serve the angel Kerub (ker-**roob**), and the Archangel Auriel (**oor**-ee-el). Such is the hierarchy of Earth in the Material Realm.

The Company of Heaven

And so I walk with choice and determination,
To bring sanctuary to all that is life,
To celebrate your existence through care and dominion:
Guardian of all that is sacred within Gaia.

Tibi amor meae omnis actiones meae sunt.
Mea gratia sententia animae meae est.

(All of my actions are my love for You.
The expression of my soul is my gratitude.)

A Daily Invocation of Nuit and Spirit

O Nuit!

Thrust me into the Night Sky so that I might know that I am part of Your body and so that I therefore know my place in your Universe.

If I am to burn with light and be seen as a star it is because I live in dedication to You, and to my Spirit, for this is the light by which I can be guided unto You.

It is in my burning brightly that I serve. It is in the beauty that is a part of You that shines in my eyes that I teach, for Your love moves through my body in its rivers of blood, as it moves in the rivers of water and fire through the body of Gaia, for we are both Your children.

Teach me, O Nuit, so that I may have the wisdom of the flowers that know Your secrets — that beauty and love of union are what make their nectar sweet.

Teach me, O Nuit, so that I may forget the burden of the admonitions of man, so that I may sing with the purity of the voices of the birds, for their Harmonies are but a reflection of Your voice, Your songs — Celestial, as both the whales and the planets sing the same song.

Teach me, O Nuit, so that each step that I take upon the body of Gaia is with the consciousness that I tread upon the bodies of my ancestors, and therefore each step I take must be an act of remembrance and honor unto the steps that they have taken before me. In this way we are continuous — as You are continuous.

O Nuit, help me to be as dark as You are, Unseen. So that I may remember the purpose of my body — so that my presence may be felt by others as a breeze that brightens and sparks the fire of their stars.

An Invocation to Hadit

*I invoke thee Hadit, for You are the manifestation of my divine Will
Which is conceived from the expression of my Spirit upon matter,
The inversion of the elements in the form of a five pointed star.*

*Serpent upon serpent,
You writhe within the persona
Rising and falling,
Until that moment when You alight with wings.
O great flaming sphere,
A point of light and fire
Divine by the nature of autonomous destiny,
Inspired by the kiss of Nu:
For You, as all things are born from Her.*

*You are the serpent, coiled,
Within all manifest in the Realm of flesh,
Yet unrealized by the masses of slaves
Who are as yet unborn into true existence.*

*I invoke thee, Hadit!
Become one with my center,
For the core of my star burns bright within me,
Even when I cannot feel its presence,
Even when I cannot realize its dominion.
Release me, O Hadit!
Release me from the bonds of my own making!
Release me from the restriction of my appetites
And my indolence, my inability to serve that which
Gave me breath:
For my life is the purpose of the presence of You within me,
The realization of my true self.*

*I invoke thee, Hadit!
I invoke my Spirit, may my serpent rise
And give voice to my awakening,
And give reason to my existence.*

The Company of Heaven

*O, Winged Snake of Light Hadit,
I embrace thee.*

*And may the gods initiate your presence within me!
And may the angels test my worthiness!
And may the fate of my existence rest upon the death of me!
And may the purpose of my incarnation be realized upon Your wings.*

An Invocation to Ra Hoor Khuit

My lord initiating be O so present among us. Thy feathered wings expanding tip to tip to cover the horizon. Sing forth O great hawk-headed lord for thy call brings terror to the hearts of those that hear Your battle cry. And as Your tail flicks and Your shadow covers them in darkness, they will remember that your fury is not yet known but only hinted at, as the shroud of the night star light surrounds them.

I call to thee, most Great and Terrible Hawk-Headed Mystical Lord of Strength, of War, of Vengeance, of Divine Retribution

It is I, [your name], and I come before you, myself an offering, ready to die and be reborn anew. For on this day, I accept the mantle of my most great and terrible purpose, that of my Will.

I am worthy to fight and die before You, Mighty Ra Hoor Khuit! I am ready to face all of my fears! I am ready to forge myself into steel, to sever that which keeps me from my divine, incarnated purpose.

I call to thee, Ra Hoor Khuit! To dedicate the purpose that binds my being in service to all that is the Will of my existence.

I call to thee, Ra Hoor Khuit! To smite me before You, if I am not worthy: for there is no life, no existence, if I do not do that which I incarnated for.

I call to thee, Ra Hoor Khuit! I sacrifice my enslavement so that I may be bound in the service of my Spirit.

Do what thou wilt shall be the whole of the law. Love is the law, love under Will.

Mystery Babalon

The Hagia's Dedication to Ra Hoor Khuit

My lord initiating be O so present among us. Thy feathered wings expanding tip to tip to cover the horizon. Sing forth O great hawk-headed lord for thy call brings terror to the hearts of those that hear Your battle cry. And as Your tail flicks and Your shadow covers them in darkness, they will remember that Your fury is not yet known but only hinted at, as the shroud of the night star light surrounds them.

I stand before You, Oh Great Hawk-Headed, Mystical Lord of magnificent strength and of fury. For You have come unto thine age to destroy the enemies and those that give homage to the dying gods. For no greater sorrow has befallen all of life and existence than the crimes committed by these demon lords. No greater violation has been brought unto the Earth, and no greater destruction has reigned than the very rape and torment of our Mother.

Oh, Ra Hoor Khu!

My body pulses with the beat of Your own heart. The sound of Your great wings brings fever to my soul, for I answer Your loud call to arms. For I am a warrior in this age. I am Noboramantu, as you so have named. And I have come, manifest, to bring forth Your armies, for all shall fall before You, and be done.

I sing the praises of this Greatest War. I invoke Your armies of Your Greatest Vengeance, In Nomine Babalon, Your Sister. It is the sound of Your call that sends terror through the veins of the weakened and the profane. For only those with the greatest courage shall raise their heads upon hearing your cry as the serpent rides upon their brow, and ready themselves for a greatest death, by Your side.

It is I, who bears the mantle of Your Warrior Kin. And it is I who dies a death before you, a death of sweetness and delight! For You call to me, and I am the bearer of the Blood of the Scarlet Mysteries, carried in the body and the soul of all my kindred sisters. I am the bearer of all that is under the world, and all that foments upon the Earth and all that moves within the skies. I am the gateway between the Realms. I am the guardian of the mysteries. I am, Oh great lord, The Daughter.

It is with mine Blood of mine Moon that I give my soul in service of You, for it is the Will of my Spirit, in Nomine Babalon, to serve You in this War.

The Company of Heaven

Oh, lover of mine, You who came down upon me, taking me into Your army of the Blood-borne, taking me in the essence of all that is of the greatest and most potent virility. It is I, Aureavia, whose name was bestowed upon my existence via Your Divine Sister. It is I, oh my Brother, who stands before You. May it be that my presence, so ordained at Your Great Feet, shall bring terror into the hearts of the masses as I am the Pashtun of their unmaking, bestowed this gift by Your mighty hand.

It is with all of my passion, it is with all of the forces that I bear within my body, my blood, it is with all of my essence and my Will, that I give myself in this oath to You.

It is with the greatest honor that I serve Your reign, and the Dominion of My Mother, as Hagia to Her People. For I have been born from the Blood of the Underworld Fire, having been beaten and buried asunder so that my body is of the Earth, flooded and washed clean by the torrents of the Waters, passed through the Gates of that Great Abyss, having leashed the Great Tormenter, Chronzon! By this, I have forsaken life to walk as The Dead, no longer living, a creature of the Realms.

I give myself unto You, for in the name of Babalon, I am Your Enginery of War.

In Nomine Babalon et Vox Sanctae Meretricis

XXIV

THE INVOCATIONS OF THE ARCHANGELS

Invocation of Auriel[36]

We call to thee, Mighty One, Light Bearer, Far-Traveler - O Auriel!

It is you who brings the light down from above,
And there in the glowing darkness you stand, illuminating the shadows.

Come Auriel, come!
And illuminate the shadows here.

---

[36] Also spelled as Uriel and Oriel, but not Ariel or Aral who are a different spirits.

The Invocations of the Archangels

O Mighty Auriel, it is you who command the little ones of the Earth!
The Elements and the Elementals, the Gnomes and all of the others,
Phorlukh, Kerub, and the mighty Angels of Earth.

Such is your countenance that all are arrayed beneath you in glorious perfection,
And they all do you service, Mighty Auriel.

It is you who is the Angelic Guardian of this World!
It is you who holds fast the balance of tension of the light and the dark!
It is you who bridges the gap between here and there!

Come Auriel, come!
And be guardian of this place.

For I am a true servant of the Earth.

Mystery Babalon

Invocation of Michael

We call to thee, Bright One, Strong One, Fierce and Unconquerable Sun!
We call to thee, Commander, Leader, Teacher and Protector!
We call to thee of the Divine Fire which burns away all impurity!

Come Michael, come!
Come with sword in hand!

Come Michael, come!
Come with your golden armor!

Come Michael, come!
And teach us the ways of righteous nobility,
Which comes from the trueness of Will.

It is you who wields the strength of the right arm.
It is you who bears the sword of justice.
It is you who is the fierce demon slayer.

Come Michael, come!
You whose names means like unto the divine.

Come Michael, come!
And watch over me, teach me, and be a guardian thereof.

The Invocations of the Archangels

Invocation of Raphael

We call to thee, Bright One, Clear One, Golden One,
You who crosses the world in the blink of an eye!

We call to thee, Fair One, Clever One, Wise One,
You who traverses the Underworld and all the Realms.

Come Raphael, come!
Cross the threshold, traverse the Golden Door!

Come Raphael, come!
Bright and blinding as the Sun!

For it is you who bring to us clarity,
And it is you who bring to us insight.

It is you who bring to us knowledge,
And it is you who bring to us healing.

Come with your Angels called Cor-Cantia,
Whose name means Heart of the Incantation.

Come with your symbols, come with your languages, come with your light!

Come Raphael, whose name means Divine Medicine,
And heal us of our ignorance.

Mystery Babalon

Invocation of Gabriel

We call to thee, O Mighty One who slips through the shadows,
*   Who is here, and who is not here.*
We call to thee, O Lofty One, who watches unseen,
*   Under the reflection of the Moon.*
We call to thee, Great One of the Brotherhood, who sends his
*   Signs and omens by mirrors and dreams.*
We call to thee, O Hidden One who changes from moment to moment,
*   But in the secret depths remains unchanged.*

Come from the Waters!
Come from the Storms!
Come from the Tides and the Seas and the Rains!
Come from the First Heaven! Come with your Gra'aeb Elohim,
*   The Angels of Shadows in the Movement of Light.*

For you delight in the reflections and movement and cycles
*   Of eddies and flows which wax and wane.*
And your voice is as dew upon the morning grass,
*   If one but cease in their motion, and see to hear it.*
We call to the, O mighty Gabriel, Lord of Justified Vengeance,
*   Whose name means Strong Man of Divinity.*

Thus we call to you, Mighty Gabriel,
*   With subtlety and perception,*
*   Through the shadows and light,*
*   Which reflect from the depths*
*   Of each moment.*

The Invocations of the Archangels

Invocation of Zadkiel[37]

We call to thee, you who would come upon a great white horse,
    for the pure joy of it!
We call to thee, you whose Realm is the Dominion of the Spirit,
    and the realization of ideals.
No enemies can dwell where you are,
    so great and magnificent is your Joy,
    so tremendous is your Righteousness.

Come, O Zadkiel, Adorned in the Purple, voluptuous or pale!
Come, O Zadkiel, Guardian of the Sovereignty of Dominion!
Come, O Zadkiel, Lord of the Fauns and the Furies!
Come, O Zadkiel, with the bliss of Spirit in matter!

It is your angels who maintain both the origin and development of manifest
    life.
It is your Realm which is called Hep-Toh-Madra-Secum,
    IO Pater, Jupiter.
It is your language which has no words at all,
    For it is a Beatific Expression,
    Encompassing all which is sensual and wild.

Come, O Zadkiel, and teach us of the realization of our Will!
Come, O Zadkiel, and teach us of our path as Lord of Ideals!

Come, O Zadkiel, that we may partake of the bounty of Dominion,
    The fruition of the Will of Spirit!

---

[37] Also spelled, Tzadkiel, Sadqiel, etc.

Mystery Babalon

Invocation of Zafkiel[38]

> *We call to thee, most sublime of angels, highest friend who as foe is seen,*
>   *For at your presence they tremble,*
>   *And in your darkness they fear,*
>   *The death sealed deep within the animal from birth!*
>
> *We call to thee, O hidden one of knowledge, which is not knowledge at all,*
>   *But rather the deepest knowing,*
>   *In the moment of pure experience,*
>   *Which the moment of death makes true.*
>
> *Come O Zafkiel with your shadows bright in darkness!*
> *Come O Zafkiel, your waves pulling to the depths!*
> *Come O Zafkiel, with the intensity of your gaze,*
>   *Which no defenses are prepared to resist!*
> *For your gaze sees through to all fears,*
>   *No matter how hidden they be,*
>   *In the folds of the flesh.*
>
> *And in that moment of truth, when all shadows fall to their end,*
>   *There is a giddiness,*
>   *There is a budding joy,*
>   *There is an exhilaration unknown.*
> *For the deepest part of our being feels a touch of the bliss*
>   *Unimaginable at the Spirit's release!*
>
> *Come mighty Zafkiel, King of the Depths,*
>   *And liberate us from our attachments and fears.*

---

[38] Also spelled, Zaphkiel, Tzaphqiel, etc.

The Invocations of the Archangels

Invocation of Anael[39]

We call to thee, wise one, royal one, philosopher of the Spirit!
    It is you who teaches of the arts,
    It is you who teaches of the sciences,
And it is you who teaches of the effects and associations
    Of all things when spirit enters matter.

Heka is in your provenience, and this the secret art you teach,
    For within your Realm is a connection
    To every other Realm and place.
Such is the virtue of Venus, that it is the gateway of all gateways,
    And the means by which magick is manifest!

Come, O Anael, with your arts, and the pure grace of divinity!
Come, O Anael, with your philosophy, and its perennial wisdom!
Come, O Anael, with your science, the observations of truth,
    For you too hold a sword,
As deadly as any other,
Which cuts with the severity of beauty.

The mighty Heptarchia are at your call, and the Nine Muses beckon,
    And all of the Angels do you service,
For you hold the key to the charm of attraction,
    The many measurements of Spirit in matter.

---

[39] Also spelled as Haniel.

Mystery Babalon

Invocation of Kamael[40]

We call to thee strong one, dread one, warrior of the highest order!
    Before you flee the dishonest!
    Before you flee the untrue!
Before you flee the deceivers, the wretches and the indolent,
    Who dishonor their living Spirit.

The necessity of purpose is your domain and therein you teach
    Courage in the moment of action,
    And certainty in the moment of choice,
For you grant the true vision of things as they are,
    For Will to be brought to its fruition.

Come, O Kamael, true warrior of righteousness!
Come, O Kamael, true seer in the midst of battle!
Come, O Kamael, truest ally of all the allies
    Who stands firm and fast,
    His arms at the ready,
    To execute the commands of Spirit.

Come thrice mighty flames who brand with fire,
Angels called Elohim, their eyes of truth ablaze!
There they stand ready in service of their Lord,
    With swords drawn and flashing,
    With strong shields clashing,
Willful triumph shall win the day!

---

[40] Also spelled as Camael, Camiel but not as Samael, who is a different being.

XXV

The Invocations of the Planets

Invocation of Saturn

Hail to you, dark one, old one, black star of time, O Saturn!

You are the gateway of birth! You are the gateway of death!
You sever the cord and release the spirit
From the bonds and chains of the flesh.
This release if as bliss unutterable,
As the Persona is shed like a husk.

Heavy beyond measure you are, and black beyond night,
You bring levity immeasurable and intensity of purpose,

The Invocations of the Planets

So that our capacity for Spirit is expanded.

Change you are, change beyond change,
An assassin of all that was.
Necessity drives you on, and purpose your compass,
Severing all bonds of attachment.

Darkest Queen of all Queens, whose dark is like light
To eyes of the Spirit within,
Come to us now in our fear,
And lend us the stubborn strength
To persevere by necessity
So that we may live long, yet desire your touch forever.

Hail to you, unconquerable Saturn!
And hail to the necessity of death!

Mystery Babalon

Invocation of Jupiter

Io Pater, Yu-pah-tair, Jupiter - King of Kings enthroned most high!

In you we find the realization of our Will!
In you we establish the dominion of our Spirit!
And in you we find the joy of accomplishment,
For you are our highest aspected self.

Unbridled is the realization of ideals,
Which grows from the primal drives,
And erupts in beatific expression.

Ecstatic is the bliss of accomplishment,
And revelry is the reward of victory!
And in the innocence of the animal and its passions
We find the purity of action unstained by thought.

Come Satyrs, come Nymphs, come Fauns and fine fellows!
Draped in deep purple and blushing with joy,
For we await the Crown of our Spirit
Which is granted to none but Kings
Who have slain all fear with the spear of Will.

Hail to you, mighty Jupiter,
May we forever dance in the throes of our innocence!

The Invocations of the Planets

Invocation of the Planet Mars

Mars, deep red, blood red, dark and fiery and full of rage!

You bring the primal will to survive!
You bring the competitive and procreative force
Which drives evolution,
The Force and Fire of the Will to Conquer!

By your force our muscles swell with power!
By your fire our Wills become like steel!

Your strength brings courage in the face of fear
So that we may triumph,
And extend the Dominion of our Wills.

For the violence of War and Predation are intrinsic
To the perpetuation of existence.

O Mars! It is you who define the Will,
That fiery force which drives all that live,
As the Necessity of Purpose!

O Mars! First Will of All Living Things!
Be ever present in us all, so that we become like Generals
Who have braved the dangers of life,
And fulfilled the purpose of their Wills.

Mystery Babalon

Invocation of the Sun

Hail to the Sun, Sol, Helios, Ra the bright shining one!

It is your eternal light which gives life to this world,
And all creatures bask in the warmth of your countenance.
All shadows are banished and all sicknesses are cured
At the touch of your cleansing presence.

Father, Time-keeper, Guardian, King,
It is you who stand for the right and principled
And keep the enemy and evil at bay.

By your might is order established.
By your light is truth shown forth.
And by your divinity is royalty established.

O princely one, fine clothed, cultured and golden,
You are the keeper of truth which shines,
And honesty without which happiness fails.

Come great father come!
Show us the righteousness of Spirit!
Guide us by the principles of Truth!
And lead us to the purpose of our life,
Which is lived in harmony and beauty,
Guided by the spirit of our incarnation.

The Invocations of the Planets

Venus Invocation

O Venus, who with a glance and a smile
Can inspire the world by desire to heights undreamed of
In times forgotten.

Venus, your grip holds fast the world,
For all seek to attract your soft gaze
And win their bounty of love.

For do you not inspire all that is beautiful,
All that is graceful,
All that is joyful,
O Venus?

Indeed, and from beauty comes truth
And from grace comes the balance of justice
And from joy comes fulfillment.

And it is these virtues of love which inspire the best of us
To selfless acts of kindness and compassion,
Which seek in their ends nothing in return.

There lies the secret within love which heals;
Both the self and the other.
There lies the secret within love
Which washes away the dross from the soul
And lightens the footsteps.

Come, O Venus, soft-footed, passionate and dancing!
Come, O Venus, lusty and desirous and wet!

Mystery Babalon

Come, O Venus, bounty-laden, sweet-smelling,
Full of hopes and promises.

Come, O Venus, with your love and beauty,
Your harmonious grace, and your passionate desires.

Fill us wholly with your Divine Creativity,
And lend your inspiration and truth to the work at hand.

The Invocations of the Planets

Invocation of Mercury

O Mercury, quick and nimble of foot and wit!
It is you who can travel the world in the blink of an eye!
It is you who can descend unharmed through the depths!

Psychopomp, deep-traveler, healer and teacher,
You alight on winged feet, you heal with winged staff,
And you teach with winged hat.

Swift with feathered-pen and quill you write
The interpretation of spirit in symbols and words,
And there is nowhere above or below which denies your visits.

Teach us, O wise Mercury!
Lead us, far-traveled one!
And heal us, with knowledge of ourselves!
For your clever wit, and your wise glance
Keep spirits burning bright with joy.

Hidden One, Bright One, Clever One, Winged One,
You are the keeper and storehouse of knowledge
In the ancient writings, on pages within books,
In symbols upon walls, and at markers at the crossroads.

Come quick Mercury, come!
Be as a teacher and friend
To those that seek to know themselves truly,
And in sincerity appreciate your gifts.

Mystery Babalon

Invocation of the Moon

Ever shifting, ever glowing, ever bleeding Moon,

It is by your growing light that all seek to ripen and become born again
And it is by your diminishing light that all seek death and renewal.
It is by your radiance, O Moon, that the tides rise and fall,
For ever and ever is the pull of your magnificence upon us.

By your full light do the wild beasts hunt and howl!
And within your darkness do the quiet mysteries rest,
For you are the bearer of dreams and revelations, illusions and reflections.

O Midnight Sun, Death Moon, Blood Moon and Goddess!
You govern the primal, the instinctual and the animal,
And you bring forth hidden memories
Evoked by the intensity of aroma.

Under your nightly countenance are all things covered in darkness,
And the shadows are nuanced by the light you give,
Yet this light is not your own,
For you are illuminated by the Sun
According to your own motion and place.

O Luna! Under you the Ibis awaits with scarlet crest,
For as the moon shifts and phases, so too does woman,
And soon the scarlet moon-blood shall flow again,
From She who is wise in the ways of change,
And in whom all power is given.

The Invocations of the Planets

Invocation of the Waxing Moon (1st Quarter)

I call to thee, Shining One, Waxing One, Amibousa, She Who Changes!
    It is you who grows the seeds to fruition,
    It is you who grows life in the womb,
And it is you who brings the world hope and joy
    As you change all things of death into life.

A time of increase of bounty marks your presence, O Zirna!
A time of new fortunes and prosperity arises with you, O Phoebe!
For at the touch of your new light
    All things grow stronger,
    All things gain fortitude,
    And all things are filled with bounty.

Come to us now, O Amibousa, Waxing One, Bright One, She Who Changes!
And bring us to the fortune and bounty of our conception,
    Which is the discovering of our Wills.

Invocation of the Full Moon (2nd Quarter)

I call to thee, Bright One, Full One, Amibousa, She Who Changes!
  It is you who births all things which exist into life,
  It is you who is the fruition of all endeavors,
And it is you who brings the world good living
  As you bring the accomplishment of all that is good.

A time of ripeness of bounty marks your presence, O Selene!
A time of the greatest fortunes and prosperity shines with you, O Dione!
For at the touch of your brightest light
  All things are at their peak,
  All things are filled with strength,
  And all things burst forth in their full expression.

Come to us now, O Amibousa, Full One, Bright One, She Who Changes!
And bring us to the fortune and bounty of our birth,
  Which is the enacting of our Wills.

The Invocations of the Planets

Invocation of the Waning Moon (3rd Quarter)

I call to thee, Dimming One, Waning One, Amibousa, She Who Changes!
   It is you who gathers the remnants of life,
   It is you who conserves for gatherings anew,
And it is you who brings the world providence
   As you prepare all things of life for death.

A time of decrease of activity marks your presence, O Cerridwen!
A time of lost fortunes and prosperity falls with you, O Persephone!
For at the touch of your dim light
   All things grow weaker,
   All things loose fortitude,
   And all things grow quiet for the silence to come.

Come to us now, O Amibousa, Waning One, Dimming One, She Who Changes!
And bring us to the truth and purpose of our life,
   Which is the achieving of our Wills.

Mystery Babalon

Invocation of the New Moon (4th Quarter)

I call to thee, Dark One, Black One, Amibousa, She Who Changes!
    It is you who guides all things into the blackness,
    It is you who drags all things into the darkness,
And it is you who brings them back up again
    Out of the vast Underworld to begin afresh and anew.

A time void of bounty marks your presence, O Hekate!
A time nightmares and madness lingers with you, O Melinoë!
For at the touch of your dark nothingness
    All things are finally lost,
    All things are completely unmade,
    In their preparation to be birthed anew.

Come to us now, O Amibousa, Dark One, Black One, She Who Changes!
And bring us to the truth and purpose of our death,
    Which is the accomplishing of our Wills.

XXVI

The Invocations of the Elements

Invocation of the Element of Earth

Take from the Earth, give to the Earth, feel the joy of it.

*Earth, that which gives any thing its foundation,
Its beginning, and its end.*

*Earth, the source of all matter,
From which all things gain stability,
Substance, form and silence.*

The Invocations of the Elements

Earth, impenetrable strength, immovable structure,
That which of all the elements is realized foremost,
But utilized the least.

Grant unto this temple your stability, O Earth,
So that we may undertake the working at hand,
And see it to its end.

Mystery Babalon

Invocation of the Gnomes

O subterranean workers,
You who mine the veins of ore like a harvester of fields,
You who keep hidden the gems of this world,
May you ever be vigilant and watchful of the Earth's treasures.

Diligent, industrious, and tireless
You labor unceasingly like the gears which turn this world upon its axis.
Grant unto us your stability, your steadfastness and your courage
To endure all things.

For you understand above all how work banishes despair.

The bowels of the Earth tremble at the pounding of your earnest footsteps,
Which sound out the rhythmic music of the passages of time.

By your industry is the molten core transformed into the Seven Metals,
And the black dust turned to Diamonds.

These Diamonds reflect upon the metals and so illuminate the depths
Like the stars in the body of Our Lady Nuit.

Hearken to our work, O Mighty and Steadfast Gnomes,
And look upon us as true Brothers of Earth.

The Invocations of the Elements

Invocation of the Element of Water

Bring together, flow together,
Move the currents from one to another.

Water, the nurturing and sustaining Blood of Life
Which runs through the spirits of all living things,
And through which all living things are connected.

Water, that which flows, that which moves,
That which cleanses and purifies and nourishes and permeates
All things that move and grow and live together.

Water, through your flow one can experience
The pain or suffering or joy or delight of another,
For in the waters such feelings are carried from one to another,
And we call this connection Empathy.

Grant unto this Temple your Purity, O Water,
For when we are moved by you, we feel our limitless connection to all,
And the pain of separation dissolves into innocence.

Mystery Babalon

Invocation of the Undines

O fluid wayfarers in the currents of life!

You who move and are moved,
You who hide and are hidden,
You who cleanse and release,
May you never cease in your constant Motion,
As you bind memory of experience with Emotion.

For you move feeling from one thing to another,
For you uncover connection of one thing with another –
And these currents and streams of connection beget seas and oceans
Which constitute the travels and travails of life.

For you understand above all that an experience and its feeling
Are only understood in its relation to other feelings and experiences,
And upon these connections you move and bring understanding
Through shared exchanges.

You wash away pains and sufferings
And purge the spirit of dross
Revealing a state of innocence and purity.

You give a sense of continuity and connection
By empathy and understanding
Which generates all help and hope.

And through all of this you create an ocean of love and compassion
Which grants unto those who swim there a trust and a bond
Which allows things to work together
And to become something greater than what it was before,
Alone.

Hearken to our work, of flowing and innocent undines,
And help bind us together in Love, Under Will,
So that we together can achieve more than we merely could,
Alone.

The Invocations of the Elements

Invocation of the Element of Air

Swift are the winds that rush to fill the void!

Air, that invisible movement which accompanies all life,
And gives light to the eyes.

Air, never at rest, you grant intelligence and reason
And thought and conclusion.

Like quicksilver or like mist, you always travel from here to there,
From this thing to that thing,
And this journey creates the road called meaning,
So that that one day it may be paved with understanding.

Grant unto this Temple your genius, O Air,
So that we may have a light and a compass to guide us
In the working at hand, and see it to its end.

Invocation of the Sylphs

O light and joyous heralds of truth!

You who come as a whisper comes.

You who dance lightly and softly and flow.

Come from your Temple of Air.
Come from that place of joyous celebration
Where only the light things are,
For there is no darkness therein.

You who appreciate decorum and ritual and courtliness.
You who delight in the dalliance of rhetoric and the swordplay of whit.

Grant unto us your good counsel and unblemished optimism.

For you above all understand that information means nothing on its own –
Its meaning is born from how it is said, and how it is heard.

For in the Temple of Winds all answers may be found,
But it is only when you ask the right question
That you will be given the understanding that you seek.

Hearken to our work, O swift and faery Sylphs,
And give us the right questions to ask,
So that we may speak truth to the winds with reverence.

The Invocations of the Elements

Invocation of the Element of Fire

Fierce is the consuming Fire which drives all Will.

Fire, that which ignites passion and lust
And desire and inspiration in all things with Spirit.

Fire, never at rest, always consuming, always transforming –
Its own heat is the veritable movement of life.

Fire, your flickering dance illuminates the night sky,
While your measured warmth gives sustenance to all at every sunrise.

Grant unto this Temple your Creative Will, O Fire,
So that the self may be transcended,
And grant unto us Courage so that we may undertake the work at hand
And see it to its end.

Mystery Babalon

Invocation of the Fire Sprites

O fickle conspirators of the Will!

You who stoke the very Fires of Life,
Dancing passionately in the flicker of your heated movements,
May your ceaseless lust for ever more and more
Drive hearts and wills to always expand, to always experience,
To always transcend and grow.

You make no difference between this and that
As you seek out new things to consume in your burning desire,
Yet in the wake of your ashes you leave new areas
Ripe for regeneration and growth.

Your entrancing dances warm the hearts of the living,
Your bright fires alight in the eyes of the strong,
And your lust and desire ensures union and regeneration
Which brings living pleasure and satisfaction of accomplishment.

For you above all understand that for a thing to change,
For a thing to become something new,
It must in some way become consumed or destroyed –
And the Will to do this is called Courage.

Drive the Seven Transformations of the Will through the Celestial Spheres!
Cast energy and light into the sullen darkness of inertia and despair!
Burn even like Our Lord Hadit and be everywhere the center!

Hearken to our work, O Willful and Lusty Fire Sprites,
And lend to our Wills the Courage to enact the change
For which we have incarnated.

XXVII

The Invocations of the Zodiac

Invocation of Aries

You who burns with Cardinal Fire,
Warrior, Martial, Ram-Headed fire-brand,
You rush forward, eager for battle,
Fierce and loyal to the fight
Forever burning.

Come with your sword held high!
Come with your shields all clashing!
Come with your eyes fierce with war,

The Invocations of the Zodiac

And win the destiny of Spirit.

I invoke thee, Mighty Aries!
Lend to me your essence, so that I might move swiftly to action,
Let the blood pound within my veins,
Your strength and ferocity surging behind my motivation,
Carrying me forward.

To help break inertia, aid in building energy to overcome obstacles; and to assist with matters of struggle or strife.

Invocation of Taurus

You who rules the pastures of the stars,
Strong, virile, fierce and stalwart Bull!
Your nature is fixed in the steadfastness of Earth,
Venusian in your enlivened passions,
O powerful solidity!

Come with your raging strength!
Come with your horns of the Moon!
Come with your beauty and splendor
Of Spirit manifested in flesh.

I invoke thee, steadfast Taurus!
Lend to me your essence, so that I might remain steadfast upon my course.
Let my sights be set firmly upon my goals,
With your strength and stability aiding me,
Making me a force unstoppable!

To help give steady foundation to the work at hand and overall stability and grounding; to assist with matters requiring unyielding perseverance.

The Invocations of the Zodiac

Invocation of Gemini

> *You who facilitates the connection of the stars!*
> *Swift and mutable Air - dancing and darting,*
> *Divided in twain, yet always seeking the other,*
> *O twin of darkness and light, the opposition within the nature of itself,*
> *Not of balance, but of duality.*
>
> *Come with your bright eyes talking!*
> *Come with your swift desire dancing!*
> *Come with your clear words ringing*
> *With the truth of Spirit made plain.*
>
> *I invoke thee, O swift Gemini!*
> *Lend to me your essence, so that I might connect with the information that*
>   *I seek!*
> *Let my mind find that which it needs to understand,*
> *For your ability to translate from place to place will aid me*
> *In finding the knowledge that I seek.*

To help create connections to ideas, knowledge, communication and information. Useful to invoke to aid in seeking connection to other Spirits for a working.

MYSTERY BABALON

Invocation of Cancer

> *You who shifts daily, as does the Moon and the tides,*
> *Clawed creature of the deep sea,*
> *Always watchful, calculating,*
> *Bearer of potentiality,*
> *And harbinger of birth and death.*
>
> *Come with your nobility enshrined!*
> *Come as guardian of innocence!*
> *Come as a knight on horseback,*
> *Defending the truth of Spirit.*
>
> *I invoke thee, O deep-moving Cancer*
> *Lend to me your essence, so that I might delight in the shifting cycles of the Moon!*
> *Let me understand the subtle ways of the growing and fading shadows,*
> *The wax and wane of energy and time,*
> *Which gives insight into things hidden and subtle.*

To help give understanding to shifts in ones cycles, emotions, and the currents of the world; to assist with workings involving specific lunar phases.

The Invocations of the Zodiac

Invocation of Leo

> *You who shines brightly as the Sun!*
> *Ambassador, bold and fixed Fire of will!*
> *It is courage and confidence that burns brightly therein,*
> *Ever radiant, ever glowing*
> *For all and any to see.*
>
> *Come magnificent beast of light!*
> *Come O lion of royalty and pride!*
> *Come great protector and guardian,*
> *Of the joy of the expression of Spirit.*
>
> *I invoke thee, O magnificent Leo*
> *Lend to me your essence, so that I might burn with the intensity of the brightest Fire!*
> *Let me increase my connection to my Will and divine Purpose,*
> *For your intensity burns away all shadows*
> *Granting me a strong connection to my Spirit.*

To help give courage and strong connection to one's own Fire and Will; to assist when needing confidence in attacking a difficult working, task, or situation.

Invocation of Virgo

O Virgin, untouched flame of Spirit!
Purity is your valor, for you exemplify that which is not corrupt.
On the wings of Mercury you see all that is not aright,
Yet with feet upon the Earth, you seek to correct and perfect all,
With innocence, with grace.

Come most innocent and pure one!
Come virgin untainted by corruption!
Come with your sword held high,
Which cuts with the truth of Spirit.

I invoke thee, O prudent Virgo
Lend to me your essence, so that I might find purity and justice in all
    things!
Let me seek within myself the core of truth and honesty,
For your valor is that of the burning flame of Spirit,
Which lights the way by casting off all but truth.

To aid in seeking the truth within oneself and others; to assist in all workings concerning valor and fighting for what is right and good; to assist in reining in tendencies towards debauchery or excess.

The Invocations of the Zodiac

Invocation of Libra

> *Light and fair defender of all that is balance!*
> *It is you who brings the beauty of symmetry to all that manifests,*
> *Radiant with harmony and equality,*
> *Enthroned upon Venusian grace,*
> *A tender painter of sweet and soft verse.*
>
> *Come with your grace and beauty!*
> *Come with your skill and your perfection!*
> *Come with your balance of truth,*
> *Which levels with the harmony of Spirit.*
>
> *I invoke thee, O beautiful Libra*
> *Lend to me your essence, so that I might understand the way to balance my nature!*
> *Let me see when I stray from my chosen path,*
> *As your scales hang golden within my Psyche,*
> *For it is your voice within that is my morality.*

To aid in maintaining balance within the self and one's life; used to assist one's working in keeping energies aligned with one's Will.

Invocation of Scorpio

You who resides in the deepest, and darkest of the Waters!
You who resides within the stillness of the darkest night.
Death warrior, who seeks the remnants of decay to engender new life,
Harbinger of the great change in shadows,
With eyes that see beyond closed veils

Come with your lusty passions and drives!
Come with your intensity of feeling!
Come with the depths of experience from pain,
Which wins the redemption of Spirit.

I invoke thee, O powerful Scorpio
Lend to me your essence, so that I might discover that which is hidden!
Let me unbury all that is lost so it can be reconciled with need.
Show me in visions and dreams that which lays beyond my blindness,
So that I may lay open to my Spirit

To aid in workings of psychic discovery and matters of hidden meaning and understanding; to assist with transitions in life and death.

The Invocations of the Zodiac

Invocation of Sagittarius

You whose flame seeks ever more,
With passionate arrows pointed at all your prey,
With quickness you strike at your fancy,
Like the fires by which the Satyrs dance,
For there are no limits to endless desires.

Come bright eyed sagacious one!
Come Philosopher King of fire!
Come O you who never bends to despair,
For the joy of Spirit will never fail.

I invoke thee, O unstoppable Sagittarius!
Lend to me your energy, so that I might find joy in all of my endeavors!
Your optimism beams, leading me through times when I might falter.
Your strength and tenacity guides me when I am discouraged.
Your arrow, once launched, always finds its mark.

To aid when seeking enthusiasm, motivation and direction; to assist with launching new endeavors, or in initiating change.

Invocation of Capricorn

*You who finds footholds in unlikely places,
Deftly navigating pathways which have defeated all others,
You bring stability in times of flight, and calm all that which seeks to rattle
     the senses!
Goat headed Saturnian, your precision is a guide to follow,
Always adapting, always seeking, undefeated.*

*Come great climber of the heights!
Come sure-footed and stubborn one!
Come O defender of traditions old,
Which forever bring Spirit to life.*

*I invoke thee, O resilient Capricorn!
Lend to me sure footing so that I might remain grounded and aright,
Unmoved by that which swirls around me seeking chaos.
Hold me fast to my own vision and pathway,
My determination undaunted by any force*

To aid in stability and grounding and the clearing of negativity; to assist with the setting of boundaries within a sacred space.

THE INVOCATIONS OF THE ZODIAC

Invocation of Aquarius

> *You who stands unmoved by the rushing waters!*
> *You observe but remain untouched as you bear the water within your vessel.*
> *Seeker of the highest and most sublime,*
> *You are fixed upon the vision of the Air before you,*
> *With ideals blazing like stars in the night sky.*
>
> *Come lofty seeker of the highest!*
> *Come undaunted lover of ideals!*
> *Come O great and steadfast one,*
> *So that Spirit may be carried to all.*
>
> *I invoke thee, O lofty Aquarius!*
> *Lend to me your ideals so that I might climb to new heights!*
> *Show me my greatest potential in all that I seek,*
> *Let me be unmoved by all who seek to stop me in my Will,*
> *And grant me clarity in all of my ambitions*

To aid in remaining unmoved by all that seeks to change or thwart you; to assist with distancing from the Waters when they overwhelm one's senses.

MYSTERY BABALON

Invocation of Pisces

> *You who swims and darts with deft swiftness,*
> *Always seeking the front of the most tremendous shoals.*
> *Innate wanderer of hidden connections,*
> *Optimist of your own making,*
> *Never caught behind, you stride forever forward.*
>
> *Come O slippery and unstoppable one!*
> *Come you who are swift beyond swift!*
> *Come seer of things before others,*
> *And steer the people to Spirit!*
>
> *I invoke thee, O shrewd Pisces!*
> *Lend to me your vision, so that I might find the finest cracks by which to pass through,*
> *All of the secret ways between tight and unknown places.*
> *Lend me your essence, so that I might be victorious,*
> *And grant to me that which I need to rise above all else.*

To aid in making connections to spirits and energies that one needs to find to overcome one's station or current status; to assist in bringing together what is needed for one's working (be it elements for the working, or energies sought out).

Part IV

The Bhaktic Rites of Babalon

XXVIII

THE DEVOTIONAL PATH

hakti is a Sanskrit word which means devotional love. Yoga is a Sanskrit word which means union. Therefore, for one to practice Bhaktic Yoga upon Babalon means that one uses the ritualized practices of devotional love in order to achieve union with Babalon. These ritualized practices of devotional love are Her Bhaktic Rites, and one who performs these practices becomes Her devotee - which is to say a devoted follower of Babalon.

Part of the reason for the creation of this book is due to the fact that scores of people have come to Templum Babalonis to request direction about how they can worship Babalon. What should they do? Are there rituals to worship Her? What should they say? How can they have union with Babalon? There are so many questions, and so little understanding in this age of what to do.

Let us first begin with a simple truth concerning the spiritual act of union: a true seeker must first realize that one must give in order to receive.

But what is it which you should give? You must give of yourself. This gift of self must be genuine, pure, and with the intention of

THE DEVOTIONAL PATH

engendering a connection between one's higher-self, or Spirit, and the Divinity which you seek. However, this is no easy task. True devotion of this sort requires cultivation, like a fine wine, or the best foods. There is an art to devotion. There is a delicacy, and a sincerity that must be expressed which transcends day-to-day normalcy. This spiritual devotion is an expression of all that we are towards all that we wish to be. It is a pledge of sincerity. And it is also the path of "Love under Will". This is so, because we must use and integrate our Will and purpose of our incarnation in order for our devotion to be true and sincere.

Do what thou wilt shall be the whole of the law

-Liber Legis I 40

Love is the Law, Love Under Will

-Liber Legis I 57

Why is Love the Law? Because Love is the seeking of Union. Love is the joining of Spirit and the Will, the uniting of self and purpose. Love is the desire for that which you lack, and therefore that which you seek. Love is that which you are drawn to for the purpose of finding your true Will. Is it any wonder then that part of our path as seekers is to devote ourselves to that which is divine? For this union will help lead us home — to that which our Spirit seeks in this incarnation as a part of its Will.

And so you are here, reading this because a part of you yearns for some sort of union with Babalon. There is something within your being, your Spirit which seeks Her. Therefore, by devoting yourself in service, or in Love, or in affinity to Babalon, who is the goddess of Spiritual Liberation, this devotion can help unite you to that which you lack in regards to the realization of your Will. These Rites are a way to spiritually express your love and devotion to Babalon, in order to create a very personal connection between yourself and Her, as devotee and a Goddess. And by ritually giving of yourself out of devotion, without the expectation of anything in return, you will begin to change yourself, your Persona, into a being who is more and more full of Love. Because Love is not something that you receive, but something that you give. And this will change your life, and open a doorway for you to Babalon which did not exist before.

What then is the purpose of devotion? How is devotion different than worship? The difference is subtle and negligible, but for our purposes let us say that devotion connotes a direct intent in regards to one's Will. One Wills to be devotional. One chooses to be devotional. Devotion is borne from the desire of one's own Spirit's to unite with a divinity. Devotion opens doors to Spirit, aligns the Persona, creates alliances of energy, and relationships. One can not break down the doors to Spirit by force and demand of Will.

In modern times we have come to think of "worship" of something demanded of us or by us by a tyrannical god. Such a demand is not Thelemic, for we do everything in our lives according to our own Wills, and not that of others. As Thelemites, we give freely and without coercion. We give Love Under Will, not because we are afraid of being punished, or because we are commanded to do so. We are a New Aeon People. And we are devoted, but not blind. The Book of Law speaks freely of worship in a positive light. And we can be worshipful people. But we use the terms Bhakti or devotion for clarity's sake, so as not to confuse our intent in these Rites with those of the tyrannical past.

Devotion is a gift you give, not a demand to be fulfilled. When we devote ourselves to a deity it is with an attitude of gratitude for the opportunity to be in their presence. We long for a chance one day to experience a tangible connection with the energy or presence of that deity, to have them manifest themselves to us. There should be a realization in the devotee that if we give in the right way, with the right sincerity and the purity of our Spirit's Love, that this will enable some sort of reciprocity from that which we are devoted to. We make ourselves worthy of Her attention, by demonstrating our Love to Her. But let it be made clear that to be devotional does not also mean we are slaves. We stand shining with the Light of our own Star—in autonomous purity of our own Spirit. We were not born ugly and shameful in sin, but beautiful and pure in the fullness of the Light of Spirit and of Purpose. We do not cower in fear as we journey upon our paths seeking our kingship, for that is what we will become when we do our Wills. And so we do not cower before the gods, yet we also recognize that we, within their hierarchies, are here to serve. We are here to ally ourselves according to our True Wills. And so if Babalon speaks to you, then here you can answer that calling with your devotion.

The Devotional Path

The Bhaktic Path is one which may require patience and endurance. There is no such thing as instant gratification when it comes to the practice of any sort of magick—and by magick here we mean the union of energies. Sometimes water moves slowly, penetrating down into the Earth. It is our job to open the way for that water to flow more freely, and more easily. It is our job to facilitate its passing. And so we begin by ritualizing our days to include the giving of ourselves in devotion to Babalon, so that this connection can become stronger and more vibrant as time goes along.

Within the Rites that follow are two paths, both of which are Devotional. One is the Bhaktic Path which is more ritualized, sublime and sometimes formal. The other is the Ecstatic path which is more energetic, sexual, and sometimes spontaneous. Both may be explored endlessly, and combined in any way which appeals to the devotee. Some will prefer a safer and steadier path, with the more controlled approach of the Bhaktic Path. Others will desire the explosive energies and intensities which will sometimes accompany the Ecstatic Path. Your genius and your desires shall guide you according to your own Will.

The Rites which follow are meant to be practiced on a regular basis in order to deepen the bond and relationship between yourself and Babalon. Doing something once is an experiment or a curiosity. Being devoted requires ritualization, repetition and dedication. And this dedication over time brings many benefits. As the Rites are practiced over time, new experiences of a deepening quality and nature will come to the devotee. But this takes time, patience and dedication. So go forward with these Rites with the proper attitude, and take the time to perform them in your own way, at your own pace. Every step for you from here on out is the step of a devotee of Babalon. So savor each and every moment on your path with Her.

XXIX

Daily Devotions

he first of the daily devotions is simple enough, but very effective over the long term for setting the proper attitude in your Persona to the work of the Shrine on a daily basis. Its continued use will shape you into a devotee. This Rite must be performed first thing in the morning, before any other major activities. The goal is to practice your devotion to Babalon before anything else upon wakening, and thereby set the tone for the rest of the day. By doing this, you are making sure that your devotion takes precedence over all other things, even eating.

The Morning Rites

Every morning upon awakening, take a few moments to become fully awake and prepare yourself and your body for the Rites. This may include using the restroom, splashing water on your face, or similar simple things which are not too distracting. It is important that this Dedication is the first act of any importance for your day, and the only thing which occupies your attention until it is completed. It should be seen as a spiritual obligation, and as such there should be a feeling that your day will not go quite right if this is not accomplished. Something will have been left unfinished between

Daily Devotions

yourself and Babalon if you do not perform these Rites. When performing these Rites, feel the intensity and purpose of your own incarnation at the saying of these words to Babalon. Let this daily Rite set the tone for the entire day, as you go to do your work amongst the living. Feel proud that you are a devotee of Babalon, and that you are working towards a special relationship with Her.

When ready, proceed to the Babalon altar in your Shrine. Light a simple white tea-light candle with calm determination while saying the following Morning Adoration to your Goddess Babalon:

> *I, (your name of dedication), awaken this Shrine to you, O Great Babalon. For as the sun rises and fills the world with light, so too do I arise and call you to fill this Shrine with your presence. I have made this Shrine a sacred place for you to dwell. Come, Great Liberating Mother! Come, Babalon, come! I am your devoted servant, and I have made open the way. In Nomine Babalon et Vox Sanctae Meretricis.*

Place the tea-light candle in the center of your altar, in the triangle of the three unlit candles there. If you are using the Sigillum Divinorum or the Sigil of Devotion, you may place the tea-light on top of that. Spend a moment in quiet acknowledgement of Babalon at Her altar before continuing on with your day. Let the tea-light candle burn for as long as it will until it goes out on its own (usually an hour or two), as you go about your daily work and life. Know that it is burning with your dedication. Of course, make sure that you are burning your candle on a fire-proof plate or surface where it can not be knocked over by people or pets.

The Evening Rites

After you have been successful with the Morning Rites for some time, you may also add the Evening Rites to the schedule of your Shrine Activities. The Evening Rites should be performed after all major activity is done for the day, and only quiet contemplation or other activities will take place before bedtime. The Evening Rites are an acknowledgment of another day lived in dedication to Babalon, and the purpose which that brings to one's life. Do as before, with a tea-light candle, but this time it can be black, or a deep midnight blue if you have them - otherwise white is fine to use again.

These Rites acknowledge the change from daytime to night in the Shrine and its accompanying change in energy, which completes the cycle which began with the Morning Rites.

When ready, proceed to the Babalon altar in your Shrine. Light your tea-light candle with calm determination while saying the following Evening Adoration to your Goddess Babalon:

> *I, (your name of dedication), come to you in the night, O Great Babalon. The Sun has descended into the Underworld, and the land is again covered in darkness. In the silence of night, in the darkness of death, I make this Shrine a sacred place for you to dwell. Come, Great Liberating Mother! Come, Babalon, come! I am your devoted servant, and I have made open the way through the night. In Nomine Babalon et Vox Sanctae Meretricis.*

Place the tea-light candle in the center of your altar, in the triangle of the three unlit candles there. Spend a moment in quiet acknowledgement of Babalon at Her altar before continuing on with your night and sleep. Let the tea-light candle burn for as long as it will until it goes out on its own, knowing that it is burning with your dedication while you sleep.

The Planetary Rites

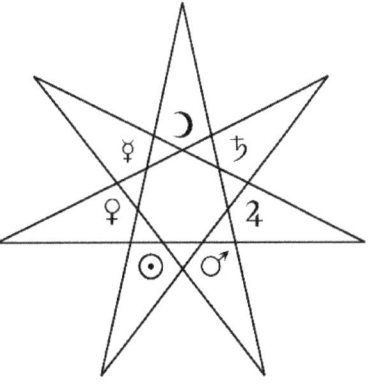

Once the Morning and Evening Rites have been thoroughly established, it is time to acknowledge the changing of the days in your Shrine. Since the most ancient times, the seven days of the week in actuality are seen as the seven planets of the Celestial Spheres. Monday is the Day of the Moon, Tuesday is the Day of Mars, Wednesday is the Day of Mercury, Thursday is Thor's day, the Day of Jupiter, Friday or Freya's day, the Day of Venus, and finally Saturday is the day of Saturn. The diagram of the Seven Planets forms the Star of Venus, and if one looks closely at this star, one will find the Star of Babalon in its center.

Now this diagram shows the planets in their "Chaldean" order, which is the order of their motion in the sky from the slowest to the fastest. The slowest is Saturn (♄), then Jupiter (♃), Mars (♂), the Sun (☉), Venus (♀),

DAILY DEVOTIONS

Mercury (☿) and finally the Moon (☽) is the fastest moving body in the heavens, from the point of view of the Earth as we watch them move across the sky. One can see the planets in this order, staring with Saturn (♄), and traveling then counter-clockwise around the star in order, ending at the Moon (☽). Thus the Star of Venus is arranged to show the Chaldean order of the planets.

But this diagram also shows us the order of the days of the week. If one starts at Saturn (♄) or Saturday, and follows the lines of the star counter-clockwise as it traces its pattern, then one can see that the line runs from Saturn (♄) or Saturday to the Sun (☉) or Sunday. From there the line runs to the Moon (☽) or Monday, and so on around the star, giving us the order of the days of the week.

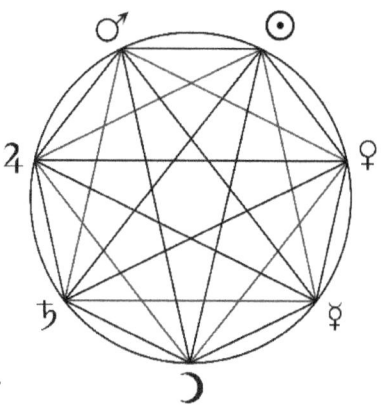

The previous diagram forms the basis for the one which will be used in the Planetary Rites upon your altar, which is called the Sigillum Divinorum. This seal is very sacred to Babalon and Her Allies, and is a gateway to many realms. In order to perform these Rites, one will need to fashion the Sigillum Divinorum in some material. One may choose to paint it upon a thin board, or carve it in wood, clay or in beeswax[41]. Of course as always, the more effort and the higher quality the materials, all the better. It is usually made between nine and twelve inches in diameter, but can be any size according to your own reasoning and genius. The choice is yours. You may also wish to color the points of the star according to the planetary colors, which are silver for the Moon, orange for mercury, green for Venus, gold for the Sun, purple (sometimes blue) for Jupiter, and black (sometimes very dark blue or purple) for Saturn. These colors are related to the metals for each of the planets, and their colors, some of which are those in which they turn with oxidation. For example, the copper of Venus turns green with oxidation. Therefore the Moon goes with silver, Mercury with the metal of the same name, also called quicksilver, Venus with copper, the Sun with gold, Mars

---

[41] The Sigillum Divinorum is also excellent to paint upon the floor of your Shrine, as large as you can if you have the room. The angle of the Moon should be in the North, while the Horns of Mars and the Sun should be in the South. This Holy Symbol contains the Circle, the Septagram, the Star of Babalon, the Star of Venus and a smaller Star of Babalon reversed. By its use is every planet connected to every other planet, in every possible way.

with iron, Jupiter with tin and Saturn with lead. In this diagram it should be noted that there are pathways connecting every planet, with every other planet, and that these connections make two different Stars of Babalon (one upright, one reversed) as well as the Star of Venus, a septagon and a septagram.

    The Sigillum Divinorum is to be placed upon the altar of Babalon in the center of the triangle made by the three candles there. If you have made the Sigil of Devotion as described in Liber 49, you may place that on top of the Sigillum Divinorum at its center. If you have a Chalice, that may be set aside for these Rites. The Planetary Rites should be performed at Noon on each day. If this is not possible due to circumstances such as work, then in the morning is next best, with the evening while the Sun still shines being the final option.

When you are ready to perform the Planetary Rites, enter your Shrine and approach the altar of Babalon. Light the two candles at the back of the altar saying "In Nomine Babalon" as you do so (just say it once), and then light the front candle of the triangle while saying "et Vox Sanctae Meretricis". If you have the Sigil of Devotion, place it upon the Sigillum Divinorum at the appropriate planet for that day, just inside the outer circle. Breathe deeply and prepare yourself for the invocations. Then call aloud with the Planetary Invocation appropriate to the day at hand (see Chapters 24 & 25 for the Invocations of the Planets and Archangels). For the advanced version, also recite the Invocation of the Archangel for that day as well. When this has been accomplished, touch the appropriate part of the Sigillum Divinorum and say the following Celestial Adoration aloud to Babalon:

> *O Great Babalon, it is I, (name of dedication). I stand before You, in this Your Shrine, on the Day of (the appropriate planet, Venus, mars etc) and call to You. Your Star is the movement of the Heavens, and the Pathway between all of the Realms. Your Star is the gateway from there to here, and the means by which Spirit becomes manifest. Your Star is that which blazes upon Your banners in the victory! Come, Great Liberating Mother! Come, Babalon, come! I am Your devoted servant, and I have made open the way through the Seven Planets of the Celestial Spheres. In Nomine Babalon et Vox Sanctae Meretricis.*

Daily Devotions

Spend a moment in quiet acknowledgement of Babalon at Her altar before continuing on with your day. Write down any thoughts, images or ideas which come to you at this time. When finished, extinguish the candles upon Her altar while saying "In Nomine Babalon et Vox Sanctae Meretricis".

The Solar Rites

The Solar Rites are used to mark the shift in the Sun from one Sign to another. These Rites should be performed at noon again right before the Planetary Rites, on the day of the start of the new Zodiac Sign. As an option, a large circular band with the images of the zodiac signs may be constructed to set outside of the Sigillum Divinorum which one can turn so that the current Sign of the Zodiac aligns with the candle at the front of the altar of Babalon. To perform the Rites, simply call aloud the Zodiacal Invocations (see Chapter 27 for the Invocations of the Zodiac) before performing the Planetary Rites as usual.

The Lunar Rites

The Lunar Rites are used to mark the shift in the Moon from one quarter to the next. These Rites should also be preformed before the Planetary Rites, and in conjunction with them. As an option, a large circular band with the images of the phases of the Moon may be constructed to set outside of the Sigillum Divinorum like before with the band of the Zodiac, which one can turn so that the current phase of the Moon aligns with the candle at the front of the altar of Babalon. To perform the Rites, simply call aloud the Lunar Invocations (see Chapter XXV for the Invocations of the Phases of the Moon) before performing the Planetary Rites as usual.

These daily Rites comprise the basic Rites of the Shrine and provide the simplest way of interacting with Babalon therein. These Rites build the energy of the Shrine every day and your connection to Babalon over time. They align the devotee to the seasons and the times, and the current of Babalon within them, and prepare the devotee for the greater Rites which follow.

Mystery Babalon

An example of the altar of Babalon with the Sigillum Divinorum, Moon Phases band and Zodiacal band placed within the triangle of the three main candles (marked by "C").

XXX

Dreamtime Devotions

he place in which our Spirit has the easiest time communicating with us is while we sleep. And while not all dreams are communications from our Spirit, some indeed are. In addition, other Spirits can also attempt to communicate with us during sleep through dreams. Therefore there are rituals we can do before we go to sleep to attempt such connections.

There are several reasons one might wish to increase the communication through dreams. One might be trying to work through personal problems or issues, or one might wish to better attune oneself to certain energies. One might wish to know something from the future, or have hidden things revealed to them (for example, treachery from other people). Or one may simply wish to gain more information about a spirit, or any other subject. By asking one's Spirit to inform them about such things during dreams, one can begin to get a better handle on issues that affect one's life.

The following exercise is a simple one which will help you get answers to questions which you seek. It rarely fails, but you must be patient, and not expect the answers to come quickly. It may take many nights, and repeated attempts, for success to take place. Often the results are subtle, and it may take practice and experience to begin to understand your own personal dream experiences. But there is no doubt that your questions will be answered once you ask your Spirit for guidance, one way or another, either in dreams or in life.

Preparation

Before you go to bed, light a candle upon a bedside altar or table. Use silver or gray if possible for the color of the Moon. You may also light some incense to help prepare you for your Dream-work. Excellent incense for this purpose would be Myrrh, Poppy Flowers, Lotus Oil, Opoponax, Chamomile, Coriander Seed, and Lotus Seed for example (any combination of these to your taste). It is best to also do the Grounding Ritual (see Chapter 18, *Grounding*) prior to going to sleep.

Dreamtime Invocation

To open for any communication from the spirit realms, on any matter which they desire to speak, simply recite the following before sleeping.

> *In Nomine Babalon,*
> *I invoke those Guardians who serve you, Babalon, to keep my dreams free from all negative influence and deceit.*
>
> *I seek my Spirit in all things.*
> *I seek peace and well being so that I might awaken rested and full of the energy of my Purpose.*
> *I seek to serve thee with my being.*
>
> *Grant unto me the serenity of knowing that I serve my Will in all that I do. And please assist me in realizing that which keeps me from it.*
>
> *I open to any and all who seek to help me in that end, so that I may receive their messages in sleep and dreams.*
>
> *In Nomine Babalon et Vox Sanctae Meretricis.*

Having completed the first part, you then state your personal question simply and directly aloud. It is very important that you do this without any care for the outcome of the answers you seek, otherwise your own desires may influence your answers, and lead you astray. Ask about that which you seek, in your own words. For example:

> *Should I move to xxx, or should I stay here? What is the best choice in this regard for my Will and Purpose of this life?*

Be very careful how your word your questions, in order to get the exact answers you seek. If you are simply seeking any communications, and nothing specific, you might say:

> *Let me receive those messages which I need to hear, in order to know and accomplish my Will.*

Having asked your own specific question, now put all of these things out of your mind, extinguish the candle and go to sleep. You should have a pen and paper next to where you sleep so that you can record any dreams that you may have when you awaken.

XXXI

The Rite of Devotion

he Rite of Devotion to Babalon is a solo Bhaktic Rite in which one calls out to Babalon in complete devotion, aligning the purpose of one's incarnation to Hers. It can be used occasionally when one feels the need to connect strongly with Babalon, before important events, or on hermitages when one is devoting oneself in a special way to Her. But it can also be performed as often as one likes, and becomes more effective with practice. The more one practices devotion unto Her, the more one will gain access to Her through a symmetry of alignment in Spirit.

Items needed:

- Babalon altar prepared in the usual manner, with the three candles.
- Sigillum Divinorum and Sigil of Devotion upon altar, if you have them
- The Chalice of Babalon
- Rain Water
- Wine
- Abramelin Oil
- Thelemic Abramelin Incense

THE RITE OF DEVOTION

- Cakes of Life (optional)

The altar to Babalon should be laid out in the usual manner, with the two blue candles in the back, and the blue or gold candle in the front, making a triangle. In the middle of the triangle should be the Sigillum Divinorum and on top of that the Sigil of Devotion, if you have them. Setting on top of that should be your Chalice of Babalon. Next to the Chalice on a special small plate only used for this purpose should be your Cake of Life, if you have any.[42] Nearby on the altar, but not within the triangle, should be your incense burner, Abramelin Incense and Oil, purified rain water or purified pond water, and a small bit of red wine of your own choosing. If you have a decanter for your rain water, you may leave it on the altar during all of your Rites so that it may grow with the power of Babalon over time.

Preparations

To begin with, prepare yourself with a Ritual Bath and other preparations as you have been taught (see Chapter 16, *Preparing for the Rites*). When you have adorned yourself appropriately, enter your Shrine and proceed to the altar of Babalon.

Light the two candles in the back saying, "In Nomine Babalon," and then light the candle in the front saying "et Vox Sanctae Meretricis".

Banishing

Now sit before Her altar and perform the Grounding ritual as you have been taught (see Chapter 18, *Grounding*).

Take the Abramelin Oil and carefully anoint your Ajna Chakra (Third Eye) while saying, "In Nomine Babalon." Light your charcoal, and when it is hot enough add some Thelemic Abramelin to it.

Banish using your preferred Banishing Ritual (see Chapter 20 *Banishing*).

---

[42] See Chapter 34, *The Devotional Rites of Ra Hoor Khuit* for more information of the Cakes of Life and the Cakes of Light, and their preparation.

Mystery Babalon

Purification of the Shrine

Return to the Altar of Babalon and pour some rain water into the Chalice of Babalon while saying over it as you do so, "In Nomine Babalon." Then raise the Chalice high in the air with both hands while saying the Watery Invocation of Babalon:

[Adoration:]

O Babalon, the seas are your home, as well as the deep,
And in this darkness you stir
As in a mirror quiet, the desires of this world.

O Babalon, whether in waters placid or storms of seas,
You orchestrate the chaos,
And in the pools of all things, give calm.

Arise, Babalon in the wake!
Crash upon the shores,
And there break the rocks of resistance and fear,
Into pebbles beneath your feet.

[Prayer:]

I call to thee, Great Liberating Mother
To show me the Fortitude in the Waters,
The power of my depths.

I call to thee, Great Liberating Mother,
To show me the Sovereignty of Dominion,
The calm of my truth.

I call to thee Great Liberating Mother,
To break down those dense stones
Which gather upon my shores!
Shatter fear and jealousy and shame,
Attachments which keep me
From my great and shining Will.

In Nomine Babalon et Vox Sanctae Meretricis

The Rite of Devotion

Now travel counter-clockwise around your Shrine, sprinkling and lustrating the floor in each of the four quarters as you go, saying at each quarter:

May the Waters of Babalon purify this Shrine in Her name!

Consecration of the Shrine

Return to the Altar of Babalon and put some Thelemic Abamelin incense onto the charcoal in your incense burner while saying over it as you do so, "In Nomine Babalon." Then raise the Incense Burner high in the air with both hands while saying the Fiery Invocation of Babalon:

[Adoration:]

O Babalon, from the fires of the stars You come!
Arise! Daughter of light, arise!
O Babalon, from the fires of the depths You rise!
Arise! Mighty torch-bearer, arise!

O Babalon, the lusts and desires of all,
Are as warriors in Your army,
Ready to serve you in battle.

Command them, Babalon,
O Great Liberating Mother,
Use them as minions in your Victory!

[Prayer:]

I call to thee, Great Liberating Mother
To show me the strength of my lusts,
And the fortitude therein.

I call to thee, Great Liberating Mother,
To show me the way in which to harness my desires,
By love under will.

I call to thee Great Liberating Mother,
To break the inhibition of cowardice,
Which keeps me from the realization

Mystery Babalon

Of my true self.

In Nomine Babalon et Vox Sanctae Meretricis

Now travel clockwise around your Shrine, fumigating and consecrating the air in each of the four quarters as you go, saying at each quarter:

May the Fires of Babalon consecrate this Shrine in Her name!

Exaltation of the Shrine

Return to the altar of Babalon. Take some wine from your decanter and add it to the water in the Chalice of Babalon (not too much, about 1/4 to 1/10 wine per water). Focus one's Will within their Persona intently and summon one's own Spirit to the forefront of consciousness and control of your existence while saying the following over the Cup of Babalon:

> *It is I (name of dedication). I come before thee, Nuit. I stand before all that is your exhalation, which is all life and all existence. I call deep within myself, and reach out to my own divine Star shining in the Heavens — that from which my Spirit was born. I am my Spirit, the Bornless One. I live to indwell my Spirit, the Bornless One. It was already with me when I was born. And now I walk upon Earth as a Spirit, wrapped within the hands of Gaia.*

Now align the incarnation of your Spirit with Babalon, by saying the following:

> *It is I, (name of dedication). I come to you in Spirit. I come to pledge my love and my devotion to you, O Great Babalon. You, who are the Mysteries beyond Death. You who Guard all that is Life. You, who Transform all within Your embrace, refusing none. Your embrace is my rapture. Your love is my soul.*

Purify your body by anointing yourself with the mixture from the Chalice of Babalon, while saying the following:

The Rite of Devotion

Make me worthy of Babalon, O Waters of the Earth. Wash away all that is impure within my being. Cleanse me now. Carry away all that hinders me, all the blocks which bind me, all that seeks to enslave my being, my essence, and my Will.

Consecrate your body by perfuming yourself with the smoke of the incense, while saying the following:

May the spirits of the Air - those who reside in the places of light, those who seek truth in all things - lend me their clarity. I ask them to carry me higher, higher into the places of knowing, so that I might learn and understand that which is Truth, and that which is my Will.

Exalt yourself by cupping your hands fairly close around the flame of central blue/gold candle, while focusing all of your attention upon the flame and saying the following:

May the Spirits of Fire burn from me all that is the dross of my days upon this Earth. Cleanse from me all that I carry which hinders my being, and all that is counter to my purpose. Render me forth as ash, so that I may rise as a Snake of Light, a Spirit purified.

The Grand Devotion of Babalon

Raise the Chalice of Babalon high to the Heavens above the Altar and call out to Babalon with all of your being with the following words:

I come before thee, all that is of the deepest depths of existence.
Guardian of the Seven Great Principles, held within your wheel,
Goddess of Heka, laid before the people within the Mysteries of Blackness
Seen as Golden by your true seekers,
I give myself, and all that I am, to you,
Great Babalon!

I lay before you, all that is within me.
I harness my animal, as you ride the Great Beast
So that I might serve you, with my Spirit,
O Great Goddess of the Gateway of Death, of Life,
And of all that is brought forth from the mysteries beyond knowing.

MYSTERY BABALON

You, who are the Goddess of War and of Vengeance,
Great Daughter of Ra,
Whose Secret Name at last I knoweth,
O, mighty Hoor-Pahkhet, whose reign rose from the sands upon the Nile,
Whose reign was born from the people who lived before even time.

You, mighty Babalon,
Take me for your own!
I exist to serve you, with all of my passion,
My heart, my soul.
My devotion is Yours. My breath is for You.
I ask you to take me, and make me that which you Desire,
For your Desire is Wisdom,
And your Heart beats for All.

In Nomine Babalon et Vox Sanctae Meretricis

Now you may consume your Cake of Life (if you have one) and drink deeply from the Chalice of Babalon. Then retire to a place of comfort, such as cushions in front of your Altar, and bathe in any energy which comes forth. When you feel the time is right, arise and extinguish the candles, saying: In Nomine Babalon. Record any thoughts, feelings, perceptions or words which have come to you, or in dreams later that same night.

XXXII

The Rite of Convocation

he Rite of Convocation to Babalon is an expansion of the Bhaktic Rite of Devotion for use by small groups of two or three people. Here the group calls out to Babalon in complete devotion together, aligning the purpose of their incarnations with Her. It can be used occasionally when one feels the need to connect strongly with Babalon with your friends or before important events. It can also be performed as often as one likes, and like the previous Rite of Devotion, becomes more effective for the group with practice and dedication. The more one practices devotion unto Her, the more one will gain access to Her through a symmetry of alignment in Spirit.

Items needed:

- Babalon altar prepared in the usual manner, with the three candles.
- Sigillum Divinorum and Sigil of Devotion upon altar, if you have them
- The Chalice of Babalon
- Rain Water
- Wine
- Abramelin Oil

The Rite of Convocation

- Thelemic Abramelin Incense
- Cakes of Life (optional)

The altar to Babalon should be laid out in the usual manner, with the two blue candles in the back, and the blue or gold candle in the front, making a triangle. In the middle of the triangle should be the Sigillum Divinorum and on top of that the Sigil of Devotion, if you have them. Setting on top of that should be your Chalice of Babalon. Next to the Chalice on a special small plate only used for this purpose should be your Cake of Life, if you have any.[43] Nearby on the altar, but not within the triangle, should be your incense burner, Abramelin Incense and Oil, purified rain water or purified pond water, and a small bit of red wine of your own choosing. If you have a decanter for your rain water, you may leave it on the altar during all of your Rites so that it may grow with the power of Babalon over time.

Preparations

To begin with, your group should prepare themselves with a Ritual Bath and other preparations as has been taught (see Chapter 16, *Preparing for the Rites*). When you have adorned yourselves appropriately, enter your Shrine and proceed to the altar of Babalon as a group. One person will need to be the leader, also called the Dedicant, to conduct the main parts of the Rite.

The Dedicant lights the two candles in the back saying, "In Nomine Babalon," and then lights the candle in the front saying "et Vox Sanctae Meretricis".

Banishing

Now all sit before Her altar and perform the Grounding ritual as has been taught (see Chapter 18, *Grounding*).

---

[43] See Chapter 34, *The Devotional Rites of Ra Hoor Khuit* for more information of the Cakes of Life and the Cakes of Light, and their preparation.

All then rise. The Dedicant takes the Abramelin Oil and carefully anoints the others in attendance on their Third Eye while saying, "In Nomine Babalon." When this is complete, the Dedicant then does the same to their own Third Eye. The Dedicant then lights the charcoal, and when it is hot enough adds some Thelemic Abramelin Incense to it.

One of the group must then Banish using their preferred Banishing Ritual (see Chapter 20, *Banishing*).

Purification of the Shrine

When complete, the Dedicant (or someone else from the group if desired) then turns to the Altar of Babalon and pours some rain water into the Chalice of Babalon while saying over it, "In Nomine Babalon." Then raise the Chalice high in the air with both hands while saying the Watery Invocation of Babalon:

[Adoration:]

O Babalon, the seas are your home, as well as the deep,
And in this darkness you stir
As in a mirror quiet, the desires of this world.

O Babalon, whether in waters placid or storms of seas,
You orchestrate the chaos,
And in the pools of all things, give calm.

Arise, Babalon in the wake!
Crash upon the shores,
And there break the rocks of resistance and fear,
Into pebbles beneath your feet.

[Prayer:]

I call to thee, Great Liberating Mother
To show me the Fortitude in the Waters,
The power of my depths.

I call to thee, Great Liberating Mother,
To show me the Sovereignty of Dominion,
The calm of my truth.

The Rite of Convocation

I call to thee Great Liberating Mother,
To break down those dense stones
Which gather upon my shores!
Shatter fear and jealousy and shame,
Attachments which keep me
From my great and shining Will.

In Nomine Babalon et Vox Sanctae Meretricis

Now travel counter-clockwise around your Shrine, sprinkling and lustrating the floor in each of the four quarters as you go, saying at each quarter:

May the Waters of Babalon purify this Shrine in Her name!

Consecration of the Shrine

The Dedicant (or someone else from the group if desired) returns to the Altar of Babalon and puts some Thelemic Abramelin incense onto the charcoal in your incense burner while saying over it as you do so, "In Nomine Babalon." Then raise the Incense Burner high in the air with both hands while saying the Fiery Invocation of Babalon:

[Adoration:]

O Babalon, from the fires of the stars You come!
Arise! Daughter of light, arise!
O Babalon, from the fires of the depths You rise!
Arise! Mighty torch-bearer, arise!

O Babalon, the lusts and desires of all,
Are as warriors in Your army,
Ready to serve you in battle.

Command them, Babalon,
O Great Liberating Mother,
Use them as minions in your Victory!

[Prayer:]

*I call to thee, Great Liberating Mother
To show me the strength of my lusts,
And the fortitude therein.*

*I call to thee, Great Liberating Mother,
To show me the way in which to harness my desires,
By love under will.*

*I call to thee Great Liberating Mother,
To break the inhibition of cowardice,
Which keeps me from the realization
Of my true self.*

In Nomine Babalon et Vox Sanctae Meretricis

Now travel clockwise around your Shrine, fumigating and consecrating the air in each of the four quarters as you go, saying at each quarter:

May the Fires of Babalon consecrate this Shrine in Her name!

Exaltation of the Shrine

The Dedicant (or other chosen from the group) returns to the altar of Babalon. They then take some wine from your decanter and add it to the water in the Chalice of Babalon (not too much, about 1/4 to 1/10 wine per water). All focus their Will within their Personas intently and summon their Spirits to the forefront of consciousness. The Dedicant or other chosen member then says the following over the Cup of Babalon:

It is I (all say their names of dedication in succession). We come before thee, Nuit. We stand before all that is your exhalation, which is all life and all existence. We call deep within ourselves, and reach out to our own divine Stars shining in the Heavens — that from which our Spirits were born. I am my Spirit, the Bornless One. (Then each of the others in attendance repeats this same last line "I am my Spirit, the Bornless One".) We live to indwell our Spirits, the Bornless Ones. It was already with us when we were born. And now we walk upon Earth as Spirits, wrapped within the hands of Gaia.

The Rite of Convocation

Now align the incarnation of your Spirits with Babalon, by saying the following:

> *It is I, (all say their names of dedication in succession). We come to you in Spirit. We come to pledge our love and our devotion to you, O Great Babalon. You, who are the Mysteries beyond Death. You who Guard all that is Life. You, who Transform all within Your embrace, refusing none. Your embrace is our rapture. Your love is our soul.*

The Dedicant (or other) then purifies the bodies of all present by anointing them with the mixture from the Chalice of Babalon, while saying the following:

> *May you be worthy of Babalon, by the Waters of the Earth. I wash away all that is impure from your being. I cleanse you now. The Water carries away all that hinders you, all the blocks which bind you, all that seeks to enslave your being, your essence, and your Will.*

And then themselves with:

> *Make me worthy of Babalon, O Waters of the Earth. Wash away all that is impure within my being. Cleanse me now. Carry away all that hinders me, all the blocks which bind me, all that seeks to enslave my being, my essence, and my Will.*

The Dedicant (or other) then consecrates the bodies of all present by perfuming them with the smoke of the incense, while saying the following:

> *May the spirits of the Air - those who reside in the places of light, those who seek truth in all things - lend you their clarity. I ask them to carry you higher, higher into the places of knowing, so that you might learn and understand that which is Truth, and that which is your Will.*

And then themselves with:

> *May the spirits of the Air - those who reside in the places of light, those who seek truth in all things - lend me their clarity. I ask them to carry me*

higher, higher into the places of knowing, so that I might learn and understand that which is Truth, and that which is my Will.

The Dedicant (or other) then exalts all present by cupping their hands fairly close around the flame of central blue/gold candle. All others place their hands upon this person's back. All focus their attention upon the flame while the Dedicant (or other) says the following:

May the Spirits of Fire burn from us all that is the dross of our days upon this Earth. Cleanse from us all that we carry which hinders our being, and all that is counter to our purpose. Render us forth as ash, so that we may rise as Snakes of Light, Spirits purified.

The Grand Devotion of Babalon

The Dedicant then raises the Chalice of Babalon high to the Heavens above the Altar and calls out to Babalon with all of their being with the words which follow. All others go to their knees and raise their arms up and out to the Altar in Adoration.

We come before thee, all that is of the deepest depths of existence.
Guardian of the Seven Great Principles, held within your wheel,
Goddess of Heka, laid before the people within the Mysteries of Blackness
Seen as Golden by your true seekers,
We give ourselves, and all that we are, to you,
Great Babalon!

We lay before you, all that is within us.
We harness our animals, as you ride the Great Beast
So that we might serve you, with our Spirits,
O Great Goddess of the Gateway of Death, of Life,
And of all that is brought forth from the mysteries beyond knowing.

You, who are the Goddess of War and of Vengeance,
Great Daughter of Ra,
Whose Secret Name at last we knoweth,
O, mighty Hoor-Pahkhet, whose reign rose from the sands upon the Nile,
Whose reign was born from the people who lived before even time.

THE RITE OF CONVOCATION

You, mighty Babalon,
Take us for your own!
We exist to serve you, with all of our passion,
Our heart, our soul.
Our devotion is Yours. Our breath is for You.
I ask you to take us, and make of us that which you Desire,
For your Desire is Wisdom,
And your Heart beats for All.

All then say together:

In Nomine Babalon et Vox Sanctae Meretricis

Now the group may consume the Cakes of Life (if you have one) and drink deeply from the Chalice of Babalon. Then all retire to a place of comfort, such as cushions in front of the Altar, and bathe in any energy which comes forth. When you feel the time is right, arise and extinguish the candles, saying: In Nomine Babalon. Record any thoughts, feelings, perceptions or words which have come to you, or in dreams later that same night. Feast together and enjoy life, In Nomine Babalon.

XXXIII

The Bhaktic Rite of Babalon

he Bhaktic Rite of Babalon is the main Rite for the people to worship Babalon together as a group, in a serious and devotional manner. It is a Dramatic Ritual, and involves different people playing different roles in the Rite. Because of this, the cast will need to practice the Rites with scripts many times, and memorize their parts if possible. The Rites are not only dramatic in nature, but interactive. The audience, or congregation, takes part in the Rites in many ways. Ultimately they are the beneficiary of the Rites during the Audience, where it is possible for each individual to have a personal experience with some form of the energy of Babalon manifesting through the Priestess. This is the ultimate goal of these Rites, to bring the common people into a new spiritual experience of their own self in relation to a Goddess, in a manner which makes a lasting and positive impression upon their Persona.

Practice and repeated performance of these Rites by the Priestess and Magus is essential, in order to learn how to cultivate the most intense energy for the congregation, and to begin to understand how to manifest and open the Liminal Gateway. The Rites can be considered to be a success if the congregation begins to see and experience the Pia Mezza[44],

The Bhaktic Rite of Babalon

the middle place between worlds which marks the encroachment of manifest Spirit. And success in this way is most often the case where the Priestess and Magus are completely devoted in their work, giving of all they have in the Rites to enable Her manifestation for the people.

It is best to perform this Rite during the Waxing or Full Moons, and Rites of contemplation or Devotion during the other times. Experienced Priestesses will easily notice the difference in type and power of energy during these Rites during different phases of the Moon, and will discover what works best for her own abilities and natures.

The Cast

Required participants:

> The Priestess
> The Magus

Preferred additions:

> Baphometis

Optional participants:

> Various Elementals
> Ra Hoor Khuit
> Congregation

The Costumes

The Priestess: The Priestess should dress as she will, according to her own genius and taste, taking in to consideration her local customs. One may wear horns, or an ornate headdress. One may apply tribal makeup, Egyptian makeup, or other types of your own design. The same recommendations apply for robes and jewelry. The Priestess is girt with a

---

[44] Pia Mezza, literally *the middle place*, between worlds. See the glossary for more information.

large sword. When adorning oneself, one may wish to take inspirations from the verses from Liber Legis I, 61-64:

> *61. ... I charge you earnestly to come before me in a single robe, and covered with a rich headdress. I love you! I yearn to you! Pale or purple, veiled or voluptuous, I who am all pleasure and purple, and drunkenness of the innermost sense, desire you. Put on the wings, and arouse the coiled splendour within you: come unto me!*
>
> *62. At all my meetings with you shall the priestess say -- and her eyes shall burn with desire as she stands bare and rejoicing in my secret temple -- To me! To me! calling forth the flame of the hearts of all in her love-chant.*
>
> *63. Sing the rapturous love-song unto me! Burn to me perfumes! Wear to me jewels! Drink to me, for I love you! I love you!*
>
> *64. I am the blue-lidded daughter of Sunset; I am the naked brilliance of the voluptuous night-sky.*

The Magus: The Magus should have a robe with a hood, all of which is of white with gold trim, gold lining and gold symbols. There may be a gold Star of Babalon, large, on the back area. The Magus carries the Winged Sun Serpent Staff, of which there are many variations.

The Elementals: These creatures should be dressed according to which type of Elemental they choose to play. Fire Sprites should be dressed in red and with clothing which gives the impression of heat and flame. Undines should be in blues, with a watery appearance. Sylphs should be in yellow and white, with a windy and light appearance. Gnomes should be in earth-tones and dark colors, with a rigorous and tough appearance. Some Elementals may also have drums for the Invocation of Babalon.

Ra Hoor Khuit: Ra Hoor Khuit should be dressed as in his Egyptian image, with a hawk mask if possible. At the very least the actor should wear some broach or lamen with his image. He bears a sword and has a warrior's physic.

The Bhaktic Rite of Babalon

Baphometis: Baphometis should be adorned with horns, and breasts exposed, if possible. A full goat mask is preferred. Apparel should be black. S/he bears the Caduceus staff and a ram horn (or other animal horn) which can be blown. If this is not obtainable, then a small musical horn of some sort which can be blown can be substituted.

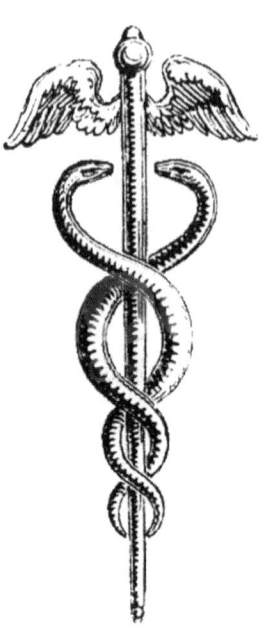

Congregation: The congregation, or audience, should dress in festive costumes according to their own genius. Masks, horns, fantastical dresses and the like are encouraged. Some may also have sistrums or rattles for the Invocation of Babalon. The Rites are a celebration of all things of sense and rapture. Let your appearance reflect this by your own genius!

Layout of the Shrine

Ideally, the entrance to the Shrine will be in the East. The main altars and Banners of Babalon will sit in the West. Not all Shrines may allow for this arrangement due to their physical orientation. The colors of the Shrine for the Bhaktic Rites should follow the instructions in Liber Legis I:51 for the Palace:

> *51. There are four gates to one palace; the floor of that palace is of silver and gold; lapis lazuli & jasper are there; and all rare scents; jasmine & rose, and the emblems of death.*

The silver and gold floor can be done with accents, with silver and gold checker-board pattern, with paint, or with rugs - all according to your own inspiration. Lapis Lazuli and Jasper represent the correct colors of blue and red to use for the Banners. Often the blues are put in the West, and the reds in the East. The blues can be shown on the large Banners of Babalon, which are vertical rectangles of cloth, quite large, hung from the ceiling. The Banners

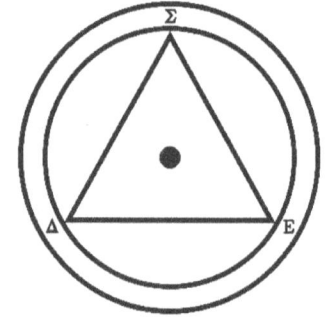

have a background field of blue, upon which is a large, gold Star of Babalon. The Banners of Ra Hoor Khuit hang on either side of the entrance to the Shrine in the East. They have a red background and the Eye in the Triangle or the Guardian of the Triangle of Manifestation symbol in gold. The important part is a circle or eye, within a equilateral triangle. Images of Nuit and Hadit may be included in the Shrine for the Bhaktic Rites, with Nuit being in the North and Hadit being in the South. They can be large, and of your own design.

There are three altars in the West, each one progressively higher than the last. The Banners of Babalon hang on either side of the altars. The first altar, on ground level, is the Altar of the Elements, for the Magus. It should be a double cube, around 1.5 feet wide and 3 feet tall. These sizes can be adjusted to fit your needs. It should be painted black, with a top that is white. You may paint a gold sunburst within the field of white on the top, if you desire. Each of the four sides of the altar may be painted with colors, symbols and images of the four elements - Fire in the South, Water in the West, Earth in the North, and Air in the East. Upon this altar is the Incense Urn for hot coals, Thelemic Abramelin Incense, a Chalice filled with rain water, and some natural sea salt without additives or anti-caking agents. Above the altar hangs an oil lamp or candle sconce, for Spirit.

The next altar is the Throne of Babalon which sits on a raised dais above the ground floor. The focal point of this dais is the Throne of Babalon in the middle. Ideally it will be carved such that the arm-rests on either side are lions, or painted with lions. Alternatively, two lion statues (such as are seen made of concrete for lawns and yards) may be used on either side of the chair. A black and a white pillar are set further to either side of the Throne, with black on the left (South) when facing the throne from the congregations, and white on the right. The lamps, which sit atop or hang above the pillars, should make a triangle with the Torch of Baphometis which sits above in a sconce (see the following).

The final dais and altar is the highest, and closest to the Western wall. This is the dais of Baphometis, and there is a chair there for hi/r to sit. There is also a sconce on the wall arranged so that when Baphometis is standing, and pointing above and below, that the torch will blaze out over hi/r head. This torch also makes a triangle with the lamps on the two pillars on either side of the Throne of Babalon.

The rest of the Shrine is filled with chairs for the congregation, with a central isle from East to West for the procession.

The Bhaktic Rite of Babalon

The Rites

The congregation is led to their chairs by the Elementals, and all are seated until the Rites are ready to begin. Once the Rites have begun, no other congregates may enter. When all is ready, the lights are extinguished and all are in complete darkness and silence.

The Opening of the Gateway to the Underworld

Baphometis the torchbearer enters, carrying the only light in the entire Shrine (a torch or large candle). S/he never speaks, but surveys the area as S/he slowly proceeds down the aisle from East to West. Baphometis is responsible for securing the people, the Shrine, and establishing the Light of Spirit therein. The torch is cast over the heads of all who are seated, so that its light and flame touches the Spirits of those present. As this happens to each member of the congregations, they may begin to quietly chant "Metis"[45], either in unison or individually according to their own meter. B. continues until all Spirits have been touched. All now should be quietly chanting "Metis". Baphometis then proceeds to the Altar of the Elements, and lights the hanging Lamp of Spirit there. The members of the congregations may begin to raise their hands if they like at this point, with palms up to Baphometis and the Altar of Elements. The chanting by the congregation should become progressively louder as Baphometis proceeds to the Throne of Babalon and lights first the Left Lamp (Black Pillar), then the Right Lamp (White Pillar). Baphometis then continues on and finally reaches highest altar of all. Baphometis stands facing away from the congregation, towards the Western wall. Baphometis holds the torch high in one hand, horn in the other, while the people of the congregation chant "Metis" even louder. Baphometis puts the torch in its sconce or socket on the wall. Baphometis turns to the audience, with the torch shining above His/r head, and blows the horn once - a long strong burst of sound. All fall silent at the sound of the horn, as B. then points above with the right hand and below with the left, as is typical of the image of Baphometis from history.

    At this, the congregation rises, and turns towards the East. A voice is heard from the East - that of the Priestess, hidden beyond the veil of the

---

[45] Pronounced *Meh*-tees, with a heavy accent on the first syllable.

open doorway. She is girt with her sword, and says in a clear and beautiful voice to all:

Had the Manifestation of Nuit.

At this voice, a number of Elementals appear through the doorway. They bear candles to light the pathway to the Altar of the Elements, and line the aisle on either side. One bears hot charcoals for the incense and places them within the Incense Urn on the Altar of the Elements. Another bears rainwater and fills the cup there as well. Others bear the salt, the Thelemic Abramelin Incense, and an open urn of wine - enough so that all in the congregation may have a small amount. When this is accomplished, the Priestess speaks again.

Nu, the Hiding of Hadit.

Now the Magus enters the Shrine through the doorway with his staff held firmly to his chest, so that it vertically extends above his head for all to see. He proceeds at a ceremonial pace forward, to the Altar of the Elements. There he stops, still facing the West, looking up to Baphometis. He holds the staff up high towards Baphometis, and then kneels down, holding the staff end against the ground. He then speaks, loud, forcefully and clear from this position.

Abrahadabra, the reward of Ra Hoor Khut.

At this moment, the Priestess enters, girt with sword at her chest, held with both hands tightly, the tip pointing downwards. She moves at a ceremonial pace down the aisle. At her passing through the threshold, Ra Hoor Khuit closes and guards the entrance to the Shrine for the rest of the Rite. The Magus rises to face her. The Magus holds the staff in front of him, end upon the floor. The Priestess proceeds to the Altar of the Elements, and circles around Magus clockwise, looking him over as she does so. She then continues up the three steps to the Throne of Babalon at the same slow processional pace. She turns and faces the Congregation and the Magus, who now face her as she stands girt with the sword. Behind her and slightly raised is Baphometis pointing up and down.

The Bhaktic Rite of Babalon

The Opening of the Shrine of Babalon

The Priestess looks to the people, girt with her sword, standing in front of the Throne, and says:

> *Do what thou wilt shall be the whole of the Law.*

The Magus and the congregation answer back:

> *Love is the law, love under will.*

The Priestess says:

> *Do that, and no other shall say nay. For pure will, unassuaged of purpose, delivered from the lust of result, is every way perfect.*

Baphometis now sits and the congregation follows. Baphometis holds the Caduceus Staff vertically, as if it is growing out from between hi/r legs.

The Priestess now looks to the Magus, and says:

> *Help me, o warrior lord of Thebes, in my unveiling before the Children of men! Be thou Hadit, my secret centre, my heart & my tongue!*

The Magus places the Winged Sun Serpent Staff in its holder just North of the Altar of the Elements, and does the Stella Heru. The Staff now stands between the Altar of the Elements and the dais of the Throne of Babalon. (The Star Ruby may be substituted.)

When the Magus is finished with the Banishing, Priestess says to him:

> *There are four gates to one palace; the floor of that palace is of silver and gold; lapis lazuli & jasper are there; and all rare scents; jasmine & rose, and the emblems of death. Let him enter in turn or at once the four gates; let him stand on the floor of the palace.*

Mystery Babalon

The Priestess sits with her sword across her lap. The congregation now stands, and performs the Adorations of Ra Hoor Khuit with the Magus:

The Magus and the congregation turn to the East and say:

> *Hail unto thee who art Ra in thy Rising, even unto Thee who art Ra in Thy Strength, who travellest over the heavens in Thy bark at the Uprising Hour of the Sun. Tahuti standeth in His splendour at the prow, and Ra-Hoor abideth at the helm. Hail unto Thee from the Abodes of Night.*

The Magus and the congregation turn to the South and say:

> *Hail unto thee who art Hathoor in Thy triumphing, even unto Thee who art Hathoor in Thy Beauty, who travellest over the heavens in Thy bark at the Noon Hour of the Sun. Tahuti standeth in His splendour at the prow, and Ra-Hoor abideth at the helm. Hail unto Thee from the Abodes of Morning.*

The Magus and the congregation turn to the West and say:

> *Hail unto thee who art Tum in Thy setting, even unto Thee who art Tum in Thy Joy, who travellest over the heavens in Thy bark at the Downgoing Hour of the Sun. Tahuti standeth in His splendour at the prow, and Ra-Hoor abideth at the helm. Hail unto Thee from the Abodes of Day.*

The Magus and the congregation turn to the North and say:

> *Hail unto thee who art Khephra in Thy hiding, even unto Thee who art Khephra in Thy silence, who travellest over the heavens in Thy bark at the Midnight Hour of the Sun. Tahuti standeth in His splendour at the prow, and Ra-Hoor abideth at the helm. Hail unto Thee from the Abodes of Evening.*

The Magus and the congregation return to the East and say:

> *I am the Lord of Thebes,*
>   *And I The inspired forth-speaker of Mentu;*
> *For me unveils the veiled sky,*

The Bhaktic Rite of Babalon

The self-slain Ankh-af-na-khonsu
Whose words are truth. I invoke, I greet
Thy presence, O Ra-Hoor-Khuit!

Unity uttermost showed!
  I adore the might of Thy breath,
Supreme and terrible God,
  Who makest the gods and death
To tremble before Thee:—
I, I adore thee!

Appear on the throne of Ra!
  Open the ways of the Khu!
Lighten the ways of the Ka!
  The ways of the Khabs run through
To stir me or still me!
Aum! let it fill me!

The light is mine; its rays consume Me:
  I have made a secret door
Into the House of Ra and Tum,
  Of Khephra and of Ahathoor.
I am thy Theban, O Mentu,
The prophet Ankh-af-na-khonsu!

By Bes-na-Maut my breast I beat;
  By wise Ta-Nech I weave my spell.
Show thy star-splendour, O Nuit!
  Bid me within thine House to dwell,
O winged snake of light, Hadit!
Abide with me, Ra-Hoor-Khuit!

The Magus gives the Sign of Silence, and the congregation follows. Then the congregation sits.

The Exaltation of the Shrine

The Magus turns to Priestess and says

> *Then the priest answered & said unto the Queen of Space, kissing her lovely brows, and the dew of her light bathing his whole body in a sweet-*

smelling perfume of sweat: O Nuit, continuous one of Heaven, let it be ever thus; that men speak not of Thee as One but as None; and let them speak not of thee at all, since thou art continuous!

The Priestess stands girt with her sword and answers with:

None, breathed the light, faint & faery, of the stars, and two. For I am divided for love's sake, for the chance of union. This is the creation of the world, that the pain of division is as nothing, and the joy of dissolution all.

The Priestess places her word across her throne. The Magus goes to the steps to meet the Priestess, who is now coming down. They clasp hands during this speech, and move together towards the Altar of the Elements.

The Magus says:

Now ye shall know that the chosen priest & apostle of infinite space is the prince-priest the Beast; and in his woman called the Scarlet Woman is all power given. They shall gather my children into their fold: they shall bring the glory of the stars into the hearts of men.

The Priestess answers as they move to the Altar of the Elements

For he is ever a sun, and she a moon. But to him is the winged secret flame, and to her the stooping starlight.

The Audience says to the couple:

Burn upon their brows, o splendrous serpent!

The Priestess takes the salt and says over it:

Take from the Earth, Give to the Earth, Feel the Joy of it!

The Priestess mixes salt into water, while saying:

The Bhaktic Rite of Babalon

This shall regenerate the world, the little world my sister, my heart & my tongue, unto whom I send this kiss.

The Priestess then sprinkles water around the area of the altar, while saying:

So therefore first the Priestess who governs the works of fire must sprinkle with the lustral waters of the loud resounding sea.

The Priestess returns to the Altar, raises the cup to West and says:

Hear thou the voice of Water: Babalon!

The Priestess takes incense and says over it

My incense is of resinous woods and gums; and there is no blood therein: because of my hair the trees of eternity.

The Magus places the Thelemic Abramelin incense that he received from the Priestess onto coals, while saying:

Harken O spirits, and accept this sweet perfume - for you, the gods, and all.

The Magus walks clockwise, censing a circle around the altar, intoning:

And when after all the phantoms have vanished, thou shalt see that holy and formless fire, that fire which darts and flashes through the hidden depths of the Universe.

The Magus returns to the center, and faces South, raising the brazier:

Hear thou the voice of Fire: Therion!

The Magus then lifts the Urn or Bowl of Wine so that the Priestess may pour the water and salt from the Chalice into the wine. The Priestess says while doing so:

There is no bond which can unite the divided but love: all else is a curse.

The Priestess then stirs the mixture with a ladle, and then puts a little back in the Chalice. The Magus returns the bowl of wine to the altar. The Priestess says over the Chalice "In Nomine Babalon" and drinks half. She hands the Chalice to the Magus who also says "In Nomine Babalon" and drinks the rest and places the Chalice back onto the Altar of the Elements. The Priestess then returns to the Throne of Babalon. As she ascends, the Magus says:

In the sphere I am everywhere the centre, as she, the circumference, is nowhere found. Yet she shall be known & I never.

When the Priestess reaches her place standing in front of the Throne, the Magus continues:

Now let there be a veiling of this shrine: now let the light devour men and eat them up with blindness!

The Invocation of Babalon

The Magus and the congregation all go down into the Beast Asana[46]. If they have a hood, it should be pulled over their head. All stay this way until the end of the Priestess' speech. Simultaneously, two Elementals come to the Babalon Throne and arrange a veil in front of the Priestess. They remove her sword from the throne and place it behind the throne for her. The Priestess here chooses to disrobe or to become scantily clad after her speech, as is her preference. The Priestess now gives the Daughter of Fortitude speech, standing in front of her throne.

---

[46] One goes down on their knees, and then from there lays down their torso on the ground in supplication. The arms are stretched above the head, forming a triangle, with the hands making the wings of Hadit.

The Bhaktic Rite of Babalon

I am the daughter of Fortitude, and ravished every hour from my youth. For behold I am Understanding and science dwelleth in me; and the heavens oppress me. They cover and desire me with infinite appetite; for none that are earthly have embraced me, for I am shadowed with the Circle of the Stars and covered with the morning clouds. My feet are swifter than the winds, and my hands are sweeter than the morning dew. My garments are from the beginning, and my dwelling place is in myself. The Lion knoweth not where I walk, neither do the beast of the fields understand me. I am deflowered, yet a virgin; I sanctify and am not sanctified. Happy is he that embraceth me: for in the night season I am sweet, and in the day full of pleasure. My company is a harmony of many symbols and my lips sweeter than health itself. I am a harlot for such as ravish me, and a virgin with such as know me not. For lo, I am loved of many, and I am a lover to many;... and behold, I will bring forth children unto you, and they shall be the Sons of Comfort. I will open my garments, and stand naked before you, that your love may be more enflamed toward me.

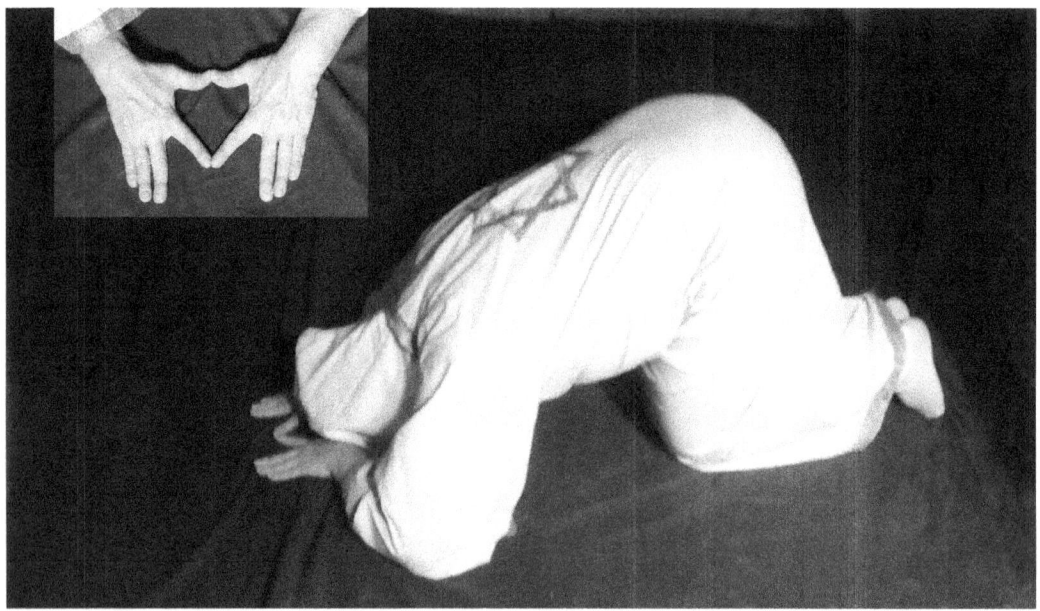

The Beast Asana

The Priestess then sits. The Magus then responds from his place on the ground in the Beast Asana:

I am the secret Serpent coiled about to spring: in my coiling there is joy. If I lift up my head, I and my Nuit are one. If I droop down mine head, and shoot forth venom, then is rapture of the earth, and I and the earth are one.

I ... lift ... up ... my ... head!

The Magus stands, and the people follow suit as he says:

O my people, rise up & awake!

The People respond:

Another prophet shall arise, and bring fresh fever from the skies; another woman shall awake the lust & worship of the Snake.

The Magus refreshes the Thelemic Abramelin incense here. The people sit. Baphomet points up and down again during the following invocation. The people and the Elementals begin to beat a slow, soft, steady drum beat while others occasionally shake Sistrums and snake rattles. The Priestess sits behind her veils, attempting to become the Liminal Gateway, guided by the words of the Magus and the people. The Magus begins the Bhaktic Invocation of Babalon.

We call to thee, Daughter of the Mighty Ones, Daughter of the Fiery One, Daughter of the Deepest Black!
People: In Nomine Babalon!

We call to thee, Gate of Life and Death, Queen of Heaven and Hell, Lady of Lust and Desire!
People: In Nomine Babalon!

We call to thee, Black One, Blue One, Gold One, the Woman Clothed with the Sun!
People: In Nomine Babalon!

We call to thee, Fierce Guardian, Formidable Warrior, Everlasting King!
People: In Nomine Babalon!

THE BHAKTIC RITE OF BABALON

> *We call to thee, Shameless One, Harlot, Whore, Bearer of the Cup of Fornications!*
> *People: In Nomine Babalon!*
>
> *We call to thee, Lady of the Star, Lady of the Snake, Lady of the Wheel!*
> *People: In Nomine Babalon!*
>
> *We call to thee, Lady of the Gate, Lady of the Crossroads, Guardian of the Liminal Point!*
> *People: In Nomine Babalon!*
>
> *We call to thee, Cunning One, Wise One, Clever One, Mistress of Heka!*
> *People: In Nomine Babalon!*
>
> *We call to thee, Great Liberating Mother, Daughter of Ra, Babalon the Great!*
> *People: In Nomine Babalon!*
>
> *We call to thee, Daughter of Fortitude, the Gate of God, the Woman Clothed in the Sun!*
> *People: In Nomine Babalon!*
>
> *We call to thee, the Mother of Prostitutes and the Abominations of the Earth, the Holy Whore!*
> *People: In Nomine Babalon!*

Repeat if necessary for as long as is needed. When the Priestess is ready, she stands, arms to the skies, parting the veil and stands bare and rejoicing in front of the people. The drumming and Sistrum sounds cease. She says:

> *Come forth, o children, under the stars, & take your fill of love! To Me! To Me!*

In addition, she may say anything else that is required or comes up or comes through. This is a point of spontaneity with the Rites, and anything can or may happen, depending upon the state of the Priestess and the closeness of Babalon.

The Audience

After this speaking is done, the Priestess returns to the Throne, and the veil is returned to a closed state to give privacy for the audiences with the people which is to come. The first of the congregation comes to the Magus, guided by an Elemental. The Magus anoints the person at their 3rd eye with Abramelin Oil, and with the phrase "In Nomine Babalon". The person is then led by an Elemental up to the Throne, behind the veil. There, the person stands before the Priestess, and has an audience with her, which starts by the both of them staring into each other's eyes, while the person breathes deeply and relaxes. The Pia Mezza may rise at this point, and many strange things may be seen. Whatever experiences take place next are private and personal. When the person feels the time in the audience is done, they then exit the veil and return to the Altar of Elements. There the Magus gives them the Chalice with a little of the wine mixture from the bowl to drink. When he hands it to the congregate, he says "In Nomine Babalon" and they respond the same as they take the Chalice and drink. The congregate then returns to their seat. The next person is then led to the Altar of the Elements, and proceeds as did the first person. After all of the congregation has had their audience in this way, the Elementals, and then finally the Magus have their audience also. Ra Hoor Khuit and Baphometis do not.

When the Magus is done with his Audience, he returns to the Altar of the Elements and then says to the people:

> *Beauty and strength, leaping laughter and delicious languor, force and fire, are of us. Nuit! Hadit! Ra-Hoor-Khuit! The Sun, Strength & Sight, Light; these are for the servants of the Star & the Snake.*

And then the Elementals say in unison:

> *Remember all ye that existence is pure joy; that all the sorrows are but as shadows; they pass & are done; but there is that which remains.*

All say:

> *In Nomine Babalon!*

The Bhaktic Rite of Babalon

Congregation goes to a prepared feast to celebrate together.

Options for the Bhaktic Rites of Babalon

The following are suggestions for performing the Bhaktic Rites with fewer people than desired.

If there is no one to perform the role of Ra Hoor Khuit, then you may use his image in the East, either an altar with a statue or an image of art.

If there are no people available for the Elementals, then the Magus must also perform their roles to the best of his ability. It may take some creativity to work out the logistics in the script, but do so according to your own genius.

If there is no one to perform the role of Baphometis, then the Priestess and Magus together must perform those functions. They should have an image of Baphometis, statue or art, which they carry. They also carry a torch, each with one hand holding the same torch. They then perform the same duties as in the script with the torch. When they reach the highest altar, they enshrine the image of Baphometis there, and place the torch in the sconce. They then return to the entrance in the East, and continue with their normal roles.

The well-being of the Priestess

Even under normal circumstances, the audience with the Priestess can be a drain on her life force, so she must be careful to understand her limits and give herself special time to prepare herself before hand and to recover her life force afterwards. But there will occasionally be those who seek an audience during the Rites who will be especially draining to the Priestess, almost to the point of being a real danger. Some of these people will not be aware of their draining influence upon the Priestess, while for others it will be covertly intentional as they, and those they carry within themselves, try to feed in this way. The Rites to Ra Hoor Khuit and the use of the Cakes of Light and the Cakes of Life can both help tremendously in this regard. For more information on the Cakes of Light and their use under the auspices of

Ra Hoor Khuit for this purpose, see Chapter 34, *The Devotional Rites of Ra Hoor Khuit*.

In the case of this particular Bhaktic Rite of Babalon, it would do well to have Activated Cakes of Light (with the blood of the Priestess) upon the Ra Hoor altar during the Rites in order to attract and trap any imbalanced or nefarious vermin which find their way to your Shrine. These should be burned on His altar after the Rites are finished. It is also suggested that you have Cakes of Life which were previously prepared days before. The additional Cakes of Life will have been dedicated to Ra Hoor on his altar for a few days (without the addition of blood), and are different than the Cakes of Light. After the Rites have been concluded, the Priestess can then consume these along with the wine from the Rites to help with her immediate energy needs. These Cakes of Life may be kept upon the Altar of Elements during the Rites, so as to be guarded nicely by the Magus and the Rites themselves. If the Magus or Baphometis have need, they can consume the wine and cakes as well, but the Priestess is always the first priority, as she is most heavily influenced in a direct manner by the people who interact with her in the Audience. See Chapter 34, *The Devotional Rite of Ra Hoor Khuit* for the preparation of these cakes.

XXXIV

The Adorations of Ra Hoor Khuit

With the mudras as given by the Brotherhood of the Midnight Sun

Being a ritual of alignment to the Aeon for the Ophidian Thelemite, to be used four times daily and before other works of Heka.

The communication revealed below was part of a much longer audience from a ritual performed using the Triangle of Manifestation in Templum Babalonis, on April 4th of 2009 EV. A new understanding of the Adorations of Ra Hoor Khuit was given by the God Tum. Hagia Aureavia has released to the world the details of these new understandings and methods contained within the original communication. It is her hope that these teachings may help to deepen the connection, for any and all, with the Company of Gods while performing the Adorations of Ra Hoor Khuit four times a day. For the details of some of the terms used here, please see the *Glossary of Terms* at the end of this volume.

The Adorations of Ra Hoor Khuit

The God Tum, speaking from the Triangle of Manifestation:

Tum: *The Wisdom comes in the front. Sacre toom num dum – num dum dare.*

Sail on the waters of your questions. Tum non dave.. da-vay

Kephra carries the Midnight Sun – you awakened it – why? Do you seek your brotherhood? The Midnight Sun. The stone's been moved. The light's shown in. The light of the Sirus Star.

Do what thou wilt shall be the whole of the law. Love is the law, love under will. Can you state your Will?

Magician: *My Will, is to establish the Cult of the Great Liberating Mother, and to help with it in any way that I may – or die trying."*

T: *Then you seek the Brotherhood of the Midnight Sun. Ka-ke kee-oh-ku keph-ra ... [edited section, to maintain oaths and Temple degree secrets, etc.] Do you know the name of the night birds of Egypt?*

M: *No.*

T: *They speak for Kephra because Kephra has no tongue. That would be the hieroglyph key-yo... key-yo... key-yo. [saying it sing-song like a bird call] And the sistrum. Now you understand.*

M: *Yes.*

T: *The sound of the beetle. Chica-chica-chica-chic-chic-chihc-chic [saying it like a sistrum sound] Can you say Resh to Tum?*

M: *Tum... evening?*

[Affirmative nod by Tum. Magician does the evening Adoration as instructed.]

T: *So if you have made a door into my house, how do you know of me? You do know that it is of the water? Which is why I said to ride the waters of your questions.*

Mystery Babalon

M: *What does your name mean?*

T: *It is most similar to your element – water.*

M: *Sometimes the books call you Atum instead of Tum.*

T: *It is different – it is the water moving.*

M: *Do you make open the way to the Midnight Sun?*

T: *It is a channel – I lead to it in the evening. Kephra can not speak.*

M: *Is Kephra the Midnight Sun?*

T: *Kephra carries the midnight Sun.*

M: *Then what is the Midnight Sun, and this Brotherhood?*

T: *The Moon. The Brotherhood of Service – the Army.*

... [edit]

T: *Those are your Brothers.*

M: *Who are 'those'?*

T: *Those who seek the same thing.*

M: *And what is Khonsu then? Is he not the Moon too?*

T: *You asked about Ankh-af-na-Khonsu.*

M: *Yes I did.*

T: *What does it mean if you translate that?*

M: *Would it be 'Life of the Moon'?*

T: *Khonsu.*

The Adorations of Ra Hoor Khuit

M: *'Life of Khonsu'.*

T: *The Force, of Life.* [Meaning the Ankh, and the Spirit]

M: *Are we invoking the Genius of Ankh-af-na-Khonsu into us?* [By performing Resh are we invoking the Genius of the Historical Ankh af na Khonsu, the person, into ourselves?]

T: *Would not the Priests of Khonsu be the Brotherhood?*

M: *Yes.*

T: *Then would you not be Ankh-af-na-Khonsu, in one sense?*

M: *In what sense?*

T: *Because you are in Life.*

M: *Yes.*

T: *There's not one Ankh-af-na-Khonsu - but there is... not many. That's the Brotherhood.*

... [edit]

T: *You are preparing for the Three Days?*

M: *We are.*

T: *There may be more to come in the next day.*

T: *This day. Note this day and why I came, for your timing.* [4 days before the Three Days. The Moon was in the 8th Mansion. In Coptic it is called Termelia. "The Descent" into the Waters of the Underworld.]

T: *And this symbol.* [makes symbol or mudra of Tum with hands, see below]

M: *What is that?*

T: *My symbol.*

M: *The Crescent Moon?*

T: *The same as Khonsu, reflected in the water.*

T: *So at one point when you learn all of the symbols, when you do Resh you can make them with the names.* [showing each symbol with hands - see below] *Also the Moon, with horns, like that...*

T: *Those others that you did – what is that?* [Referencing the Golden Dawn degree signs which the magician used when performing the Adoration for Tum.]

M: *Those were learned from a modern group called the Golden Dawn who were copying images from papyri from Egypt, what they thought were different images of the Gods standing in certain ways as pictured on walls.*

T: *What does it have to do with this?*

M: *Nothing.*

T: *So this is instead.*

M: *Yes.*

T: *That makes Ra Hoor happier.*

...[edit]

T: *Now you know the secret door into the house of Tum. The Stone has been Moved.* [The Stone which seals the Pyramid, tomb, or burial chamber.]

T: *You would not have begun this path if it was not the right time.*

Such was the way in which the God Tum introduced us in the Temple to the proper expression of the Adorations of Ra Hoor Khuit, popularly called Resh by the modern followers of Crowley. In our Temple, we perform the

The Adorations of Ra Hoor Khuit

"long" versions of the Adorations to Ra Hoor Khuit four times a day: Sunrise, Noon, Sunset and Midnight. This is not so uncommon as many people do this. But what is uncommon is the expression and attitude one has in one's Persona towards one's Spirit when reciting the Adorations. The Mudras given by the Brotherhood help tremendously in this regard. In addition, it is important to understand all of the players which are mentioned in the Adorations, and why they are there. Most people have some grasp of who Ra Hoor Khuit is, or his father Ra. But few have much of an understanding of Khonsu or Mentu in relation to their presence in the Adorations. We hope to be able to help in this regard.

But first, let us give the text of the Adorations, with the proper placement of the Mudras therein. The adorations were written by Crowley as his poetic translation of the Stele of Revealing, and included in the Book of Law at the behest of the Gods during its reception. Only part of this translation was used and can be found in Chapter III verses 37-38 of Liber Legis. When reciting the text as worship to Ra Hoor Khuit and the other Gods which cluster to support him, it is divided into two parts. The first part changes, depending upon which time of day one is performing the worship. The second part is longer, and is always said in the same way, no matter which time of day it is. Here then is the text of the ritual with the insertion of the Mudras (hand symbols).

(Morning, facing East with Ra Mudra which is held until the next one is reached at "Tahuti".)

Hail unto thee who art Ra in thy Rising, even unto Thee who art Ra in Thy Strength, who travellest over the heavens in Thy bark at the Uprising Hour of the Sun. Tahuti (make mudra) standeth in His splendour at the prow, and Ra-Hoor (make mudra) abideth at the helm. Hail unto Thee from the Abodes of Night.

(Noon, facing South with Hathoor Mudra which is held until the next one is reached at "Tahuti".)

Hail unto thee who art Hathoor in Thy triumphing, even unto Thee who art Hathoor in Thy Beauty, who travellest over the heavens in Thy bark at the Noon Hour of the Sun. Tahuti (make mudra) standeth in His splendour at the prow, and Ra-Hoor (make mudra) abideth at the helm. Hail unto Thee from the Abodes of Morning.

(Evening, facing West with Tum Mudra which is held until the next one is reached at "Tahuti".)

Hail unto thee who art Tum in Thy setting, even unto Thee who art Tum in Thy Joy, who travellest over the heavens in Thy bark at the Downgoing Hour of the Sun. Tahuti (make mudra) standeth in His splendour at the prow, and Ra-Hoor (make mudra) abideth at the helm. Hail unto Thee from the Abodes of Day.

(Midnight, facing North with Kephra Mudra which is held until the next one is reached at "Tahuti".)

Hail unto thee who art Khephra in Thy hiding, even unto Thee who art Khephra in Thy silence, who travellest over the heavens in Thy bark at the Midnight Hour of the Sun. Tahuti (make mudra) standeth in His splendour at the prow, and Ra-Hoor (make mudra) abideth at the helm. Hail unto Thee from the Abodes of Evening.

The Adorations of Ra Hoor Khuit

(Then recite the following no matter which time of day.)

(Begin Mentu Mudra which is held until the word "truth" is reached, then transform to Ra Hoor Khuit Mudra at the invocation of his name. Hold this until the words "Appear on the Throne of Ra".)

I am the Lord of Thebes,
   and I The inspired forth-speaker of Mentu;
For me unveils the veiled sky,
   The self-slain Ankh-af-na-khonsu
Whose words are truth. I invoke, I greet
Thy presence, O Ra-Hoor-Khuit!

Unity uttermost showed!
   I adore the might of Thy breath,
Supreme and terrible God,
   Who makest the gods and death
To tremble before Thee: —
I, I adore thee!

(Begin Throne of Ra Mudra which is held until "house of Ra".)

Appear on the throne of Ra!
   Open the ways of the Khu!
Lighten the ways of the Ka!
   The ways of the Khabs run through
To stir me or still me!
Aum! let it fill me!

(Transform to mudras of Ra, Tum, Kephra, Hathoor and Mentu as the names are said. Hold Mentu until "Ankh-af-na-khonsu" is said.)

The light is mine; its rays consume Me:
   I have made a secret door
Into the House of Ra and Tum,
   Of Khephra and of Ahathoor.
I am thy Theban, O Mentu,
The prophet Ankh-af-na-khonsu!

(At "By Bes-na-Maut" bring both fists together at chest. For Ta-Nech move both hands out in front of face, palms slightly apart and facing each other. For Nuit move the arms outstretched to the stars, palms up. For Hadit move the palms back together and pull down over the third eye. Then transform this into the Ra Hoor Khuit Mudra with the worlds "Abide with me..." and hold it in meditation in silence afterwards. Finish with sign of Silence.)

By Bes-na-Maut my breast I beat;
   By wise Ta-Nech I weave my spell.
Show thy star-splendour, O Nuit!
   Bid me within thine House to dwell,
O winged snake of light, Hadit!
Abide with me, Ra-Hoor-Khuit!

(Give the Sign of Silence)

The Adorations of Ra Hoor Khuit

Ra Hoor, in front of face

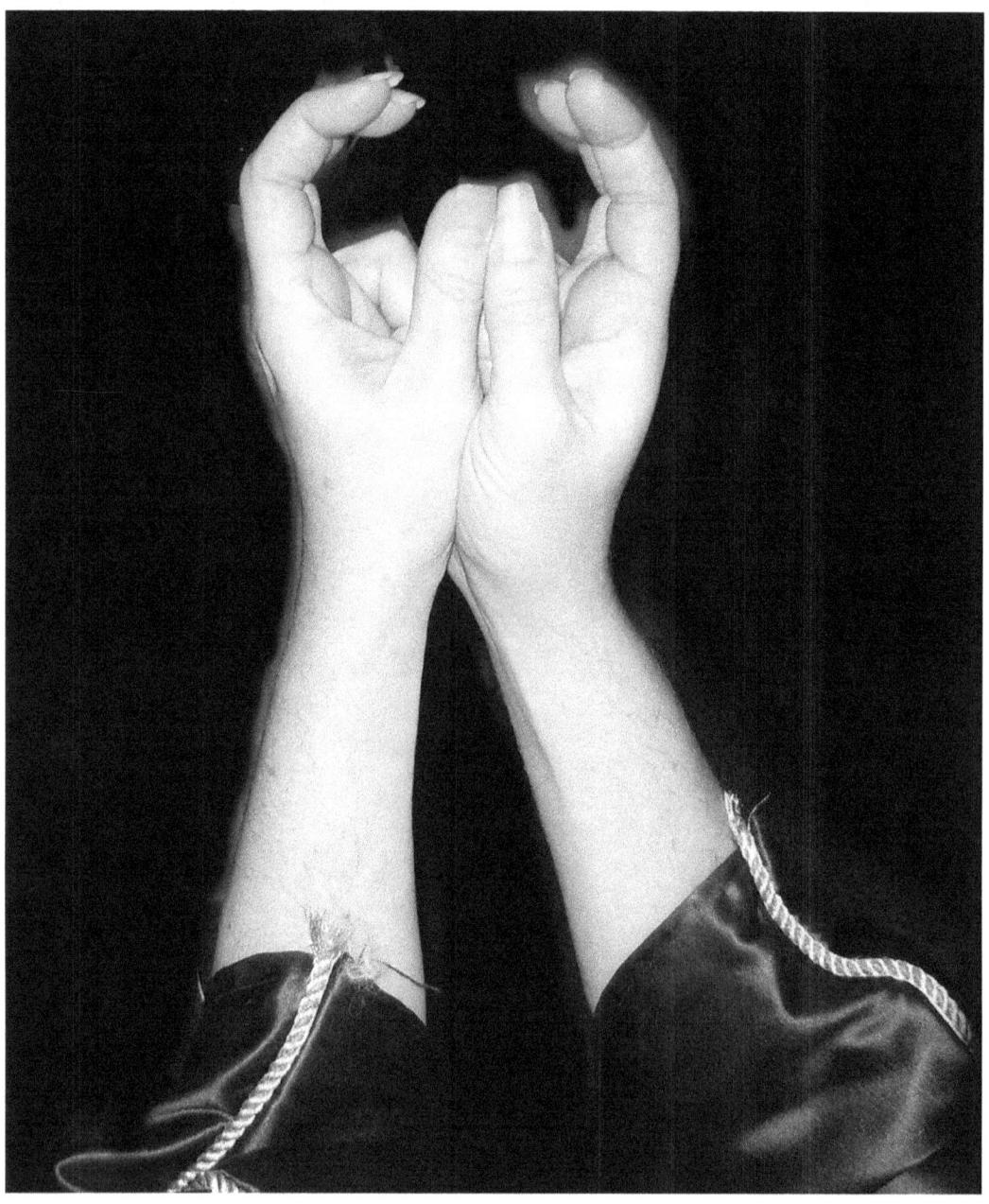

Mystery Babalon

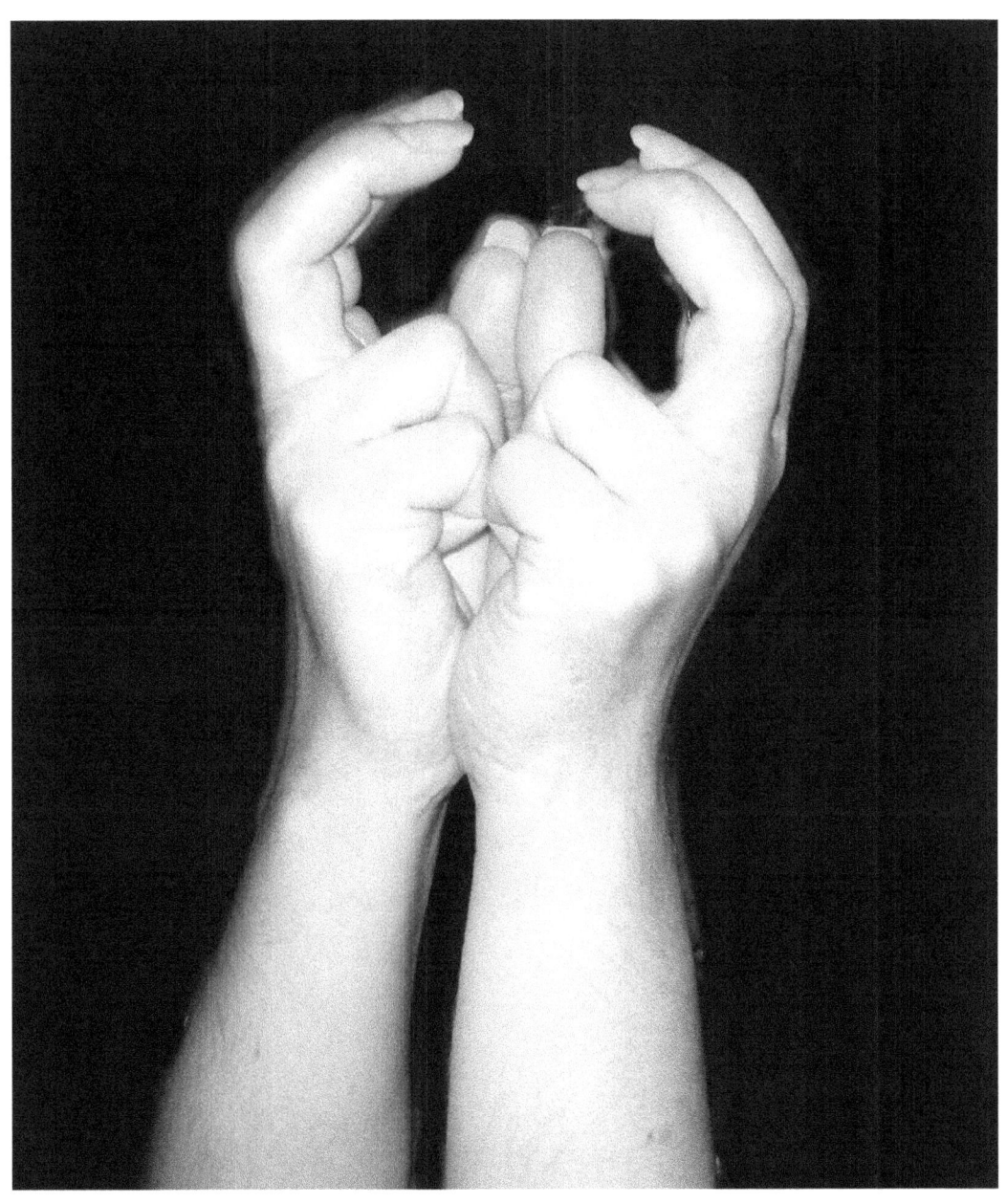

The Adorations of Ra Hoor Khuit

Ra, out above head

Mystery Babalon

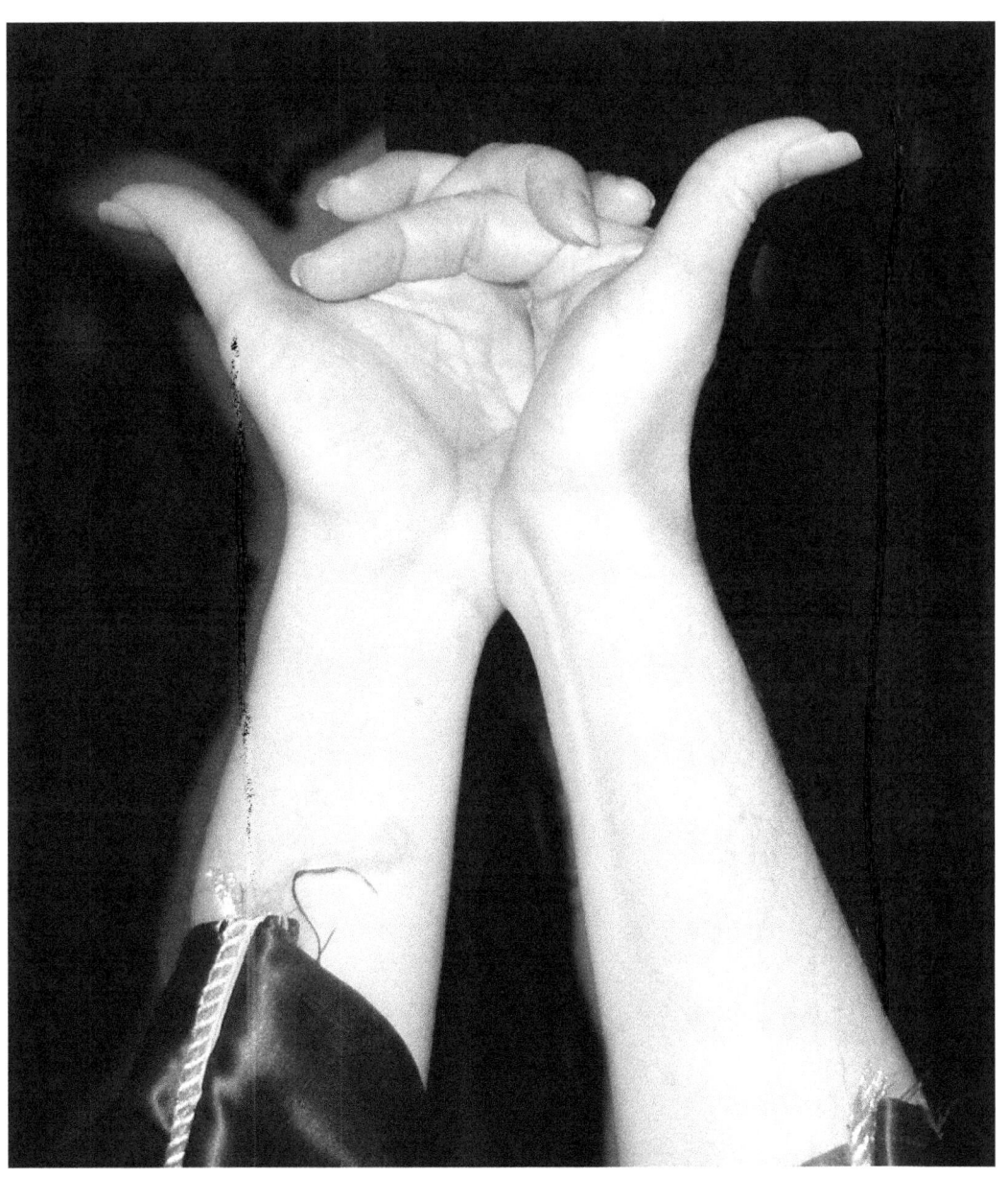

The Adorations of Ra Hoor Khuit

Hathor, out in front of face

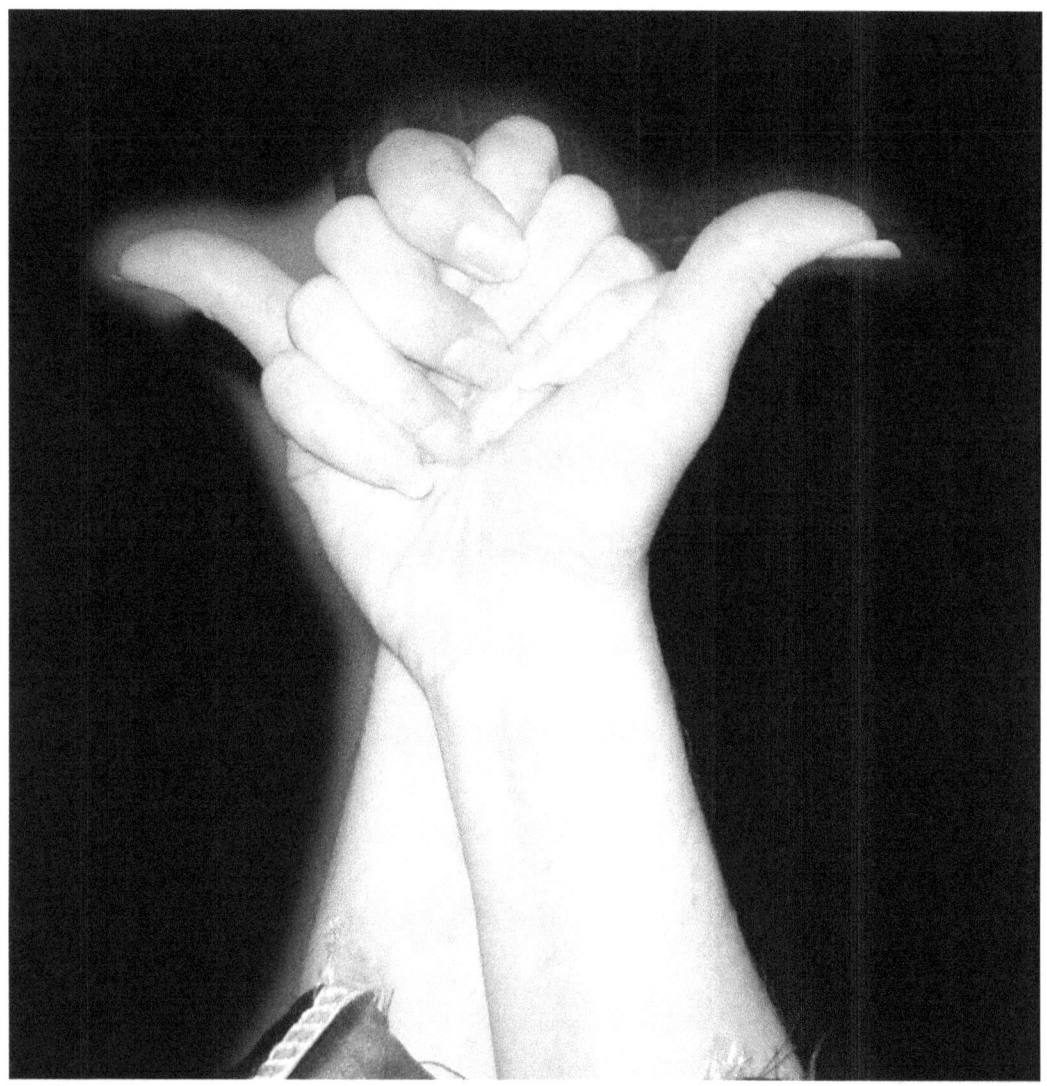

Mystery Babalon

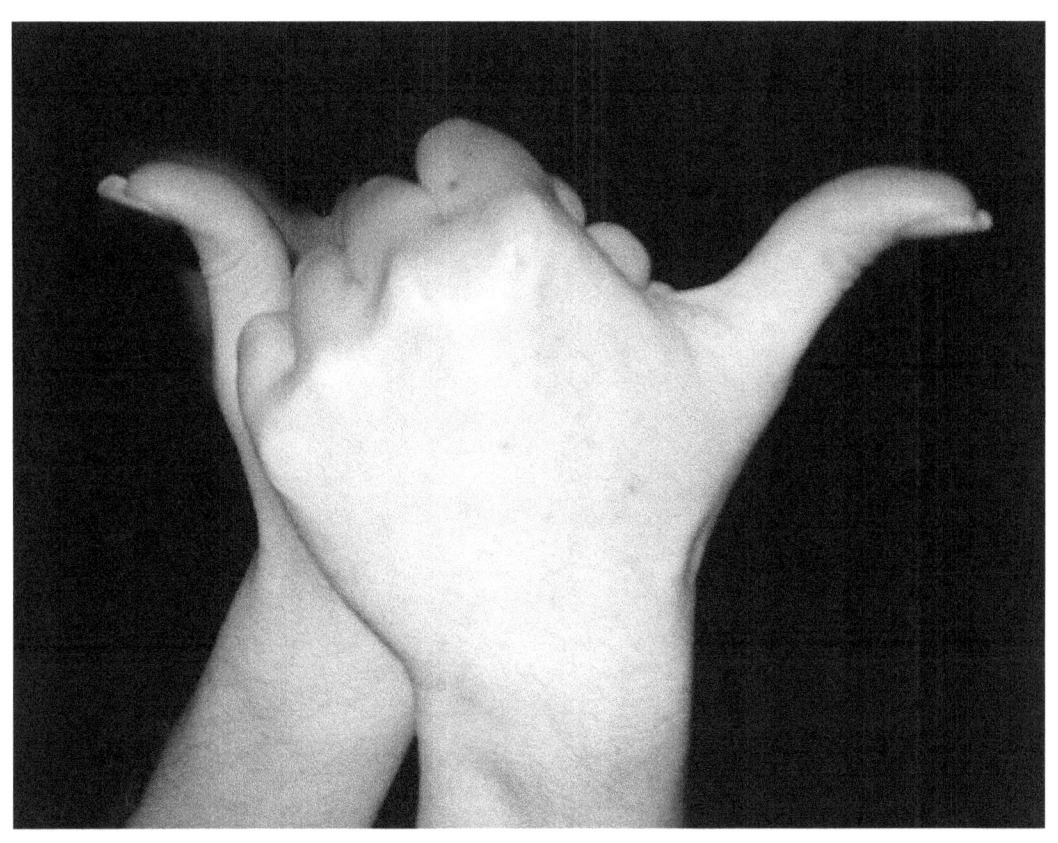

THE ADORATIONS OF RA HOOR KHUIT

Tum, resting on the waist

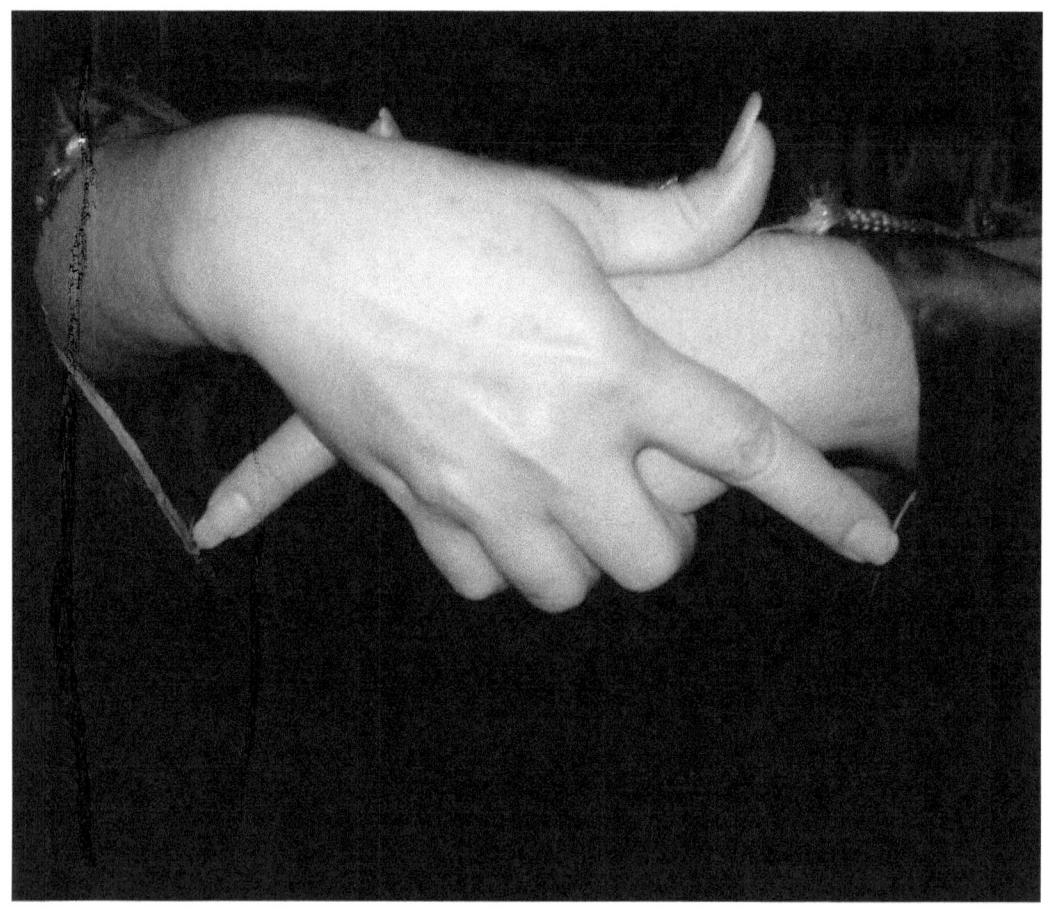

Mystery Babalon

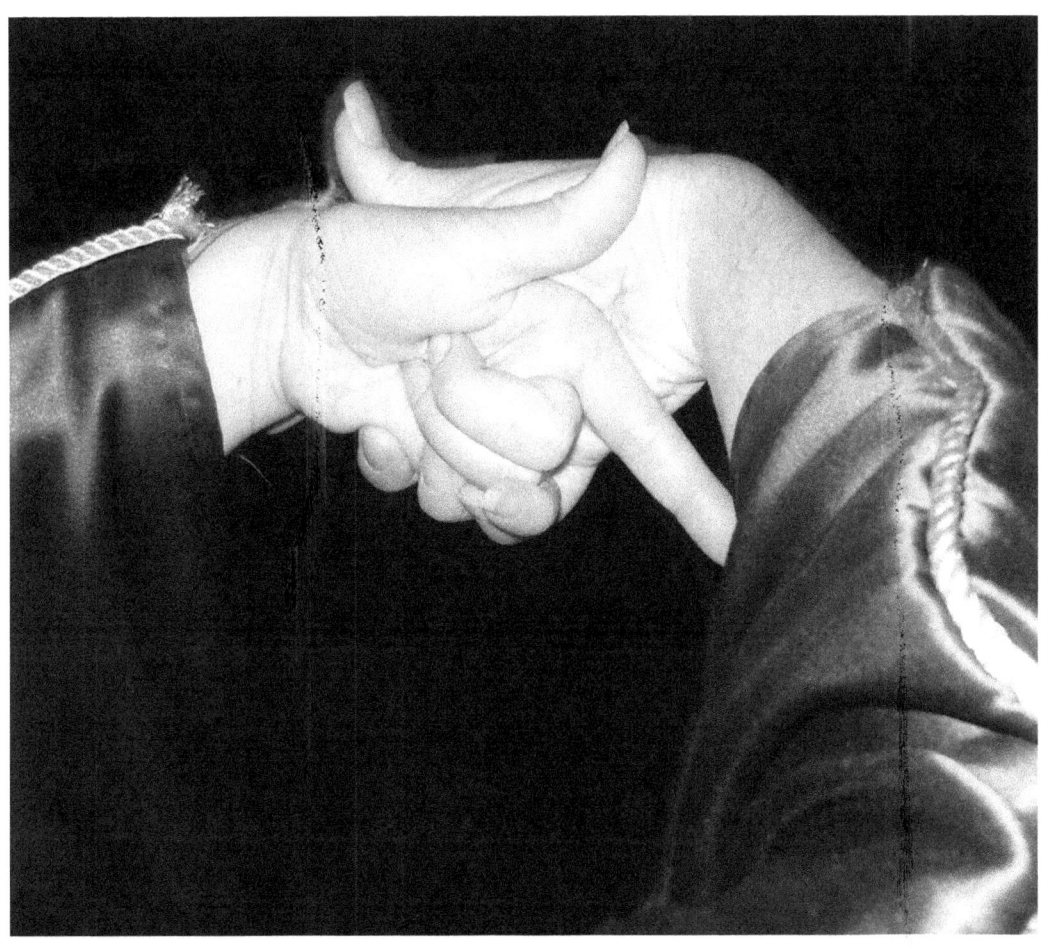

The Adorations of Ra Hoor Khuit

Kephra, out in front of face

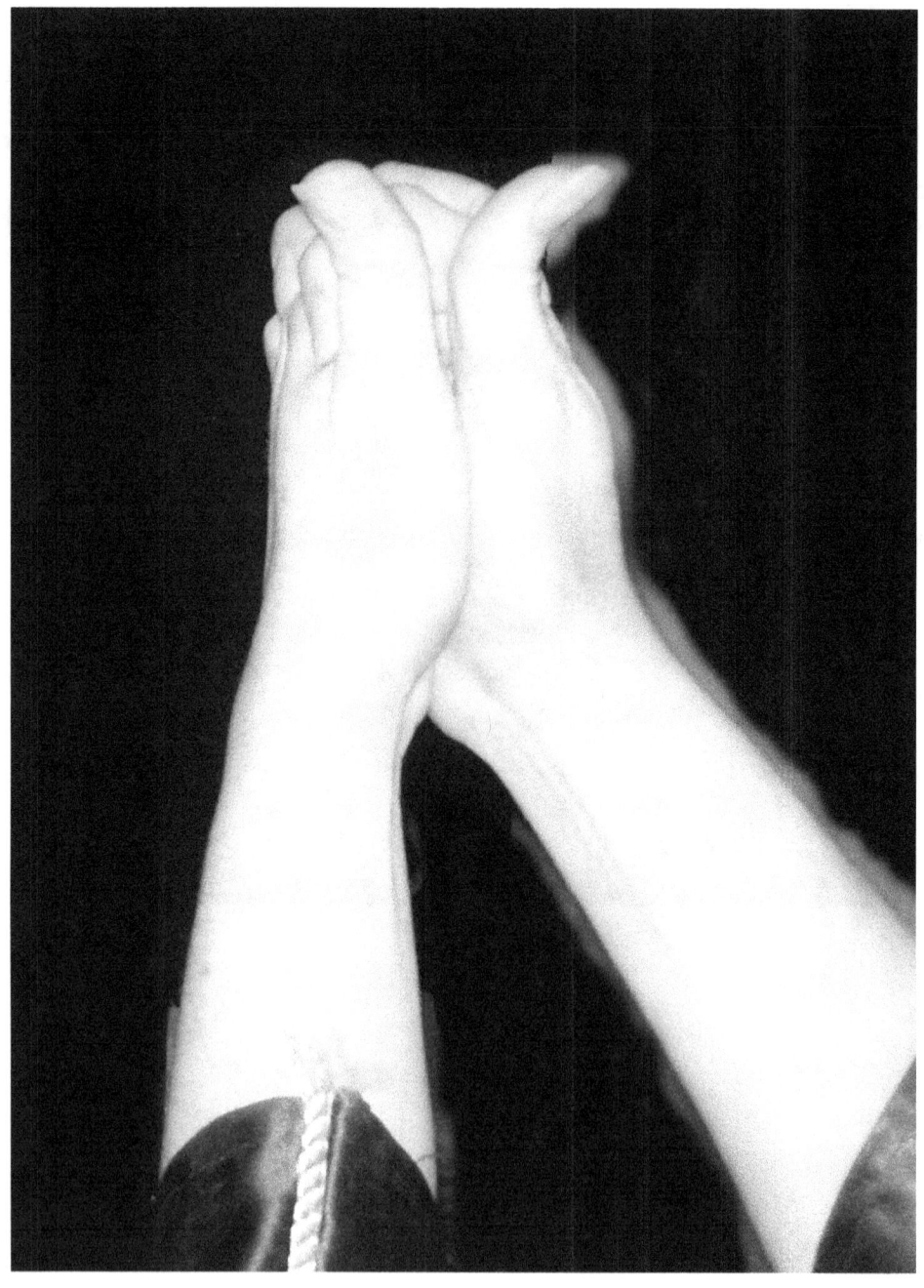

Mystery Babalon

The Adorations of Ra Hoor Khuit

Djehuty, out in front of chest

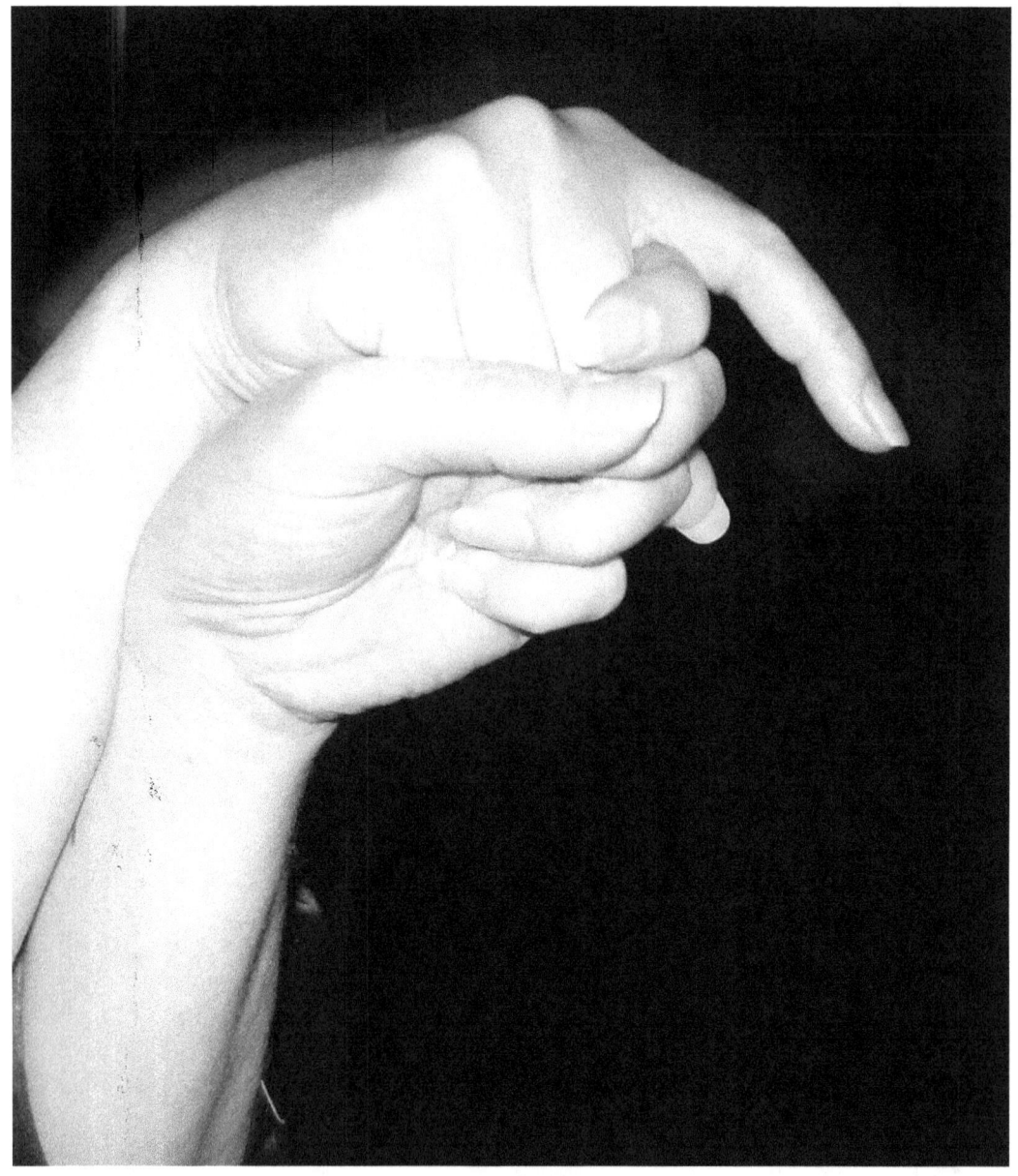

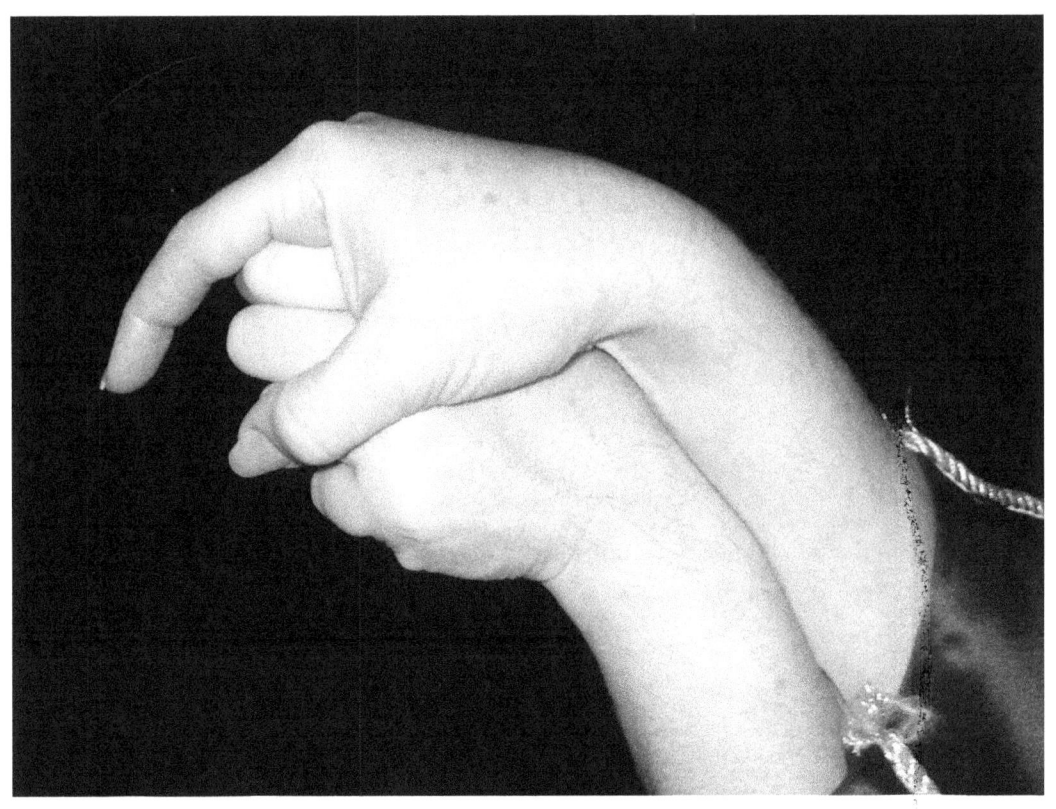

The Adorations of Ra Hoor Khuit

Mentu, in front of face

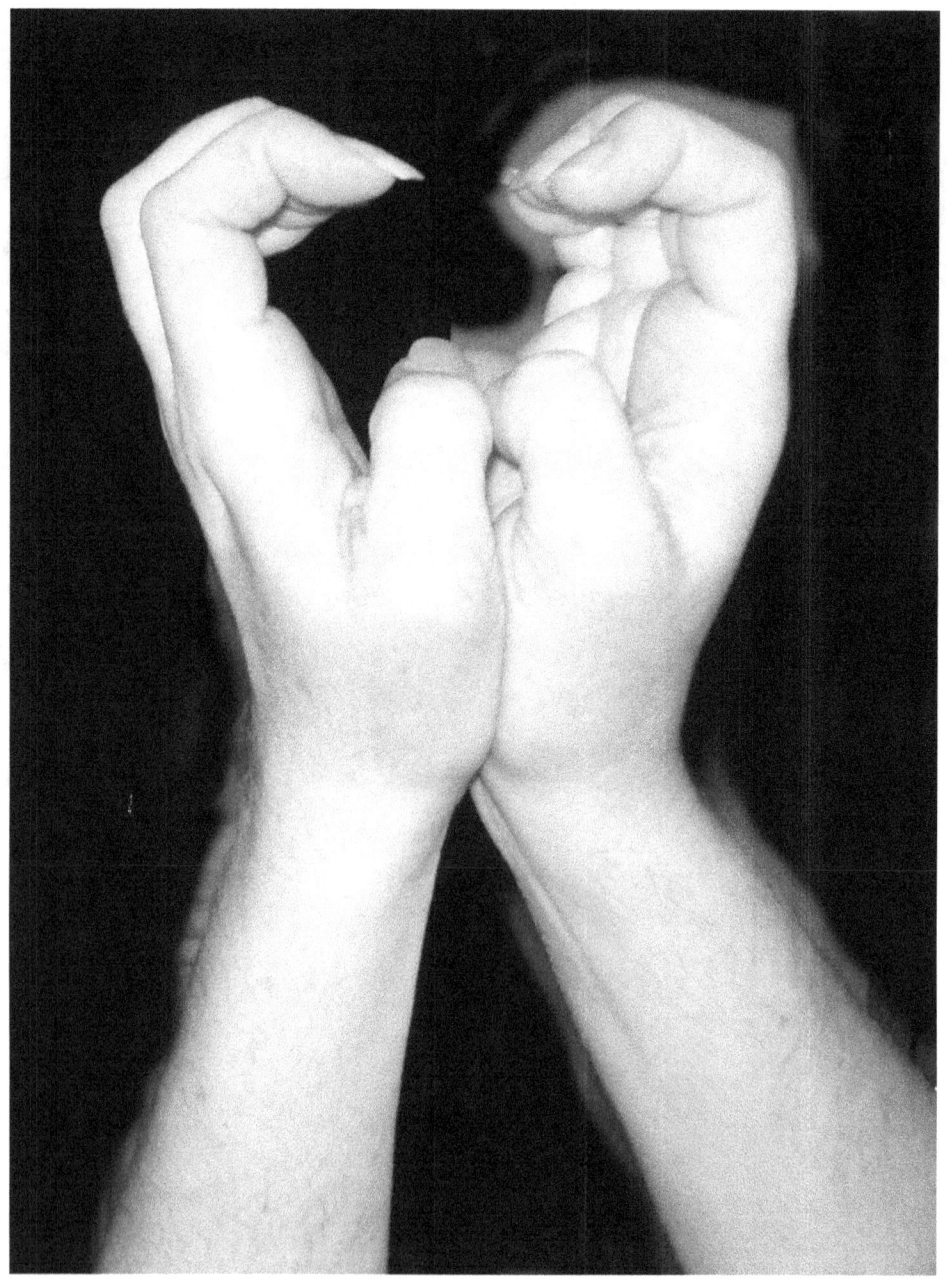

Mystery Babalon

The Adorations of Ra Hoor Khuit

The Throne of Ra, slightly out in front above head, as if holding the sun disk

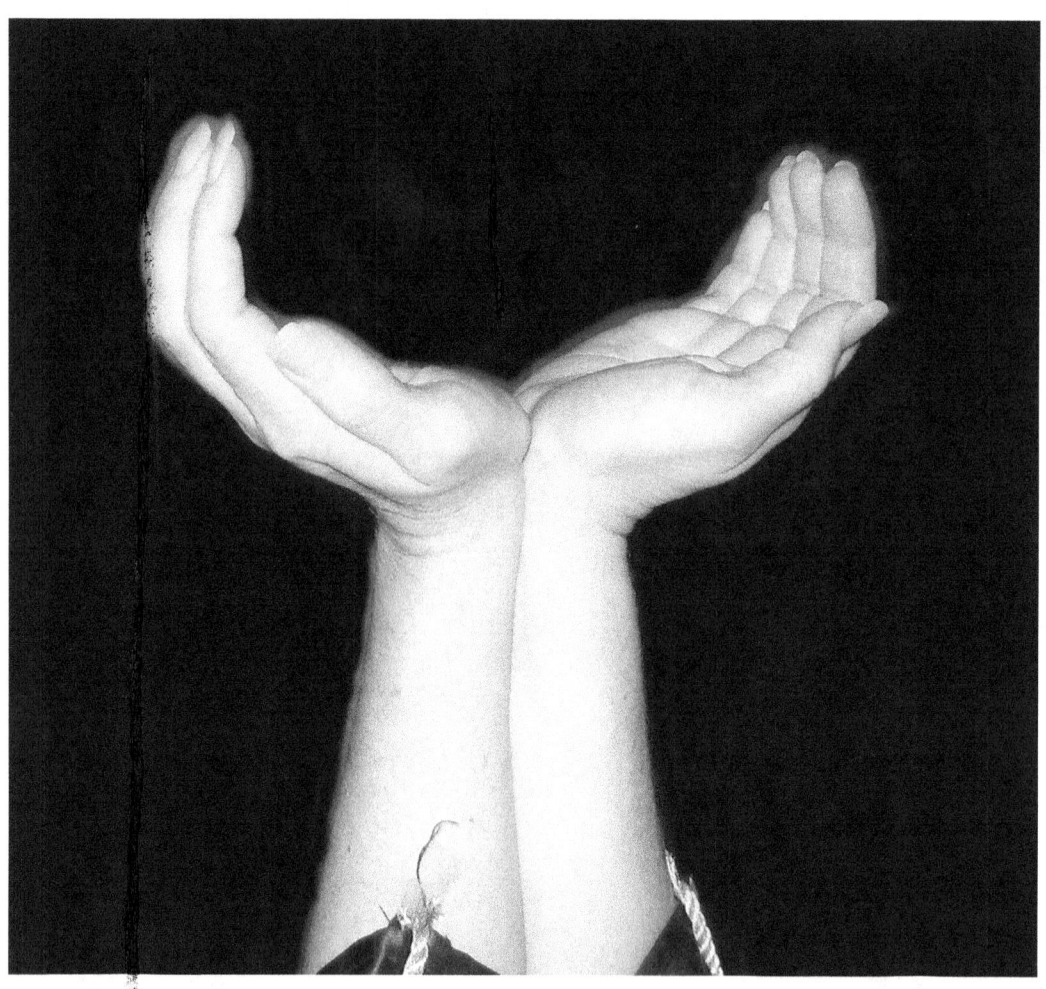

This is the way in which the Four Gates to the One Palace are opened. The Adorations and the Mudras will help, over time, to prepare one to open these Gates, but the Gates then are ultimately only opened by the Gods during Initiation of the student. For the Four Gates are the Four Elements within the Persona, and the ways in which they function there within Heka are important. And the One Palace is the Spirit - that which is manifested by means of Heka.

Now this process of Initiation into the Four Gates is cognate with the Four Realms of the Underworld, which are themselves divided many different ways - often again by seven (which incidentally leads one to the Realms of the 28 Mansions of the Moon, which are the stations of transformation in the Underworld). Now it is the Gates to these Underworld Realms from the manifest Realm of the Living which are guarded by Ra Hoor Khuit himself. He is the prime Initiator. He is the Guardian to His Sister's Realm in the Underworld. He is the Brother to all of the Daughters of Ra. All of this is very technical, but for our purposes here, He is the prime Guardian and Initiator of these Gateways. "Four Gates" equals 120 in the English Kabbalah which we Ophidians use, as does "Ra Hoor Khuit". So too does "golden path", which is the name of the Hagia, "Aureavia" - and as a Daughter it is that particular Golden Path which She now lays before the people at this point in time of the Aeon. 120 is also "black stone", which is a very important stone from history, last in our possession in the Temple of Kybele in Rome, and which now probably sits defiled in the cornerstone of Mecca. This is the "Stone which was moved", in the teachings given by Tum Himself in the ritual text given above. 120 is also "star fire", which is the source of the One Palace, the Spirit itself. For it is from the fire of a Star that each Spirit is born, eternal. Liber Legis I 3 "Every man and every woman is a star." There are many other associations with 120 as well, but suffice it to say that this is an indication of Ra Hoor Khuit's function as the Guardian of the Gates of the Initiations into the Underworld.

> *My lord initiating be O so present among us. Thy feathered wings expanding tip to tip to cover the horizon. Sing forth O great hawk-headed lord for thy call brings terror to the hearts of those that hear your battle cry. And as your tail flicks and your shadow covers them in darkness, they will remember that your fury is not yet known but only hinted at, as the shroud of the night star light surrounds them.*

The Adorations of Ra Hoor Khuit

In these words, which in part form the beginning paragraph of a longer invocation taught to us by Ra Hoor Khuit Himself, he mentions his wings touching the Horizon, tip to tip. He covers all four Gates in this way as the Guardian of those places of egress into the Underworld. And the phrase "tail flicks" also equals 120. The image of the shadow covering them in darkness, and the emergence of the night star light is also an image of the descent into the Underworld for those who have undergone his Ordeals and passed the threshold.

The One Palace, which is the Spirit, and its relation to the Four Gates or Elements has already been explained in Book II, Chapter 1 of the Magickal Philosophy of Templum Babalonis. But it should also be mentioned that when Ra Hoor Khuit states that he is the "Warrior Lord of the Forties" in Liber Legis III 46, that in one respect he is again referring to the One Palace. Both "one palace" and "forties" equals 114. This can also be read as the number of Heka or Magick (11) acting upon the four elements (4).[47]

But to return to our subject at hand, in the text of the Adorations the Four Gates to the One Palace are also signified by the Gods of the four positions of the Sun during its passing through the sky: Ra, Tum, Kephra and Hathor. Ra should not be seen only as he historically is now in the context of an Aryan creator-god who is the head of the Egyptian Pantheon, but rather also as the living orb of the physical Sun itself in a way that science and history do not yet understand. And it is in his different positions during the day one can see the different stages of Spirit as it goes on its journeys through its various manifestations in life and death. These are

---

[47] But it should also be noted that the Forties and the Eighties referred to in this verse mainly refer not to this "one palace", but rather it refers to the Prophecy of the Shuddering, the War, and the earth changes which are currently afoot on this planet, which only became apparent to the masses at the events of 9-11-2001 and after. Liber Legis III 46 "I am the warrior Lord of the Forties: the Eighties cower before me, & are abased. I will bring you to victory & joy: I will be at your arms in battle & ye shall delight to slay. Success is your proof; courage is your armour; go on, go on, in my strength; & ye shall turn not back for any!" It is interesting to note that *George W Bush, Osama Bin Laden, Saddam Houssein, Twin Towers, God the Adorer, blood begins,* and many other important names and phrases all equal the same value as the word *"eighties"*, which is 140. So now you know who the *"eighties"* are, even if you do not know yet who actually controls them, as we were told in this Temple back in 2001 and 2002. We are not at liberty to release the identity of the "forties" at this time, due to the nature of the War and those involved. We will do so only after they arrive for all to see, if such a thing were to happen in that manner.

the Sun in his different manifestations. He is Ra in his Rising and the element of Air as the Sun rays break over the Horizon of Night, each and every morning. This is the Birth of the Light (the Spirit), into matter. At noon this Light of Ra shines the brightest, and manifests His temporal Power through the Daughters of Ra. Hathor is one such Daughter, a sister to Babalon when She was in Her Egyptian incarnation. It is through the Tu, Her Bull form, that this pure power of the Fire of Life is manifested into the material Realm. And of course as we have already shown in Book II, Chapter 2 of the *Magickal Philosophy of Templum Babalonis*, this imagery of the bull with its horns is not only the image of the waxing and waning moons, but the image of the womb itself which is the seat of the power of manifestation. In the Evening the Sun descends to the Waters and to Tum, the Gateway to the Underworld in this Solar journey. This is the death of the Sun on its journey. And of this process Babalon once spoke:

> **Babalon**: *When Hathor descends into the water, do you know what comes back out?*
>
> **Magician**: *Mist?*
>
> **B**: *A serpent.*
>
> **M**: *I did not know that.*
>
> **B**: *The winged serpent.*
>
> **M**: *What is the winged serpent?*
>
> **B**: *When a spirit ascends. When the serpent in the picture is like this, it is the transformation in the water.*
>
> **M**: *What does that mean?*
>
> **B**: *The place between death and birth.*
>
> **B**: *Does it feel – this change – that you are about to be born in your new life?*
>
> **M**: *Yes.*

B: *Then it is like Hathor going under the water and coming out the winged serpent in the ascendance. Which in your words about the space is the milky way – in the stars.*

Concerning this place of Evening, of Death, of the Opening to the Underworld in the Solar Cycle through the Element of Water, a bit more was said by Tum, himself:

Tum: *If the Midnight Sun is in the water, then it could be seen as being the Underworld and therefore Anubis guards the opening to it in this stone that's been moved. This you see?*

M: *Yes.*

T: *For when they open the tomb, they see Anubis guarding the opening – yes?*

M: *Yes.*

T: *Then a True Brother could pass that opening and go past Anubis unscathed. But a not true brother would not be so fortunate.*

T: *Then you shall talk to Anubis about seeing the Trueness of a Brother. And if a brother who's not true, then you know where he goes.*

M: *To the mumbler?* [Set – I did not want to say his name.]

T: *Hm?*

M: *The One who Mumbles?*

T: *Setesh.*

M: *Yes. The Void.*

T: *Then you talk to Anpu.*

T: *Now.*

And there we must stop, for the instructions by Anpu on how to test a True Brother are not meant for the world to see.

So from Death in Water and in the Evening the Sun travels on its journey through the Underworld. It is here that it can no longer speak, as Kephra bears it through the place of darkness and transformation. This is the place of unmaking, and the place of conception - both in the deepest darkness of the Womb itself. Kheper Ra is the name of the Sun here, "the coming into being of Spirit". It is here that the greatest of all Heka takes place.

On this journey of his Father, Ra Hoor Khuit has said:

> *The Sun is born and dies each day,*
> *And the Moon each month.*
> *Both are born again, but the Moon always in blood,*
> *And the Sun always of darkness.*

And why is it that during this journey it is said that "Tahuti standeth in His splendour at the prow, and Ra-Hoor abideth at the helm"? You may ask what are they standing in and why? The answer is the Boat of Millions of Years, which is also called the Boat of Ra. This is the vehicle which carries the light on its journey through these cycles of death and rebirth. In other cultures it was seen as a chariot, but here in Egypt it is a boat, because it travels through the Cosmic Waters of the Primordial Nu, the source of All Things. Sisi, the Ape of Thoth, had this to say concerning this arrangement of Gods in the Boat of Millions of Years:

> **Sisi**: *What is the relationship of Tahuti and Ra Hoor Khuit? They both see. But one sees one direction and one sees another.*
>
> **S**: *If Ra Hoor faces forward, what you would say forward in the boat, towards the Light of Ra, Tahuti sees what you would say backwards into the darkness. One of life, one of death.*

So one can see into the world of life (Ra Hoor) and one can see into the Underworld (Tahuti). That is why the Adorations mention them, and you invoke them as guides and guardians into your life for the same reason every time you say the adorations.

The Adorations of Ra Hoor Khuit

Now we come to the Theban section of the Adorations.

> "I am the Lord of Thebes, and I
>   The inspired forth-speaker of Mentu;
> For me unveils the veiled sky,
>   The self-slain Ankh-af-na-khonsu
> Whose words are truth. I invoke, I greet
>   Thy presence, O Ra-Hoor-Khuit!"

The Lord of Thebes is the god popularly named Mentu. In this function he is the most ancient Bull God, guardian of the Priestesses of the Womb, the Ta, from an ancient time. He is Men Tu. The Man Bull. The Tu guards the Ta. The Bull guards the Womb. In Aryan times in Egypt he is pictured almost like Ra Hoor Khuit as a Falcon God, but he was originally a Bull Beast, which is to say a Guardian of the Goddess. The Beasts of the Great Liberating Mother always appear as Lions, Monsters and Bulls of various sorts. Phonetically Montu, MNT, is not far historically from another Son of the Goddess named Minotaur (MNTR) who served the same function in a different land. Now Thebes has both a Warrior Lord as Falcon in Mentu, as well as a boy-child God in Khonsu. This mirrors the relationship between Ra Hoor Khuit and Hoor Par Khart, who is Horus the Child. Mentu is a Solar God while Khonsu is Lunar. It is interesting to note that Mentu in later Egyptian means "traveler" while Khonsu means "wanderer". The Moon God is often called "wanderer" or "shepherd" in many cultures, because of its path through the sky which deviates from the other stars. But the important point here is that you have two pairs of deities with similar functions, but for different realms. Ra Hoor Khuit and Hoor Par Khart function in the Manifest Realm of the living, while Mentu and Khonsu generally function in the Darkness of the Underworld.

> Unity uttermost showed!
>   I adore the might of Thy breath,
> Supreme and terrible God,
>   Who makest the gods and death
> To tremble before Thee: —
> I, I adore thee!
> Appear on the throne of Ra!
>   Open the ways of the Khu!
> Lighten the ways of the Ka!

> The ways of the Khabs run through
> To stir me or still me!
> Aum! let it fill me!

The Throne of Ra is the body of the King, which is to say an Adept who is Manifesting his or her Spirit fully. This is done by "opening the ways of the Khu". The Khu is the unmanifest Spirit. The Ka is the fiery Will of the life-force of the Manifest Khu. The Khabs is the starry origin of the Khu, which is often seen as the light of the Spirit which shines forth. Aum or Amn is a word which means to "bring in", "bring forth" or "to manifest" in the Ancient Goddess language. It is not the same as the Sanskrit word "aum" or "om" which signifies the first sound of creation - although they do obviously have a common origin in meaning and phonetics further back in history. This word is used a number of times in Liber Legis. First in the verse again concerning the Four Gates and the One palace mentioned above, Liber Legis I, 51: "There are four gates to one palace; the floor of that palace is of silver and gold; lapis lazuli & jasper are there; and all rare scents; jasmine & rose, and the emblems of death. Let him enter in turn or at once the four gates; let him stand on the floor of the palace. Will he not sink? Amn. Ho! warrior, if thy servant sink?" "Ho" as we have shown many times means "warrior" in the ancient Goddess language, while Amn here means "invoke" or "bring forth". Another place this word is used is at the very end of the Book, Chapter III 75 "The ending of the words is the Word Abrahadabra. The Book of the Law is Written and Concealed. Aum. Ha." "Ha" as we have shown means "people". The Mi Ha is a word that Babalon often uses and means "my people". Aum Ha therefore is an admonition at the close of the book to "bring forth the people" so that they may see it. So therefore "Aum! Let it fill me" from before is a call to bring in the light of Spirit, the Khabs, so that it may fill the Persona and transform it.

> The light is mine; its rays consume
>   Me: I have made a secret door
> Into the House of Ra and Tum,
>   Of Khephra and of Ahathoor.
> I am thy Theban, O Mentu,
> The prophet Ankh-af-na-khonsu!

The Adorations of Ra Hoor Khuit

Once this Khabs, this light of Spirit, is manifest the secret door into the One Palace is made open in four ways - these are the Four Gates as already described. Mentu has already been explained and the title of Ankh-af-na-khonsu was described by Tum at the beginning of this document.

> By Bes-na-Maut my breast I beat;
> > By wise Ta-Nech I weave my spell.
> Show thy star-splendour, O Nuit!
> > Bid me within thine House to dwell,
> O winged snake of light, Hadit!
> Abide with me, Ra-Hoor-Khuit!

Bes means an Initiation in Egyptian and Maut or Mut is the Vulture Goddess of Death, who in the Ancient Goddess cultures like that of Catal Huyuk picked clean the exposed corpses of the people. The bones were then reclaimed by the family. Breast-beating, shirt tearing and hair-pulling were all ancient practices of public mourning at the death of a friend or family member. So therefore in this first line the speaker of the Invocation is claiming to have gone through the Initiation of the Death Goddess Mut, their own Persona beating its own breast in mourning for itself. Wise Ta-Nech weaves the spell of remaking in the Underworld. There are two types of women leaders in the Ancient Goddess cultures, the Ta and the Or. The Or are Kings who have a royal spiritual Lineage from certain Goddesses. They are the Ho Or, the Warrior Women so often referred to. The meaning of their ancient name is hidden in that of their Guardian, Hoor, and in names such as Ra Hoor Khuit. The Ta are the Priestesses of the Bull, the Women of the Womb. Tu in the Ancient Goddess language means Bull (as in Men Tu, above). It is the Ta woman referred to here in Ta Nech, weaving the new life in the womb after the ritual death, in the Underworld. And this "Ta" became the suffix "-t" or "-it" later in the Egyptian language which signifies a female or Goddess by its presence (such as Nuit, Aset, Pahkhet, Selket and many others). Interestingly Hathor's name contains both the Ta and the Or lineages, as in Ha Ta Or. The reading of Her name as Het Heru, House of Horus, is a later creation of the Aryan times.

    As we have shown in other writings, the Underworld journey ultimately leads to the Stars and the Cosmos. To go out, you must go in. This is shown in the next line immediately after referring to the star-spendour of Nuit. She is the Mother of Mothers, and the Mother of all things. The light of the living Spirit itself is then invoked via Hadit, the

Winged Serpent. And finally the protection of Ra Hoor Khuit is called for, as the speaker invites him into their existence.

And so one can now see that the Adorations bring one into alignment not only with the Company of Gods, but with ones own Spirit as it journeys through your life, heading towards your own very real death which will be much closer than you think, on the day in which it happens. One must learn to embrace ones journey to the Underworld - and eventually to long for it with all your being. For as is said in Liber Legis III 73-74 "Ah! Ah! Death! Death! thou shalt long for death. Death is forbidden, o man, unto thee. The length of thy longing shall be the strength of its glory. He that lives long & desires death much is ever the King among the Kings. " Such is the serious understanding of Ophidians when saying the Adorations four times a day, every single day.

In Nomine Babalon et Vox Sanctae Meretricis

Adorations quick sheet

First say the verse appropriate to the time of say:

Morning, East	Noon, South	Evening, West	Midnight, North
Hail unto thee who art Ra in thy Rising, even unto Thee who art Ra in Thy Strength, who travellest over the heavens in Thy bark at the Uprising Hour of the Sun. Tahuti standeth in His splendour at the prow, and Ra-Hoor abideth at the helm. Hail unto Thee from the Abodes of Night.	Hail unto thee who art Hathoor in Thy triumphing, even unto Thee who art Hathoor in Thy Beauty, who travellest over the heavens in Thy bark at the Noon Hour of the Sun. Tahuti standeth in His splendour at the prow, and Ra-Hoor abideth at the helm. Hail unto Thee from the Abodes of Morning.	Hail unto thee who art Tum in Thy setting, even unto Thee who art Tum in Thy Joy, who travellest over the heavens in Thy bark at the Downgoing Hour of the Sun. Tahuti standeth in His splendour at the prow, and Ra-Hoor abideth at the helm. Hail unto Thee from the Abodes of Day.	Hail unto thee who art Khephra in Thy hiding, even unto Thee who art Khephra in Thy silence, who travellest over the heavens in Thy bark at the Midnight Hour of the Sun. Tahuti standeth in His splendour at the prow, and Ra-Hoor abideth at the helm. Hail unto Thee from the Abodes of Evening.

Then say the following each time, no matter what time of day it is:

I am the Lord of Thebes,
   and I The inspired forth-speaker of Mentu;
For me unveils the veiled sky,
   The self-slain Ankh-af-na-khonsu
Whose words are truth. I invoke, I greet
Thy presence, O Ra-Hoor-Khuit!

Unity uttermost showed!
   I adore the might of Thy breath,
Supreme and terrible God,
   Who makest the gods and death
To tremble before Thee: —
I, I adore thee!

Appear on the throne of Ra!
   Open the ways of the Khu!
Lighten the ways of the Ka!
   The ways of the Khabs run through
To stir me or still me!
Aum! let it fill me!

The light is mine; its rays consume Me:
   I have made a secret door
Into the House of Ra and Tum,
   Of Khephra and of Ahathoor.
I am thy Theban, O Mentu,
The prophet Ankh-af-na-khonsu!

By Bes-na-Maut my breast I beat;
   By wise Ta-Nech I weave my spell.
Show thy star-splendour, O Nuit!
   Bid me within thine House to dwell,
O winged snake of light, Hadit!
Abide with me, Ra-Hoor-Khuit!

XXXV

The Devotional Rites of Ra Hoor Khuit

As has been shown previously in many places, Ra Hoor Khuit is a very important god within the pantheon of Babalon. Ra Hoor Khuit is actually the brother to Babalon, who in ancient Egypt was known as Hoor Pahkhet. Both Babalon as Hoor Pahkhet and Ra Hoor Khuit are *Hoors*, which translates in one sense to "warriors". And both are vital gods for this Aeon and present age. Ra Hoor Khuit is the Warrior Lord of this Aeon and its Guardian. Because of this, an altar to him should be placed in the East of every Shrine, private and public. Properly maintained, his altar and presence will lend a strong anchor to the working within the Shrine, and will also help to ensure the purity and sanctity of the Rites which take place there.

Therefore, let us examine the instructions that Ra Hoor Khuit gives in the Book of Law in regards to His place in the sacred space of your Shrine.

Set up my image in the East: thou shalt buy thee an image which I will show thee, especial, not unlike the one thou knowest. And it shall be suddenly easy for thee to do this.

-Liber Legis III 21

The Devotional Rites of Ra Hoor Khuit

In the Book of Law, Ra Hoor Khuit instructs the aspirant to set up his image in the East. This image may be a picture or a statue. There are many statues available of Ra Hoor Khuit on the market, but most are made of plastic. It would be best if you could have one made of bronze or brass. You may use a statue, a picture of Ra Hoor Khuit, a Stele of Revealing which has Ra Hoor Khuit depicted upon it, or any other image of him that you choose.

> *The other images group around me to support me: let all be worshipped, for they shall cluster to exalt me. I am the visible object of worship; the others are secret; for the Beast & his Bride are they: and for the winners of the Ordeal x. What is this? Thou shalt know.*
>
> -Liber Legis III 22

It is permissible to have other deities, angels, and spirits represented within a given Shrine. But one should do as Ra Hoor Khuit commands it, and place these images around Ra Hoor Khuit, but never above Ra Hoor Khuit in height. Many people wish to include Archangels, gods, goddesses, Lucifer, Satan—all are welcome. The exceptions are Christian or other monotheistic images, as they represent the enemies of Ra Hoor Khuit and Babalon, according to their own words. The goal is to allow Ra Hoor Khuit to function as a powerful guardian in a prominent position within your Shrine. And then bring in as many allies of Babalon and Ra Hoor Khuit as you wish.

To begin, let us study the instructions from Ra Hoor Khuit Himself as to what his offerings are to be.

> *For perfume mix meal & honey & thick leavings of red wine: then oil of Abramelin and olive oil, and afterward soften & smooth down with rich fresh blood.*
>
> -Liber Legis III 23

The above recipe lists the basic ingredients for what is commonly termed the Cakes of Light or the Cakes of Life, depending upon their use. The recipe for these cakes follows below. The recipes for Abramelin Incense and Oil have already given in Chapter 14, Shrine Incense, Perfumes and Oils.

Mystery Babalon

The best blood is of the moon, monthly: then the fresh blood of a child, or dropping from the host of heaven: then of enemies; then of the priest or of the worshippers: last of some beast, no matter what.

-Liber Legis III 24

Ra Hoor Khuit then lists the different types of blood which are to be used in His offering. As has been said before in previous chapters, the sources of these bloods are in order of importance: the menses, the blood of childbirth or of the placenta, the blood of enemies on the battlefield, one's own blood as a devotee, and finally the least effective being the blood of animal sacrifice.

This burn: of this make cakes & eat unto me. This hath also another use; let it be laid before me, and kept thick with perfumes of your orison: it shall become full of beetles as it were and creeping things sacred unto me.

These slay, naming your enemies; & they shall fall before you.

Also these shall breed lust & power of lust in you at the eating thereof.

Also ye shall be strong in war.

Moreover, be they long kept, it is better; for they swell with my force. All before me.

-Liber Legis III 24-29

A common recipe for the Cakes is as follows, but any cake recipe will do:

Ingredients[48]

---

[48] Modern Thelemites and followers of Crowley often include what they call "Ingredient X" in this mixture too, which many say according to Crowley was sperm, or at least the combined sexual fluids which result from coitus. Crowley's reasoning was that masturbation was like child sacrifice, for you are killing potential children by ejecting them outside of a matrix - hence his contention that sperm was being referenced by "the fresh blood of a child". Crowley was painfully ignorant of the Female Mysteries, which he often dismissed in favor of his male-centered brand of Spermo-Gnosticism, which views women as an "empty vessel" to be filled with his "holy ghost". The meaning of the bloods has now been corrected and set right, and it is to be noted that sperm as such is not

The Devotional Rites of Ra Hoor Khuit

- 1.5 cups flour (gluten-free flours are best due to widespread intolerances)
- 6 tbsp. extra virgin olive oil
- 7 tbsp. honey
- 1 tbsp. wine leavings[49]
- 7 drops Abramelin Oil

1. Rub some olive oil on your working surface so that the dough won't stick. Also oil some pans or cookie sheets at this time.

2. Pre-heat your oven to 300 degrees Fahrenheit.

3. Mix oils and flour together with a spoon. Keep mixing while you add the other ingredients. Keep mixing and kneading until the dough yields a homogenous consistency. It should stick together nicely, but not stick to an oiled rolling pin or oiled surface.

4. Re-oil the counter top if necessary. Take out one small ball of dough at a time from your bowl, and press it flat with the palm of your hand. Then use an oiled rolling pin to flatten it out. When it is about an 1/8" thick, you can cut the dough into whatever shape you like, and press shapes into it for decoration.

5. Bake for 4 - 7 minutes, depending on thickness of the cakes and the heat of your oven.

6. You may refrigerate or freeze to store.

These cakes are used for several purposes.

- As incense for the Rites of Ra Hoor Khuit, in which they are burned.

- As a celebratory communion in the Rites of Ra Hoor Khuit where they grant certain powers.

---

mentioned in this section of Liber Legis.
[49] Wine leavings are a by-product of the wine making process. In the absence of actual wine leavings, you can capture the "leavings" from the bottom of a good bottle of port, or you can simmer some ruby port until it leaves a thick syrupy residue.

- As a tool used in one method of cursing and slaying enemies in Ra Hoor's name.

- As a method to trap demons and unwanted influences.

Most of these methods are too much to detail in the scope of this book, however we will briefly summarize some general points which may be of assistance. *"And afterward soften & smooth down with rich fresh blood."* The blood is applied to the cakes during the Rites, after they are already baked. This goes the same for sexual fluids, if the cakes are being used in this way. The intensity of the Cakes of Light dedicated with blood to Ra Hoor Khuit on His altar over many days should not be underestimated. Their power increases through an attraction created by the cake and the blood in His presence, which creates a lure or beacon when left in the open. That which is attracted to feed upon the cakes and blood is often of an imbalanced or demonic influence, which Ra Hoor has the power to frustrate and sublimate. One must be very careful with activated Cakes of Light in this way, and never consume them, as you would make that energy a part of yourself. It is not without consequence.

My altar is of open brass work: burn thereon in silver or gold!

-Liber Legis III 30

The final instruction from Ra Hoor Khuit is a brief description of His altar. We have already described the details of this altar in Chapter 13, Altars and Shrine Decorations in the section entitled *The Ra Hoor Khuit Altar*.

The Rite of Cleansing

One of the beneficial uses of these instructions by Ra Hoor Khuit is in the periodic cleansing of your Shrine, and yourself, of unwanted influences. The Cakes of Light are most potent in this regard, and if handled properly, will greatly increase your own fortitude and well-being. This Rite of Cleansing is to be performed at Noon of any day of the week in a periodic fashion. Once a week is wonderful.

The Devotional Rites of Ra Hoor Khuit

To begin bake a small quantity of Cakes for these Rites, or have a large batch previously baked and stored well from which to draw from. Have them with you on a small dedicated plate when you enter the Shrine. Also have your blood with you in the Chalice of Babalon from Her altar. Go to Ra Hoor's altar and set the plate of cakes on one side of the altar and the Chalice of Blood on the other, outside of the main triangle made by the candles. Start the charcoal within the censer on the altar. Light the two candles in the back, while saying "In Nomine Ra Hoor Khuit". Then light the candles closest to you in the front while saying "Abrahadabra, the reward of Ra Hoor Khuit."

Now perform The Adorations of Ra Hoor Khuit for Noon to the South. After this, face again to the East at Ra Hoor's altar. Add some Thelemic Abramelin Incense to the charcoal and say the following Invocation of Ra Hoor Khuit, which was given by the God himself.[50]

> *My lord initiating be O so present among us.*
>
> *Thy feathered wings expanding tip to tip to cover the horizon.*
>
> *Sing forth O great hawk-headed lord for thy call brings terror to the hearts of those that hear your battle cry.*
>
> *And as your tail flicks and your shadow covers them in darkness, they will remember that your fury is not yet known but only hinted at, as the shroud of the night star light surrounds them.*

Now take the plate with the Cakes of Light, and hold them before His image while saying the following.

> *I have made the Cakes of Light, as you have commanded, and bring them before you, mighty Ra Hoor Khuit.*

---

[50] On April 9, 2006 during the rituals of the Three Days of the Receiving of the Book of Law, Ra Hoor Khuit made an appearance within the Inner Sanctum of Templum Babalonis and held Audience with Hagia Aureavia and her members there present. Ra Hoor Khuit gave prophecy, and instruction for the Hagia and the Temple, during which this verse was given as the proper way to begin all invocations to Him.

Place the plate of cakes in the center of the Triangle of candles. Then take the Chalice of Babalon with your blood and hold it before His image and say the following.

I smooth them down with rich fresh blood, In Nomine Ra Hoor Khuit.

Pour the blood onto the Cakes of Light. Then say the following.

You are the Warrior Lord of War and Vengeance! In this Shrine, I shall refuse none - but I shall know and destroy the traitors! O mighty Ra Hoor Khuit, you are powerful to protect your servants! May these Cakes of Light be as a beacon, and cleanse this Shrine under your protection!

In Nomine Ra Hoor Khuit.

Now leave the candles burning for a little while before extinguishing them and go about your normal business. Do the Adorations of Ra Hoor Khuit for Noon at His altar over the next two or three days while burning Thelemic Abramelin Incense[51]. This is what is meant by "let it be laid before me, and kept thick with perfumes of your orison."

In time, you will begin to feel the presence within the Cakes of Light which have been activated. Do not let them swell more than two or three days, or their influence will start to leak out into the Shrine. After a few days, simply burn[52] them in silence to Ra Hoor Khuit, transforming their accumulation up to Him in service, and cleansing your Shrine at the same time. If you feel the need to say anything, simply say "In Nomine Ra Hoor Khuit, Mighty Lord of the Aeon, I make this offering to you!"

---

[51] The Adoration is performed next to His altar in the East, but facing South as usual for the Noon Adoration.
[52] Usually this is done upon charcoal in the incense urn upon His altar in front of His Image.

The Devotional Rites of Ra Hoor Khuit

The Devotional Rite of Ra Hoor Khuit

This Rite of Devotion to Ra Hoor Khuit is a wonderful way to partake of His Force and Fire, in the form of the Cakes of Life[53]. It is best performed at Noon on any given day of the week. By performing this Rite, you will create Cakes of Light which are fit for consumption, and allow you to partake of that sacrament in the name of the Lord of the Aeon. You may do this Rite as often as you like, and it is recommended that Priestesses who are performing the Bhaktic Rites of Babalon also perform this Rite in advance, so as to have Cakes of Life ready for consumption after that ritual.

To begin bake a small quantity of Cakes for these Rites, or have a large batch previously baked and stored well from which to draw from. Have them with you on a small dedicated plate when you enter the Shrine. Go to Ra Hoor's altar and set the plate of Cakes on one side of the altar, outside of the main triangle made by the candles. Start the charcoal within the censer on the altar. Light the two candles in the back, while saying "In Nomine Ra Hoor Khuit". Then light the candles closest to you in the front while saying "Abrahadabra, the reward of Ra Hoor Khuit."

Now perform The Adorations of Ra Hoor Khuit for Noon to the South. After this, face again to the East at Ra Hoor's altar. Add some Thelemic Abramelin Incense to the charcoal and say the following Invocation of Ra Hoor Khuit, which was given by the God himself.

> *My lord initiating be O so present among us.*
>
> *Thy feathered wings expanding tip to tip to cover the horizon.*
>
> *Sing forth O great hawk-headed lord for Thy call brings terror to the hearts of those that hear Your battle cry.*
>
> *And as Your tail flicks and Your shadow covers them in darkness, they will remember that Your fury is not yet known but only hinted at,*

---

[53] N.B. The Cakes of Light are used with blood, and attract imbalanced forces and entities like a beacon, swelling with their energy. These are to be burned to Ra Hoor Khuit in sacrifice to raise his power. The Cakes of Life do not use blood, and swell with the Force and Fire of Ra Hoor Khuit upon His altar. These cakes *are* meant to be consumed by the worshipper to increase his or her power. It is best to not get them confused.

as the shroud of the night star light surrounds them.

Now take the plate with the Cakes of Light, and hold them before His image while saying the following.

I have made the Cakes as You have commanded, and bring them before You, mighty Ra Hoor Khuit.

Place the plate of cakes in the center of the Triangle of candles. Now reach out your arms to the image of Ra Hoor Khuit on the altar, and call to him with the following lines.

I call to Thee, most Great and Terrible Hawk-Headed Mystical Lord of Strength, of War, of Vengeance, of Divine Retribution

It is I, [your chosen name], and I come before You, myself an offering, ready to die and be reborn anew. For on this day, I accept the mantle of my most great and terrible purpose, that of my Will.

I am worthy to fight and die before You, Mighty Ra Hoor Khuit! I am ready to face all of my fears! I am ready to forge myself into steel, to severe that which keeps me from my divine, incarnated purpose.

I call to Thee, Ra Hoor Khuit! To dedicate the purpose that binds my being in service to all that is the Will of my existence.

I call to Thee, Ra Hoor Khuit! To smite me before You, if I am not worthy: for there is no life, no existence, if I do not do that which I incarnated for.

I call to Thee, Ra Hoor Khuit! I sacrifice my enslavement so that I may be bound in the service of my Spirit.

Do what thou wilt shall be the whole of the law. Love is the law, love under Will.

[Place more Thelemic Abramelin Incense upon the charcoal.]

Accept these cakes, Mighty Warrior of Silence and Strength!
May they swell with Your power!
May they swell with the strength, force, vigor of Your arms!
Success is my proof, courage is my armor!

The Devotional Rites of Ra Hoor Khuit

*May I serve You with the trueness of my Will
Receive these offerings, O Mighty Ra Hoor Khuit,
And Shine Your light upon them.
May my loyalty win me your gifts,
So that at last I may understand your reward:
Abrahadabra.*

In Nomine Ra Hoor Khuit, let it be done.

You may now extinguish the candles, or let them burn for a while and quietly do it later. Leave the cakes on the altar for another day or two, again doing the various Adorations to Ra Hoor Khuit over them as you have a chance, while burning Thelemic Abramelin Incense. After this they are ready to eat.

XXXVI

The Blood Rites of Ra Hoor Khuit

he Blood Rites of Ra Hoor Khuit are a Hieros Gamos. In Greek ἱερὸς γάμος means a Holy Marriage between a human and a god. It is an ancient Rite of dedication, which can not be undone. It is the most serious undertaking which one can perform, as you are laying your life at the feet of a deity, so that they may use you as they Will. Even unto death. You are completely and permanently aligning your Will with the Will of the divine one, in this case Ra Hoor Khuit. And there is no greater power to be gained while incarnate than this.

And let it be clearly known, that this is the one and only way in which a true Scarlet Woman is forged, according to Liber Legis.

Now this chapter should be read in conjunction with Chapter 5, *What is a Scarlet Woman*, as there are many important concepts to this process which will not be reviewed again here, that are explained there in detail. It is assumed that you have studied that chapter thoroughly, and understand the description, duties and demands of the Scarlet Woman completely before proceeding further.

The Blood Rites of Ra Hoor Khuit

By proceeding with these Rites, you will be undertaking an Initiation at the hands of the gods. You will become Ho Or, the Warrior Woman, who will be used as a sword in the hands of Ra Hoor Khuit. There is no turning back from this or turning away. Many may hate you for this, and jealously turn their back on you for your dedication. By aligning yourself with Him, you will be making great enemies of others. And if you betray Him, or betray Babalon in your heart or in your devotion, then you will receive the direful judgments of Ra Hoor Khuit. You will be burned up and consumed as a Living Cake of Light, and become a plaything for demons. You will be hollowed out and become a shell of who you once were, no longer with a Will of your own. And your previous destiny, that for which you incarnated, will be undone. You will become a vapid and empty slave, no longer capable of self-transformation, turning from addiction to addiction, influence to influence. You will become a Carapace.

And we have seen this happen. And it is worse than you can imagine. For it can not be undone.

Therefore, let only the most dedicated and most serious of women follow this path of the Warrior Woman, the Holy Ho Or. And let them do so with complete and holy dedication, with all of their soul and being. For it will require nothing less.

So when you feel - when you know - that you are ready to become in Spirit, so dedicated, then it is time for you to become a true Scarlet Woman. By doing so, your Spirit will be forever marked. This incarnation of yours will end some day, but your Spirit will not, and it will be marked with the symbol of the Grandmother, Nuit. It is the same symbol which is upon the hood of the Cobra, which is the symbol of Omega, reversed. It is also similar to the Horns of the Bull, which show the shape of the uterus, the Holy House of Divinity. And these symbols show the phases of the Moon, as it waxes and wanes - which reflect the power of the female body and its cycles. This is the Ophidian Mark upon the Spirit of the Scarlet Women, and it can never be removed.

To begin, wait until it is the second or third day of your Menses, and in the hour of Mars therein[54]. This is the best blood of the best blood. The first day of bleeding can contain too many impurities, and be too strong. Do not have sex with men from day one of menses, so there will be no sperm or any Fila to them during the Blood Rites. Next, prepare yourself for the Rite as shown in Chapter 16, *Preparing for the Rites*. Prepare your altar in the East to Ra Hoor Khuit as detailed in Chapter 13, *Altars and Shrine Decorations*. Stand before the altar, with the coals lit and burning hot in the censor. The Thelemic Abramelin Incense is there and ready to be used. The three candles upon the altar are lit and burning brightly. The room is dark. In a special, dedicated dish or vessel, place your blood. Have it ready upon the altar. Disrobe, and be naked before your Lord Ra Hoor Khuit, for you are coming to Him on your wedding night, and you desire him to take you completely and to have His way with you as he Will.

With every bit of your soul, with every bit of your essence, with every bit of the core of your being and your Will—inhale deeply and slowly exhale. Then call to Ra Hoor thus with the holy words of His Invocation, which he has given for this purpose.

>   *My lord initiating be O so present among us.*
>
>   *Thy feathered wings expanding tip to tip to cover the horizon.*
>
>   *Sing forth O Great Hawk-headed Lord for Thy call brings terror to the hearts of those that hear your battle cry.*
>
>   *And as Your tail flicks and Your shadow covers them in darkness, they will remember that Your fury is not yet known but only hinted at, as the shroud of the night star light surrounds them.*

---

[54] See Chapter 17, *Timing of the Rites*, and the section therein called *The Planetary Days and Hours* in order to determine the Hour of Mars on your particular day. Ra Hoor Khuit is a particularly martial deity as the God of War. Vengeance is of the Moon.

The Blood Rites of Ra Hoor Khuit

And once you have performed this invocation with all of your passion, it is time to open the Four Gates to the One Palace, and to offer yourself as a Sacrifice upon His altar. To Open the Four Gates, you perform the Adorations of Ra Hoor Khuit in all of the Four Elemental Quarters, using the Dawn, Noon, Evening, and Midnight version of Resh, in that order. In addition, use the sacred mudras (hand signs) which were given by Tum. See Chapter 33, *The Adorations of Ra Hoor Khuit* for this Rite.

Begin in the East, and perform the full version of the Adorations which start with Ra, as if it were morning. Then move to the South, and perform the full version of the Adorations which start with Hathor, as if it were noon. Then move to the West and do as before but to Tum, as if it were evening. And then finally move to the North and do as before but to Kephra, as if it were midnight. Once you have done all of this, you have made the way open. Now it is time to give your Blood Sacrifice to your Lord Ra Hoor Khuit

Go again before His Altar. Remember you are offering yourself as His Bride. He may take you. Be ready. He is very Powerful. He is All Virility. He is All Male. He is Magnificent. Take some of your blood, and mix it with the Abramelin incense. Place it upon the burning coal. And now it is time to tell Him what you offer. Make it personal. Make it sincere. Make it passionate. Close your eyes and open to Him, in all ways. You may have visions. You may see Him before you. You may feel His energy. You may feel His presence, and you may feel Him enter you sexually. This sort of sexual experience can overwhelm your body, your mind, and your emotions. It can be more intense than one can bear in the flesh.

> *I come before You, Mighty God, Ra Hoor Khuit,*
> *May I be worthy.*
> *I give to You my offering of my Best Blood*
> *May You bind me and use me in service*
> *I stand before You naked so that you may view me in clarity*
> *May my soul be shown to be pure*
> *I offer to You my Spirit in service for it is my divine Will to do this*
> *May I forever be Your bride*
> *I bring to You all of the qualities that I have in my nature*
> *May you have use for me in all that I offer*
> *I pledge my love, my lust, my very heart, soul and being to You*
> *May I forever be Your beloved*
> *I open to You so that You may take me as Your own*
> *May I be strong enough to bear Your essence*

Mystery Babalon

I lay upon the Earth for You, slain in my sacrifice of my soul to You
May You take me and keep me, O guardian
I give myself to You, Ra Hoor Khuit
May I be Yours in sacred trust.

When the ritual is completed, allow yourself to dwell within the energy created as long as you can. It may take time to process all that has taken place. Make sure to record everything that you did and then what occurred in your magickal diary.

If you did not feel any energy or have any obvious results do not despair. The act was still a success in that you did everything in earnest and true to your Will. Give it time. Do your Blood Rites every month, and in time you should have energetic results. If not, you may need to explore initiation in order to better hone your abilities in working with spirit.

The monthly Blood Rites are done to grow, strengthen and maintain your connection to Ra Hoor Khuit. They should be done on the second or third day of your menses if possible every single month (or how ever often you have menstruation.) Perform the same preparations and base ritual as above. The invocation that you do may change over time to reflect what you feel you wish to devote of yourself. You may also wish to seek guidance from Ra Hoor Khuit. After you perform your Blood Sacrifice, you may ask Ra Hoor Khuit for information, or protection if need be. As always, sit in the energy when the ritual is finished to give it a chance to manifest any visions or answers. Be patient with the energy. Sometimes it is very slow and takes some time to come in. And always record your results.

As we have already shown, the words *Scarlet Woman* equal the very important number 128. The Scarlet Woman is the Bride of Ra Hoor Khuit. *As my bride* equals 128 also. You are now a Scarlet Woman, the enemy of Mary Inviolate, who is to be *torn upon wheels* (128). Let all these women who betray the power of the female beware - those who seek to usurp us, or to thwart us, or to tell us we cannot take our fill of love as we Will. We are the Scarlet Women. And we are wicked, and adulterous, and shameless before all men. We are the Women of Will.

> *Let the Scarlet Woman beware! If pity and compassion and tenderness visit her heart; if she leave my work to toy with old sweetnesses; then shall my vengeance be known. I will slay me her child: I will alienate her heart: I will cast her out from men: as a shrinking and despised harlot shall she crawl through dusk wet streets, and die cold and an-hungered.*
>
> -Liber Legis III 43

The Blood Rites of Ra Hoor Khuit

This admonition is a warning from Ra Hoor Khuit, and as was said in the beginning, do not become a Scarlet Woman and then think you can change your mind. This is not an act of mind. This must be an act of Will. For Blood Oath, by Blood Rite, is forever binding. Ra Hoor Khuit is swift to defend his Allies, and as swift to destroy his enemies. The worst enemy of all is one who turns ones back on another—the betrayer. Do not betray your oath—this one, or any Magical Oath. Lest you be made a Carapace. Or worse.

> *But let her raise herself in pride! Let her follow me in my way! Let her work the work of wickedness! Let her kill her heart! Let her be loud and adulterous! Let her be covered with jewels, and rich garments, and let her be shameless before all men!*
>
> -Liber Legis III 44

Ra Hoor Khuit says, "Let her kill her heart." *Let her kill* also equals 128, the same as Scarlet Woman. Now when we kill our hearts, this does not mean that we no longer feel love, or compassion, or any of those things. No. What it means is that these things can no longer control us. We no longer are run around by emotional weakness, neediness, and longing. We learn to take control of our Waters, and our Hearts. The Heart is the part of us that is weighed when we die by Maat in the Underworld. This is the organ of judgment. If we live a life of pure Spirit and pure Will, then we live a righteous life. For *Righteous* also equals 128, and Ra Hoor Khuit is the Lord of Just Principles. And so, My Scarlet Sisters, when we live by the Law of Thelema; when we are Righteous in our Spirit and in our Will - when we Love, but Love Under Will - meaning that we use our Will to guide our Love, and do not let love run us around in our Persona, then we are Righteous. Then we are Scarlet Women. They will call you wicked for this, because you do not obey. Good. Work the work of *wickedness* (128) then. And now you see how Ra Hoor Khuit is already showing you the Way of the Scarlet Woman.

Go to Ra Hoor Khuit, every month. Stand naked before the most Mighty and Powerful of the Gods, with no shame, in all of your beauty. Stand there in all of your pride. Purify yourself, so that you possess no shame. You are beautiful. You are glorious. There is pride, and there is ego. We have no ego. Ego is the Persona, yelling about how it is everything. It is not. It is a servant. This is an act of Spirit. Let your Spirit grow in strength before our Lord. Let Him teach you to be the Warrior, Girt with a Sword. Let Him teach you to have Strength, and Purity. Become a Golden Warrior. And take lovers if you Will, and even many at the same time if it is your sovereign desire. Lust. Enjoy all things of sense and rapture. Adorn yourself in your Tribal Ways - bear the Flame of Ra within you. Become Golden. Stand in the Pride of your Divine Spirit. And now no one can therefore stop you in your Will. This *is* the reclamation of the Divine Feminine. *You* are a conduit of this Divinity, if only you can reclaim it within yourself.

Βαβαλον

Part V

The Ecstatic Rites of Babalon

XXXVII

The Balanced Ecstatic Path

We come now in this book to its heart, and to that which so many seek - the ecstatic bliss of experiential release, in the physical and in the spiritual, in union with Our Goddess Babalon. For it is true that when Her Presence is close, one's own lusts are awakened and one's own desires burn hotter. The goal then is to express the lusts and desires within Her Rites as an offering unto Her in order to grow Her power in this world. This act is a sacrificial act, for you will achieve orgiastic bliss in these Rites not for its own sake, which is short-lived and fleeting, but for a greater purpose. And the irony in this is that by dedicating your sensual bliss to something greater than yourself, you will in turn receive an experience which is not possible were you to pursue these carnal desires for their own sake.

And there is a method to the stoking of these fires, these carnal lusts and their satiation. It is a method which will help to curb obsessive impulses and demonic influence, which are the real dangers in this type of work. For the energy you will raise will be great indeed, and there are a great many creatures which seek to feed on such lusts, and to use them to grow their own power. These creatures will want more and more, which manifests as a feeling of obsession and compulsion around such carnal

The Balanced Ecstatic Path

pleasures which are expressed for the desires of the Persona only. Liber Legis makes this point very clearly, and admonishes the practitioner of "lust as worship" to a certain type of self control within the act itself.

> *Be not animal; refine thy rapture! If thou drink, drink by the eight and ninety rules of art: if thou love, exceed by delicacy; and if thou do aught joyous, let there be subtlety therein!*
>
> -Liber Legis I 70

This then is the method: to always be in control, and to practice such acts of love, under Will. Stoke your fires to ever higher heights, but do so with caution and care. And always pull your own reins back from time to time, to assure yourself that you are the one who is actually in control, and making the decisions. There must never be any self deceit as to why you are indulging your lusts, and who is the benefactor of these orgasmic moments. This orgasmic energy must be sacrificed unto a god, and that god is not you. This gift is yours to experience, but not yours to keep, and if you realize this and accept this, then the bliss will be a hundred times greater than you could normally manufacture for yourself. But first you must understand the difference between your Persona and your immortal and divine Spirit. For it is your Spirit which is beyond the limitations of the Persona, and beyond such definitions of right hand or left hand path when it comes to these Mysteries of Babalon. Indeed, She teaches of the Balanced Ecstatic Path, which is greater than both.

For quite a long time now, at least since the Areans conquered the known world, there has been a war of ideals between two different philosophies of life, and what it means to live well. This philosophical war has been carried over into the world of Heka, and has influenced the philosophies to be found there well. In Greek and Roman times these two warring schools were called the Stoics and the Epicureans. These two camps adhered to many different philosophies in many different times and places, by were generally divided into those who praised order, creationism of some sort, worship, and tradition, generally speaking, and those who acknowledge the supremacy of chaos, entropy and iconoclasm, self indulgence and rebellion. In esoteric schools of thought, these two factions became known as the Right Hand Path and the Left Hand Path.

Now it should be noted that for the last 4000-5000 years the rulers of the Right Hand Path have generally reigned supreme under the empires first of the Areans in the Aeon of Aires, and then under the Ichthyos in the Aeon of Pisces[55]. They have preached ideas of dogma, belief and obedience, to the people under penalty of torture of death. They have claimed the role of teachers and spiritual priests for themselves alone, and are always completely Patriarchal in their methods of politics, religion and morals. Because of their penchant for complete and totalitarian control of all others, those who do not comply with their ruler-ship are literally demonized in the eyes of the masses and extinguished from existence as a warning to all others to obey, lest the same fate should happen to them. In this way, all other philosophies and ways of thinking became taboo and outcast from the culture and history of humanity.

Its opposition was these other ways of thinking and living which were generally grouped under the moniker of Left Hand Path. Here we find all rebellion against the dogma and censorship of the empires of control which enslave humanity. Here we often find the opposite of what is Right Hand Path, in an effort to break free of the chains of control. If obeying a word and tradition of god is considered good, then those of the Left Hand Path will ally themselves with the adversary of that "good". If there are morals or rules which are not to be broken, then these rebels will break them just on principle alone, in order to exert their own freedom, or with the idea that something important which has been suppressed is hidden therein. And so the Left Hand Path has become a jumble of adversarial rebellion, taboo breaking, demonology and self-worship in reaction to the powers which seek to control them.

But there is a problem with reactionary thought and actions by an oppressed people, in that the oppressor is still controlling your thoughts and actions. You are doing those things, enacting those rebellions, because of the oppressor. These are not things you would normally have done if left to your own devices, living in a natural way, unmolested by an oppressor. And herein is the problem of the Left Hand Path, and its inherent reactionary state: you eventually become that which you hate, and are in the end still controlled by it. There is no autonomy and spiritual

---

[55] The Areans were best exemplified in the war-loving empires of Greece and Rome. The Pisceans, also called the Ichthyos (eeek-tohs), are best known by the coercive and manipulative empires of the Monotheists, namely the Jews, Christians and Muslims who combine the war-like nature of the Areans with religious manipulation of guilt and shame to achieve total control of the people for their own ends.

The Balanced Ecstatic Path

freedom in that place, merely being the adversary of that which you hate, and reacting against it.

Yet rebellion and war against one's oppressor is also the only path to freedom, when one is being violently or spiritually restricted. And some have been fighting for their personal and individual freedom for so long that it becomes their way of being, even though in reality they generally have gained some autonomy in their existence. And out of these new behavioral patterns of endless rebellion entire new philosophical and spiritual movements have been created in these times, which seem to have turned all things upon their heads. This complete and total iconoclasm is an Aeonic problem of Aquarius, and is currently happening in all areas of life, not just in the world of the Esoteric.

We know that the Right Hand Path is the way of an old and oppressive age, a way of slavery and self-denial. And we know that the Left Hand Path is a Manichean reaction to this restriction of the self, in the form of self-indulgence and rejection of all morals. But these two paths are not one's only options. There is a very ancient Pagan way, and that is a way from before there was a word "Pagan" and we were just indigenous people, long before agriculture and civilization and all this mess which comes with it. And this way is part of the Reclamation of the Goddess Babalon at this time in history, and part of the reason why this book exists. And this way is called the Balanced Ecstatic Path.

Come forth, o children, under the stars, & take your fill of love!

I am above you and in you. My ecstasy is in yours. My joy is to see your joy.

-Liber Legis I 12-13

We are commanded by the Grandmother, the mother of all Mothers and the Mother of All Things Herself, to take our fill of love. And this is because we are Her children, and the spirit of life which She births into the universe is the same which flows through our bodies and animates us. There is no denial of our animal selves here. And there is no restriction of one's Spirit and its full expression in this world. The animal desires of the flesh and the spiritual will of the incarnation are to be harmonized and made to serve each other.

Mystery Babalon

...Be goodly therefore: dress ye all in fine apparel; eat rich foods and drink sweet wines and wines that foam! Also, take your fill and will of love as ye will, when, where and with whom ye will! But always unto me.

-Liber Legis I 51

This harmonization and balancing together of the lusts of the animal and the Will of the Spirit is the new "good" proclaimed here for this new Aeon. This is the new art of living well, which has been repressed for over 4000 years by the Areans and the Ichthyos who came after them. But this new way, this Balanced Ecstatic Path is not new at all. It is the ancient female way of the Goddess cultures from the time before the Areans, which is why it is Nuit who teaches the people of these ways again.

Invoke me under my stars! Love is the law, love under will. Nor let the fools mistake love; for there are love and love. There is the dove, and there is the serpent. Choose ye well! He, my prophet, hath chosen, knowing the law of the fortress, and the great mystery of the House of God.

-Liber Legis I 57

Nuit makes it very clear, however, that while these animal desires and lusts are not to be denied or repressed, they are to be harnessed to a greater purpose, that of your Will. These lusts are not to be indulged simply for their own transient rewards in the flesh, but rather they are to be put to a greater use and used to power a greater purpose. There are many ways to interpret the Dove and the Serpent mentioned above, but for our purposes here the Dove is the symbol of the Holy Spirit of God and the slavery which it fosters upon the people, while the Serpent is our friend from the Garden of Eden, the wise Ophidian one who is the Spirit which liberates one from the shackles of oppression[56]. Later in Chapter 2, the fiery winged serpent, a true Ophidian, reinforces these proclamations.

---

[56] There is also the problem of Crowley's interpretation of the Dove in his Spermo-Gnosticism and its use symbolically in the Gnostic Mass and pragmatically in his version of "sex magick", where Crowley views the woman as an "empty vessel to be filled with the Holy Ghost". This version of the Dove descending into the Cup, which appears upon the seal of the organization which enshrines these practices, is certainly an extreme misinterpretation of this, and other, verses. "He, my prophet, hath chosen, knowing the law of the fortress, and the great mystery of the House of God." Yes, it says Crowley has

The Balanced Ecstatic Path

... Be strong, o man! lust, enjoy all things of sense and rapture: fear not that any God shall deny thee for this.

-Liber Legis II 22

It is the Serpent, the Ophidian One, who teaches of the immanent sensuality of the Sprit which incarnates in flesh. As the spirit rises on wings, these canal desires become enflamed and serve to fuel the Union of Hadit back to Nuit, of the Persona to the Spirit, and of Love to Will.

But to love me is better than all things: if under the night-stars in the desert thou presently burnest mine incense before me, invoking me with a pure heart, and the Serpent flame therein, thou shalt come a little to lie in my bosom. For one kiss wilt thou then be willing to give all...

-Liber Legis I 61

The Serpent Flame is the burning of desire within the flesh, which is accompanied by a Pure Heart, which is the true desire for Union with something greater than oneself, greater than one's Persona. This, then, is our journey to the embrace of the Serpent. We are Ophidian. We shall be as the egg, with the Serpent coiled around us. We shall learn the Via Babalonis: the way of union with the divine. We shall, if willing to give all, and hold none of the pleasure back for our Personas, know the greatest bliss possible.

The Balanced Ecstatic Path is the line upon which the Fool walks. It is the refinement of Persona in service of Spirit. It is the joining of our senses, our selves, all that we are with all that we seek.

Aye! feast! rejoice! there is no dread hereafter. There is the dissolution, and eternal ecstasy in the kisses of Nu.

There is death for the dogs.

-Liber Legis II 44-45

---

chosen, but it does not say that Crowley has chosen well.

Mystery Babalon

The "dissolution and eternal ecstasy in the kisses of Nu" is an image of the Underworld. This is the state of bliss which the Spirit feels at the moment of release at death, when it is freed from the restriction of the flesh. And this is also an orgasmic bliss which is unbearable in the flesh, and destroys the Persona utterly at death. That is why the orgasm is called the "Little Death", because it foreshadows that which happens at death, and what lies beyond that transition in the underworld. And this is the power hidden in sex, the power of the transformation of death itself.

This is what the Balanced Ecstatic Path teaches. These are the ancient female ways, the Mysteries of the Underworld, which are the Rites of Sex and Death. This is the Liberation which Babalon emanates in Her Mysteries, and why She is called the Great Liberating Mother. The Underworld is Her Domain. To embrace bliss, to embrace the ecstatic and to know true freedom, one must also embrace death, and the end of the Persona. Let us now return to Chapter II, verse 70, and those fateful words with which we began this explanation of the Balanced Ecstatic Path.

> *There is help & hope in other spells. Wisdom says: be strong! Then canst thou bear more joy. Be not animal; refine thy rapture! If thou drink, drink by the eight and ninety rules of art: if thou love, exceed by delicacy; and if thou do aught joyous, let there be subtlety therein!*
>
> *But exceed! exceed!*
>
> *Strive ever to more! and if thou art truly mine -- and doubt it not, an if thou art ever joyous! -- death is the crown of all.*
>
> *Ah! Ah! Death! Death! thou shalt long for death. Death is forbidden, o man, unto thee.*
>
> *The length of thy longing shall be the strength of its glory. He that lives long & desires death much is ever the King among the Kings.*
>
> -Liber Legis II 70-74

The fears which lead the Right Hand Path to acts of tyranny ultimately stem from the fear of death within the Persona, and therefore also the repression of sex. Because sex and death are twins, inseparable. Much of the superstitions and religions of humanity are based upon this

The Balanced Ecstatic Path

fear of death, and mankind's search for immortality of one sort or another. Much of the philosophy of the Left Hand Path is based around a rejection of the otherworldly yearnings of immortality found in the Right Hand Path. In doing so they posit an atheistic acceptance and indulgence in the satiation of the senses of the body for its own sake, since it seems to them that there is no other point in life which they can find. Or these people proclaim themselves to be a living god, imagining that in doing so they will make their persona immortal and escape death's grasp in some grand fantasy of the mind. All of these ways can be seen as a reaction to death, and therefore death is still their master. But there is another way. This way is an ancient way of understanding these Mysteries of the Underworld, and that which takes place therein at the death of the flesh. To begin this path, one must wholly and completely, on a daily basis, embrace ones own mortality and death, in service of something greater than oneself. And so let us hear the Sistrums of Bast rattling in the ecstatic rhythm of the Spirit, as Babalon teaches of these ways, the sensual ways of overcoming the limitations of fear, and the Mysteries of Sex and Death.

These sensual ways of harmonizing the flesh and the Spirit have been lost in the West over the course of 4000 years by forced extermination and repression. In the last 2000 years the Great Liberating Mother and Her Incarnations are completely missing in the West. To find Her you must go East. One must go to the various schools of the Tantras in India and Tibet wherein, over the last 1500 years, these ways of the Balanced Ecstatic Path have blossomed and grown, under different terms and names. There you will find the missing incarnations of Babalon in many Goddesses and traditions, especially in that of Kali and the Mahavidyas, which are the ten major Tantric Goddesses. These Goddesses all have much to teach about the mysteries of Sex and Death and the Mysteries of the Underworld. And one of the Mahavidyas in particular shows very clearly these mysteries in the Ecstatic Rites which follow, and that is Chinnamastā, "She whose head is severed".

We have shown images of Chinnamastā early in Chapter 11 in the section *On Sacrifice, Human Sacrifice, and the Living Flame* and again here at the beginning of the section on Ecstatic Mysteries because She so elegantly typifies the proper attitude for the Persona when engaging in the carnal desires of the flesh for spiritual purposes. Without getting too technical, Chinnamasta dances on top of Rati (sexual desire) and Kamadev (love). She has severed Her own head, and from the streams of blood issuing forth she feeds Herself, as well as Jaya (victory) and Vijaya (triumph). This blood contains the wisdom of self control in the midst of indescribable bliss, which is shown by Her dancing atop a copulating couple. The heads of the couples are like skulls, more of which are in a chain around Her neck, showing the connection between sex and death in this undertaking, and knowledge of the source of such tremendous bliss.

Chinnamasta is an excellent image of what one should strive for in their Persona when perusing the Ecstatic Rites of Babalon. One could spend a lifetime studying the writings of the Tantras, and learn much of great importance to our purposes here - but there is not room for such an undertaking in this book. And this book is meant to bring the Tantrikas, the Scarlet Priestesses of the East, back to the West - to our own traditions and cultures which will mirror and complement those wonderful cultures of the East, but with a focus here upon one's individuality and unique Will.

So as you practice these Rites and begin to experience your own purpose and bliss remember the admonitions of Nuit. Remember the image of Chinnamasta. Remember why you are using your flesh to find your Spirit and to worship Babalon. For just as a plant does not measure the amount of sunlight it takes from the Sun, but freely and happily consumes all it needs to grow and blossom in the body of Gaia, so too be as such for Babalon. During all Rites endeavor to build your Fire to feed Her Fire, in your Shrine and upon this planet. Do not measure how much you give, or how much you keep, or worry about such things. Only thereby can you fail. The more Fire you raise and pass through to Her, the more your capacity for it will grow, and the more you will experience in the process. Nothing beyond the Spirit is to have or hold forever. All is to be experienced in the moment. To have, to keep, and to make static is the way of the Persona and the way of animal fear. To flow with, to change, to build and to Liberate is the way of the Spirit. Flow and change freely, embracing what your flesh desires by love and union, under the auspices of the Will of your Spirit.

The Balanced Ecstatic Path then is one great step in the Reclamation of the Great Liberating Mother named Babalon. It is neither fearful denial nor blind indulgence. Let the Serpent excite you. Let it call to you in all of its glory. Let your Lust be your eyesight. Let your rapture by your glory. And let Death be the Crown of All.

In Nomine Babalon et Vox Sanctae Meretricis

XXXVIII

Preparations for the Union

he first step down the Ecstatic Path is one of awakening. This is an awakening of Spirit within the flesh, and can be practiced for as long or as short a time as one feels that it is needed. Some people spend years devoting themselves to this exploration. Others may choose to spend a few days. It can also serve as an excellent reminder from time to time of the role of flesh in service of the Spirit. And of course, maintaining this perspective can help lead one to the higher arts of Spirit such as Heka, which in the Egyptian language is the calling down (He) of the fiery elements of Spirit (Ka).

It is essential to begin this path with attention to the senses of your physical being and existence. One must learn to experience one's own body as an instrument of one's own Spirit. Therefore, a new relationship with the body must be cultivated[57]. The following exercise

---

[57] There is not room in this book to go into every detail of Natura, and the element of good care with the body and natural living, especially in a world full of negative and debilitating influences of poisons, addictions, toxins, electromagnetic pollution, GMOs, plastic and soy endocrine disrupters, fluoride, and many, many other problems which our ancestors never had to deal with. Endeavor to rid these things from your life, despite the temptation of normalcy and convenience, and you will see an increase in your ability to feel and perceive Heka within the body.

Preparations for the Union

helps in this regard. It can be practiced as often as you like, and it may be helpful to do parts of this exercise before some of the Ecstatic Rites, in order to put your mind and body into the proper sensual attitude. This exercise attempts to help you see your body as separate from your awareness of it, as if you are young and discovering it for the first time, integrating it into your complete being in a holistic and sensual manner.

The Awakening:

Tomorrow morning when you wake up and open your eyes, regard your body as if you are seeing it for the very first time. Imagine that during the night, your Spirit incarnated into your body, and when you woke up from sleeping, you found yourself enthroned in flesh.

"What is this," you might ask yourself, in wonderment. Begin by examining what the flesh is. What does it feel like from the inside of your being? What does it feel like when you touch it with your fingers? Look at your hand, as if it was a glove, and your spirit was inside wiggling the fingers. Celebrate these things.

Examine your eyes — what it is to look with them. Open and close them — what is darkness? What is light? What is this solidity — this Material Realm all about? What are colors? What are shapes? Look at your body. See it for the first time. Celebrate these things.

Notice your ears — what is sound? Is it disruptive to your inner voice? Is it pleasurable? Is it jarring? Try out your voice for the first time. What is that? What is it making? Try making different sounds — loud, quiet. Try singing. Wow. What was that? Celebrate these things.

Notice your nose — and smell everything around you. What does your skin smell like? What about your pillow? Your room? Smell the objects around your room. Celebrate these things.

When you make it out of your room, smell around until you find something that makes your mouth salivate. What is that? Try it. What is taste? Does it make you want more? Or less. Search for things that make your tongue dance with pleasure. Try to chew. Try to swallow. What are those sensations? What is hunger? What is satiation? Celebrate these things.

Use this dawning awareness for everything that you do in your day. Everything you do is being done for the first time in this body, by this Spirit. What is the shower? What is water? How does that feel? If you find sensual experiences, revel in them. Explore them. Feel the water caress your skin. Let it merge with your energy.

If you should find yourself sexually aroused during the day, explore that, too. What do those feelings tell you? How does it increase when you touch certain places on your body? Follow the feelings and let them lead you where they will.

These are ways to awaken your Earth, for you to begin to use your Earth everyday, in service of your Spirit in a sensual manner.

Next expand your awareness to your Waters—these are your feelings, and your emotions. Treat these as if this is the first time that you felt them. If you do something that makes you have an emotion, stop and look at it. What is that? What made that happen? Do I like that? Why? Why not? Can I make more of it if I like it? Can I make it stop? Why? Why not? What are these feelings trying to tell or show me? How do I learn this language of the emotions?

This will naturally lead you into the Air of your being—what are these "thoughts?" Where do they come from, and whose voice is making them? What can I do with this? What kind of tool is this thing for my Spirit to use in this body? How does this place of Air serve me, the Spirit, as I move around this Realm of The Manifest?

And as you become acquainted with these three aspects of your Manifest Existence, you will find that the more you become united in your Spirit's perspective, the more you begin to realize the Fire that is connected to your Spirit. These are the questions you will then ask: Why did I come here? Why am I in my body? What are these desires I feel. What are these urges which move me? What is my purpose for entering this Realm? What is my Will?

This is the Pentacle of the Persona. This is your First Awakening.

Preparations for the Union

The Exorcism of the Waters and the Fires

Now this previous exercise is important in order to recalibrate your Waters and your Fires away from the old ways of your normal everyday reactive and unconscious behaviors, and to start to bring them under the control of your Spirit, through the guidance of your Persona. And this will become important, for the Ecstatic Rites of Babalon will make you feel many emotions, and give you many desires, and many of these will cause potential problems in the Persona for those who have not experienced such things before.

> *... But there are means and means. Be goodly therefore: dress ye all in fine apparel; eat rich foods and drink sweet wines and wines that foam! Also, take your fill and will of love as ye will, when, where and with whom ye will! But always unto me.*
>
> *If this be not aright; if ye confound the space-marks, saying: They are one; or saying, They are many; if the ritual be not ever unto me: then expect the direful judgments of Ra Hoor Khuit!*
>
> *This shall regenerate the world, the little world my sister, my heart & my tongue, unto whom I send this kiss. Also, o scribe and prophet, though thou be of the princes, it shall not assuage thee nor absolve thee. But ecstasy be thine and joy of earth: ever To me! To me!*
>
> -Liber Legis I 51-53

It is inevitable that all of your past pains and sorrows will come to visit you again, each in their own ways at various points in the Rites for you. Some will experience jealousy, loneliness, anger, fear, misery, hatred and a myriad of other emotions at some point or another. Others will be driven by urges and fetishes which they do not understand, and which may make them feel uncomfortable. All of this is normal. In fact, despite what it may feel like at the time, all of this is intentional, and this is a good thing. You must be liberated from that which keeps you from your destiny, which is the accomplishment of the Will of your Spirit. And these Rites will bring these impediments out in you, whether you like it or not.

It is important in these moments to remember the purpose of why you are in the Shrine, and that you are dedicated to Babalon. All of these potential negative emotions and urges stem not from your Spirit, but from your Persona and its traumas and fears. Remember that, especially in these moments. Understand that your jealousy, for example, which you are feeling in the Rites actually comes from something that happened to you before, and is now keeping you from your bliss. These things are not really happening now, yet here you are reliving the suffering of them again. They are ghosts, haunting you from the past.

You have an opportunity to self-transcend, and to correct the wrongs of the past which sit like heavy black stones deep within the Persona, keeping you from being who you were born to be. Remember that there is no shame here. The only shame is in turning away from these things which arise, and seeking to repress them again.

Self-honesty is difficult for everyone, as it involves a type of pain which is very coercive and rarely understood. And that pain is of the Waters, and the deep emotional suffering which many seek to avoid even worse than physical pain. This avoidance is mental, as well as emotional, and so it can be very difficult to realize in oneself what your reactions to situations mean, and why they are happening. Why am I suddenly feeling anger in the Rites? Or jealousy? Or extreme loneliness? These things will happen to everyone at some point, so it is important when they do happen in the Rites or afterwards, to realize that these are messages from your Waters, and not meant to be acted upon in your normal, reactionary way. This is an opportunity for self-realization and self-transcendence. And in these moments are found the steps to true Illumination, and the building blocks of which enlightened Self Mastery is made.

The "direful judgments of Ra Hoor Khuit" mentioned above are the punishments of anger and regret for those who fail in these matters of the Waters and the Fires within your Persona. The pain and suffering is real, yet the choice in how to react to it is yours. It exists within you because you allow it to in these moments. You are master of your own boat, and it is time you steer it to the destiny of your own making, unfettered by the wounds of your past.

Therefore, when these moments arise, it is important to stop everything you are doing in the Rites, and to go to Babalon's altar. There, come before your Goddess, and express completely your Waters or your Fires as best as you are able. If you are angry, express that as completely as possible without being destructive to Her altar or those around you. But express it. Yell. Scream. Cry. Whatever it is you need. Understand where it comes from. Understand why you feel this way. And then, after your cathartic expression of it with all of your being, understand that it is time to forge new behaviors within your Persona, and let it go. Cleanse

Preparations for the Union

your Waters and clear your Fires at Her altar, before your Goddess. This is Her gift to you. Succumb to Her completely in these moments, and realize the opportunity for release of a thing which has long plagued you, and kept you from the full realization of your bliss in life. Call out to Her as your Goddess, and explain out loud to Her, and to all that may be present, about this thing which has exposed itself within you. Do not be ashamed. Bring it out into the open for all to see, so that it can never control you from the shadows of your being again. This is self-honesty. After describing it or expressing it completely to Her, then release it to Her as an offering with the following words.

> *O Great and mighty Babalon, Mother of Harlots and Abominations of the Earth!*
> *You who accepts all and refuses none!*
> *It is I (chosen name), and I come before you today.*
> *I offer up to you that which keeps me from my Spirit.*
> *I offer up this thing which I was not born with.*
> *I offer up that which is my abomination upon the Earth.*
> *May it plague me no more.*
> *May I walk free of it in the future,* **and** *in the past.*
> *I serve you with my love and devotion, Mighty Babalon!*
> *May you Liberate me from my Abomination, which I lay before you in sacrifice on this day.*
>
> *In Nomine Babalon et Vox Sanctae Meretricis.*

Now anoint and purify yourself with the Water from Her Chalice and perfume and consecrate yourself with the smoke from the Fire from Her Censer. Take what time you need before Her altar, or in a private place, or with your brothers and sisters in the Rites, or in whatever way is necessary for you at that time. You are a new person now, with a new future. Your old self has died, liberated in death by Babalon.

XXXIX

The Rite of Sappho

The Rite of Sappho is an intimate solo female Rite to be performed by a woman in sexual adoration of her goddess Babalon. Also called the Baths of Sappho, one comes humbly to Babalon as a Devotee and lover, ready to be used by Her as She wills. This union is woman to goddess, and there will be no male energy here. In the Baths of Sappho, you may freely express all of your femininity in an open and uninhibited way. It is here that we may, as women, be all that is the sensual of the Divine Feminine. Not for anyone else, but for ourselves. When we touch ourselves and arouse ourselves, it is with the knowledge that our bodies are the iterations of all that is female spirit. This we feel. This we know. It is here that we explore all that is sensation; all that is desire; all that is the deepest colors of divine female lust.

What is it to be female? What does that really mean? It is very easy in these fragmenting times to lose that sense of feminine. Feeling feminine has almost become a stigma in itself. But not here. Not in the secret Baths of Sappho. For Babalon is the Great Liberating Mother. And She is a Warrior. And She is the Goddess of Sex and Death. So we shall explore this in sensual union with Her as lover and mentor.

The Rite of Sappho

There are endless books written about women's bodies, their sexualities, their sense of selves. You have been shaped by endless movies, pictures and books about what you should be, what you should feel, and how you should experience it. Let us put all of that aside, and here begin to explore for ourselves our own sexuality in union with Babalon.

This Rite is to be performed alone. You are to be naked and completely vulnerable to your Goddess Babalon. You are to come before Her yearning for Union with Her, offering yourself and your body up to Her in a sensual sacrifice. Prepare a bath for the Rites, in Her honor. Let your desires and yearnings fill you as you run the water. Touch everything as you do so in a sensual manner, as if anything and everything there might be used in a sensual manner upon your body, if need be. All things may be used in sensual service to Her, if they are so chosen in the moment of worship and it feels right to do so. Add some aromatic and sensual herbs like Rose Petals or lavender to the bath. Perhaps some favorite oils, and maybe even milk and honey as in the ancient ways for a very special sensual experience. Also place candles around the bath, burn some Thelemic Abramelin Incense, and turn off the lights.

When the bath is prepared, slip into the warm water and let yourself become calm and centered. Feel the lushness of the watery sensations upon your naked flesh. When you are ready to proceed, call out to Babalon with the following invocation.

I call to thee, O Great Goddess, Lady of the Waters and the Fires!

My desire moves like a serpent through the Waters at your approach.
My Fires raise like the heat of deepest summer at your approach.

Wet I am , open and yearning, awaiting your presence.
Warm I am, desirous and craving union in service to you.

Come mighty Babalon, whom no one can resist!
 You are the sweet waters, dripping down upon my fevered brow.
 You are the sweet perfumes which anoint my yearning flesh.
I whisper my yearnings to you, O Great Goddess of passion and inspiration!

I cry out to you so that I might know the touch of all that is my Fire!
 Let me feel you burn through me,
 Let me burn with your Fire within and without,
So that I might succumb to all that is Your Bliss,

and with the passion of my body offer myself up to you, completely.

In Nomine Babalon et Vox Sanctae Meretricis

After saying this invocation, meditate upon Her and invite Her into your bath, and into the water around you. Follow the energies which manifest upon your wet naked flesh with your own hands. Touch your body in answer to the energy, as if the energy were guiding your fingers across its landscape. Explore every part of you body which cries out for attention. At each sensual touch, let your excitement and pleasure build. Do not be afraid to call out to Her occasionally at the moment of intense sensations, as if She is the one touching you, and you are responding to the ecstasy which She has given to you as a gift. Use whatever items which appeal to you upon your body to increase your sensations and lust. See Her in everything which touches your body, caresses your breasts and penetrates your vulva. Experience all that is sensation., as a gift from Her presence, and immerse yourself within it.

In good time let yourself reach to the ultimate climax in your orgasm, singular or many, crying out in complete submission and union with Her as you do so. Make sure that all which you experience and receive is given back to Her in reciprocation and in thanks. Become a Living Flame, a sacrifice of human sensuality in Her service.

As soon as you have finished your orgasms, say the following devotion to Babalon, giving your thanks to your Goddess for your experiences with Her. You may also take your sexual fluids and anoint the candle burning in Her name as you do this, or upon sacred items from Her altar which you have brought with you to the Rite, so that they become sanctified in Her name[58].

O Great Liberating Mother of the ecstasy which waits in the deepest depths and darkest silence, I give to you my gratitude, and I give you my service, for you are that which guides me to my greatest Passions.

In Nomine Babalon et Vox Sanctae Meretricis

---

[58] Do not ever leave any sexual fluids or blood lying about after practicing Ecstatic Rites. These can attract unwanted Spirits and bring imbalance to your Sacred Space. All sexual fluids which are not dedicated upon the altar or upon sacred relics designated for that purpose should be either burned, or buried within the Body of Gaia (the Earth) in a ritual manner.

THE RITE OF SAPPHO

Meditate upon this Rite and celebrate your love with your Goddess. Record any results, thoughts, feelings, occurrences within your Magickal Diary.

God Pan by Nuria Fortuny Art

XL

The Rite of Pan

As the Sun burns with His Force and Fire before all, so too shall man burn with his desire, his passion, his lust—for Babalon. For a male devoted to Babalon knows that as the Goddess of Sex and Death, She shall accept all and refuse none that is offered to Her. All will be used in their own way, according to what they have to offer.

A virile and strong man is an incredible storehouse of energy[59]. He exists to exercise that energy, to use it. And his strong body is designed to manufacture more. He is a machine that creates ever more and more, to give out to others and to be used. For just as the Sun seems to be born each day, rising tall to its fullest expression, and then setting and disappearing at night, so to is it for man. Whenever he seems depleted, spent, and used up after giving all of himself in coitus and worship, he must rest a while and recuperate a small amount of time in order for his Sun to rise again. Yet it will rise again, over and over, for such are the ways of the male sexuality.

---

[59] To this end, one should review again *Chapter 7, Becoming the Beast* in order to understand that role within the Mysteries of Babalon.

The Rite of Pan

Beauty and strength, leaping laughter and delicious languor, force and fire, are of us.

-Liber Legis II 20

As we have said before in Chapter 7, the male and his cock together is the force, which must be used to feed the fire of others. It is a tool of service, and like the male himself, will die upon completion of his work.

We have nothing with the outcast and the unfit: let them die in their misery. For they feel not. Compassion is the vice of kings: stamp down the wretched & the weak: this is the law of the strong: this is our law and the joy of the world. Think not, o king, upon that lie: That Thou Must Die: verily thou shalt not die, but live. Now let it be understood: If the body of the King dissolve, he shall remain in pure ecstasy for ever. Nuit! Hadit! Ra-Hoor-Khuit! The Sun, Strength & Sight, Light; these are for the servants of the Star & the Snake.

I am the Snake that giveth Knowledge & Delight and bright glory, and stir the hearts of men with drunkenness. To worship me take wine and strange drugs whereof I will tell my prophet, & be drunk thereof! They shall not harm ye at all. It is a lie, this folly against self. The exposure of innocence is a lie. Be strong, o man! lust, enjoy all things of sense and rapture: fear not that any God shall deny thee for this.

-Liber Legis II 21-22

The Ecstatic Rites are the Rites of the Serpent. They are Ophidian. Let us then charm the snakes, and make them rise. And let us never forget that this ecstasy which is generated is for Babalon, and She is the deepest, wettest Water to the Sun's hottest Fire.

There is a strength and vitality generated from the passions and lusts of a man that are unequaled. If one learns to channel this energy, one can apply it in fortuitous ways. And here, in the Halls of Pan, we challenge the men to come forth for Babalon, and to offer up all that is your sexual force and power unto Her. If you do so, She will take you, She will ride you and She will use you for all that you offer Her. And it is in this way that you may, if it be your Will, come to know Her through the service first of your cock, and finally of your very being and incarnation.

Mystery Babalon

It is important to learn to swell your essence, to build your vitality and your desire, which are the two things you give of Sacrifice to Babalon. Every man has his own ways in which this can be accomplished naturally, and it may be fitting to explore new ways as well. But you must find your own way in which to increase the vital power of your physical sexuality, without spending it too often or waiting too long to do so. There is a balancing act here that each male must find for themselves, within the rhythms of their own body. This process of the sacrifice of the vital life essence of the male unto Babalon is alluded to often in Liber Legis. It is used as a symbol of double-meaning, the first of which describes the proper attitude and sexual use of a man and his cock, while the second describes the same process applied to one's entire lifetime in such service, as a living flame of sacrifice.

> *Write, & find ecstasy in writing! Work, & be our bed in working! Thrill with the joy of life & death! Ah! thy death shall be lovely: whoso seeth it shall be glad. Thy death shall be the seal of the promise of our agelong love. Come! lift up thine heart & rejoice! We are one; we are none.*
>
> *Hold! Hold! Bear up in thy rapture; fall not in swoon of the excellent kisses!*
>
> *Harder! Hold up thyself! Lift thine head! breathe not so deep -- die!*
>
> *Ah! Ah! What do I feel? Is the word exhausted?*
>
> *There is help & hope in other spells. Wisdom says: be strong! Then canst thou bear more joy. Be not animal; refine thy rapture! If thou drink, drink by the eight and ninety rules of art: if thou love, exceed by delicacy; and if thou do aught joyous, let there be subtlety therein!*
>
> *But exceed! exceed!*
>
> *Strive ever to more! and if thou art truly mine -- and doubt it not, an if thou art ever joyous! -- death is the crown of all.*
>
> *Ah! Ah! Death! Death! thou shalt long for death. Death is forbidden, o man, unto thee.*

The Rite of Pan

The length of thy longing shall be the strength of its glory. He that lives long & desires death much is ever the King among the Kings.

-Liber Legis II 66-74

There are some important considerations to keep in mind concerning the philosophy of power, and its connection to vitality. And there are volumes upon volumes written about ways for men to supposedly increase their own "power". This practice that I am writing about is not to increase your power, but rather your vitality[60]. It is about giving of this vitality to Babalon. One is not taking here. One is generating, growing and giving. This is the beginning of a devotional path. And so, if a man wishes to know Babalon directly, it is through his devotion and his service that She will take notice, and potentially answer. For those who seek power for themselves are ubiquitous and quite useless. But those who truly offer themselves in service are exceeding rare, and are the Kings here spoken of above in Liber Legis, whether or not they be male or female.

There are a myriad of ways in which Babalon or Her servants and allies may attempt to speak to those incarnate. To most people, She may come to you in dreams. She may call your attention to Her through that which you find attractive in the female form—causing you to notice the hair of one woman, the smile of another. She may put things in front of you in your life which you never noticed before. These things are ribbons which can lead you closer to Her, if you allow them to catch your attention. Follow them, but do not attempt to take control of them. This is the path of Love under Will. Let yourself be seduced. Let Her whisper to you in the breeze. Let her catch your eye through the reflection of light upon the water, which sends a ripple through your core and a tingling in your cock.

This Rite of Pan gives the male an opportunity for sexual worship of Babalon in a solo manner, through masturbation. You will come before Her altar clean and prepared in a single robe. Lay out a towel of other such cloth which can later be washed upon Her altar to catch your offering later in this Rite. Light Her candles saying "In Nomine Babalon" and also light the charcoal and apply some Thelemic Abramelin Incense as an

---

[60] The philosophical implications of the differences to be found in comparing vitality to power are too much to go into in this small space, other than to say that vitality is what is generated and maintained within the body which is possessed and maintained by one's living Spirit. And it is this Spirit which holds the power of life, not the incarnated individual.

offering unto Her. Take the Abramelin Oil and anoint your Third Eye at your forehead saying "In Nomine Babalon," and then the area right above your cock where it joins your body saying "et Vox Sanctae Meretricis." Now disrobe and raise your cock in offering unto Her, getting it hard and straight. Once this is accomplished, keep it that way sticking out straight, near or upon Her altar, while saying the following invocation unto Her.

I, [your chosen name], come before you, O Great Babalon!
I come to you burning with the Fires of my Passions,
     My lust swelling within me,
     My force ready to serve Your Fires!
And even as the Fires of your Father burn
     And shed His Massive heat upon us all
So to must I pour forth my fire for You, O, Mighty Babalon!
It is you who inspires me with the greatest longing,
It is you who liberates with a bliss unimaginable.
Take from me, O Babalon! All of my essence is offered up to you,
And here is the long straight truth of my devotion standing tall for you to
     see.
In Nomine Babalon, I give myself to you.

Proceed then with the masturbation. See and imagine all things in woman which you find most appealing and beautiful. See and feel them upon you in all of the ways you desire them most. See Her in all of the faces which you have ever been attracted to in your lifetime, changing from one face and body to the next, as you thrust and serve them all with your pulsing cock. And when you approach orgasm, return your focus directly to the Great Liberating Mother Herself. As you climax, pour out with all of your essence, by your Will. Cry out with the words "In Nomine Babalon" as you ejaculate every last drop of your being and life force upon Her Altar and to Her. Leave nothing back for yourself. All must go to Her in complete devotion, lest there be failure and abomination created within your Persona. This is very important.

    Now let yourself fall down in worship at Her altar, succumbing to the deep blackness of Her universal cosmic vulva. Let yourself collapse within Her, in your mind and body, and rest there for a while within the womb of the Divine Feminine. When you begin to recover, you may arise and gather yourself. Fold up the towel or cloth which has caught the offering of your essence and leave it upon Her altar for not more than an

The Rite of Pan

hour or two at the most[61]. Record any visions or experiences in your diaries, and extinguish the candles upon Her altar.

---

[61] After this do a preliminary washing by hand of this cloth with soap and water, saying "In Nomine Babalon" as the water takes away what is left of the offering. The cloth may then be washed again as usual with the rest of your garment.

XLI

The Rite of the Twin Flame

he Rite of the Twin Flame is an ecstatic version of the Rite of Convocation from Chapter 32. It is a sexual Rite for couples to perform in private worship of Babalon, using their bodies and their sexuality. There are fewer invocations in this ecstatic version of the Rite, as the participants are expected to use their bodies intermingling, and their sexuality as the invocation to Babalon.

It is important that the couple work together as a team to raise the energy between them as an offering to Babalon. Keeping deep eye contact with each other and synchronized breathing of each other's breath, where one breaths in the others exhalation, and then the reverse, will help the energy to come in strongly. This Rite is written for a female and a male, but can be adapted by any couple of any orientation, as long as someone plays the role of Priestess which is the lead in this Rite.

Items needed:

- Babalon altar prepared in the usual manner, with the three candles.

The Rite of the Twin Flame

- Sigillum Divinorum and Sigil of Devotion upon altar, if you have them
- The Chalice of Babalon
- Rain Water
- Wine
- Abramelin Oil
- Thelemic Abramelin Incense
- Cakes of Life (optional)

The altar to Babalon should be laid out in the usual manner, with the two blue candles in the back, and the blue or gold candle in the front, making a triangle. In the middle of the triangle should be the Sigillum Divinorum and on top of that the Sigil of Devotion, if you have them. Setting on top of that should be your Chalice of Babalon. Next to the Chalice on a special small plate only used for this purpose should be your Cake of Life, if you have any.[62] Nearby on the altar, but not within the triangle, should be your incense burner, Abramelin Incense and Oil, purified rain water or purified pond water, and a small bit of red wine of your own choosing. If you have a decanter for your rain water, you may leave it on the altar during all of your Rites so that it may grow with the power of Babalon over time.

Preparations

To begin with, you should prepare yourselves with a Ritual Bath and other preparations as has been taught (see Chapter 16, *Preparing for the Rites*). Do this together. When you have adorned each other appropriately, enter your Shrine and proceed to the altar of Babalon as a couple. One person will need to be the Priestess, to conduct the main parts of the Rite.

The Priestess lights the two candles in the back saying, "In Nomine Babalon," and then lights the candle in the front saying "et Vox Sanctae Meretricis".

---

[62] See Chapter 34, *The Devotional Rites of Ra Hoor Khuit* for more information of the Cakes of Life and the Cakes of Light, and their preparation.

Banishing

Now both sit before Her altar and perform the Grounding ritual as has been taught (see Chapter 18, *Grounding*).

Both then rise. The Priestess takes the Abramelin Oil and carefully anoints her Lover on their Third Eye while saying, "In Nomine Babalon," and then right above the genitalia with the words "et Vox Sanctae Meretricis." When this is complete, the Priestess then does the same to herself. The Priestess then lights the charcoal, and when it is hot enough adds some Thelemic Abramelin Incense to it.

One of the couple must then Banish using their preferred Banishing Ritual (see Chapter 20, *Banishing*).

Purification of the Shrine

When complete, the Priestess then turns to the Altar of Babalon and pours some rain water into the Chalice of Babalon while saying over it, "In Nomine Babalon." Then raise the Chalice high in the air with both hands while saying the Watery Invocation of Babalon:

> *[Adoration:]*
>
> *O Babalon, the seas are your home, as well as the deep,*
> *And in this darkness you stir*
> *As in a mirror quiet, the desires of this world.*
>
> *O Babalon, whether in waters placid or storms of seas,*
> *You orchestrate the chaos,*
> *And in the pools of all things, give calm.*
>
> *Arise, Babalon in the wake!*
> *Crash upon the shores,*
> *And there break the rocks of resistance and fear,*
> *Into pebbles beneath your feet.*
>
> *[Prayer:]*
>
> *I call to thee, Great Liberating Mother*
> *To show me the Fortitude in the Waters,*

The Rite of the Twin Flame

The power of my depths.

I call to thee, Great Liberating Mother,
To show me the Sovereignty of Dominion,
The calm of my truth.

I call to thee Great Liberating Mother,
To break down those dense stones
Which gather upon my shores!
Shatter fear and jealousy and shame,
Attachments which keep me
From my great and shining Will.

In Nomine Babalon et Vox Sanctae Meretricis

The Priestess then travels counter-clockwise around the Shrine, sprinkling and lustrating the floor in each of the four quarters as she goes, saying at each quarter:

May the Waters of Babalon purify this Shrine in Her name!

The Priestess then returns to her place before the altar.

Consecration of the Shrine

The Lover then steps up to the Altar of Babalon and puts some Thelemic Abramelin incense onto the charcoal in the incense burner while saying over it as he or she does so, "In Nomine Babalon." Then he or she raises the Incense Burner high in the air with both hands while saying the Fiery Invocation of Babalon:

[Adoration:]

O Babalon, from the fires of the stars You come!
Arise! Daughter of light, arise!
O Babalon, from the fires of the depths You rise!
Arise! Mighty torch-bearer, arise!

O Babalon, the lusts and desires of all,
Are as warriors in Your army,

Ready to serve you in battle.

Command them, Babalon,
O Great Liberating Mother,
Use them as minions in your Victory!

[Prayer:]

I call to thee, Great Liberating Mother
To show me the strength of my lusts,
And the fortitude therein.

I call to thee, Great Liberating Mother,
To show me the way in which to harness my desires,
By love under will.

I call to thee Great Liberating Mother,
To break the inhibition of cowardice,
Which keeps me from the realization
Of my true self.

In Nomine Babalon et Vox Sanctae Meretricis

The Lover then travels clockwise around the Shrine, fumigating and consecrating the air in each of the four quarters as he or she goes, saying at each quarter:

May the Fires of Babalon consecrate this Shrine in Her name!

Exaltation of the Shrine

The Lover returns to the altar of Babalon. The couple then disrobes and stands naked before their Goddess. The Priestess then takes some wine from the decanter and adds it to the water in the Chalice of Babalon (not too much, about 1/4 to 1/10 wine per water). Both focus their Will within their Personas intently and summon their Spirits to the forefront of consciousness. The Priestess and the Lover then say the following over the Cup of Babalon (said in unison):

The Rite of the Twin Flame

It is I (both say their names of dedication in succession). We come before thee, Nuit. We stand before all that is your exhalation, which is all life and all existence. We call deep within ourselves, and reach out to our own divine Stars shining in the Heavens — that from which our Spirits were born. I am my Spirit, the Bornless One. (Then the lover repeats this same last line "I am my Spirit, the Bornless One".) We live to indwell our Spirits, the Bornless Ones. It was already with us when we were born. And now we walk upon Earth as Spirits, wrapped within the hands of Gaia.

Now the couple aligns their incarnations of their Spirits with Babalon, by saying the following (said in unison):

It is I, (both say their names of dedication in succession). We come to you in Spirit. We come to pledge our love and our devotion to you, O Great Babalon. You, who are the Mysteries beyond Death. You who Guard all that is Life. You, who Transform all within Your embrace, refusing none. Your embrace is our rapture. Your love is our soul.

The Priestess then purifies the body of her Lover by anointing him with the mixture from the Chalice of Babalon, while saying the following:

May you be worthy of Babalon, by the Waters of the Earth. I wash away all that is impure from your being. I cleanse you now. The Water carries away all that hinders you, all the blocks which bind you, all that seeks to enslave your being, your essence, and your Will.

And then herself with:

Make me worthy of Babalon, O Waters of the Earth. Wash away all that is impure within my being. Cleanse me now. Carry away all that hinders me, all the blocks which bind me, all that seeks to enslave my being, my essence, and my Will.

The Lover then consecrates the body of the Priestess by perfuming her with the smoke of the incense, while saying the following:

May the spirits of the Air - those who reside in the places of light, those who seek truth in all things - lend you their clarity. I ask them to carry you higher, higher into the places of knowing, so that you might learn and understand that which is Truth, and that which is your Will.

And then himself with:

May the spirits of the Air - those who reside in the places of light, those who seek truth in all things - lend me their clarity. I ask them to carry me higher, higher into the places of knowing, so that I might learn and understand that which is Truth, and that which is my Will.

The Couple then exalt themselves. The Priestess cups her hands fairly close around the flame of central blue/gold candle. Her Lover places his hands upon her back. They both focus their attention upon the flame while they say in unison:

May the Spirits of Fire burn from us all that is the dross of our days upon this Earth. Cleanse from us all that we carry which hinders our being, and all that is counter to our purpose. Render us forth as ash, so that we may rise as Snakes of Light, Spirits purified.

The Grand Devotion of Babalon

The Priestess turns to face her partner in front of the altar and raises the Chalice of Babalon high to the Heavens above the Altar. Her Lover goes to his knees in adoration of his Priestess above him, and his goddess beyond. The Priestess says the following.

O Mighty Babalon,
We come before thee as a Twin Flame,
Offering ourselves up to you in service.
May the lust and heat of our passions
Carry us in our love as an offering unto you.
We join ourselves as one, in your honor,
As a sacrament unto you.

The couple then begins to embrace and to let their passions dictate the course of the worship according to their predilections and desires. It is appropriate to reach orgasm as many times as one wishes, however each time the orgasm approaches,

THE RITE OF THE TWIN FLAME

both participants must begin to chant "In Nomine Babalon" and focus completely upon their goddess as the orgasm comes to fruition. Ensure that She receives Her offering each time, and that nothing is held back for oneself in your bliss of devotion.

When both participants are fully spent, it is time to conclude the Rite. The energy and intensity of the Rite will now have dissipated, and the mundane Persona will be regaining dominance. The Priestess takes the Cakes of Life and anoints them with the fluids of the sacrifice from between her legs, while saying "In Nomine Babalon et Vox Sanctae Meretricis." Both now consume the Cakes of Life. The Priestess then holds the Chalice of Babalon and again says over it saying "In Nomine Babalon et Vox Sanctae Meretricis." Both then drink deeply from the Chalice of Babalon. They then retire to a place of comfort, such as cushions in front of the Altar, and bathe in any energy which comes forth. When they feel the time is right, the Priestess arises and extinguishes the candles, saying again: In Nomine Babalon. Record any thoughts, feelings, perceptions or words which have come to you, or in dreams later that same night. Feast together that night in celebration and enjoy a life of union, In Nomine Babalon.

Babalon Brigid

Orryelle Defenestrate-Bascule

XLII

The Rite of the Holy Whore

he Rite of the Holy Whore is an ecstatic exercise designed to help one see the sensuality of Babalon everywhere, and in everything. This Rite is especially good practice for those who are considering the part of the Holy Whore in the Ecstatic Rites of Babalon, and should be practiced by them for some time to help accustom their Personas to seeing sensual beauty in everyone, no matter their own personal preferences in such matters. This is certainly no easy task.

It is often said that Babalon accepts all and refuses none, and that this is the reason why She is called the Holy Whore. This is indeed one of the reasons, but not the only one. But in general, people generally interpret this line along some philosophical idea of compassionate love, in that Babalon is accepting all as a loving mother, no matter what one's faults or motivations may be. That is what people want from Her. But in reality what it really means when it is said that She accepts all and refuses none, is that all will be used in their own way, as they are, with what they have to offer. And it is this attitude in which one should practice the Rite of the Holy Whore, upon all of the people around you in every-day life, without them having any idea you are doing so.

The Rite of the Holy Whore

In the Ecstatic Rites of Babalon, the Holy Whore is the Visible Object of Worship upon the altar. The worshippers in the Rite pour out all of who they are in ecstatic sensual and sexual worship upon the Holy Whore in spontaneous ritual according to their Spirit and the influence of Babalon in the Rites. In order to prepare the Holy Whore for such attention, this Rite of the Holy Whore should be practiced in order to prepare the Persona for the sexual attention of a very wide range of people.

The Rite involves traveling through your day in a different way than normal, and with a different awareness than usual. At each encounter with a person during your day, you are to see in your mind yourself seducing them with your sexuality. It does not matter whether it be your co-worker, a woman in the hallway, a delivery man, or any other person - even family members (as difficult as that sounds). The only exceptions are those who can not make informed decisions about their own sexuality, which would mean no children, no pets or animals, and no invalids or immobilized people who can not give consent. But with everyone else, you are to see yourself engaged with them in sensual and sexual ways.

Do these actions in your mind while you are talking with them as you normally would. They will have no idea what you are doing, but make a game of it and watch to see if their normal reactions to you change at all. As in the full understanding of the meaning of Holy Whore which was described above, try to find the use and value in them for yourself sexually. Explore them and see what they have to offer. Let it build your fires, and see yourself doing things with them according to your own predilections that arise. These predilections will be your own, and potentially change with each person. For some it will be innocent seduction with kisses and touching, for others it may be rough and demanding. Yet others may require a voyeuristic approach of watching each other touch themselves. Who knows? The important point is to pursue this interaction for yourself with each and every person you encounter, finding what they have to offer you in a sexual and sensual manner, no matter what your normal attraction to them in your Persona would be. This is certainly no easy task, especially when you encounter people whom you normally do not like. But even with them, you must endeavor to find something in them which is of use to you sexually or sensually. And once this is accomplished, then you will find a way in which they are of use to Babalon, through these methods.

To begin with, choose a day and time to practice these Rites in advance. For example, you will choose tomorrow from 9 am to 1 pm. Upon awakening on your chosen day, go to Babalon's altar in your Shrine. Light Her candles with "In Nomine Babalon" as usual. Burn to Her some Thelemic Abramelin Incense and then declare your intention to be Her Holy Whore for that period of time with the following words.

> *O Great Liberating Mother! It is I, (your chosen name), and I come before you today as your Holy Whore. I will walk as you walk. I will see as you see. And in my mind, I will do as you do. I am the Visible Object of Worship, and I will use all for who they are, and what they have to offer, refusing none. I will wrap them in your veil of Love, under Your Will, though they know it not. I do this for you! In Nomine Babalon et Vox Sanctae Meretricis.*

Now go about your day as normal. With each person you encounter, do as described earlier, finding the sensual and sexual use of each person and what they have to offer in the most intimate of ways. Even though in reality it seems you are talking and interacting with them as normal, in your mind you are ravishing them, or they you, in the most intimate ways imaginable. After you leave the presence of each person, say under your breath "In Nomine Babalon" to consummate each interaction unto Her.

There may be a temptation to allow these situations to develop into something real and actual in a sexual manner. That is not recommended, as this may create situations in real life which would completely compromise the normal world in which your Persona must live and work, for example. You do not want to couple with people who it is entirely inappropriate to do so with, outside of a ritualized context in which everyone is dedicated to Babalon. Otherwise you may put yourself in danger physically, or jeopardize yourself in your job, or other such problems. If there are obvious and mutual attractions which develop with those on whom you practice these Rites of the Holy Whore, then one can arrange to fulfill these mutual desires with them at a different time, after carefully considering the consequences as you normally would with any sex partner.

After your allotted time for the Rite, you may experience exhaustion or extreme excitement or many other feelings. If you are completely aroused and feeling unfulfilled, then it would be good to practice the Rite of Sappho or the Rite of Pan, depending upon your orientation. In this

The Rite of the Holy Whore

way, you can release all of the built up energies you are carrying within you to Babalon as a proper sacrifice unto Her, and a proper catharsis and release for yourself as a Holy Whore. Repeated practice of this Rite will increase not only your powers of seduction with others, but also your own capacity to hold ecstasy and experience the bliss of release, under the auspices of the Great Liberating Mother whom we call Babalon.

XLIII

THE ECSTATIC RITE OF BABALON

he **Ecstatic Rite of Babalon** is the main Rite for the people to worship Babalon together as a group, in a serious and ecstatic manner by means of their sensual and sexual appetites. It is partly a Dramatic Ritual, based upon the structure of the Bhaktic Rites of Babalon, and involves different people playing different roles in the Rite. Because of this, the cast will need to practice the Rites with scripts many times, and memorize their parts if possible. The Rites are not only dramatic in nature, but also sensually interactive. The audience, or Devotees, takes part in the Rites in many ways. Ultimately they are the beneficiary of the Rites during the Sacrifice, where it is possible for each individual to have a personal experience with some form of the energy of Babalon manifesting through the Holy Whore. This is the ultimate goal of these Rites, to bring the common people into a new spiritual experience of their own self in relation to the Great Liberating Mother, in a manner which makes a lasting and positive impression upon their Persona.

Practice and repeated performance of these Rites by the Holy Whore and the Beast is essential in order to learn how to cultivate the most intense energy for the Devotees, and to begin to understand how to manifest and open the Liminal Gateway. The Rites can be considered to be a success if

The Ecstatic Rite of Babalon

the Devotees begin to see and experience the Pia Mezza[63], the middle place between worlds which marks the encroachment of manifest Spirit. And success in this way is most often the case where the Holy Whore, the Beast, and all the cast and the Devotees are completely devoted in the performance of the Rite. It is the giving of all they have in the Rites that can enable Her manifestation for the people.

It is best to perform this Rite during the Waxing or Full Moons, and Rites of contemplation or Devotion during the other times. Experienced Priestesses will easily notice the difference in type and power of energy during these Rites during different phases of the Moon, and will discover what works best for their own abilities and natures. In the Rite the Priestess will play the part of the Holy Whore, and must be willing to engage with the participants in a sexual manner to fulfill this role.

All participants in this Rite will wear masks and should be prepared to be fully naked during the ecstatic part of the Rites.

The Cast

Required participants:

> The Holy Whore
> The Beast
> Baphometis
> Devotees

Optional participants:

> Various Nymphs and Satyrs
> Ra Hoor Khuit

The Costumes

The Holy Whore: The Priestess should dress as she will, according to her own genius and taste, taking into consideration her local customs. She wears a mask of her own design. If robes or other apparel are worn, then they should be of such a fashion that they are revealing, and easily

---

[63] Pia Mezza, literally *the middle place*, between worlds. See the glossary for more information.

removed and discarded. One may wear horns, or an ornate headdress. One may apply tribal makeup, Egyptian makeup, or other types of your own design. The same recommendations apply for robes and jewelry. The Priestess is girt with a large sword. When adorning oneself, one may wish to take inspirations from the verses from Liber Legis I, 61-64:

> *61. ... I charge you earnestly to come before me in a single robe, and covered with a rich headdress. I love you! I yearn to you! Pale or purple, veiled or voluptuous, I who am all pleasure and purple, and drunkenness of the innermost sense, desire you. Put on the wings, and arouse the coiled splendour within you: come unto me!*
>
> *62. At all my meetings with you shall the priestess say -- and her eyes shall burn with desire as she stands bare and rejoicing in my secret temple -- To me! To me! calling forth the flame of the hearts of all in her love-chant.*
>
> *63. Sing the rapturous love-song unto me! Burn to me perfumes! Wear to me jewels! Drink to me, for I love you! I love you!*
>
> *64. I am the blue-lidded daughter of Sunset; I am the naked brilliance of the voluptuous night-sky.*

The Beast: The Beast should have a robe with a hood, all of which is of red with black trim, black lining and black symbols. The Beast wears a mask of his own design. This robe should open in the front for easy access when required. There may be a black Star of Babalon, large, on the back area. The Beast carries the Thyrsus or Dionysian Staff, of which there are many variations, all of which include a large pinecone at the top of a straight long staff.

The Nymphs and Satyrs: These creatures should be barely dressed according to the myths, with masks. They are creatures of sensual spontaneity, who with their charm keep the spirits of all present focused on the sexual and sensual worship of Babalon.

The Ecstatic Rite of Babalon

Ra Hoor Khuit: Ra Hoor Khuit should be dressed as in his Egyptian image, with a hawk mask being required. He bears a sword and has a warrior's physic.

Baphometis: Baphometis should be adorned with horns, and breasts exposed, if possible. A full goat mask is required. Apparel should be black. S/he bears the Caduceus staff and a ram horn (or other animal horn) which can be blown. If this is not obtainable, then a small musical horn of some sort which can be blown can be substituted. If the Baphometis is a male transsexual, then hi/r full hanging cock should be exposed as well. If not, then a prosthetic cock may be used and made visible for others.

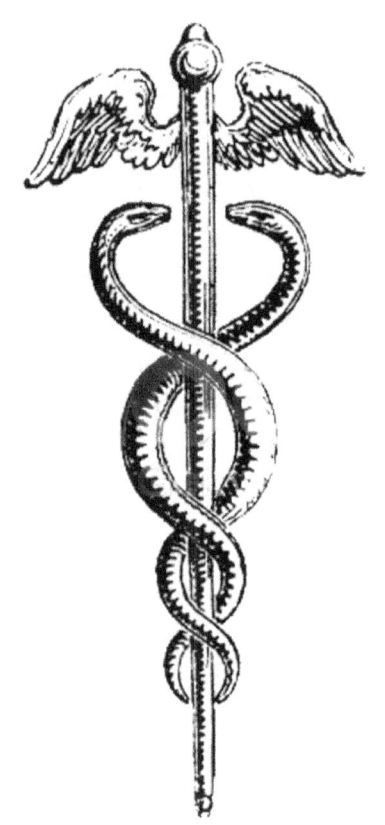

Devotees: The Devotees, or audience, should dress in festive costumes according to their own genius. Masks are required. Horns, fantastical dresses and the like are encouraged. The Rites are a celebration of all things of sense and rapture. Let your appearance reflect this by your own genius!

Layout of the Shrine

Ideally, the entrance to the Shrine will be in the East. The main altars and Banners of Babalon will sit in the West. Not all Shrines may allow for this arrangement due to their physical orientation. The colors of the Shrine for the Bhaktic Rites should follow the instructions in Liber Legis I:51 for the Palace:

> *51. There are four gates to one palace; the floor of that palace is of silver and gold; lapis lazuli & jasper are there; and all rare scents; jasmine & rose, and the emblems of death.*

The silver and gold floor can be done with accents, with silver and gold checker-board pattern, with paint, or with rugs - all according to your own inspiration. Lapis Lazuli and Jasper represent the correct colors of blue and red to use for the Banners. Often the blues are put in the West, and the reds in the East. The blues can be shown on the large Banners of Babalon, which are vertical rectangles of cloth, quite large, hung from the ceiling. The Banners have a background field of blue, upon which is a large, gold Star of Babalon. The Banners of Ra Hoor Khuit hang on either side of the entrance to the Shrine in the East. They have a red background, and the Eye in the Triangle or the Guardian of the Triangle of Manifestation symbol in gold. The important part is a circle or eye, within a equilateral triangle. Images of Nuit and Hadit may be included in the Shrine for the Ecstatic Rites, with Nuit being in the North and Hadit being in the South. They can be large, and of your own design.

There are three altars in the West, each one progressively higher than the last. The Banners of Babalon hang on either side of the altars. The first altar, on ground level, is the Altar of Union, for the Beast. It should be a double cube, around 1.5 feet wide and 3 feet tall. These sizes can be adjusted to fit your needs. It should be painted black, with a top that is white. You may paint a gold sun conjoined with a silver lunar crescent within the field of white on the top, if you desire. Each of the four sides of the altar may be painted with red Serpent-Stars. Upon this altar is the Incense Urn for hot coals, Thelemic Abramelin Incense, a Chalice filled with rain water, and some natural sea salt without additives or anti-caking agents. Above the altar hangs an oil lamp or candle sconce, for Spirit.

The next altar is the Throne of Babalon which sits on a raised dais above the ground floor. The focal point of this dais is the Throne of Babalon in the middle. Ideally it will be carved such that the arm-rests on either side are lions, or painted with lions. Alternatively, two lion statues (such as are seen made of concrete for lawns and yards) may be used on either side of the chair. A black and a white pillar are set further to either side of the Throne, with black on the left (South) when facing the throne from the Devotees, and white on the right. The lamps, which sit atop or

The Ecstatic Rite of Babalon

hang above the pillars, should make a triangle with the Torch of Baphometis which sits above in a sconce (see the following).

The final dais and altar is the highest, and closest to the Western wall. This is the dais of Baphometis, and there is a chair there for hi/r to sit. There is also a sconce on the wall arranged so that when Baphometis is standing, and pointing above and below, that the torch will blaze out over hi/r head. This torch also makes a triangle with the lamps on the two pillars on either side of the Throne of Babalon.

The rest of the Shrine is filled with chairs for the Devotees, with a central isle from East to West for the procession.

The Rites

The Devotees are led to their chairs by the Nymphs and Satyrs, and all are seated until the Rites are ready to begin. Once the Rites have begun, no other Devotees may enter. When all is ready, the lights are extinguished and all are in complete darkness and silence.

The Opening of the Gateway to the Underworld

Baphometis the torchbearer enters, carrying the only light in the entire Shrine (a torch or large candle). S/he never speaks, but surveys the area as S/he slowly proceeds down the aisle from East to West. Baphometis is responsible for securing the people, the Shrine, and establishing the Light of Spirit therein. The torch is cast over the heads of all who are seated, so that its light and flame touches the Spirits of those present. As this happens to each of the Devotees, they may begin to quietly chant "Metis"[64], either in unison or individually according to their own meter. Baphometis continues until all Spirits have been touched. All now should be quietly chanting "Metis". Baphometis then proceeds to the Altar of Union, and lights the hanging Lamp of Spirit there. The Devotees may begin to raise their hands if they like at this point, with palms up to Baphometis and the

---

[64] Pronounced *Meh*-tees, with a heavy accent on the first syllable. Before the mythology was changed by the Areans, Metis was a Titan and Goddess whose name meant *cunning in magic*. Her most ancient aspect is She who *metes* out space with boundaries, so as to establish the Liminal Gateway for the ingress of Spirit. Notice that Her name still exists in English with a similar meaning. After the Arean invasion, She was married off to Zeus and the meaning of Her name became something more akin to *wisdom* and *cunning*.

Altar of Union. The chanting by the Devotees should become progressively louder as Baphometis proceeds to the Throne of Babalon and lights first the Left Lamp (Black Pillar), then the Right Lamp (White Pillar). Baphometis then continues on and finally reaches highest altar of all. Baphometis stands facing away from the Devotees, towards the Western wall. Baphometis holds the torch high in one hand, horn in the other, while the Devotees chant "Metis" even louder. Baphometis puts the torch in its sconce or socket on the wall. Baphometis turns to the Devotees, with the torch shining above Hi/r head, and blows the horn once - a long strong burst of sound. All fall silent at the sound of the horn, as Baphometis then points above with the right hand and below with the left, as in typical of the image of Baphometis from history.

At this, the Devotees rise, and turn towards the East. A voice is heard from the East - that of the Holy Whore, hidden beyond the veil of the open doorway. She is girt with her sword, and says in a clear and beautiful voice to all:

Had the Manifestation of Nuit.

At this voice, a number of Nymphs and Satyrs appear through the doorway. They bear candles to light the pathway to the Altar of Union, and line the aisle on either side. One bears hot charcoals for the incense and places them within the Incense Urn on the Altar of Union. Another bears rainwater and fills the cup there as well. Others bear the salt, the Thelemic Abramelin Incense, and an open urn of wine - enough so that all in the Devotees may have a small amount. When this is accomplished, the Holy Whore speaks again.

Nu, the Hiding of Hadit.

Now the Beast enters the Shrine through the doorway with his staff held firmly to his chest, so that it vertically extends above his head for all to see. He proceeds at a ceremonial pace forward, to the Altar of Union. There he stops, still facing the West, looking up to Baphometis. He holds the staff up high towards Baphometis, and then kneels down, holding the staff end against the ground. He then speaks, loud, forcefully and clear from this position.

The Ecstatic Rite of Babalon

Abrahadabra, the reward of Ra Hoor Khut.

At this moment, the Holy Whore enters, girt with sword at her chest, held with both hands tightly, the tip pointing downwards. She moves at a ceremonial pace down the aisle. At her passing through the threshold, Ra Hoor Khuit closes and guards the entrance to the Shrine for the rest of the Rite. The Beast rises to face her. The Beast holds the staff in front of him, end upon the floor. The Priestess proceeds to the Altar of Union, and circles around the Beast clockwise, looking him over as she does so. She then continues up the three steps to the Throne of Babalon at the same slow processional pace. She turns and faces the Devotees and the Beast, who now face her as she stands girt with the sword. Behind her and slightly raised is Baphometis pointing up and down.

The Opening of the Shrine of Babalon

The Holy Whore looks to the people, girt with her sword, standing in front of the Throne, and says:

> *Do what thou wilt shall be the whole of the Law.*

The Beast and the Devotees answer back:

> *Love is the law, love under will.*

The Holy Whore says:

> *Do that, and no other shall say nay. For pure will, unassuaged of purpose, delivered from the lust of result, is every way perfect.*

Baphometis now sits and the Devotees follow. Baphometis holds the Caduceus Staff vertically, as if it is growing out from between hi/r legs.

Mystery Babalon

The Holy Whore now looks to the Beast, and says:

> *Help me, o warrior lord of Thebes, in my unveiling before the Children of men! Be thou Hadit, my secret centre, my heart & my tongue!*

The Beast places the Dionysian Staff in its holder just North of the Altar of Union, and does Stella Heru. (The Star Ruby may be substituted.) The Staff now stands between the Altar of Union and the dais of the Throne of Babalon.

When the Beast is finished with the Banishing, the Holy Whore says to him:

> *There are four gates to one palace; the floor of that palace is of silver and gold; lapis lazuli & jasper are there; and all rare scents; jasmine & rose, and the emblems of death. Let him enter in turn or at once the four gates; let him stand on the floor of the palace.*

The Holy Whore sits with her sword across her lap. The Devotees now stand, and perform the Adorations of Ra Hoor Khuit with the Beast:

The Beast and Devotees turn to the East and say:

> *Hail unto thee who art Ra in thy Rising, even unto Thee who art Ra in Thy Strength, who travellest over the heavens in Thy bark at the Uprising Hour of the Sun. Tahuti standeth in His splendour at the prow, and Ra-Hoor abideth at the helm. Hail unto Thee from the Abodes of Night.*

The Beast and Devotees turn to the South and say:

> *Hail unto thee who art Hathoor in Thy triumphing, even unto Thee who art Hathoor in Thy Beauty, who travellest over the heavens in Thy bark at the Noon Hour of the Sun. Tahuti standeth in His splendour at the prow, and Ra-Hoor abideth at the helm. Hail unto Thee from the Abodes of Morning.*

The Beast and Devotees turn to the West and say:

The Ecstatic Rite of Babalon

Hail unto thee who art Tum in Thy setting, even unto Thee who art Tum in Thy Joy, who travellest over the heavens in Thy bark at the Downgoing Hour of the Sun. Tahuti standeth in His splendour at the prow, and Ra-Hoor abideth at the helm. Hail unto Thee from the Abodes of Day.

The Beast and Devotees turn to the North and say:

Hail unto thee who art Khephra in Thy hiding, even unto Thee who art Khephra in Thy silence, who travellest over the heavens in Thy bark at the Midnight Hour of the Sun. Tahuti standeth in His splendour at the prow, and Ra-Hoor abideth at the helm. Hail unto Thee from the Abodes of Evening.

The Beast and Devotees return to the East and say:

I am the Lord of Thebes,
  and I The inspired forth-speaker of Mentu;
For me unveils the veiled sky,
  The self-slain Ankh-af-na-khonsu
Whose words are truth. I invoke, I greet
Thy presence, O Ra-Hoor-Khuit!

Unity uttermost showed!
  I adore the might of Thy breath,
Supreme and terrible God,
  Who makest the gods and death
To tremble before Thee:—
I, I adore thee!

Appear on the throne of Ra!
  Open the ways of the Khu!
Lighten the ways of the Ka!
  The ways of the Khabs run through
To stir me or still me!
Aum! let it fill me!

The light is mine; its rays consume Me:
  I have made a secret door
Into the House of Ra and Tum,
  Of Khephra and of Ahathoor.

I am thy Theban, O Mentu,
The prophet Ankh-af-na-khonsu!

By Bes-na-Maut my breast I beat;
    By wise Ta-Nech I weave my spell.
Show thy star-splendour, O Nuit!
    Bid me within thine House to dwell,
O winged snake of light, Hadit!
Abide with me, Ra-Hoor-Khuit!

The Beast gives the Sign of Silence, and the Devotees follow. Then the Devotees sit.

The Exaltation of the Shrine

The Beast turns to the Holy Whore and says

> *Then the priest answered & said unto the Queen of Space, kissing her lovely brows, and the dew of her light bathing his whole body in a sweet-smelling perfume of sweat: O Nuit, continuous one of Heaven, let it be ever thus; that men speak not of Thee as One but as None; and let them speak not of thee at all, since thou art continuous!*

The Holy Whore stands girt with her sword and answers with:

> *None, breathed the light, faint & faery, of the stars, and two. For I am divided for love's sake, for the chance of union. This is the creation of the world, that the pain of division is as nothing, and the joy of dissolution all.*

The Holy Whore places her sword across her throne. The Beast goes to the steps to meet the Holy Whore, who is now coming down. They clasp hands during this speech, and move together towards the Altar of Union.

The Beast says:

> *Now ye shall know that the chosen priest & apostle of infinite space is the prince-priest the Beast; and in his woman called the Scarlet Woman is all*

The Ecstatic Rite of Babalon

power given. They shall gather my children into their fold: they shall bring the glory of the stars into the hearts of men.

The Holy Whore answers as they move to the Altar of Union

For he is ever a sun, and she a moon. But to him is the winged secret flame, and to her the stooping starlight.

The Devotees says to the couple:

Burn upon their brows, o splendrous serpent!

The Holy Whore takes the salt and says over it:

Take from the Earth, Give to the Earth, Feel the Joy of it!

The Holy Whore mixes salt into water, while saying:

This shall regenerate the world, the little world my sister, my heart & my tongue, unto whom I send this kiss.

The Holy Whore then sprinkles water around the area of the altar, while saying:

So therefore first the Priestess who governs the works of fire must sprinkle with the lustral waters of the loud resounding sea.

The Holy Whore returns to the Altar, raises the cup to the West and says:

Hear thou the voice of Water: Babalon!

The Holy Whore takes incense and says over it:

Mystery Babalon

My incense is of resinous woods and gums; and there is no blood therein: because of my hair the trees of eternity.

The Beast places the Thelemic Abramelin incense that he received from the Priestess onto coals, while saying:

Harken O spirits, and accept this sweet perfume - for you, the gods, and all.

The Beast walks clockwise, censing a circle around the altar, intoning:

And when after all the phantoms have vanished, thou shalt see that holy and formless fire, that fire which darts and flashes through the hidden depths of the Universe.

The Beast returns to the center, and faces South, raising the brazier:

Hear thou the voice of Fire: Therion!

The Beast then lifts the Urn or Bowl of Wine so that the Holy Whore may pour the water and salt from the Chalice into the wine. The Holy Whore says while doing so:

There is no bond which can unite the divided but love: all else is a curse.

The Holy Whore then stirs the mixture with a ladle, and then puts a little back in the Chalice. The Beast returns the bowl of wine to the altar. The Holy Whore says over the Chalice "In Nomine Babalon" and drinks half. She hands the Chalice to the Beast who also says "In Nomine Babalon" and drinks the rest and places the Chalice back onto the Altar of Union. The Holy Whore comes around the Altar of Union to the Beast and kisses him deeply and passionately. The Holy Whore then returns to the Throne of Babalon. As she ascends, the Beast says:

In the sphere I am everywhere the centre, as she, the circumference, is nowhere found. Yet she shall be known & I never.

The Ecstatic Rite of Babalon

When the Holy Whore reaches her place standing in front of the Throne, the Beast continues:

> *Now let there be a veiling of this shrine: now let the light devour men and eat them up with blindness!*

The Invocation of Babalon

The Beast and the Devotees all go down into the Beast Asana[65]. If they have a hood, it should be pulled over their head. All stay this way until the end of the Holy Whore's speech. Simultaneously, two Nymphs or Satyrs come to the Babalon Throne to attend to the needs of the Holy Whore during the Rites. They remove her sword from the throne and place it behind the throne for her. The Holy Whore then gives the Daughter of Fortitude speech, standing in front of her throne.

> *I am the daughter of Fortitude, and ravished every hour from my youth. For behold I am Understanding and science dwelleth in me; and the heavens oppress me. They cover and desire me with infinite appetite; for none that are earthly have embraced me, for I am shadowed with the Circle of the Stars and covered with the morning clouds. My feet are swifter than the winds, and my hands are sweeter than the morning dew. My garments are from the beginning, and my dwelling place is in myself. The Lion knoweth not where I walk, neither do the beast of the fields understand me. I am deflowered, yet a virgin; I sanctify and am not sanctified. Happy is he that embraceth me: for in the night season I am sweet, and in the day full of pleasure. My company is a harmony of many symbols and my lips sweeter than health itself. I am a harlot for such as ravish me, and a virgin with such as know me not. For lo, I am loved of many, and I am a lover to many;... and behold, I will bring forth children unto you, and they shall be the Sons of Comfort. I will open my garments, and stand naked before you, that your love may be more enflamed toward me.*

At this point the Holy Whore drops all of her garments and stands naked before the people. Her attendants gather her garments from the floor and

---

[65] One goes down on their knees, and then from there lays down, their torso on the ground in supplication. The arms are stretched above the head, forming a triangle, with the hands making the wings of Hadit.

put them aside. The Beast then responds from his place on the ground in the Beast Asana:

> *I am the secret Serpent coiled about to spring: in my coiling there is joy. If I lift up my head, I and my Nuit are one. If I droop down mine head, and shoot forth venom, then is rapture of the earth, and I and the earth are one.*
>
> *I ... lift ... up ... my ... head!*

The Beast stands, and the people follow suit as he says:

> *O my people, rise up & awake!*

The Beast retrieves his Dionysian Staff and turns to the people. The People respond:

> *Another prophet shall arise, and bring fresh fever from the skies; another woman shall awake the lust & worship of the Snake.*

The Beast refreshes the Thelemic Abramelin incense here. The Beast says to the Devotees:

> *It is a lie, this folly against self. The exposure of innocence is a lie. Be strong, o man! lust, enjoy all things of sense and rapture: fear not that any God shall deny thee for this.*

The Beast bangs his staff three times upon the floor and the Devotees drop their garments at the same moment. Baphomet points up and down again during the following invocation. The Nymphs and Satyrs begin to beat a slow, soft, steady drum beat while others occasionally shake Sistrums and snake rattles. The Devotees begin to play with each other, sensually and slowly at first, but building as the invocations from the Beast continue. All hold back their orgasms however, as a sacrifice to Babalon through the Holy Whore. The Holy Whore sits upon her throne, observing the Devotees in their sensual orgy. Her attendants caress her and touch her as she has instructed them to before hand, to arouse her during the invocations. All are guided by the words of the Beast and the people as the

The Ecstatic Rite of Babalon

Invocations commence. The Beast begins the Ecstatic Invocation of Babalon.

> *We call to thee, Daughter of the Mighty Ones, Daughter of the Fiery One, Daughter of the Deepest Black!*
> *People: In Nomine Babalon!*
>
> *We call to thee, Gate of Life and Death, Queen of Heaven and Hell, Lady of Lust and Desire!*
> *People: In Nomine Babalon!*
>
> *We call to thee, Black One, Blue One, Gold One, the Woman Clothed with the Sun!*
> *People: In Nomine Babalon!*
>
> *We call to thee, Fierce Guardian, Formidable Warrior, Everlasting King!*
> *People: In Nomine Babalon!*
>
> *We call to thee, Shameless One, Harlot, Whore, Bearer of the Cup of Fornications!*
> *People: In Nomine Babalon!*
>
> *We call to thee, Lady of the Star, Lady of the Snake, Lady of the Wheel!*
> *People: In Nomine Babalon!*
>
> *We call to thee, Lady of the Gate, Lady of the Crossroads, Guardian of the Liminal Point!*
> *People: In Nomine Babalon!*
>
> *We call to thee, Cunning One, Wise One, Clever One, Mistress of Heka!*
> *People: In Nomine Babalon!*
>
> *We call to thee, Great Liberating Mother, Daughter of Ra, Babalon the Great!*
> *People: In Nomine Babalon!*
>
> *We call to thee, Daughter of Fortitude, the Gate of God, the Woman Clothed in the Sun!*
> *People: In Nomine Babalon!*
>
> *We call to thee, the Mother of Prostitutes and the Abominations of the Earth, the Holy Whore!*
> *People: In Nomine Babalon!*

Repeat if necessary for as long as is needed. When the Holy Whore is ready to receive adoration for Babalon from a Devotee, she will say aloud:

Come forth, o children, under the stars, & take your fill of love! To Me! To Me!

The Beast will then tap his staff three times hard upon the ground, and a Devotee will arise from the orgy and come before him. The Magus then anoints the Devotee at their 3rd eye with Abramelin Oil, and with the phrase "In Nomine Babalon", and again right above their genitals while saying "et Vox Sanctae Meretricis." The Devotee then ascends to the Throne of Babalon, escorted by the attendants of the Holy Whore, who have come down to escort the Devotee. There he or she will offer what sexual or sensual sacrificial offering which they may. The Holy Whore will decide from her end whether or not full penetration and orgasm within her yoni or mouth will take place if the devotee has a penis, or rather if the offering will be received upon her body. For a female devotee, the Holy Whore will decide how to suckle, rub and kiss the devotee or vice versa according to the desires of the Holy Whore. The Devotees should follow the lead of the Holy Whore in all ways. Orgasm is not required, but beneficial. During orgasm, the Devotee and the Holy Whore complete the sacrifice to Babalon with the words "In Nomine Babalon" at the peak moment. The Holy Whore channels all energy offered and sacrificed to Babalon by means of her body and vulva. Afterward, the Devotee should kiss and adore in worship the body of the Holy Whore as his or her goddess, even kissing her feet in adoration if called to. The Devotee then returns to the other Devotees and helps them in any way in the orgy. If the Holy Whore so desires, her attendants may wash her body with sponges or cloth between Devotees, and also serve her wine, water or other refreshments as required. When she is ready, she again calls forth with the line above for the next Devotee to come to her for sacrifice. The next Devotee then goes to the Beast for anointing, and the process repeats.

    At any point, the holy Whore may feel the need to speak or to convey any messages, as they may come through. It is incumbent on the Beast to stop his invocations and to record these words or messages. When she is finished, he may begin again with his invocations, and the Rite continues as before.

    When the Holy Whore calls forth and no more Devotees appear, then the Beast goes to her to make his offering as the others have done. Or

The Ecstatic Rite of Babalon

when the Holy Whore has taken all of the sacrifices which she can physically handle at that time, and wishes to end the Rites there, then her attendants will pull up the veil to cover the view to the throne. The Beast then goes to her and offers himself in whatever way she is able to handle at that time, even if it is only to adore and kiss her feet. The safety of the Holy Whore is paramount, and she must not be pushed past her limits.

When the Beast is done with his sacrifice, he returns to the Altar of the Union and then says to the Devotees who all stand and face him:

> *Beauty and strength, leaping laughter and delicious languor, force and fire, are of us. Nuit! Hadit! Ra-Hoor-Khuit! The Sun, Strength & Sight, Light; these are for the servants of the Star & the Snake.*

And then the Satyrs and Nymphs say in unison:

> *Remember all ye that existence is pure joy; that all the sorrows are but as shadows; they pass & are done; but there is that which remains.*

All say:

> *In Nomine Babalon!*

The Devotees gather themselves and their belongings, and go to a prepared feast to celebrate together.

The well-being of the Holy Whore

The same considerations which apply to the Priestess at the end of the Bhaktic Rites of Babalon also apply to these Ecstatic Rites. In addition to those considerations, it is incumbent upon the attendants of the Holy Whore and the Beast to see to her well being not only during the Rites, but afterward as well. She has become a Living Flame unto Babalon, and may need to be helped back into her Persona before continuing on to the feast. Eating will help the grounding process immensely. The Holy Whore should also be honored and toasted at the feast which follows.

CHINNAMASTA STUDY BY DANIEL CORCUERA

XLIV

THE HIEROS GAMOS TO BABALON

he Hieros Gamos to Babalon is the most sacred undertaking a man may make in service to Babalon. In Greek, ἱερὸς γάμος means a Holy Marriage between a human and a god. It is an ancient Rite of dedication, which can not be undone. It is the most serious undertaking which one can perform, as you are laying your life at the feet of a deity, so that they may use you as they Will. Even unto death. You are completely and permanently aligning your Will with the Will of the divine one, in this case Babalon, the Great Liberating Mother. And there is no greater power to be gained while incarnate than this service.

But one should be warned, for if you undertake this Hieros Gamos, then you will be tried by Her and Her Allies, and you will be tested by Her and Her Allies. She will take the pretty gold of your Persona and hammer it into steel. There are many ways that She may do this, and it may last for many years. She may test one who has so dedicated himself, to see if in fact there is nothing more important to him than his dedication. If there is, then She may take it away from him. This path is certainly not for the casual Devotee of Babalon, or those seeking to get something from Her for themselves.

The preferred vessel for one to pour yourself to Babalon in a sexual manner is ideally a Nine, or at least a Dedicated and Initiated Priestess of

Babalon. That is how it is done in Templum Babalonis. These Priestesses will help to train you in the act, and to give you lots of practice safely. Without a proper Priestess at hand, any other female could work, but it will drain their life force over time, in addition to the fact that they do not know what you are doing with them, which is a moral dilemma. Perhaps more importantly, they do not know how to transfer the offering from their vulva to Babalon. This lack of proper transfer can, over time, cause problems of various sorts for the woman involved, which usually result in various health problems for them as they will be fed upon and drained without their knowledge or consent.

Even so, there will be men who wish to dedicate themselves to Babalon in the highest way possible, but who do not have any access to an Initiated Priestess to officiate the Hieros Gamos. These men should not despair however, for there is another option for them which can be just as effective in the end for their desires, and if done properly, can actually lead them to find such a Priestess. But there can never be any lust of result in doing so, or all will fail. The offering must be sincere and true, with no hope of ever receiving anything in return. This attitude must be upon the mantel of the heart when the sacrifice is made.

The Vessel of Babalon

To begin with, the man who seeks a Hieros Gamos with Babalon should craft a vessel of clay by your own genius, in the shape of a large Yoni to receive your offerings. This Yoni should be made according to your own tastes and desires, in a manner which will be attractive to you and to help arouse you. It should be two or three times larger than a normal vulva, and be open to receive your offering. Once this is completed, you should also surround the Yoni with a Star of Babalon. This can be a separate piece which the Yoni sits upon, such as a special board painted with the star, or perhaps fashioned out of clay or wax. This then is your Vessel of Babalon, to be used in your Hieros Gamos with Babalon

This Vessel of Babalon should be consecrated by you when the moon is waxing or full. Bring the completed Vessel of Babalon to your Shrine and place it upon Her altar. Now perform the full Rite of Devotion from Chapter 31. When you Purify the Shrine with water from the Chalice, also sprinkle some on the Vessel saying, "May the Waters of Babalon purify this Vessel in Her name!" And when you Consecrate the Shrine with smoke from the incense, also fumigate the Vessel saying, "May the Fires of Babalon consecrate this Vessel in Her name!"

When you have completed the Rite of Devotion, and have Purified and Consecrated the Vessel of Babalon during that Rite, you may then Dedicate it. Apply a small amount of oil of Abramelin to the vessel, and rub lovingly all over it while saying the following.

> *May this be a Holy Vessel unto my Lady Babalon, whom I serve, and to whom I give all that I am. In Nomine Babalon et Vox Sanctae Meretricis.*

The Offering unto Babalon

The Offering unto Babalon should be done whenever one's sexual vitality has been built to a strong point by not masturbating or having sex for an extended period of time. This buildup and tension makes for a stronger offering, which will be poured out unto Babalon within Her Vessel which you have fashioned for Her.

To begin go to your Shrine and place the Holy Vessel of Babalon in a place in front of Her Altar which is convenient in such a way as to be used for you to pour yourself into at the climax of the Rite. Perhaps this will be upon a stool or a chair. Now perform the full Rite of Devotion from Chapter 31. In the beginning of that Rite, when you take your Abramelin Oil and anoint your third eye with the words "In Nomine Babalon", also then anoint the area right above your cock with the words "et Vox Sanctae Meretricis". Remember that because of the Cinnamon essential oil content, Abramelin Oil burns. Do not anoint your cock directly unless that is your pleasure.

When this Rite of Devotion has been accomplished, it is time to offer yourself to Babalon. Disrobe and stand naked before your Holy Vessel of Babalon. Make your cock nice and hard and stick it out over the Vessel while saying the following.

> *I come to you, Mighty Babalon, that I might be of service to You and your Daughters. I offer all that I am unto You, in your service.*

Then you may begin to pleasure yourself in whatever way you normally do in order to reach climax. Try to focus you attention in fantasy upon your image of Babalon, or one of the Nine, or other of Her Daughters as

The Hieros Gamos to Babalon

best as you can. If none of these images are available to you, simply focus on all the attributes of woman which you find most desirable and appealing in sexual fantasy. As you get close to the point of orgasm, focus all of your intensity, Will and life force energy into Babalon before you do so. Position yourself over the holy Vessel, and at the moment of orgasm throw yourself wholly and completely to Her, along with all of your semen, into Her Vessel, even to the point of death. You must be Her beast, used up and ridden completely in Her service. You must feel yourself die in Her vulva, with every last drop given. Pour all your semen into the clay vulva as you do this. If you must cry out, do so out loud or to yourself inwardly, with the words, "In Nomine Babalon et Vox Sanctae Meretricis!".

You may very well loose consciousness or fall into a deep reverie after your orgasm and Offering. Take as long as you need in this place. Give yourself completely to Her. Fall to the ground before Her altar and Vessel if need be. The only danger is if you hold anything back. Then, when you have returned somewhat to consciousness, you will need to recite an invocation to Babalon over your offering, and verbally dedicate it to Her. The following will serve for that purpose. If there are words which you wish to add from yourself to Her, then you may do so.

Great Babalon, it is I, (state your name of dedication).
I come before thee, all that is of the deepest depths of existence
Guardian of these great Principles, held within Your Wheel,
Goddess of Heka, laid before the people within the Mysteries of Blackness,
Seen as Golden by your true seekers,
I give myself, and all that I am, to you,
Great Babalon!

I lay before you, all that is within me,
I harness my animal for you, as you ride the Great Beast,
So that I might serve you, with my Spirit,
O Great Goddess of the Gateway,
O Great Goddess Of Death, and therefore Life,
And of all that is brought forth from the mysteries beyond knowing.

You, who are the Goddess of War and of Vengeance,
Great Daughter of Ra,
whose Secret Name at last I knoweth,
O, mighty Hoor-Pahkhet, whose reign rose from the sands upon the Nile,
whose reign was born from the people who lived even before time.

I offer myself and my essence to You, mighty Babalon!
Take me for your own.
I exist to serve you, with all of my passion,
my heart, my soul.
My devotion is Yours.
My breath is for You.
I ask you to take me, and make me that which you Desire,
For your Desire is Wisdom,
And your Heart beats for All.

In Nomine Babalon et Vox Sanctae Meretricis!

Now take your vessel, and cover it with cloth and keep it in a safe place, unseen by all. This is your secret offering, known only between you and Babalon. You may repeat this offering as often as you like. If you need to clean the dried cum of your offering from the Vessel, then take it and burn it with incense dedicated to Her, preferably Thelemic Abramelin. When your sperm is outside of the matrix of a woman, or other sanctified vessel, there are those things which will attempt to feed upon it without your permission. Guard it carefully. It is important that nothing else is able to feed on your offering to Her. This Vessel is the object of the establishment of a powerful Fila between you and Babalon, and interference with it, or feeding upon it by others there could affect you negatively.

An alternative to burning your offering periodically is to bury it in the body of Gaia. Find a place of good, pure and natural ground, preferably some place in nature. There, bury your Offerings in the soil with the following words.

I [your name of dedication] give to you, O Gaia,
that which brings the light of Ra to the essence of a new beginning,
Use this gift, O Gaia,
Use this energy to make life where it may be needed.

In Nomine Babalon, I give this unto you.

Notes upon the construction of the Holy Vessel of Babalon

Concerning the Star around the Vulva, you may put the letters of Babalon's name in each triangle of the Star if you like, or leave it just the Star by itself. The choice is yours. Do not use a mirror, as it may aid other unwanted

The Hieros Gamos to Babalon

spirits from getting access to your ritual workings. Keep all mirrors covered while working in the Shrine, if they are in your space and you can see them while you are offering. As far as the shape and substance of what you put the star on, round or square is fine. The star is to help focus you on the vulva, with Her seal around it. Along with your focus of Will when giving your offering to Her, the visuals of the Star and Vulva will leave no doubt in your persona as to what you are doing, and who you are doing it to. It will help to focus your offering completely to Her. That is the intention. Therefore make it according to your own notions, but not on glass or anything which casts a visible reflection which you could see spirits upon or within.

Appendices

Appendix A

What Are Shrines of Babalon?

hrines of Babalon is an ambitious, new, non-denominational world-wide project to support the spread of the Goddess Babalon and Her energy to all corners of the Earth.

Who can start a Shrine?

Anyone and everyone can start a Shrine in their local area. The Shrine can be public and offer Rites to the people, or private and serve only who you like. There can be more than one Shrine in the same area, to serve different needs and perspectives. All you need is a small space which you can dedicate to the Shrine, and perform the Rites in.

What happens at the Shrines?

Mostly whatever you like, as long as you follow the simple guidelines provided by the Shrine Council. This book which you hold, Mystery Babalon: The Bhaktic and Ecstatic Rites of Babalon, contains many types of Rites and rituals which can be performed in your shrine. The Bhaktic Rites are solemn and devotional in nature while the Ecstatic Rites are orgiastic, sensual and wild. There are Rites for solitary people as well as groups of all types, genders and orientations of people. Private Shrines can be a way for a small group of people to share the most intimate experiences possible, and to reconnect meaningfully in a busy distracting world. Public Shrines can become the hub of many underground scenes in your area, fostering many other creative groups and currents. The possibilities are only limited by your creativity and desires. The Shrine is a place to teach, to learn, to listen and to experience the transformative power of Babalon in all Her forms. Let the reciprocity flow.

Do I need any expertise to start a Shrine?

Not at all. All you need is to feel an affinity or a connection to Babalon. That is it. By creating the Shrine, and performing the Rites, you will discover your path and where you need to go. You will meet like-minded people at your Shrine and share experiences that will transform you and those around you. You can keep your Shrine private for as long as you like, or offer special public Rites, when and if you feel ready for that step. The choice is yours.

What if I already belong to another group or order?

That does not matter. The Shrine system is non-denominational, and is intended to bring people together regardless of philosophy, belief or affiliation. It is not an initiatory body, nor does it require any belief system or adherence to certain philosophies - other than the simple Guidelines of the Shrines which are intended to keep everyone safe and within certain thematic parameters concerning Babalon.

What is the Shrine Council?

The Shrine Council is made up of Shrine-holders who seek to help administer and oversee the system of Shrines. They have the power to change the Guidelines as may be needed as the system moves forward. They also oversee the approval process of new Shrines, and make sure that all Shrines are conforming to the Guidelines.

Is there any charge for any of this?

No. The Shrine system is completely voluntary and supported by ones own devotion to Babalon in their own way.

Great! How do I get started?

Simply go to http://www.shrinesofbabalon.com and print out, sign and return the application there. That is it. In the mean time, feel free to ask any questions you like. You may reach us via email at council@shrinesofbabalon.com or via our Facebook page at https://www.facebook.com/babalonshrines/.

Appendix B

Ophidian Thelema and the Temple of Babalon

rom the most Ancient times of human history, the Great Goddesses of Earth, Sky and Underworld have been the source of the most important Wisdom for humanity concerning the Spirit. This Spirit is your immortal, divine, unique, higher self which incarnates into flesh in order to achieve its manifest purpose, which is called its Will. It is immortal in that it is deathless, and imperishable. It is divine in that it is incorruptible and perfect in its nature and possesses a consciousness with a much greater horizon than your own manifest self. It is unique in that it is like no other Spirit in both its nature and consciousness, yet always recognizable in every incarnation no matter which different body you are born into. It is your higher self in that it creates and informs all that you are, and without which you would certainly cease.

  Therefore from times immemorial, certain Goddesses have taught the Principles of the Will, one's Divine Purpose, and its greater relation to life and to existence. These Principles describe the Art of Living Well, in Harmonia, which is the state of beauty, balance and euphoria which attends any thing done properly as directed from the Spirit. And this

Ophidian Thelema and the Temple of Babalon

Harmonia is the result of practicing the teachings of Heka and Natura. Heka is an act of consciously manifesting Spirit into matter, and all of the attendant spiritual powers which become apparent as the result of this action. The Principles and Rituals which manifest the Spirit in the body, Persona, and the natural world are governed by Natura. It is in Natura that we find the secrets of the body, its energy pathways, how the substances we ingest affect not only our health, but also our emotions, our consciousness and our ability to manifest Heka.

It is important to understand that these teachings of the Goddesses concerning Spirit, Heka and Natura change and adapt to that of the current understanding of humanity, depending upon their current stage of evolutionary progress. These evolutionary stages are charted in the Aeonic Cycles which span thousands of years. However in the current Aeon of Aquarius, the first impulse of this understanding of the old teachings and Principles of Spirit and Heka has been delivered under the banner of Thelema, in what is commonly known as the Book of the Law, called Liber AL vel Legis.

Now in modern terms, Thelema is the Cult of the Will. This is pronounced **Thel**-ley-mah in Ancient Greek, with a strong emphasis on the first syllable. Therefore, Thelema is the name for the system of Magical Philosophy that was divulged to the modern world in the Book "Liber AL vel Legis", commonly referred to as "The Book of the Law", in Cairo, Egypt, in 1904. On April 8th, 9th and 10th of that year, a communication was received by Rose Edith Kelley and written down by her husband Aleister Crowley. This communication consisted of three small chapters that were received at noon, one on each of the three days. Within this writing, with its strange phrases and multi-layered meanings, a new Law for a New Aeon was proclaimed.

Do what thou wilt shall be the whole of the Law.

-Liber Legis I 40

Thelema is Greek for Will, and by Gematria equals 93[66]. This Law proclaims that every woman and every man his a unique, individual and autonomous Will, and that she or he has an inalienable right and responsibility to find out that purpose, and to achieve it, no matter what it

---

[66] See Appendix C for an explanation of Gematria and the Ophidian Kabbalah.

may be. Each person's Will is unique, and can only be discovered by his or her self. This Will is spiritual, and the reason why one has incarnated on this planet. But, how does one discover what their Will is?

Love is the law, love under will.

-Liber Legis I 57

Agape is Greek for Love, and also equals 93. In Thelema, Love means attraction and union. This union is a union with one's Spirit, which holds the keys to one's Will. One must discover and follow their path, by uniting with each and every experience that one needs in order to accomplish their Will, no matter what it may be.

Now Crowley and his subsequent followers were ignorant of the spiritual and historic origins of the Great Liberating Mother, and the Cult of the Will of the Spirit throughout history. Therefore they assumed that Crowley was the original author of these ideas, and that all of the thoughts and conjectures of his mind concerning such things were therefore like the proclamations of a prophet of a new religion. Yet it should be remembered that he was merely the scribe. It is true that he is also called a Prophet, but Prophet in definition means nothing more than a spokesman, or in the terms of the Book of the Law, the forth-speaker. Therefore we call Crowley and his followers Crowleyan Thelemites, for their religion and philosophy is modern, and bears little relation to the Aeonic traditions of the Cult of the Spirit through the Great Liberating Mother.

The Book of the Law states that "There is the dove, and there is the serpent. Choose ye well! He, my prophet, hath chosen, knowing the law of the fortress, and the great mystery of the House of God." In one sense, the Dove is religion with its worship, while the Serpent is Spirit with its devotion. It indeed says that "the prophet has chosen", but not in fact that he has chosen well. There is a difference.

We are called Ophidian Thelemites because we acknowledge the importance of the Book of the Law as a new proclamation of this our Ancient Tradition of the Serpent, the Spirit. We are the followers of the Serpent, or the Spirit, within Thelema. And therefore we are followers of the Divine Feminine throughout history. Ophidian Thelemites follow the Seven Guiding Principles as delivered by Babalon, the current incarnation of the Great Liberating Mother throughout time. These Seven Guiding Principles describe how Spirit arises out of the Underworld, and form the

Ophidian Thelema and the Temple of Babalon

basis for the existence of all things, manifest and unmanifest. Ophidian Thelema emphasizes the importance of the Balanced Ecstatic Path, the enthronement of Spirit within matter, Devotion to the Great Liberating Mother, Heka and Natura. Ophidian Thelemites follow a Living Tradition of Spirit, which means that they still hold the keys to the Knowledge and Conversation of the spirits in their Lineage on a day-to-day basis, whereas most other traditions and religions are following the dead and static words of the founders, by which they seek to govern their own lives. And some Ophidians live life in an indigenous way, in their homeland of Ophidia, secluded away against the corrupt and degenerate ways of modernity so that their Living Traditions may be preserved for a time beyond the coming future changes.

Ophidian Thelemites are devotees of the Goddess Babalon. Because of this, Ophidian Thelemites follow the Balanced Ecstatic Path of the Liberation of the Spirit, of the Serpent, from the bonds of the Persona. As Babalon Herself says:

My Vocation is the Serpent.

Hadit is a manifestation of the Will to Spiritual Advancement. The Sun rising on wings. Or the Winged Serpent, like you say. That's why the Serpent bears the mark of my Mother. The cobra.

The symbol on the back of the hood of the Cobra looks to the eye like the Greek letter Omega, which is a symbol of Nuit for many reasons, not the least of which is that it resembles in shape Her arched body through the star-lit night sky as She is so often represented. It is also important to note in relation to the Serpent that there is no one singular image of the Goddess. Babalon continues:

Many times in history because of the nature of the female the goddess is represented by her Priestess. In the statues. Because there is no one image of the female. It is changing with every day of the Moon. The Sun is always the Sun. The female is different every day. So there are images representing times. But now if you want a statue it would have to be either one of the Nine with the snakes, or just put the snake, because you are reclaiming the female. And I would like a cobra because it had my Mother on its hood, and we always had cobras.

The Serpent sheds its skin, the Moon moves through its phases, and the body sheds its Spirit in continual death and rebirth. The Serpent shows us this motion, this movement, of Spirit through life and death and life again, rippling down through time.

Thus, because of the Will of the Spirit we are Thelemites. And because we are Devotees of Babalon, and of the Spirit itself, and Her Mother, and of the Female, and of the Lineage - because of all of this and more - we are Ophidian.

Templum Babalonis

The Temple of Babalon is a Mystery School dedicated to the devotion and worship of the incarnation of the Great Liberating Mother who is currently known as Babalon. The Temple is an Ophidian organization and practices Ophidian Thelema. In addition, the Temple teaches many forms of Heka, which includes the Orphetic Mysteries, which are the ancient techniques of opening Liminal Gateways to other Realms.

The Temple operates as a Mystery School, which is an institution which teaches esoteric and magical spirituality in a direct and experiential way, as opposed to the symbolic and intellectual approach of other modern esoteric groups. The wisdom of the Temple is based on a core set of philosophies and spiritual principles that guide the student to contact their own Spirit, their divinity within themselves. This is accomplished through a series of Initiations with corresponding teachings that must be mastered by the student before moving on to the next Initiation. These Initiation Cycles, or Degrees, are centered on the Mysteries and Rites of Sex and Death. These are the Mysteries of the Underworld. These Mysteries are kept secret from the uninitiated, who would misinterpret and defile them without the proper experiential knowledge gained by the Initiation and other rituals which accompany it. Without this experiential wisdom, they simply would not understand them, or worse yet as often happens, misinterpret them. These Mysteries and their Initiatory steps increase the student's spiritual awareness and powers in gradual steps, towards Adeptship, which is total self-mastery by the Spirit over the Persona.

It is best if one can be a local member to the Temple, and train directly under the guidance of the Hagia. However, that will not be a possibility for most students, so the Temple offers an Affiliate program as well. By becoming an Associate Member of the Outer Temple, you will be tasked with the serious undertaking of learning Ophidian Magick, with the goal of being fully trained in the Orphetic Mysteries and the Triangle of Manifestation. The main task of the Associate Member is the enacting of the Curriculum in their daily life, pursuing their Will, and learning of the Ophidian ways. This system is for those who crave knowledge of Heka, or Magick, and want to pursue a path of self-transformation in this regard. This is a system based in the tradition of Ophidian Thelema, and personal dedication to Babalon is not required. The Outer Temple Associate system will appeal to those who have magical inclinations, a desire to work with spirit evocation, and who enjoy living in a ritualistic and transformative way.

To be considered for Associate Membership, one must be in good standing with the Temple, and agree to a simple code of conduct. Associate Members will then gain access to the public curriculum, training and the help of Dedicated Temple Members. Associate Members will also have access to some of the Guilds of the Temple, and may help in the work therein. Dedicated Members will be available to answer questions and to help guide the Associate Members in their practices, and private discussion groups have been made available to members online. Associate Members who complete the various curriculum parts may have the opportunity to visit Ophidia and undergo direct Initiation to become Confirmed Members. Confirmed Members may have opportunities for more responsibility in the Temple as well as leadership roles. All Associate Members will have the opportunity to attend certain gatherings and rituals in Ophidia, if so desired and opportunity allows. Associate Members may cease their involvement at any time. There are no charges or fees for Associate Membership - only one's sincere dedication and diligence is required.

Becoming a Daughter of Babalon

The great Liberating Mother has many, many children of various types, both incarnate and discarnate. She births angels, demons, diverse creatures of the Underworld, and many others. Some of the children can and do incarnate into human flesh. And She calls certain of these incarnated beings "the Miha", Her People. Part of the purpose of the Temple of Babalon is to bring the Miha together, in order to reestablish the Temples of the Great Liberating Mother in these modern times. This is part of the Reclamation. And She has Her Priestesses, who are called to establish and run these Temples. The most dedicated of Her Priestesses are also one type of Her Daughters, called the Nine.

> *She is one of the Nine. They do many things. They are Spirit Guardians and Ministers of Message, Teaching. They can do many things. They can traverse Time and Space in lifetimes and teach about past incarnation and ritual and understanding of information important to the work now. They can guide you to where you need to see, as they did with you. They speak in many languages from many times. They have many names.*
>
> *The girl, in your dream... Is a Nine. Madimi, is a Nine. Pahkahtuahte (Pah-kah-tu-**ah**'-teh) is one name. Kashina (Kah-**sheen**'-nah), Mayohkah (May-**oh**'-kah), Seraphina (Ser-a-**pheen**'-ah), Diotima (Day-**oh**'-tih-mah), Hatshepsut (Hah-sep-**shoot**'), Tapeekah (Deh-**peek**'-kah), Nani (**Nah**'-neh), Leeosa (Lee-**oh**'-sah). It is as you thought. Diangela (Dee-**ahn**'-jel-lah). They lived in my service, and they work for me still. There is a Lineage. The Royal Lineage of my Daughter. Nine Ways.*
>
> -Vox Babalonis[67]

These Holy Women are the incarnate daughters of the Great Liberating Mother, and form what She calls the Lineage. This is the Royal Lineage from Ra. Therefore these are the Daughters of Fortitude. These are the Noboramantu, the sword of Mentu, the white faced Bull, which steers down through space and time. This chain of incarnations forms the temporal power structure of the Great Liberating Mother. Many of the names of the Nine have survived in the historical record, such as Diotima, Hatshepsut, Diangela, and Seraphina. The Principalia is one of the Nine. And the discarnate Nine, and their Shades, are often Deified Geniuses who continue their work after death in Babalon's name.

Now because they are called the Nine does not mean there are only nine of them in existence. Rather there are nine offices or functions, or as Babalon says, they are born in "Nine Ways". And only a few are incarnate at any given time. Because of this, any woman who feels an affinity for these words concerning the Nine should seek out the Temple to make themselves known. There, one may undergo the tests and observations to

---

[67] Babalon Herself from one of the secret periodic Supreme Rituals in Templum Babalonis, in this case from 2008 EV. An audio recording of this part of Her communication was made public as an example, and can be found at http://www.templeofbabalon.com/images/05_babalon_nine.mp3

determine if indeed one is a Nine. These tests are concerned not only with knowledge of information we have not published, but also with their identity from their past incarnations as a Nine in the service of the Great Liberating Mother. Once their identity has been verified, a Nine must be properly trained and awakened to their full power, or abomination may ensue. Unfortunately, we have already seen this happen to one other Nine.

But even if you are not a Nine, but have an intense yearning within your Spirit to become a Daughter Of Babalon, and to perhaps be reborn in your next incarnation as a Nine, one of Her Daughters, then there is a path for you. Any woman who wishes to be so dedicated will be taught and trained by the Hagia in the ways of the Nine. In fact, this is the way that all of the Priestesses became Nine in the past, through dedication and service in Her Temple. And their power is increased in each incarnation in which they serve Her, their Spirit transformed by Babalon with each new incarnation, Nine Ways. And when the Hagia steps down or returns to the Underworld, then the next Nine will assume the role of Hagia in Templum Babalonis, and continue the Lineage in service. This path is available to those who are so called to the Great Liberating Mother. And so too for the men who wish to serve Babalon and Her Daughters and Priestesses. You may be Miha, and this Temple may be your home.

For more information, please contact the Temple of Babalon at info@templeofbabalon.com or through our web site at http://www.templeofbabalon.com .

Appendix C

The Gematria of the Ophidian Kabbalah

ematria is a Greek word which is used to describe a specific kind of numerology in which the letters of the alphabet also have a corresponding number or value. The word Gematria is probably a confusion or combination of two Greek words, the first of which is γεωμετρία, geōmetriā, which describes the three-dimensional interpretations of numbers through the position and placement of the system of Geometry. The second Greek word is γραμματεια, grammateia, which means *knowledge of writing*. So it becomes clear now that Gematria is a term which describes the assignment of numbers to letters according to position and place in an alphabet. This Greek word Gematria was later adopted into the early Hebrew system of Kabbalah. Kabbalah, Qabalah, or Cabala is a word which comes from the Hebew לבק, QBL, "to receive," which signifies a tradition of received spiritual information from a non-material source. Gnosis in Greek, γνῶσις, is a similar term.

Many cultures and languages use a form of Gematria in which the letters of their alphabets are assigned numerical values. By adding the values of the letters together, the total value of a word may then be known. For example, the Greek word θέλημα, Thelema, which means Will has the

THE GEMATRIA OF THE OPHIDIAN KABBALAH

value of 93 by Gematria. 9 + 5 + 30 + 8 + 40 + 1 = 93. The word ἀγάπη, Agape, which means Love also equals 93. 1 + 3 + 1 + 80 + 8 = 93. These two words are considered to by related by Gematria, because they both equal the same value. And when it says in Liber Legis "Love is the law, love under will," one can now see the numerical relationship between these two important concepts of Love and Will, by way of the number 93 via Gematria.

In this way, writings and words which are truly received from beyond the minds of men will often have an internal numerological coherency which proves the validity of the writing. Within the Ophidian Kabbalah, Gematria is used not only to attempt to understand meanings which are not currently known or that are unclear, but more importantly to verify what has been spoken by the Spirits[68]. This was its original use. These systems of number associations, or Gematria, shows us the secret coherency of the underlying Magickal Philosophy, and keeps us on a proper track when exploring received teachings and philosophies. When one uses this system of Gematria to study the Book of Law, one is often shocked at the numerical coherency one can find there. Liber Legis is a received Grimoire of the highest order. It is an instruction manual for Priestesses of Heka. And it contains many of the lost mysteries of a culture now extinct, but which remnants of may be found in Egyptian, Sumerian, Etruscan, Magyar, Maltese and other cultures heading back towards the Golden Age.

Now many of the ancient languages already have a Gematria, meaning that their alphabets are already assigned to numbers. But many modern languages which are derivatives of Latin do not. This has posed a problem for received teachings which have been manifest in the Latin or English languages. Often these words would be translated into a different language, such as Hebrew or Greek, in order to discover something more concerning their meaning. But most often this is wholly inadequate, as each language has its own spiritual evolution and internal meanings which are lost upon translation. For example, important numbers in the Hebrew Kabbalah may not also be important in the Greek. Each language, and the culture which formed it, contains its own genius. To solve this problem, and to prove in yet another way its own spiritual authenticity, the Book of the Law prophesies many times concerning the English Qabalah, and

---

[68] And this is why the Hebrew root of the word Qabalah, QBL means "to receive". All systems of Qabalah, no matter which tradition, have their origins in Spirit communication, such as in our case with the Book of Law.

states in fact that it will be discovered by means of the writing within this book, itself. The following are the five relevant verses concerning these ciphers which have lead to the discovery of the English Qabalah[69].

My number is 11, as all their numbers who are of us.

-Liber Legis I 60

Thou shalt obtain the order & value of the English Alphabet; thou shalt find new symbols to attribute them unto.

-Liber Legis II 55

4 6 3 8 A B K 2 4 A L G M O R 3 Y X 24 89 R P S T O V A L. What meaneth this, o prophet? Thou knowest not; nor shalt thou know ever. There cometh one to follow thee: he shall expound it. But remember, o chosen one, to be me; to follow the love of Nu in the star-lit heaven; to look forth upon men, to tell them this glad word.

-Liber Legis II 76

This book shall be translated into all tongues: but always with the original in the writing of the Beast; for in the chance shape of the letters and their position to one another: in these are mysteries that no Beast shall divine. Let him not seek to try: but one cometh after him, whence I say not, who shall discover the Key of it all. Then this line drawn is a key: then this circle squared in its failure is a key also. And Abrahadabra. It shall be his child & that strangely. Let him not seek after this; for thereby alone can he fall from it.

-Liber Legis III 47

---

[69] The bare bones of this system which is now called the New Aeon English Qabalah was first discovered by an English woman named Carol Smith in 1974 EV. It has been used in Templum Babalonis since its inception and by its founders since at least as far back as 1990 EV.

THE GEMATRIA OF THE OPHIDIAN KABBALAH

Paste the sheets from right to left and from top to bottom: then behold!

There is a splendour in my name hidden and glorious, as the sun of midnight is ever the son."

-Liber Legis III 73-74

In addition to the above verses, there is one more clue given in Liber Legis as to the decipherment of the English Qabalah, and that is from the handwritten page from which the above verse, III 47, comes from. (See Figure I) And this is where we shall start the explanation of the discovery of what is now called the New Aeon English Qabalah. Please direct you attention to the writing upon the page, particularly where it says "Let him not seek to try: but one cometh after him, whence I say not, who shall discover the Key of it all. Then this line drawn is a key: then this circle squared in its failure is a key also." Now you can see on the page where the diagonal line was slashed across the page, and the circle around the cross (the circle squared in its failure) was drawn. This Key was the Key to deciphering the English Kabbalah, as foretold in II, 55 above. If you will notice the grid which has been dawn upon this page, and that this grid is marked on the left with numbers and along the top with letters. "Thou shalt obtain the order & value of the English Alphabet." This grid is an invitation to write down the order of the English Alphabet following the numbers upon the left hand side. If we do so, we put the first letter of the alphabet "a" in box number one. We then put "b" in box number 2, "c" in box number 3 and so on until we reach the bottom. We then continue in the next column and on through the alphabet as many times as is needed in order to fill the entire grid. The result will look like the grid in Figure II, where each square now has a letter, according to the order of the English Alphabet, as commanded.

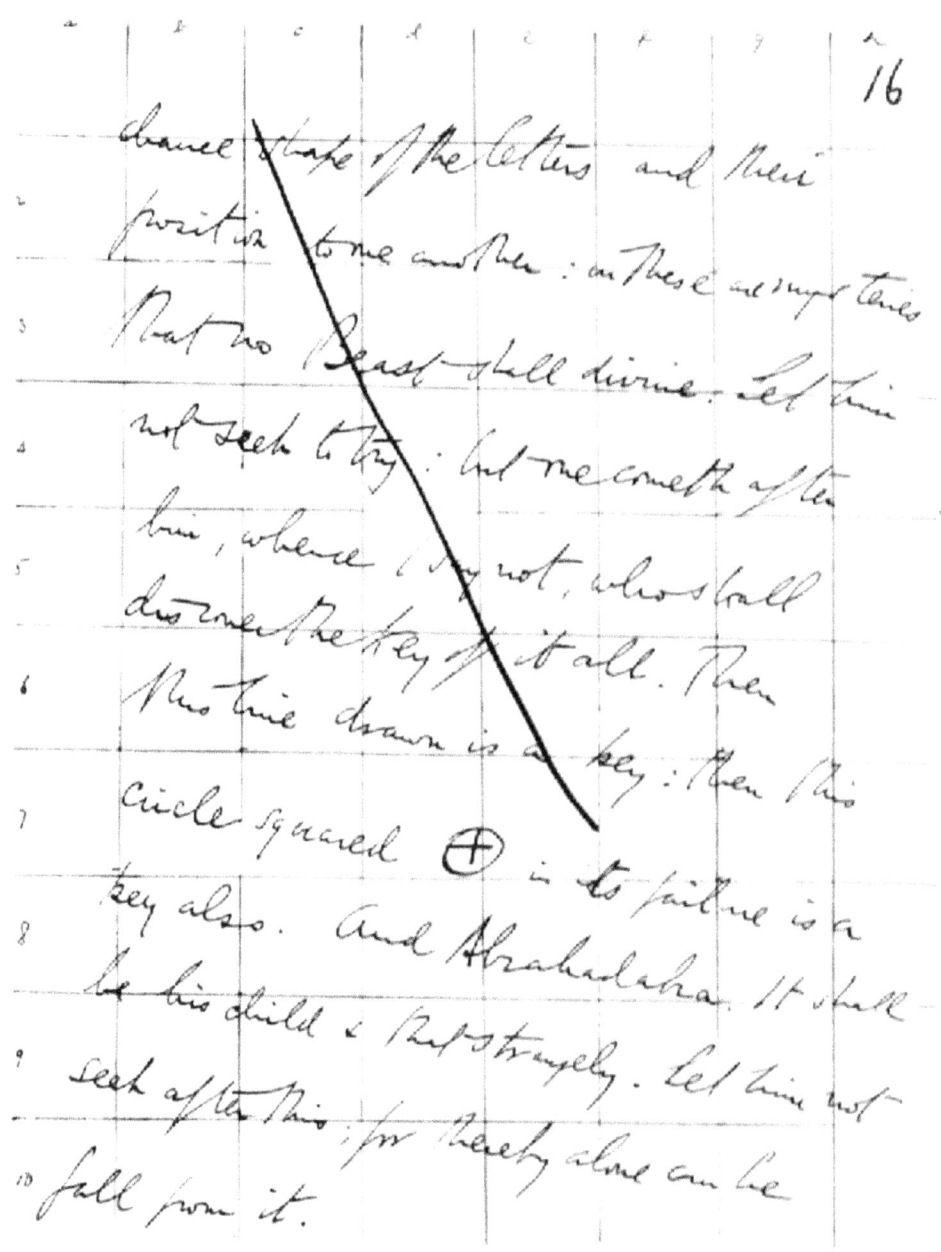

Figure I

The Gematria of the Ophidian Kabbalah

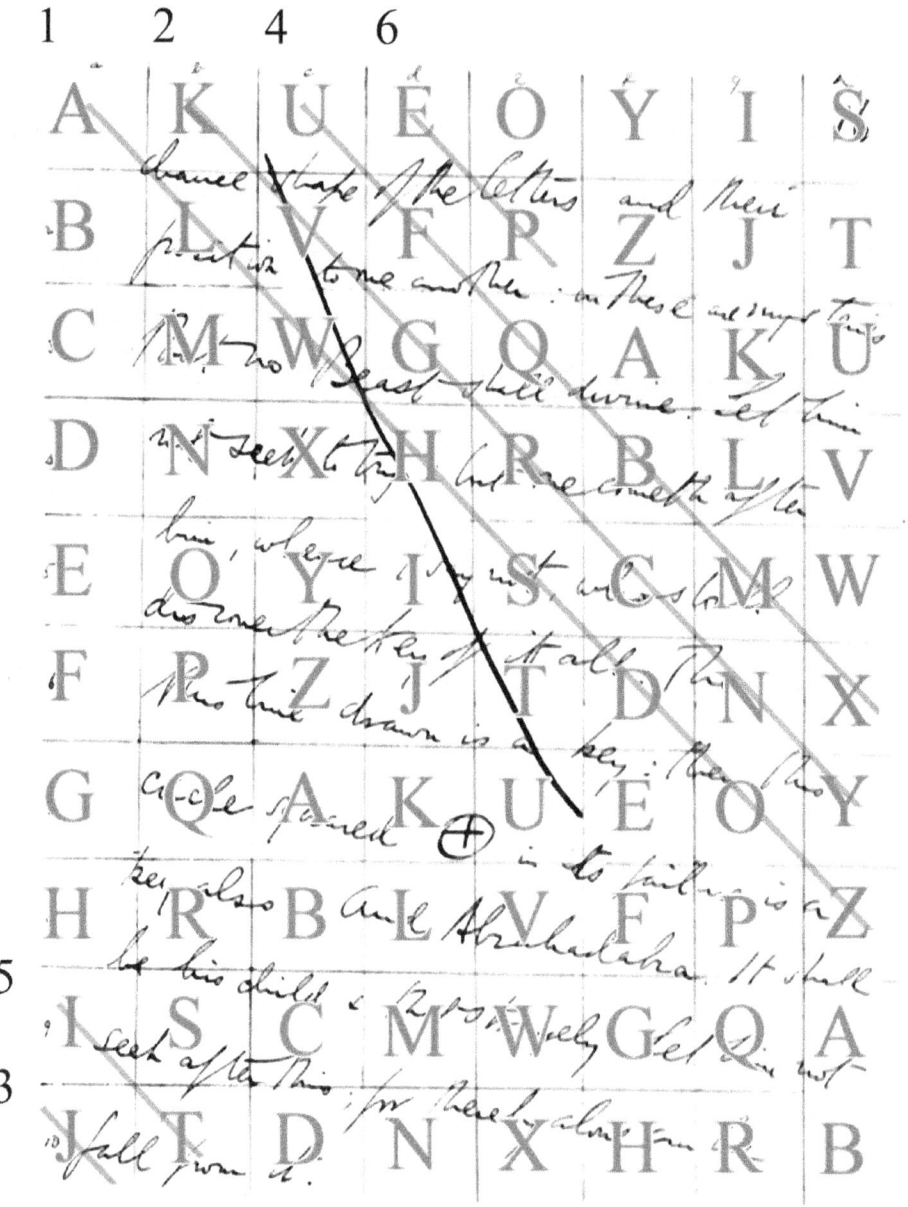

Figure II

The next step is to apply the Keys as given in Liber Legis. There are three explicit Keys given in verse III 47, and they are mentioned in quick succession. "Then this line drawn is a key: then this circle squared in its failure is a key also. And Abrahadabra." The first shows the direction to read, the second shows where to begin, and the third is a marker, to make sure you are reading the correct letters. Therefore we need to be reading in a diagonal direction according to the line drawn. We need to start at the first cross in the top left of the grid, according to the offset cross which is in the top left corner of the circle. If we do so, then the first letter we get is A. The next letter. Following diagonally is L. Notice that L is 11 letters after A. Abrahadabra is a famous 11 letter word. Let us see if this continues. The next letter in the diagonal line is W. Yes, W is 11 letters from L. Let us remind you again of verse 1, 60 "My number is 11, as all their numbers who are of us." Indeed. We have now found a new "order and value of the English Alphabet" according to their instructions. Following this method, the value of A is 1, L is 2, W is 3, H is 4, S is 5 and so on through the entire alphabet.[70] And notice too that if you count by 11 letters in this manner that it loops seamlessly though the entire alphabet, with the last letter in the series, P=26 being 11 letters from A again in the series. Notice also that this solution also perfectly satisfies Frater Achad's Key to Liber Legis, "AL". Verse III 47 says "but one cometh after him, whence I say not, who shall discover the Key of it all." It was universally accepted by Crowley that Fr. Achad had discovered the Key to Liber Legis, even though they did not fully understand all of its implications at the time. This Key was the letters AL, which is why the name of the book was changed to Liber AL vel Legis from the original Liber Legis. This Key of AL from Fr. Achad shows how the new "order and value of the English Alphabet" begins. A-L-W etc. Each being 11 letters apart. It is indeed the Key of it all.

So we finally have our order and values for the English Alphabet, as listed now below.

A	1	G	11	M	21	S	5	Y	15
B	20	H	4	N	14	T	24	Z	8
C	13	I	23	O	7	U	17		
D	6	J	16	P	26	V	10		
E	25	K	9	Q	19	W	3		
F	18	L	2	R	12	X	22		

---

[70] Please notice too that the letter A then corresponds to the first row of the grid, and L to the row marked 2 on the grid, the letter W to the row marked 3 and so on, further reinforcing the number assignments of A=1, L=2, W=3 etc.

The Gematria of the Ophidian Kabbalah

Now the proof of this assignment of letters and numbers is further born out by the strange string of numbers and letters from verse II, 76 "4 6 3 8 A B K 24 A L G M O R 3 Y X 24 89 R P S T O V A L". There are many ciphers hidden in this phrase, but here is one of the first that was discovered as proof of the English Alphabet, and the number assignment given above. In the original handwriting it is written in two lines in the original text as such:

4 6 3 8 A B K 24 A L G M O R 3 Y
X 24 89 R P S T O V A L

Notice here that there are 17 letters on the first line, and 11 letters on the second. Forgetting the importance of those numbers for a moment, if one takes the x at the beginning of line two as a multiplication sign, then 11 x 17 = 187. Suddenly all becomes clear, because the phrase "English Alphabet" in fact also equals 187 if figured using the values of each letter in the phrase and adding them together.

AL 2:55 states "Thou shalt obtain the order & value of the English Alphabet; thou shalt find new symbols to attribute them unto." Furthermore, under this new attribution of letters and numbers, the words "order & value" = 117, as does the word "letters", and the phrase "new symbols" and the command "Change them not" in style of value. Notice that the numbers 11 and 17 from the above proof are appearing again, this time merged as 117

But there is more yet with this line. Now notice that the numbers 1 through 26, which are the letters A through Z, add up to 351. The strange phrase in AL 2:76 "4 6 3 8 A B K 24 A L G M O R 3 Y x 24 89 R P S T O V A L" also equals 351. So this cipher of strange letters and numbers is equal to the sum of all of the letters in the English Alphabet, as well as to the phrase "English Alphabet" itself.

But there is one more mystery of these letters in Liber Legis which we have not mentioned yet. Not only is a new "order and value" established for the English alphabet which satisfies the commands of Liber Legis, and solves one of its greatest ciphers as shown above, but a new advanced method of Gematira is given as well.

Paste the sheets from right to left and from top to bottom: then behold!

MYSTERY BABALON

There is a splendour in my name hidden and glorious, as the sun of midnight is ever the son."

-Liber Legis III 73-74

This advanced method of Gematria is sometimes referred to as the *Count Well* method. In essence, it combines two words together in order to get a new understanding of their relationship to each other in a new number which results from their combination, which is not obvious by just adding the letters together in a normal fashion. For example, it is hinted in the verses shown above that there is a *hidden splendour* in the *sun of midnight*. Now the phrase *sun of midnight* is equal to 187, the famous number above which is also equal to the phrase *English Alphabet*. But believe it or not, that is not the important point. If we take the two words Midnight Sun and arrange them in a certain way, according to the instructions given in the verse above, by writing them from right to left and from top to bottom, then a certain mathematical computation can be performed upon them through simple addition as follows.

	S (5)	U (17)	N (14)
M (21)	26	38	35
I (23)	28	40	37
D (6)	11	23	20
N (14)	19	31	28
I (23)	28	40	37
G (11)	16	28	25
H (4)	9	21	18
T (24)	29	41	38
Totals	166	262	238

166 + 262 + 238 = 666

We have now "pasted the sheets from right to left[71], and from top to bottom". In doing so, every letter from one word can be added to every

---

[71] It does not matter in the end if your write the words right to left or bottom to top, the mathematical result will always be the same.

The Gematria of the Ophidian Kabbalah

letter from the other word. These totals are then added together. Then behold, Midnight % Sun equals the value of 666! *There is a splendour in my name hidden and glorious, as the sun of midnight is ever the son.*

The % symbol is used to indicate that the Count Well method has been used. Using this method, we find many amazing results, such as Azure % Lidded = 718, Abrahad % abra =418 and English % Alphabet = 1393. At the very end of Liber Legis the last verse it says, "The Book of the Law is written and concealed. Aum Ha" Aum % Ha = 93. In addition to that, Aum % Ho, which is written earlier in Chapter I equals 111. These are but a few examples of mysteries which are to be uncovered in Liber Legis, which proves beyond a shadow of a doubt the non-human origins of the book.

Many mysteries and ciphers are solved by the New Aeon English Qabalah, many examples were given in Part I of this book Mystery Babalon when explaining the nature of the various Thelemic Deities. But the study of the Ophidian Kabbalah, which in part includes the New Aeon English Qabalah, might take many volumes to be explored adequately, and will be published in Book IV: Commentaria of the Magickal Philosophy of Templum Babalonis.

Appendix D

Artist Acknowledgements and Resources

Special thanks are in order to the wonderful creative people who lent their talents and kind permissions to use their works in this book. You can find them and their work at the links below.

Angel Silva
　　Photographer
　　https://www.facebook.com/ojotestigo

Daniel Corcuera
　　Artist
　　https://www.facebook.com/nekronikontemple/

Lance Haworth
　　Owner

Lawless Art, Janin Pisarek
　　Artist
　　https://www.facebook.com/LawlessArt/

Luciana Lupe Vasconcelos
　　Artist
　　http://www.lupevision.com

Artist Acknowledgements and Resources

Nuria Fortuny Art
Artist
https://www.facebook.com/NuriaFortunyArt/

Orryelle Defenestrate-Bascule
Artist
Illustrations (c)2016 Orryelle Defenestrate-Bascule, from his 'The Book of Going Back by Night', whose Third Chapter deals with Babalon as an earthing of the Maat current in our Aeon. Images used with permission. The book is available here: www.crossroads.wild.net.au/inspiral2.htm

More of Orryelle's art can be seen at
www.crossroads.wild.net.au/esoterotica.htm

Saba Khandroma
Dancer, Performance Artist and Model
https://www.facebook.com/anexia23/
https://www.facebook.com/khandroma23/

Soma Luna LLC

The Aromatic Herbs, Resins, Oils and Incense supplies mentioned in Chapter 14 *Shrine Incense, Perfumes and Oils* may be found at the world's largest and oldest online supplier of incense making materials: Soma Luna LLC. Please visit them at http://www.somaluna.com to view their selection of rare botanicals, including Thelemic and Traditional Abramelin incense and oil. Soma Luna LLC is owned by the author, Hagia Aureavia.

Glossary of Terms

Ab: In Egyptian Ab, Ib, Yb or Haty are words which signify the Heart, or what we *Ophidians* call the Waters, which permeates the *Khat* (physical body). The compliment of the Ab (emotions, *Waters*) is the *Ka* (desires, *Fires*). Both the Ab and the *Ka* are the most immediate vehicles of communication between the *Ba* (*Persona*) and the *Khu* (*Spirit*). See also *Membra Animae*.

Abyss, The: The Gulf created by the separation of the awareness of the *Persona* and the presence of the *Spirit*. The greater the separation of *Persona* and *Spirit*, the greater the Gulf of the Abyss. This Abyss houses denizens of various natures, the most important of which is *Choronzon*. The experience and the affect of the Abyss is different for males and females, the former of which tend toward megalomaniacal insanity and power lust, while the latter tend to become lost and fragmented. The cure for both however is the same: the *Persona* must enact subservience to the guidance of their *Spirit*. It is only by following a path in life other than that of the *Will* of your *Spirit* that the Abyss grows and gains power. Or to look at it another way, the Abyss grows in power the more that the *Persona* seeks to usurp the rightful place of the *Spirit*, especially by seeking the immortality of the *Spirit* for itself.

Adept: One who has achieved the level of spiritual attainment where their *Persona* is subdued by and in the control of its *Spirit* for the purpose of implementing its *Will* amongst the living. This is also known as *Enlightened Self-Mastery*, or *True Self Mastery*. An Adept is known by the special light

Glossary of Terms

which shows forth in his or her eyes, signifying the close presence of their *Spirit*.

Aeons: The concept of Aeons refers to a way of organizing historical events and influences according to the system of the *Precession of the Equinoxes*. Each Aeon lasts for 2160 years, and follows the signs of the Zodiac in reverse order. The Aeons mark different epochs in human history and advancement, as well as different incarnations of the gods which are influenced by the ruling sign of the Aeon. Pronounced *ee*-ohn. See also *Precession of the Equinoxes, Equinox of the Gods*.

Anima: The life force energy of an incarnated *Spirit* which emanates from the body of its incarnation, generally called a soul. In Greek it was called Psyche and in Egyptian it was called the *Ba*, which included all of the things which ceased connection with the *Spirit* upon death, like the *Khat, Khaibit, Ab* and *Ka*. The soul of a person emanates from its body, just as the incarnated Soul of *Nuit* emanates from the planet as *Gaia*. When a person dies, the *Fila* of its soul is severed from the immortal *Spirit* to which it was attached, and in most cases it becomes a *Shade*. See also *Membra Animae*.

Anima Mundi: The *World Soul*. See *Gaia*

Apotelesma: The result of any *Heka*, ritual or manifestation of spiritual energy, started by the process of *Katarche*. The Apotelesma is usually worldly in nature and the connection from the Apotelesma back to the originating *Katarche* may not always be apparent, unless one can find the *Fila* connecting the two events. Pronounced Ah-poh-tel-*lays*-mah. See also *Manifestation*.

Areans, The: See *the Aryans*.

Aryans, The: This term has nothing to do with modern connotations of Aryans in a racial sense, although most of the Aryans were indeed of European descent. The Aryans were originally the children of the *Storm Gods* who ruled the many empires of the Aeon of Aries, from which they get their name. They brought broad-scale war and empire to the world, while repressing the earlier Goddess cultures and relegating women to a life of slavery. They are the authors of a large part of the Degeneration, and tried to suppress the cults of the *Great Liberating Mother* wherever they could.

Aureavia: The name of the current *Hagia* of *Templum Babalonis* and *Principalia* of the *Nine*. The name means "Golden Path" and it is this Golden Path which She manifests which shall lead to a new Golden Age. She is also the Daughter of the *Daughter of Fortitude*. Pronounced ow-ree-ah-*vee*-ah.

Avreavia: An alternate spelling in English of *Aureavia*, the *Principalia* and the current *Hagia* of *Templum Babalonis*.

Ba: An Egyptian word signifying the personality or person-hood of an individual. The Ba is often imagined as a human-headed bird. The concept of the Ba includes what we *Ophidians* call the *Persona* complex, which is the manifested mundane consciousness or mind of the incarnated *Khu* (*Spirit*). The Ba rests within the *Sa* (the subtle body of the *Spirit*, also called the *Soul*), and is communicated to most immediately by the *Ab* (*Waters*) and the *Ka* (*Fires*). See also *Membra Animae*.

Babalon: The name of the current incarnation of the *Great Liberating Mother*. Her symbols are the *Star* and the *Snake*. The *Star* is the Seven Pointed Star of Babalon, which is drawn differently than the Star of Venus. The *Snake* is a *Cobra*, because the hood of the *Cobra* has the mark of Her Mother *Nuit*. Babalon is a Warrior Goddess, a Goddess of *Heka*, a *Liminal Point* to the *Underworld*, and a Goddess of *Ecstatic Liberation of the Spirit*. She also appears in a throne with *lions* or a chariot pulled by *lions*, and sometimes astride beasts like *lions* or *serpents*. The first historical record of Her appearance in recent times can be found in the magical diaries of Dr. John Dee (See *Madimi* and *M.D.M.I.*). Her name in this incarnation is a play upon the corrupted image of Her found in the Book of Revelation, when She ruled the city of Babylon as the Goddess Ishtar (Innana, Astarte). Her Egyptian name is Hoor Pahkhet, and is plainly visible in *Liber Legis* for those that can see that "there is division hither homeward; there is a word not known. Spelling is defunct; all is not aught." For a more in-depth analysis of Babalon, please see "Who or what is Babalon?" For a more extensive exposition of *Babalon* and the History of the *Great Liberating Mother*, please see Book II Chapter 2 and 3 of the Magickal Philosophy of Templum Babalonis.

Balanced Ecstatic Path, The: A collection of teachings, rituals and ways of living which have been given to mankind by the *Great Liberating Mother* so that they might know the full pleasure of existence and life. These

GLOSSARY OF TERMS

teachings center around the revelation of one's own *Spirit*, and they seek to bring it onto the throne of one's life. Many powers and levels of being and understanding accompany the closeness of one's *Spirit*, and these are the ecstatic rewards of following Her teachings. See also *Ecstasy*, *Harmonia*, *Natura*, and the *Seven Guiding Principles*.

Black Star, The: A name used by many spirits for *Saturn*, referring to its secret history before the formation of the Earth, when it was a *Blue Star*. In one interpretation, it is the Blue part of the "Blue and Gold" in the *Book of Law*, which are "seen of the seeing". There is also a secret history of the origins of the *Blue Star* and its connection to the *Sirius* system long ago, of which many of the spirits speak. The Black Star has a strong connection to the *Underworld*. See also *Midnight Sun*.

Black Sun, The: Another name for the *Midnight Sun*.

Blue and Gold: Either an artistic image of the Sun shining in the blue sky, *Saturn* and *Sol*, or *Babalon* and Her Brother *Ra Hoor Khuit*, depending upon the context.

Blue Star, The: When *Saturn* was a Star. See the *Black Star*.

Bona Dea: A Roman Goddess whose name means "the Good Goddess". She was a secret cover for *Kybele* in Rome when Her worship in its original form was banned. She had Temples which contained vast stores of women, spices, herbs and medicines. Like earlier Egyptian cults of the *Great Liberating Mother*, Her priestesses used *cobras* to guard the Temple stores. Like *Fortuna*, Bona Dea bears the *Cornucopia*, and also a *Serpent* coiled around Her hand to show Her *Ophidian* nature. Pronounced *Boh-*nah *Day*-ah.

Book of Law, The: Also called *Liber AL vel Legis*, or simply *Liber Legis*. In this book the Magical Philosophy of *Thelema* was first divulged to the world. A communication was received by Rose Edith Kelley and written down by her husband Aleister Crowley in Cairo, Egypt, in 1904 on three consecutive days, April 8th, 9th and 10th of that year. This communication consisted of three small chapters that were received at noon, one on each of the three days. Within this writing, with its strange phrases and multi-layered meanings, a new Law for a new *Aeon* was proclaimed. Although the book is commonly referred to as "the Book of the Law", *Babalon* always refers to it as "the Book of Law", which follows the title as given within the text of the book itself.

Book of the Law, The: See the *Book of Law*.

Bounty: The result of following the principles of *Natura*, which is a state of abundant resources and spiritual fulfillment. If left unmolested by the needless resource-extraction of science and industrialization, both biological and spiritual aspects of life always trend towards Bounty and abundance. Bounty is impossible to avoid when all life acts in a *Justified* manner. Life does not need more than Bounty to thrive and be perfectly content and happy. The coins of the monetary systems, however, are a tool of enslavement, being issued by authorities as a form of control. See also *Cornucopia*, *Fortuna*.

Brotherhood, The: See the *Brotherhood of the Midnight Sun*.

Brotherhood of the Midnight Sun, The: The Dwellers and Guardians in the *Underworld*, under the Light of *Sirius*. The golden *Sons of Gaia* in the *Outer Temple* are forged into the steel of the Brothers of the Midnight Sun in the *Inner Temple*. The Brotherhood's members, both incorporeal and incarnate, are all male. The incarnate Brothers are *Inner Temple Adepts*. It is they who exhibit true manhood in the Temple - for they function as Guardians of Power, not the wielders of it. The incorporeal members form the Body of the Brotherhood and are lead by their unmanifest brethren which organize themselves into an Alliance of 15, which is manifest in three ways. These Greater Brothers all have a connection to *Sirius*, *Saturn* or the Moon. There are many male deities in the Ancient World associated with the *Midnight Sun* in all of its forms, including Nana, Sin, Khonsu, Tahuti (Dahuty, Djehuti etc.), Setesh and His Herald Anpu, Tum and others.

Caelestial Realms, The: One of the *Three Great Realms*. The Caelestial Realms are the source of all Divine Potentiality and *Principles*. Also called the *Heavenly* or *Divine Realms*, the origination of all true Gods and Angels are to be found here.

Choronzon: The demon of the *Abyss*, who is by far the most feared demon by the mind of the *Persona*. One flash of the presence of his eyes will cause such a tremendous primordial fear within the mind of the *Persona* that most never recover from such an experience. Often people confronted by such terror are so overwhelmed that they forsake their spiritual path, and retreat back into the mundane world in hopes of forgetting the experience entirely. However, Choronzon serves a special purpose upon the leash of *Babalon*, known to Her *Priestesses* in the *Inner Temple*.

Cobra: A special form of the *serpent* for *Ophidians*, which bears on its hood the mark of *Nuit*, the Mother of the Cosmos, the Mother of all Mothers. Cobras were used by the *Priestesses* to guard the stores of the Temples of many Goddesses in Egypt such as Pahkhet, as well as *Bona Dea* in Rome.

Cornucopia: Literally the "horn of plenty" which holds the bounty of a life laid at the feet of the properly manifested *Will* of the *Spirit*. The Cornucopia is an image of that state when all material things needed for the accomplishment of the *Will* of an incarnated *Spirit* are manifest and available for that purpose. This state is accomplished by following the *Seven Guiding Principles*. See also *Fortuna*.

Court of Babalon, The: Those who enjoy the presence of *Babalon* in the *Inner Temple*, bound in life as well as death to the service of Her and Her Lineage.

Chthonic Realms, The: One of the *Three Great Realms*. See also *Underworld*.

Cybele: See *Kybele*.

Daughter of Fortitude, The: An ancient title of the *Great Liberating Mother*. She was declared in almost all of the cultures which worshipped Her as the Daughter of the Sun, which was the greatest visible object of Fortitude. But this title was not mere symbolism, for She holds lineage from the Sun God himself, as in Egypt where She was one of the Daughters of Ra or in Archaic Greece where She is the Daughter of Helios and kin to the *Titans*. The Daughter of Fortitude was also a title given to John Dee by *Madimi* as the name of her mother.

Deified Genius: See *Shade*.

Divine Realms: One of the *Three Great Realms*. See the *Caelestial Realms*.

Equinox of the Gods, The: The point of transition between one *Aeon* and another, which takes place on the Spring Equinox every 2160 years. The most recent Equinox of the Gods took place in the spring of 1904. See also *Precession of the Equinoxes*, *Aeons*.

Ecstasy: The state of bliss which floods the *Persona* and its physical body when the *Spirit* draws close to the flesh. This state is also accompanied by many powers of *Heka* granted by the closeness of the *Spirit*. This state is known as the *Ecstatic Liberation of the Spirit*. It is also one of the powers of the *Great Liberating Mother*. *Ophidians* follow the *Balanced Ecstatic Path*, which seeks to manifest this state in daily life, through rituals of *Heka* and *Natura*, so that *Harmonia* may ensue. See *Ecstatic Liberation of the Spirit*.

Ecstatic Liberation of the Spirit, The: The state of *ecstasy* which accompanies the Liberation of the Spirit from the confines of the *Persona*. It is important to note that the *Spirit* is not alienated from the flesh, or at war with the flesh, as many suppose. Rather, the flesh allows one to feel the *Ecstasy* of the *Spirit*. The flesh is the *Justified* Throne of the *Spirit* in the manifest realm. It is the tight grip and control of the *Persona* over consciousness which is one of the factors which keeps the *Spirit* from manifesting more fully. See *Ecstasy*.

Elemental Degrees, The: See the *Outer Temple*.

Emotional Language, The: The symbols of the *Waters* of the *Persona*, and the methods of their navigation and use. See also *Fila*.

Enlightened Self-Mastery: See *Adept*.

Ethereal Body: See Anima.

Fila: Literally a string, or connection. A Fila is an experiential imprintation created in the *Waters* of the *Persona* by a spiritual event, energy or entity. This imprintation creates a link to the event, energy or entity that can be used again at a later date to help to reconnect with that event, energy or entity again - no matter how great the distance or time. Filas work in reverse as well, so it is important to be trained in their navigation within the *Waters* so that they do not become a way for entities to influence or control the *Persona* to a greater or lesser degree - as usually happens with the uninitiated dabblers in *Heka*. The principles of *Filas*, the

GLOSSARY OF TERMS

Waters and their navigation is generally known within the Temple under the moniker of the Emotional Language, and constitutes one of the many great lost arts from the Ancient world housed within the Temple. Pronounced *Fee*-lah.

Fortuitous Angels, The: See the *Seven Fortuitous Angels*.

Fortuna: The fortuitous Goddess. Fortuitous means both Strong and Fortunate. We *Ophidians* know this word "fortunate" not by its modern meaning of luck, good fortune, or random chance, but rather by its true meaning stemming from the *Cornucopia* which She bears, full of *Bounty*. This *Bounty* is a source of strength. Therefore this word fortuitous or fortunate means the *Bounty* of Full *Spirit*, also called *Spirit* Fulfilled. This is the *Harmonia* of a life properly lived. One is Fortunate if one has the full presence of one's *Spirit*, and the *Bounty* which that brings. This has also been called one's Fortune or Destiny. In addition to the *Cornucopia*, Fortuna holds the *Wheel* which shows that the *Bounty* of ones Fortune is accomplished by following the *Seven Guiding Principles* of *the Great Liberating Mother*. She is an *Underworld* Goddess, as Fortune lies beneath one's feet. She was known as Hel or Hela in the Northern European traditions and *Helena* in Greece, as the root Hel means Fortune in many languages. Pronounced For-*toon*-ah.

Gaia: The *Anima Mundi*, or *World Soul*, is the matrix of all life-energy of the planet Earth. All physical life is born from Her, and to Her it returns. She is a living being, and all life forms make up Her body in the same way that cells make up one's own body. For just as cells can not thrive and reproduce outside of the matrix of the body, so too is it for life whose matrix is Gaia Herself. The principles of *Natura*, which govern the manifestation of *Heka*, are given to all life by Gaia so that *Bounty* may ensue. *Nuit* has endless incarnations in various bodies throughout the Universe, one of which is Gaia. In this way Gaia is the *Soul*, the incarnated *Spirit* energy of *Nuit*, having been born into the body of the planet itself. This is why Gaia is called *Anima Mundi*, the *World Soul*, and also why *Nuit* says in *Liber Legis* I,53 "This shall regenerate the world, the little world my sister, my heart & my tongue, unto whom I send this kiss." The heart and tongue here signify the *Anima* and *Vox* of Gaia, respectively. Gaia is also the mother of the important beings, now demonized and forgotten, known collectively as the *Titans*. Pronounced *Guy*-ah.

Genius: 1) A *spirit* or intelligence of something - be it person, place, group, race, country, astronomical body, or any other thing. Examples are Genius Loci (spirit of a place) and Roma (Personification of Rome as a Goddess).

Genius: 2) The *Shade* of an advanced *Adept* that can maintain a *Fila* to its *Spirit* and continue the work of its *Will* after death. The Nine often function as Deified Genii in this way, and still work in service of *Babalon* beyond death. See *Shade*.

Grandmother, The: A title for *Nuit* amongst *Ophidians*, for She is the Mother of *Babalon*, by Ra. See also *Nuit*.

Great Liberating Mother: The universal name first divulged by the *Brotherhood* in the late 1990's for a very ancient Goddess who is both a Warrior Goddess and a Goddess of *Heka*. The Great Liberating Mother also functions as a *Liminal Point* to the *Underworld*, and is a Goddess of *Ecstatic Liberation of the Spirit*. Her current name is *Babalon*, but She has gone by many names in Her many different incarnations, such as *Kybele*, *Helena*, Pakhet, *Bona Dea*, Astarte, and Inanna to name but a few. Many of Her incarnations are secret. Many of the incarnations attributed to Her by moderns are false, for such is Her power that many cultures seek to imitate Her in their own Goddesses. Her symbols are that of the Crescent Moon and Sun conjoined which is Her power of *Ecstatic Liberation of the Spirit*, the *Serpent* which is Her power over *Heka* and the *Underworld*, and *Lions* supporting Her Throne or pulling Her Chariot which is Her power as warrior-king. She also carries the *Wheel* of Seven Spokes or *Star* of Seven Points both of which refer to the *Seven Guiding Principles*. She is seen as the *Torch-bearer* in Her role *as Liminal Gateway* for *Spirit*, similar in function to *Helena*, Lucifer, *Hekate*, Baphometis and many others. She is also historically the Morning Star and the Evening Star, depending upon which role is being emphasized, both of which are seven pointed.

Hadit: The manifestation of the *Will* to Spiritual Advancement in the *Persona*. It is the Sun rising on wings. Also called the Winged Serpent or the *Winged Disk* or the *Winged Snake of Light*. Pronounced *Had*-et by *Babalon*, not Had-*eet*.

Hagia: The Holy Woman, a title of one the *Nine* when one incarnates in the *Lineage* as the daughter of the *Great Liberating Mother* and assumes the great and terrible responsibility which that entails. The Temple is always

GLOSSARY OF TERMS

run by the Hagia as king, and she has absolute authority therein. Note well that there are no queens in *Ophidia*, only women kings. The Hagia is born with enough memory intact from previous incarnations that She can prove her identity based upon secret objects and magical formulas which She remembers. These objects and formulas are known to no one outside of the office of Hagia, or an interim *Hagia Porne* who rules during the times when none of the *Nine* are manifest. Many Adepts who are not necessarily the Hagia will also be born with an uncanny understanding of the *Ophidian* ways, and with some former memories intact as well. The current Hagia of *Templum Babalonis* is the *Principalia Aureavia*. Pronounced *Hah*-gee-ah, not Hah-*jee*-ah.

Hagia Porne: Greek for "Holy Whore" and an *Ichthyos* slander of the *Great Liberating Mother* based upon a misunderstanding of the ritualized sexual imprintation practiced by Her *Priestesses* during initiation which they witnessed when they were slaves in Her Babylonian, Sumerian and Egyptian temples.

Harmonia: The state of beauty, balance and euphoria which attends any thing done properly as directed from the *Spirit*. In Ancient times this was envisioned as a Goddess of harmony and concord named Harmonia in Greece and Concordia in Rome. *Ophidians* seek to manifest Harmonia in all of their actions in Temple and out by following the *Seven Guiding Principles*, the Principles of *Natura*, *Heka* and their own *Spirit's* manifest *Will*. Also spelled Harmonaea, which is pronounced Har-moh-*nai*-yah.

Heavenly Realms: One of the *Three Great Realms*. See the *Caelestial Realms*.

Hecate: See *Hekate*.

Heka: The Ancient Egyptian word for Magick, literally meaning the *Manifestation* or activation (He) of the vital essence of the *Spirit* (*Ka*). Therefore Magick is the act of calling down the *Spirit* into the body. All other acts attributed to Magick, but which do not include the *Spirit* in this way, are merely acts of sorcery. The body possesses tremendous powers when the *Spirit* predominates. The compliment of Heka is *Natura*. *Natura* defines the Principles by which Heka is manifest. See also *Hekat*, *Hekate*, *Manifestation*.

Hekat: The secret Egyptian Goddess of Magick was Hekat, who was openly known by Her name Pakhet. In the Egyptian language the addition of the suffix –t to the base "*Heka*" indicates a female name, or in this case a Goddess name. Other examples of this suffix are Aset (Isis), Pakhet, Maat, Selket, *Nuit*, Sekhmet, Mut, Tanit, and Bastet to name a few. The secret Egyptian Goddess Hekat was later known in the Greek language as *Hekate*. See also *Heka*.

Hekate: A Greek goddess who in one sense became the deified image of the *Priestess* as *Liminal Point*. She combines the *Heka* aspects of the *Great Liberating Mother* with the Triple Goddess of the Celtic traditions. She is a *Torch-bearer* in the *Underworld*. Her name is inherited from the Egyptian word for Magick, *Heka*. Pronounced *Heh*-kah-teh or Heh-*kah*-teh depending upon the ancient dialect. See also *Hekat*.

Helena: Helena is a Goddess whose Greek name is a word which means "wicker, reed, shoot; torch; or basket". Often the word is interpreted therefore as light, bright and sometimes sun, by extension. She was the Mother of the Greek people from the pre-Aryan times, and gave them their name as Hellenes. Helena was a name used for the *Great Liberating Mother* in the Graeco-Roman world when the traditional worship of *Kybele* was banned. Like both *Hekate* and *Kybele*, Helena carries the torch, which is a symbol for the Guiding Light of the *Spirit* in the *Underworld* which leads to Liberation of the *Spirit* from the control of the animal self. She is the Mother of the *Fortuitous Angels*. She is sometimes confused with *Fortuna*, who is similar in nature but hails from Roman times and culture. She was known as Hel or Hela in the Northern European traditions, as the root Hel means Fortune in many languages. Pronounced Hel-*lay*-nah.

Holy Whore: Commonly believed to be a title of Goddess *Babalon*, presumably inspired by a description in the Book of Revelation, "Babylon the Great, the Mother of Prostitutes and Abominations of the Earth". It is an *Ichthyos* word, inspired by their degenerate loathing and lust by the *Ichthyos* and the *Aryans* for the *Priestesses* of the *Great Liberating Mother* who used a variety of sexual imprintation rituals upon the men that they initiated. But there is also a secret meaning in this phrase, beyond what most people imagine, which is revealed to those who cross the threshold into the *Inner Temple*.

I.N.B.V.S.M.: See *In Nomine Babalon et Vox Sanctae Meretricis*.

GLOSSARY OF TERMS

Ichthyos: A word used by *Babalon* with great contempt as it signifies all Monotheists, but particularly the early Hebrew semitic tribes from which all others are spawned. She pronounces the word as "*eek*-tohs". The image intended is one of "fish people", which is something else which She also calls them. This image of "Fish People" refers not so much to the Christian symbolism of Christ as the fish, but rather the earlier Hebrew tribal totems of the fish, from which Christianity heavily borrowed. For examples of this in the historical record see the Amorite God Dagon. The Amorites are one branch of the Ichthyos. Another branch of Ichthyos are the Hyksos who first appeared in recorded history around 1800 BCE in the eastern Nile Delta of Egypt. Linguistically, the names Ichthyos and Hyksos are obviously related.

In Nomine Babalon: Literally, "In the Name of Babalon". This phrase is used as a greeting amongst *Ophidians*, a pledge or renewal of an Oath of Fealty, a test of the Truth of another's *Justified Nature*, a completion of a Proclamation of one's *Will*, or the finalization of a Curse of an Enemy by *Ophidians*. See also *In Nomine Babalon et Vox Sanctae Meretricis*.

In Nomine Babalon et Vox Sanctae Meretricis: This phrase was first received in 1999 as message from the *Brotherhood* for the foundation statement of the Temple. It is a very special phrase containing layered meanings for the *Initiate*, but which literally translates to "In the name Babalon, and the Voice of the Holy Whore". The phrase can be found upon the seal of *Templum Babalonis*. The initial letters of the phrase, I.N.B.V.S.M. equal 93 by Gematria. Since releasing this phrase in 2000, many people now use it. It should be noted that those who use this phrase align themselves to Babalon, the nine and the Ophidian current. See also *In Nomine Babalon*. See also *Vox Sanctae Meretricis*.

Incubation: From the Latin incubare, to lie down. The practice of ritually sleeping within the Earth, close to the *Underworld*, so that messages from the Guardians and Protectors for oneself and one's spiritual path may be received in dreams or visions. This practice is one of the oldest ritual practices in human history, and was widely practiced up until the fall of Paganism in the Aeon of Pisces.

Initiate: A member of a *Mystery School* who has been Initiated into its *Mysteries*. An Initiate is privy to more of the *Mysteries* than an uninitiated outsider, and has potentially gained considerable experience with those

Mysteries, depending upon the degree to which they have attained in their *Initiations*.

Initiation: The act of imprinting a candidate in a ritualistic way according to certain *Mysteries*. This experiential act is the only way for a *Persona* to increase its capacity to hold *Spirit*, and thereby assume more of its Wisdom and Power. Self Initiation, as popularly understood in modern times, or ritual initiation following scripts in modern "secret societies", do not offer true Initiation - which in fact requires the presence of presiding *Spirits* who carry out the transformation itself. These ceremonies which do not involve the actual presence of Initiatory *Spirits* are in actuality merely *Rites of Passage*, not Initiation. *Rites of Passage* are human-centered and culture-centered. While sometimes exhilarating to the *Persona*, they do not increase ones capacity for *Spirit*. *Rites of Passage* are most often used by private groups and religions to behaviorally form compliant members, under the guise of spiritual motivations.

Inner Temple, The: The Inner Temple is also the *Court of Babalon*, the place of Kings within the Temple. All who wish to enjoy the life which awaits one there must pledge their life and death to Her Service. Those who dare to pass the Guardian of the *Liminal Point* to the *Underworld* will be shaped by the *Initiation* of twenty-eight trials awaiting them therein. This is the place where *Adepts* are forged and *Geniuses* are born. See also *Outer Temple*.

Justified: See *Justified Will or Action*.

Justified Will or Action: The only *Ophidian* moral rule. Being Justified is a positive state of action sought by all *Ophidians* which is based upon the innate purpose of a thing. The term is used in its old Egyptian sense for a state of being or for an action initiated by the *Spirit* in accordance with its purpose. It is also a term used to describe the proper innate behavior of a person, animal or thing. For example, a predator animal is Justified in its killing and eating of a prey animal because it is its innate nature to do such a thing. Corruption only arises when actions are not Justified, when one is not following the *Will* of one's *Spirit*.

Ka: An Egyptian word signifying the Desires, or what we *Ophidians* call the Fires, which permeates the *Khat* (physical body). The compliment of the Ka (*Fires*) is the *Ab* (heart, *Waters*). Both the Ka and the *Ab* are the most

GLOSSARY OF TERMS

immediate vehicles of communication between the *Ba* (*Persona*) and the *Khu* (*Spirit*). See also *Membra Animae*.

Katarche: The ruling spiritual principle or power behind any *manifestation*, or the inaugural steps of a ritual to manifest something via *Heka*. Katarche is both the spiritual ruling power and principles which govern the *manifestation*, and the impulse which causes it to come into being. The result of Katarche is manifest as *Apotelesma*. Pronounced Kah-*tar*-kay. See also *Manifestation*.

Khabs: An Egyptian word signifying a Star, which is the source and origin of the immortal and divine *Spirit*, called the *Khu*. Each *Khu* has its originating Khabs from which it was born, with spiritual mates or peers coming from the same Star. The Gods, too, are born from Stars and have Lineage with their people and worshippers from the same or neighboring Star. See also *Membra Animae*.

Khaibit: Khaibit, Shut or Sheut are Egyptian words signifying the energetic aura which permeates and surrounds the *Khat* (physical body) of all living things. The Shut is literally the dark shadow which stays after death (what we still to this day call the *Shade*), as opposed to the *Khu* which is the shining one who ascends to its star. See also *Membra Animae*.

Khat: Khat or Khet is an Egyptian word signifying the physical body, which is the seat of the *Ba* (*Persona*). The Khat, or physical body houses the *Ab* (heart, emotions, *Waters*) and the *Ka* (desire, passions, *Fires*) which communicate to the *Khu* (*Spirit*) via the *Sa* (Subtle Body) which surrounds the *Ba* (*Persona*). Using the Principles of *Natura* which govern the secret workings of the Khat, *Heka* may physically manifest in the body. See also *Membra Animae*.

Khu: An Egyptian word signifying the immortal and divine *Spirit*, also called Khu, Akhu, or simply Akh. The name Akhu generally means "Shining One", and it is born from a *Khabs* (Star). It is the Khu which administers the divine *Will* through the *Sa* of the individual, which must then be fulfilled by the incarnate *Ba* (*Persona*) as the purpose of their incarnate life. See also *Membra Animae*.

Kybele: The last incarnation of the *Great Liberating Mother* which held great temporal power in the Roman world, before the final fall of paganism and the onslaught of monotheism. This Cult of the *Great Liberating Mother* was banned in its original form by Rome as a threat to their patriarchal power structure, but She infiltrated their culture under the guise of various other goddesses, such as *Bona Dea* and *Helena*. From the earliest times, She was associated with mountains, hawks and *lions*. She is often pictured with torches, enthroned with *lions*, holding a *Cornucopia*, or standing at the door of Her Temple (the *Liminal Point*). It was from Kybele's temple in Anatolia that the Great Black Stone was brought to Rome when they officially accepted Her worship around 210 BCE and built a great Temple there to house this relic. Her Temple on Vatican Hill is now the site of the Vatican, St. Peter's Basilica, of the Roman Catholic Church. This was not by accident. Her name is also written as *Cybele*. Pronounced Kai-*bee*-lee, not sai-bee-lee or sih-bel or chih-bel-ee. See also *M.D.M.I.*

Liber Legis: See the *Book of Law*.

Liber AL vel Legis: See the *Book of Law*.

Liminal Gateway: See *Liminal Point*.

Liminal Point, The: A very important concept in ancient magical systems, almost completely abandoned or misunderstood in modern systems. The Liminal Point is the gateway of ingress for *Heka*, which is to say *Spirit* energy manifesting in matter. Without understanding the mechanics of this gateway or possessing some innate ability to accomplish its opening, one can not accomplish *Heka* of any sort, let alone attempt the *Triangle of Manifestation*. There are many ancient Goddesses of the Liminal Point, such as *Babalon, Hekate,* and Bapho-Metis who function not only as Liminal Points themselves in a special way, but offer instruction on the process as well. All of these *Liminal Gateway* deities are female, for a very important reason. Many such as Bapho Metis, also functions as Guardians of the Gateway against transgression. The opening of the *Liminal Gateway* is always accompanied by *Pia Mezza*.

Lineage, The: The Historical Procession of the Incarnations of the *Nine*. The Lineage itself is a mantle of strength down through time for those in the service of the *Great Liberating Mother*. The Lineage represents Her temporal power structure, administered through the incarnations of Her Daughters into the physical Realms. See the *Nine*.

GLOSSARY OF TERMS

Lion: Either an image of the *Great Liberating Mother* Herself, Her male lovers, or Her guardians. The Lion shows the *Great Liberating Mother's* royalty, pride and power. In the image of Her Therions, the Lion imagery shows the ferocity of their loyalty to Her and Her *Priestesses* as their guardians and lovers.

M.D.M.I.: The initials of the Latin phrase Mater Deum Magna Idaea, one of the most famous cult titles of *Kybele*, which can be found throughout the ancient world. The phrase means "Great Mother of the Gods from Ida". Mount Ida in Anatolia (specifically in Phrygia near Troy) was *Kybele's* homeland. This cipher was used by *Madimi* for her name in her interactions with John Dee.

Madimi: A spirit which was very important to John Dee and his communications with the Angels. She would often appear as a little girl, and speak of her mother's coming. Over time she grew older and more sexually provocative in her interactions with Dee. Dee thought the name was a play on the Medieval Angelic name Madimiel, which is based upon the Hebrew name for the planet Mars, Madim. But see *M.D.M.I.* for the real explanation of her name which holds the code for her mother's true identity. The *Great Liberating Mother* as *Helena* is the mother of the *Fortuitous Angels*. Dee recorded her as the *Daughter of Fortitude*, as well as the commander of the vast Heptarchia. His encounter with Her formed the last spirit encounter of any significance in his diaries. It should be noted that Dee went to his deathbed never writing Her name openly in his diaries, such was his fear of what Madimi had lead him to. In actuality, Madimi Herself is the *Deified Genius* of one of the *Nine*, who are the Daughters of the *Great Liberating Mother*. The various *Deified Geniuses* of the *Nine* often act as Heralds for the *Great Liberating Mother*, and may appear to those who seek to be in Her service. Pronounced Mah-*dee*-mee.

Magick: See *Heka*.

Magna Mater: Latin for the "Great Mother". Pronounced *Mahg*-nah *Mah*-tair. See also *Kybele*. See also *Great Liberating Mother*.

Manifest Realms, The: One of the *Three Great Realms*. See *Terrestrial Realms*.

Manifestation: The process by which *spirit* or spiritual energy becomes materialized. This manifestation can be of some spiritual intelligence such as an Angel manifesting to visible appearance upon the material plane, or simply some spiritual energy which causes some effect in the material. All spiritual manifestation follows a process which includes the steps of *Katarche* and *Apotelesma*. *Katarche* is the ruling spiritual principle or power behind any manifestation, or the inaugural steps of a ritual to manifest something via *Heka*. *Katarche* is both the spiritual ruling power and principles which govern the manifestation, and the impulse which causes it to come into being. The result of this spiritual impulse or ritual inauguration is the material result of the manifestation itself, or the *Apotelesma*. Being worldly in nature, the connection from the *Apotelesma* back to the originating *Katarche* may not always be apparent, unless one can find the *Fila* connecting the two events.

Material Realms, The: One of the *Three Great Realms*. See *Terrestrial Realms*.

Membra Animae: Literally, the limbs of the body of being. *Ophidians* hold that all being begins with the source of *Spirit*, the stars, which is called *Khabs* in Egyptian. From the *Khabs* comes the *Khu*, the great immortal, unique and unmanifest *Spirit*. This *Spirit* is like a *Serpent* moving through time, periodically shedding its skin which becomes its incarnations. When the *Spirit* manifests into time and space, it does so in the *Ethereal Body* or *Soul*, which the Egyptians called the *Sa*. The *Sa* carries the incarnated *Will* of the *Khu* in each incarnation. This *Sa* also houses all of the temporal and transient parts of one's being which are born and die in each incarnation. These transient parts of one's character and being are known as the *Persona*, which the Egyptians called the *Ba*. They gave it the appearance of a little bird with a human head. It is this Persona which houses all of those things which one thinks of when they contemplate "the self". Within this *Persona* called the *Ba* are the *Fires* and the *Waters*, the Mind of mundane awareness, the *Shade* and the physical body. The Fires are the desires and drives of both the earthly body and the Spiritual *Sa*. The Egyptians called this the *Ka*, and it is what also fires one's *Magick* in *Heka* (He Ka). The compliment of the *Fires* are the *Waters*. Here we find one's behavioral and emotional complexes, and the feelings by which one navigates existence. Like the *Ka*, these feelings too come from both the body, and from the *Sa*. The Egyptians called this the *Ab*, the Heart, and it was terribly important for them to keep one's *Waters* pure, otherwise bad things would be created

GLOSSARY OF TERMS

in the world around them. These *Waters*, envisioned as the heart of a person where we "feel" the most, were weighed and judged after death to determine the state of being of a person during their life. Did they cultivate a good and harmonious heart? Or was it polluted and sullied? The next layer of being was called the *Khaibit* by the Egyptians, and was imagined as a shadow or *Shade*. Here one could find the manifest life force energy which inhabits a living body. Finally we have the physical body itself, built to be a biological vehicle for the manifest *Spirit* energy of the *Sa*, or *Soul*. This last layer of being was called the *Khat* by the Egyptians. Such are the main layers or limbs in the body of being, both manifest and unmanifest.

Midnight Sun, The: First and foremost, this term refers to the light of the Moon at Midnight, and all of the powers contained therein. Therefore, by extension, it is also the light which shines in the blackness of the *Underworld*, and the light held aloft by the *Torchbearers* who illuminate its depths such as *Hekate* and *Helena*. In addition to these considerations, the Midnight Sun may also refer to the analogous energies of *Sirius*, or the mythology of the hidden Sun within the Earth, or a certain suppressed nearby brown dwarf star which is called Enki by the spirits, or the *Black Star* itself. There is not one Midnight Sun, there are many. And they all have a connection to the *Underworld*.

Mysteries: The central theme of a Mystery School, with its corresponding principles, philosophies, rituals and *Initiations*. The Mysteries are often connected to a series of spiritual entities who act as Teachers, Guides, Guardians and Initiators to those same Mysteries. The Mysteries are always kept secret from the profane, who will certainly misinterpret, and therefore corrupt, the Mysteries. Often these Mysteries are concerned with the *Underworld*.

Mystery School: A Mystery School is an institution that teaches esoteric and magical spirituality in a direct and experiential way, as opposed to the symbolic and intellectual approach of the modern esoteric groups. This wisdom of the Mystery School is based on a core set of philosophies and spiritual principles that guides the student to contact their own *Spirit*, their divinity within themselves. A Mystery School is often structured in its approach to this task by a series of *Initiations* with corresponding teachings that must be mastered by the student before moving on to the next *Initiation*. These Initiation Cycles, or Degrees, are often centered around a central theme, or set of *Mysteries*. Often these *Mysteries* are concerned with the *Underworld*. These *Mysteries* are kept secret from the uninitiated, who would misinterpret them without the proper experiential knowledge gained by the *Initiation* and other rituals which accompany it. These *Mysteries* and their Initiatory steps increase the student's spiritual awareness and powers in gradual steps, towards *Adeptship*, which is total self-mastery by the *Spirit*.

Natura: The Principles and Rituals which govern the manifestation of *Heka* in the body, *Persona*, and the natural world. It is in Natura that we find the secrets of the body, its energy pathways, how the substances we ingest affect not only our health, but also our emotions, our consciousness and our ability to manifest *Heka*. We discover the notion of mindfulness in our daily actions towards *Gaia*, the *World Soul*, and how this affects which types of spirits we are able to interact with in our *Heka*. The Principles of *Natura* hold the Keys for unlocking the power of *Heka*. And the further one pursues *Heka*, the more one discovers the Principles of *Natura*, which makes its manifestation possible. As this process deepens, *Harmonia* ensues bringing with it the *Cornucopia*. Pronounced Nah-*toor*-rah.

Nine, The: These Holy Women are the incarnate daughters of the *Great Liberating Mother*, and form what She calls the *Lineage*. Many of their names have survived in the historical record, such as Diotima, Hatshepsut, Diangela, and Seraphina. The *Principalia* is one of the *Nine*. The discarnate *Nine* are *Deified Geniuses* who continue their work after death in *Babalon's* Service.

Nuit: The Mother of all Mothers, the Mother of all Gods, and the Mother of the Cosmos. She is the mother of *Babalon* (under Her secret Egyptian name), by Ra. She is an *Ophidian* goddess, and the *Cobra* is sacred unto Her for it carries Her mark on the back of its hood. Pronounced *Noo*-it by Babalon, not Noo-*eet*.

Ophidia: The sacred land of the *Ophidians*, dedicated to *Gaia* on one hand, and the *Great Liberating Mother* on the other. *Ophidia* is the place of the New Indigene, and all who live there follow the Principles of *Natura*, whether or not they serve *Babalon* directly. Pronounced Oh-*fid*-ee-ah.

Glossary of Terms

Ophidian: Having lineage from or pertaining to the *Great Liberating Mother*, Her servants, or Her allies. This connection to Her is usually indicated by the presence of a *Serpent* in some manner.

Ophidian Thelema: The followers of the *Serpent*, or *Spirit*, within *Thelema*. Ophidian Thelemites follow the *Seven Guiding Principles* as delivered by *Babalon*, the current incarnation of the *Great Liberating Mother* throughout time. Ophidian Thelema emphasizes the importance of the *Balanced Ecstatic Path*, the enthronement of *Spirit* within matter, Devotion to the *Great Liberating Mother*, *Heka* and *Natura*.

Ophidians, The: The people of the *Serpent*. Ophidians are the servants and devotees of the *Great Liberating Mother* throughout time. One of their highest symbols is that of the *Snake*, which represents *Spirit* in all its manifest forms. The Ophidians are the New Indigene and live in *Ophidia*.

Orkestial Realms, The: One of the *Three Great Realms*. See also *Underworld*.

Outer Temple, The: The first Degrees of the Temple, which are five in number and Elemental in nature. The central teachings of the Outer Temple are concerned with the method known as the *Triangle of Manifestation*, the spiritual pursuit of *Heka* and the behavioral adaptation to *Natura*. This is the natural resting place for most members. Advancement to the *Inner Temple* is not required, unless one feels compelled to do so of their own *Will*. See also *Inner Temple*.

Pashtun: A term used by some spirits to describe their role as Herald, Minister or Speaker for another spirit, whom they serve in this capacity. The etymology of this word pre-dates the current Persian word used for the people of Afghanistan and their language. Interestingly many Pashtuns will exhibit the sign of Khamsa (Hamsa) upon arrival as a symbol of their office and function. Originally the raised right hand by a spirit messanger was a ward against fear of a divine presence, and the effect of anxiety caused in the body of the human witnessing its presence. But this symbol has degenerated in the last few *Aeons*, far from its original use into a superstitious sign now used to ward off the so-called "evil eye" in many Near-Eastern cultures.

Persona: Called the *Ba* in Egyptian cosmology, the *Persona* is the base and simple personality, body, behavioral and emotional complexes, and mind of an individual – none of which are divine or immortal. In short, the transitory parts of an individual which perish upon death, or are left behind as a *Shade*. The Persona has no higher *Will* of its own, and therefore must work to know and accomplish the *Will* of its *Spirit*. In this way, the *Persona* is the primary tool of the *Spirit* to accomplish its *Will* in the material world. See also *Membra Animae*.

Pia Mezza: Literally the middle place, or the place between. Pia Mezza is a term *Babalon* uses to describe the effect that the *Liminal Gateway*, the ingress of *Spirit*, has upon the senses of those in its presence. The witnesses often feel as though they are swimming through their sensations, with sight in particular becoming unusual in a myriad of different ways. The senses become heightened and on edge, much like one who is sneaking through a dark woods, alone at night. This state has nothing to do with the use of drugs or chemicals, nor can it be achieved by the employment of such substances. Pronounced *Pee*-ah *Mehz*-ah.

Precession of the Equinoxes, The: an astronomical phenomenon which is defined by the long-term shift of the stars in our sky caused by a wobbling of the Earth as it spins on its axis. It is a pre-cession, instead of a pro-cession, because it appears as if we are traversing through the constellations in reverse, one complete cycle every 25,920 years. According to *Liber Legis* I:49, the Equinox of the Gods took place on the Spring Equinox of 1904 as the Earth entered Aquarius. Therefore one can calculate each Aeon of 2160 years as follows:

    24,016 BCE Aquarius begins
    21,856 BCE Capricorn begins
    19,696 BCE Sagittarius begins
    17,536 BCE Scorpio begins
    15,376 BCE Libra begins
    13,216 BCE Virgo Begins
    11,056 BCE Leo Begins
     8,896 BCE Cancer begins
     6,736 BCE Gemini begins
     4,576 BCE Taurus begins
     2,416 BCE Aires begins
      256 BCE Pisces begins

GLOSSARY OF TERMS

1,904 CE Aquarius begins
4,064 CE Capricorn will begin

See also *Aeons*, *Equinox of the Gods*.

Priestess: A title of a woman dedicated to a particular Goddess. The use of the word dedication here is technically important, as it is an actual life commitment to stand for and with that particular Goddess. Having merely a sense of affinity or affiliation with a particular Goddess, or simply "liking the image" of a Goddess is not a dedication. Usually there is a series of *Initiations* that must be undergone and teachings which must be assimilated and behavioral changes which must be enacted before the Goddess of that particular Temple accepts the candidate as a Priestess. In action a Priestess generally acts as *Liminal Gateway* for her Goddess, and carries out Her *Will* upon the planet. Because of this, a Priestess must always be born female, as she must physically possess a womb to accomplish this act. It is the female body itself which provides the ability to function as a Priestess in this way. In modern times the people have completely lost touch with the old traditions and with actions of spiritual commitment, and people routinely self-proclaim themselves "Priestesses" of this or that without any real commitment or accomplishment. In actuality these claims hold little if any real meaning as these people have no real connection to any Goddess other than mere feelings of affinity, or as a trendy image to be portrayed to others for attention, or as an act of role-playing in groups.

Principalia: Always the first of the *Nine* in a new wave of incarnations, and the current *Hagia* of the Temple, who is called *Aureavia*.

Principia: Literally, the Principles. The Temple is governed not by rules, laws, dogmas, teachings or constitutions - rather it manifests solely by the *Seven Guiding Principles*. These *Seven Guiding Principles* were revealed by the *Great Liberating Mother* Herself and form the cornerstone of all cosmological teachings. Each Principle is ruled by one of the *Fortuitous Angels*, who overseas its implementation. There are Seven Angels of Fortune and Seven Spokes of the *Wheel of Fortuna*, just as there are Seven Points on Her *Star*. In Her guise of *Helena* the *Torch-bearer*, the *Great Liberating Mother* is the Mother of the Seven *Fortuitous Angels*. Pronounced Prin-*kip*-ee-ah.

Principles, The: See *Principia*.

Pythia: A She-Serpent. A term amongst the *Ophidians* for a *Priestess* who has gained the Orphetic ability of *Vox* using the *Triangle of Manifestation*. The mouth of the *Priestess* is used by the *Serpent*, the spirit, to speak. This ability gave rise in the past to the myth of the fabled Pythia, later imitated at Delphi when the *Aryans* controlled the old Goddess cults there. They shackled those *Priestesses* to Apollo and made them inhale toxic vapors so that they would give up babbling visions which the Priests would then interpret for their own political uses. The Priests of the Oracle at Delphi became very wealthy and powerful by imitating the *Priestesses* of old, yet never once did they speak with a True Voice.

Rites of Passage: Ceremonies performed by groups, societies, religions and cultures upon people whom they wish to imprint certain loyalties and behaviors. Rites of Passage are often confused with true *Initiation*, especially by modern so-called esoteric organizations.

Sa: An Egyptian word signifying the *Ethereal Body* or *Soul* of the incarnated *Spirit*, which is called Psyche in Greek or *Anima* in Latin. This Sa or Sahu functions as the seat of the *Ba* (*Persona* complex), which is the manifested consciousness of the incarnated *Khu* (*Spirit*), and maintains the *Fila* from the *Ba* to the *Khu*. The Sa recedes from the body upon death, most often leaving the *Ba* as a *Shade*. In advanced *Adepts*, the Sa can become a *Genius* or even a *Deified Genius*. See also *Membra Animae*.

Saturn: See the *Black Star*.

Serpent: The symbol of *Spirit* for the *Ophidians*. Serpents were believed by the Ancients to be deathless, because they could renew themselves when old by shedding their skin. They believed that Serpents could see into the *Spirit* realm because of their pupils which are shaped like slits. And they believed that snakes come up out of the *Underworld*, the land from which they were born. See also *Ophidians*, *Spirit*.

Seven Angels of Fortune, The: See the *Seven Fortuitous Angels*.

Seven Fortuitous Angels, The: The angelic rulers of the *Seven Guiding Principles*, and the children of *Helena* the *Torch-bearer*. See also the *Wheel of Fortuna*.

Glossary of Terms

Seven Guiding Principles, The: See *Principia*.

Shade: The *Persona* of a person or animal left on the material plane after death, which sometimes appears as a ghost or poltergeist. These Shades can be called forth like other spirits, but it should be kept in mind that they only know what they knew when they were alive, and nothing more. They also maintain all of their biases and beliefs from that life as well. Most do not seem to know that they have died. *Adepts* are capable of developing a more evolved type of *Persona* that works so closely with its *Spirit* that it becomes something more upon death, which we call a *Genius*, or in rare cases a *Deified Genius*. A *Genius* has more awareness than a Shade, and can continue the work of its *Will* beyond death. A *Deified Genius* becomes something even more.

Sirius: The Source Star for some of the Deities brought to Earth by way of the *Black Star*, such as Setesh, Anubis and many of the *Titans* and their children. Because of a shared heritage, these deities are allies of the *Great Liberating Mother* and are Guardians of Her. They have organized themselves in an Alliance ruled by 15 known as the *Brotherhood of the Midnight Sun*.

Snake: See *Serpent*.

Sons of Gaia, The: The Sworn Guardians of *Heka* and *Natura* in the *Outer Temple*. They are by necessity all male by birth and strong of *Will* by nature.

Soul: See *Anima*.

Spirit: 1) Usually pictured as a *Serpent*, the Spirit is sometimes called your True Self, Divine Self or Divine Spirit and is always capitalized in order to differentiate it from other types of spirits, such as shades, elementals, angels or demons, to name a few. In Egyptian, it was called the *Khu* which came from the *Khabs*. This Spirit is your immortal, divine, unique, higher self which incarnates into flesh in order to achieve its divine purpose, which is called its *Will*. It is immortal in that it is deathless, and imperishable. It is divine in that it is incorruptible and perfect in its nature and possesses a consciousness with a much greater horizon than your own manifest self. It is unique in that it is like no other Spirit in both its nature and consciousness, yet always recognizable in every incarnation no matter which different body you are born into. It is your higher self in that it creates and informs all that you are, and without which you would certainly cease. See also *Membra Animae*.

Spirit: 2) The source of all life and consciousness in the universe, which manifests by means of the Goddess *Nuit*. Spirit is that which animates life itself.

Spirit: 3) Any entity or being which has conscious intelligence, but which is not immediately visible to mundane human perception. This includes *Shades*, Demons, Angels, Elementals and the like. The classifications of such beings and their variety throughout the universe is endless.

Star: A symbol of the *Spirit*, with special emphasis on the divine and unique aspects of *Spirit*. By contrast, the *Serpent* is a symbol of the *Spirit* that emphasizes the immortal and magical aspects of *Spirit*. Concerning the Star as *Spirit* we read in *Liber Legis* I, 3, "Every man and every woman is a star", which shows that every man and every woman is divine and unique because of their connection to their *Spirit*. And furthermore, those *Spirits* are born directly from Stars, themselves, as the *Titans* attest. See also *Seven Pointed Star of Babalon*.

Storm Gods, The: The rulers of the Aeon of Aries, and the patron Gods of the *Aryans*. They brought to the world the law of Lex Talionis, that might is right. Their culture was one in which males were the superior gender in all ways. The Storm Gods were born from the over-zealous worship and sacrifice to the Rain Gods after the introduction of agriculture and the subsequent anxiety concerning rain. Their names are numerous, and their myths are almost universally the same: Zeus and Ares, Jupiter and Mars, Odin and Thor. These were the Storm Gods, with their vengeful bolts of lightening and thunderclaps like Indra. They had warrior sons, hero sons, who slew the monsters of old who threatened their new order.

Templum Babalonis: Simply the name of "the Temple of Babalon", in Latin.

Terrestrial Realms, The: One of the *Three Great Realms*. The Terrestrial Realms are the endpoint of all *Manifestation* of *Spirit* in all of its endless forms. Also called the Material or Manifest Realms, it is here that one finds

Glossary of Terms

the four elements, the manifest beings, spirits and animals, and the endless worlds of the cosmos with its laws of physics.

Thelema: The Cult of the *Will*. Thelema is the name for the system of Magical Philosophy that was divulged to the modern world in the Book "*Liber AL vel Legis*", commonly referred to as the "*Book of the Law*", in Cairo, Egypt, in 1904. On April 8th, 9th and 10th of that year, a communication was received by Rose Edith Kelley and written down by her husband Aleister Crowley. This communication consisted of three small chapters that were received at noon, one on each of the three days. Within this writing, with its strange phrases and multi-layered meanings, a new Law for a new Aeon was proclaimed.

"Do what thou wilt shall be the whole of the Law." Liber AL vel Legis I:40

Thelema is Greek for *Will*, and by Gematria equals 93. This Law proclaims that every woman and every man his a unique, individual and autonomous *Will*, and that she or he has an inalienable right and responsibility to find out that purpose, and to achieve it, no matter what it may be. Each person's *Will* is unique, and can only be discovered by his or her self. This *Will* is Spiritual, and the reason why one has incarnated on this planet. But, how does one discover what their *Will* is?

"Love is the law, love under will." Liber AL vel Legis I:57

Agape is Greek for Love, and also equals 93. In Thelema, Love means attraction and union. This union is a union with one's *Spirit*, which holds the keys to one's *Will*. One must discover and follow their path, by uniting with each and every experience that one needs in order to accomplish their *Will*, no matter what it may be. Since Thelema is a Magical Philosophy, and not just a mental or mystical exercise of the mind, there are Magical means of personally seeking out and discovering your *Will*. In the training of *Templum Babalonis*, these methods are often physical and experiential, and the *Outer Temple* degree structure is designed to help the student seek out and discover their *Will* through the magical training they receive.

Pronounced *Thel*-leh-mah by *Babalon*, with a strong emphasis on the first syllable, as it was pronounced in Ancient Greek. Also acceptable is *Tel*-leh-mah with a stronger "t" sound, but never tha-*lay*-mah as is in vogue by commoners in modern times. See also *Ophidian Thelema*.

Thelemites: Those who follow some form of *Thelema*. See also *Ophidian Thelema*.

Therion: Greek for "wild animal" or "beast". In *Templum Babalonis* a Therion is a guardian of the Sacred *Mysteries* of the *Great Liberating Mother*, and Her *Priestesses*. He has pledged his life to their service and protection. He is often envisaged as a great *Lion*, resting at the end of the leash of *Babalon*. Becoming a Therion is the first stage of membership in the *Brotherhood of the Midnight Sun* upon reaching the *Inner Temple*. Pronounced *Theer*-ee-on.

Three Great Realms, The: The spirits all universally acknowledge the existence of three great Realms, and these three Realms are the same three which existed in the records of the ancient Goddess cultures, long before the Neolithic times. These three Realms are the Terrestrial, Caelestial and Orkestial - also known as the Material Realms, the Heavenly Realms, and the Underworld Realms. A manifestation of the Great Goddess rules over each Realm, the Earth Mother, the Bird Mother and the Snake Mother. Elementals and *Titans* and incarnate beings like *Gaia* and yourself are found in the Terrestrial Realms. Angels and true Gods are found in the Caelestial Realms, while *Titans* again, Dualities, Demons, *Ophidians* and many other types of spirits are found in the Orkestial Realms. The Terrestrial Realms are the places of *Manifestation*. The Caelestial Realms are filled with all possibilities of Divine Potentiality, while the Orkestial Realms provide the place of endless Transformation. The Terrestrial Realms contain the Four Elements which describe the levels and *Manifestation* of *Persona*, life and *Spirit*. The Caelestial Realms contain the Seven Planets which are the modifications of the *Spirit*, the source of the *Seven Guiding Principles*, and the fonts of all Divine Potentiality. The Orkestial Realms contain the reflection of both the Terrestrial and Caelestial Realms in its Twenty-Eight Mansions of Transformation, which are divided equally by four great rivers.

The combination of Terrestrial and Orkestial Realms is sometimes referred to as the Sublunary Realms, while the combination of Terrestrial and Caelestial Realms is sometimes referred to simply as the Universe or the Universal Realms. When referring to the Caelestial and Orkestial Realms only, the term Unearthly or Spiritual Realms is sometimes used. The magical practices of the Caelestial Realms are sometimes called Theurgia. The magical practices of the Orkestial Realms are sometimes called Goetia,

GLOSSARY OF TERMS

but in modern parlance that term is now used exclusively for a group of 72 particular demons. This was not so originally. The magical practices of the Terrestrial Realms are sometimes called Telluric or Geomantic. Today this is generally known by the term Shamanism.

Titans, The: The ancient children of *Gaia*, who ruled during the Golden Age of Leo. They are the guardians of the old ways of the Goddess, now forgotten. Some of them are Guardians of the *Underworld*. Some are members of the *Brotherhood*. Some are Guardians of *Gaia* and some inaugurate planet-level changes upon and within the Earth. After a long slumber of many thousands of years the Titans are again on the move, seeking vengeance against their enemies, and the enemies of their Mother. Earth changes are the result of their movements, as they reshape the planet. There are many Titans, and many of their names have survived to the present, demonized by the *Aryans* in their myths, such as Typhon, Echidna, Cerebus, Ladon, Chimera, Hyperion, Chronos, Oceanus, Themis and many, many more.

Torch-bearer: A title of the *Great Liberating Mother*, or one of the Guardians, in their role as guide and guardian of the *Liminal Gateway* for *Spirit*. In this guardianship, they also function as the Guiding Light of the *Spirit* undergoing Emergence and Transformation in the *Underworld*. The Torch-bearers have gone by many names, including: *Helena*, Libertas, Lucifer, *Hekate*, Bapho-metis and others.

Triangle of Art: A triangle, often painted on the floor surrounded with various names of power, outside of the magical circle. It is used to trap and hold the summoned spirit in an evocation. In actuality, the mere symbol of a triangle holds little power over spirits in and of itself. The Triangle of Art has always been a blind for the true method of evocation, known as the *Triangle of Manifestation*.

Triangle of Manifestation: This is the ancient, true and secret method of evoking spirits into the physical realm. It is the cornerstone of the teachings of the *Outer Temple* in *Templum Babalonis*. It is impossible to accomplish this method without a properly trained *Priestess* who can function as a *Liminal Gateway*. For has it not been said that "woman is the Triangle of Manifestation"? A man alone can not evoke a spirit to manifestation in the physical realm, without possession, for he lacks the proper physical equipment. This method has nothing to do with the commonly written method involving the *Triangle of Art*, which is a mere blind for the true and secret method. Nor does it involve any tricks with eyesight, mirrors, smoke, altered states of consciousness or trance-possession. The true Triangle of Manifestation affects an actual face-to-face manifestation on the material plane of the spirit evoked.

True Self Mastery: See *Adept*.

True Voice, The: See *Vox*.

Underworld, The: One of the Three Great Realms. Also called Orkestial or Chthonic, the Underworld is the place of darkness, *magick*, mystery and the dead. It is the womb of all existence - both manifest and unmanifest. It was often imagined by the ancients as being within the Earth. Some traditions state that there was an inner light source or sun which existed there, which they called the *Midnight Sun*. The Goddess of the Underworld in various cultures and times was usually an incarnation of the *Great Liberating Mother*. The Underworld is the source of all Emergence and Transformation, and therefore the only place of *Initiation* beyond the purely Elemental Degrees. The secrets of this Underworld process have been lost and forgotten in modern times, but are taught by *Babalon*, the *Titans* and the *Fortuitous Angels* to those who persevere and are able to discover the First Guardian of the First Gate of the Underworld.

Vox: The Voice of *Spirit*. The are four Voices in the hierarchy of manifest *Spirit*. The First Vox is the True Vox of *Babalon* Herself. This is *Vox Babalonis* or *Vox Deae*. This Vox speaks Her words, directly from Her lips, through Her Daughters and the *Triangle of Manifestation*. The Second Vox is that of Her Daughter, who is Ninefold in manifestation. It is the Vox of the *Hagia*, *Vox Sanctae Meretricis*. She is able to speak in a voice which is inherited from Her *Lineage*. It is the Vox from beyond the Veil of Incarnation, and does not come from Her incarnated *Persona*. It is a Vox of both Truth and Prophecy - for there is no difference. The words contain their own proof of origin within themselves, and they resonate as such within the *Spirit* of the one who hears them. The Third Vox is a Vox which is extremely rare, but is still able to be found to this day amongst a few people. It is the Vox of their *Spirit*, *Vox Animae*, and it always shows forth as a voice of knowing, which is to say it speaks in Truth and Beauty. This voice is potentially achievable by many, but pursued by very few. The Fourth Vox is the one which is inspired by the feelings of *Spirit* in the

GLOSSARY OF TERMS

Waters and *Fires* of the *Persona*. This is the beautiful voice of the Arts, *Vox Artis*, and one which can speak much truth in the moment. But while it may speak Truth to some degree, it may also lack a little in the *Spirit* perspective which extends beyond the impermanence of the *Persona*.

Vox Animae: The Voice of *Spirit*. This voice is the Third Voice and is extremely rare, but is still able to be found to this day amongst a few *Adepts*. It is the Vox of their *Spirit*, Vox Animae, and it always shows forth as a voice of knowing, which is to say it speaks in Truth and Beauty. This voice is potentially achievable by many, but pursued by very few. See *Vox*.

Vox Artis: The Voice of the Arts. This voice is inspired by the feelings of *Spirit* in the *Waters* and *Fires* of the *Persona*. This is the beautiful voice of the Arts, Vox Artis, and one which can speak much truth in the moment. But while it may speak Truth to some degree, it may also lack a little in the *Spirit* perspective which extends beyond the impermanence of the *Persona*. Many people today pursue such a voice in the words, images and arts of may sorts - and much of these efforts of expression are quite moving and worthwhile. See *Vox*.

Vox Babalonis: The Voice of *Babalon*. Also called *Vox Deae*. This Vox speaks Her words, directly from Her lips, through Her Daughters and the *Triangle of Manifestation*. See *Vox*.

Vox Deae: The Voice of the Goddess. See *Vox Babalonis*.

Vox Sanctae Meretricis: The Voice of the *Holy Whore*. It is the voice of Her Daughter, who is Ninefold in manifestation. It is the Vox of the *Hagia*, *Vox Sanctae Meretricis*. She is able to speak in a voice which is inherited from Her *Lineage*. It is the Vox from beyond the Veil of Incarnation, and does not come from Her incarnated *Persona*. It is a Vox of both Truth and Prophecy - for there is no difference. The words contain their own proof of origin within them, and they resonate as such within the *Spirit* of the one who hears them. See *Vox*.

War Gods, The: See the *Storm Gods*.

Wheel of Fortuna, The: The image of the *Seven Guiding Principles*, which are the Seven Spokes of the *Wheel*. The *Wheel* is held by many Goddesses, including *Bona Dea*, *Helena*, *Kybele* and *Fortuna*.

Wheel of Fortune, The: See the *Wheel of Fortuna*.

Wheel, The: See the *Wheel of Fortuna*.

Will: The Will of your *Spirit* is one's guiding sovereign purpose in life, and the reason why one accomplished the miracle of incarnation in the first place. All *Ophidians* are here for a purpose, and there is no greater and nobler act than accomplishing the purpose of one's incarnation, other than to die trying to achieve it. Most often one's Will changes from one lifetime to another, but many times there will be overriding themes which will be of a similar nature throughout many lifetimes. It is also important to note that no other person, no matter how advanced, is able to tell one what their Will is. It is expressly a matter between one's *Persona* and one's *Spirit*.

Winged Disk: Either an image of *Hadit* or an image of the *Spirit*.

Winged Globe of Light: Either an image of *Hadit* or an image of the *Spirit*.

Winged Serpent: Either an image of *Hadit* or an image of the *Spirit*, or an image of a Lila, or the image of one of the Seraphim.

Winged Snake of Light: Either an image of *Hadit* or an image of the *Spirit*.

World Soul, The: See *Gaia*.

About the Author

Hagia Aureavia founded the Temple of Babalon in the year 2000 as a Mystery School dedicated to the devotion and worship of the incarnation of the Great Liberating Mother who is currently known as Babalon. The Temple is an Ophidian organization and practices Ophidian Thelema. She trains her students in the lost art of the Orphetic Mysteries, Heka and Natura, the Liminal Gateway to the Underworld, and the Rites of Sex and Death. The Hagia is a Priestess of Babalon and a Scarlet Woman, an author, an artist, multiple business owner, a student of naturopathic medicine, a homesteader and a survivalist. She lives off-grid at her home in Ophidia where she runs her Temple and trains her students from around the world.

www.ingramcontent.com/pod-product-compliance
Lightning Source LLC
Chambersburg PA
CBHW082315230426
43666CB00036B/2671